# THE COMPLETE ILLUSTRATED GUIDE TO
# ANIMALS
# BIRDS & FISH
# OF THE BRITISH ISLES

THE COMPLETE ILLUSTRATED GUIDE TO

# ANIMALS
# BIRDS & FISH
## OF THE BRITISH ISLES

A NATURAL HISTORY AND IDENTIFICATION
GUIDE WITH OVER 440 NATIVE SPECIES FROM
ENGLAND, IRELAND, SCOTLAND AND WALES

EDITED BY DANIEL GILPIN

HERMES
HOUSE

This edition is published by Hermes House, an imprint of Anness Publishing Ltd, Blaby Road, Wigston, Leicestershire LE18 4SE

Email: info@anness.com

Web: www.hermeshouse.com; www.annesspublishing.com

If you like the images in this book and would like to investigate using them, please visit our website www.practicalpictures.com for more information.

Publisher: Joanna Lorenz
Editorial Director: Helen Sudell
Project Editor: Rosie Gordon
Artists: Mike Atkinson, Peter Bull, Peter Barrett, Penny Brown, Jim Channell, Anna Childs, Felicity Rose Cole, Julius Csotonyi, Anthony Duke, Rob Dyke, John Francis, Rob Highton, Stuart Jackson-Carter, Paul Jones, The Magic Group, Martin Knowelden, Stephen Lings, Shane Marsh, Robert Morton, Janos Marffy, Fiona Osbaldstone, Denys Ovenden, Andrew Robinson, Mike Saunders, Sarah Smith and Tim Thackeray
Designers: Ian Sandom and Nigel Partridge
Production Controller: Wendy Lawson

**ETHICAL TRADING POLICY**
At Anness Publishing we believe that business should be conducted in an ethical and ecologically sustainable way, with a proper regard to the replacement of the natural resources we employ. As a publisher, we use a lot of wood pulp in high-quality paper for printing, and that wood commonly comes from spruce trees. We are therefore currently growing more than 750,000 trees in three Scottish forest plantations. Because of this ongoing ecological investment programme, you, as our customer, can have the pleasure and reassurance of knowing that a tree is being cultivated on your behalf to naturally replace the materials used to make the book you are holding. For information about this scheme, go to www.annesspublishing.com/trees

A CIP catalogue record for this book is available from the British Library.

Previously published as part of four separate volumes:
*The Complete Book of Animals*, by Tom Jackson
*The Complete Illustrated World Guide to Marine Fish & Sea Creatures*, by Amy-Jane Beer and Derek Hall
*The Complete Illustrated World Guide to Freshwater Fish & River Creatures*, by Daniel Gilpin
*The World Encyclopedia of Birds & Birdwatching*, by David Alderton

**PUBLISHER'S NOTE**
Although the advice and information in this book are believed to be accurate and true at the time of going to press, neither the authors nor the publisher can accept any legal responsiblity or liability for any errors or omissions that may be made.

# CONTENTS

## MAMMALS, AMPHIBIANS AND REPTILES

# INTRODUCTION

Because Britain is an island the summers are warm and wet and the winters generally mild. This consistent lack of extremes provides an excellent climate for animals that know that they can rely on food being available virtually all year round. Animal evolution, physical characteristics and behaviour are partly dictated by the environment in which they live. Britain's island status meant that centuries ago its wildlife was fairly unchanging, but human movement, invasion and settlement has introduced new species, and threatened or wiped out others.

## British wildlife

From the rocky islands of Orkney and Shetland to the warm beaches of Jersey, the British Isles encompass a stunning variety of scenery. The woods, rocky cliffs, lakes, rivers and wild places are full of wildlife, as are 'artificial' habitats such as farms, hedgerows, cities and gardens. Some fauna live alongside humans very happily, but there are far more elusive animals. Only the determined will glimpse a Scottish wildcat or adder. Of course, unless you enjoy fishing, you may never even have seen the fish that inhabit our freshwater lakes and rivers, not to mention those in the depths of the North Sea and Atlantic. Many of the animals we

*Below: Hares thrive in the grasslands of the British Isles. They are the fastest-running animals in the region and can accelerate from a sitting position to 72kph (45mph) in a matter of seconds.*

*Above: From the rolling coastline of the south of England, seen here, to the wild moors and mountains of the far north of Scotland, and with marshland, woodland, farmland and urban areas inbetween, Britain offers a wide variety of habitats for its native animals.*

see in the British Isles are visitors, either stopping for the winter months or simply passing by on their migrations north or south. This is true of many marine animals and a huge number of birds.

In this book we concentrate on animals that live in Britain in the present day, whether they are native, visitors, or have become established relatively recently.

## About this book

The chapters that follow examine Britain's mammals, amphibians, reptiles, birds and fish, and aim to help you identify and understand the creatures you may see in your garden, the countryside or even the city streets. The book opens with a discussion of the major habitats of the British Isles: forest, grassland, shores, heaths and highlands, wetlands, parks and gardens, and then divides into three main sections: mammals, amphibians and reptiles; birds; and fish.

Each section begins with a clear overview about biology, behaviour, senses and other vital information to help readers understand British animal life, and the importance of wildlife and habitat conservation.

*Above: The red-legged partridge is one of several game birds that were brought to England for sport. It breeds naturally in south-western Europe and was probably introduced to southern England in the late 1600s. It has been seen breeding as far north as Lancashire.*

*Above: Amphibians, such as this frog, were the first land animals, but they have kept their close links to water, where their ancestors originated. Therefore amphibians are most common in damp places, such as ponds and rivers, where they can keep their bodies moist.*

Animals are displayed in groups, either where they are biologically related to each other, in a similar classification group or found in a similar habitat, such as within deep seas or in woodland.

Following these informative chapters, each section then contains a directory. Each entry offers a wealth of written and visual information, including distribution maps, habitat, food, size, maturity, breeding and lifespan, as well as lists of related animals, their main characteristics and behaviour.

*Above: Britain is not known for its large mammals. The red deer, seen here in the Scottish Highlands, is the largest wild land mammal likely to be encountered. Its only significant predator is man, so it is widespread, and large numbers often have to be culled.*

**Introduced animals**

There are interesting histories behind many animals of the British Isles. When Britain came under Roman control, around 60CE, rabbits, which we think of as a native British mammal, were introduced for food and sport. House mice were originally natives of Asia, but are thought to have arrived in Britain on Roman ships, as did brown and black rats. These rodents have multiplied and thrived in all sorts of British habitats, and are masters of adaptation. There are many types of bird, mainly game birds, geese and ducks, that have been introduced to hunt or for public or private ornamental bird collections, and have since gone wild. An example is the pheasant, an exotic bird from Asia that is still bred for shooting but thrives in the wild. One mammal, which was brought in by Victorians avid for novelty species, was the grey squirrel that has all but wiped out the native red squirrel.

*Above: Red squirrels can still be found in some parts of Britain.*

# WHAT IS AN ANIMAL?

*More than two million animal species have been described by scientists, and there are probably millions more waiting to be discovered. They live in all corners of the world, and come in a huge range of shapes and sizes. The largest weighs over a hundred tonnes, while the smallest is just a fraction of a millimetre long.*

The living world is divided into five kingdoms: animals, plants, fungi, protists and monerans, which include bacteria. The protists and monerans are micro-organisms. Each individual is just a single cell, and although they often form large masses or colonies – for example, yogurt contains a colony of bacteria – the micro-organisms do not form bodies. The plants, fungi and animals do grow bodies, which are made from millions of cells, all of which work together. These three types of macro-organism, as they are called, tackle the problems of life in different ways.

## The plant kingdom

Plants are the basis of life on Earth, and without them animals would not exist. This is because plants get the energy they need from sunlight (because they do not have to feed actively they are called autotrophes, meaning self-feeders). The green pigments in the plants' leaves trap the energy found in light and convert carbon dioxide and water into glucose, a simple sugar, in a process of food production called photosynthesis. Its by-product is oxygen.

*Below: Anemones are members of the group of cnidarians, like jellyfish. Starfish belong to the group of echinoderms.*

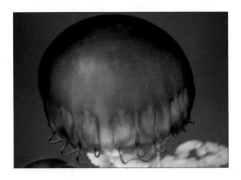
*Above: Jellyfish are very simple animals, related to corals and sea anemones. They catch food by spearing prey with tiny cells called nematocysts.*

*Above: Crabs, such as this hermit crab, are crustaceans. Other crustaceans include lobsters, prawns and krill. Their forelegs are armed with strong pincers.*

## Fungi

Largely invisible organisms, fungi live in large masses of tiny fibres which run through the soil. They only pop up

*Above: Snails belong to a large group of invertebrates called molluscs. Most live in water, but many snails, such as this giant land snail, survive on land.*

*Above: Spiders, scorpions and mites are arachnids. Many spiders build a sticky silk web to trap prey; others lie hidden and pounce on passing victims.*

above the surface in the form of mushrooms and toadstools when they are ready to reproduce. Fungi do not photosynthesize, but they are valuable as decomposers. They grow over the dead bodies of other organisms, such as trees which have fallen to the ground, secreting digestive enzymes that break down the dead body from the outside. They thereby release valuable carbon, nitrogen, phosphorus and other elements which each tree locks up in itself over its lifetime.

## The animal kingdom

Animals could not be more different. They are active feeders (called heterotrophes or 'other-eaters') which collect food from their surroundings.

Unlike plants and fungi, animals are able to swim, walk, burrow or fly.

With the exception of primitive forms, such as sponges, all animal bodies are organized along the same lines. They process their food in a gut, a tube which passes through the body. In most cases the food enters the gut through an opening in the head, that is, the mouth. Once inside the body, the food is broken down into its constituent parts. The useful parts, such as proteins, fats and sugars – made by plants during photosynthesis – are absorbed into the body. The left-over waste material passes out of the gut through the anus, a hole at the other end of the body.

The useful substances absorbed from the food then need to be transported around the body to where they are needed. This job is done by the animal's circulatory system. The insides of many animals are simply bathed in a liquid containing everything required by the body. However, larger animals, including reptiles, amphibians and mammals, need to pump the useful substances around the body in the blood. The pump is the heart, a strong muscle that keeps the blood circulating through a system of vessels.

The blood carries food for the body and also oxygen, which reacts with the sugar from the food, releasing the energy that is essential for all living things to survive. Animals get their oxygen in a number of ways. Some simply absorb it through their skin, many that live in water extract it using gills, and those that live in air breathe it into their lungs.

Compared with other organisms, animals are more aware of their surroundings and certainly more responsive to them. This is because

Above: Apart from bats, birds, such as this kingfisher, are the only flying vertebrates. Their forelimbs have evolved into wings that allow them to perform amazing feats of agility. Feathers are better than hair for keeping the body streamlined for flight.

they have a nervous system which uses sensors to detect what is happening in their environment, such as changes in temperature, the amount of light and various sounds. This information is then transmitted by means of nerves to what could be called the central control. This might just be a dense cluster of nerves, of which the animal might possess several, or it may be a single controlling brain. The brain or nerve cluster passes the information from the senses to the muscles so the body can respond appropriately, either by running away to avoid being eaten or by attacking its prey.

Mammals, reptiles and amphibians share a similar body plan having four limbs. They are members of the larger group of tetrapods, to which birds also belong. Almost all possess a visible tail. The brain and most of the sensors are positioned at the front of the body in the head. Vital organs, such as the heart and lungs (or gills), are located in the central thorax, while the gut and sex organs are found mainly in the abdomen at the rear of the body.

Above: Fish live in all corners of the world's salt-water oceans. They also live in fresh water, where they are found everywhere from submerged caves to mountain lakes.

Above: Frogs are the most familiar of the amphibians. Others include salamanders and newts. The common frog is often seen in British garden ponds.

Above: The British Isles are home to several species of lizard. Common lizards are able to deliberately shed their tails if, for example, a bird attacks, enabling them to escape to safety.

Above: Mammals are the most widespread of vertebrates. However, certain species, such as the red squirrel, decline in number when humans introduce new species to their environment.

# THE HABITATS
# OF BRITAIN

The British Isles are an archipelago of islands to the north-west of continental Europe. For the purposes of this book – to examine the area's mammals, amphibians, reptiles, birds and fish – the term 'Britain' includes all the islands lying off England and Scotland, from the Channel Islands to those of northern Scotland. The two largest islands, Great Britain and Ireland, cover 216,777km$^2$ (83,698 square miles) and 84,406km$^2$ (32,589 square miles) respectively. Within this are mountains and valleys, rivers, lakes and estuaries, rocky and sandy beaches at the base of craggy cliffs, wild mixed forests and thousands of acres of farmland. All these places harbour wildlife, as do urban centres, which have provided a lifestyle for many creatures including rodents, foxes and a great many species of bird.

It is important to be aware of the habitats these islands provide so that they can be conserved. This chapter covers each of the major types of habitat in Britain, and the types of animal they support.

*Above: Much of the British shoreline is rocky, and its sheer cliffs offer safe nesting areas to a wide variety of birds.*

*Left: Great Britain was once completely forested but has largely been cleared in order for humans to build dwellings, graze livestock and farm crops. The result is a very beautiful and diverse environment, but one that is, to a large extent, man-made. This can have a profound effect on the animals resident in the British Isles.*

# FOREST

*Britain's forests are a mixture of farmed plantations, natural habitats and managed native woodland areas. Those richest in fauna are the most undisturbed and made up of native tree species. All, however, provide a home to some wild animals, from small rodents to large herbivores such as deer and in a few places the recently reintroduced wild boar.*

Forest once covered most of the British Isles. Today it has been largely replaced by farmland, but unbroken stretches of natural forest still exist in places, particularly in Britain's wilder areas. Elsewhere, the forests have been subdivided into pockets that are commonly called woods.

The term woodland is used to mean any smaller area covered in trees, however dense. The term ancient woodland is used in British nature conservation to refer to any wooded land that has existed for a very long period. Existing undisturbed for over 400 years, the ancient woodland environment has allowed a unique range of plants and animals to survive. In most places ancient woods are managed, but they provide a vital habitat for a wide range of wildlife.

Ecologically, a woodland is an area that is covered in a variety of native, broadleaf, deciduous species, usually at low density, forming an open habitat, allowing sunlight to penetrate between the trees, and limiting shade.

Far less rich, in terms of species, are the planted areas of conifer forest that have been established with the aim of making money from the land. The trees within them are predominantly non-native. The environment that they create is only favourable to a few native creatures – crossbills, for instance. For most other creatures, with virtually no light at all reaching the forest floor, conifer plantations are almost as barren as a desert.

Britain's natural woodlands, however, are a completely different matter. They are made up of a rich

mixture of tree species and other plants, which in turn provide food and shelter for thousands of wildlife species. This is particularly true of ancient woodland, which provides a home for more wildlife than any other British landscape. Many woods contain species that only like to live in damp shady places where there is little disturbance. Some, such as the pine marten, woodcock and red squirrel are only rarely spotted outside of this habitat. But lots of woodland creatures only reside there for part of their time or search for food outside woodland. These other animals, such as the fox, the badger and many birds, have adapted to the world beyond the wood, and are therefore a much more familiar sight to the human inhabitants of the British Isles.

# GRASSLAND

*Britain is not famous for its wide open spaces, although in fact much of the land today is farmed rather than forested. The long occupation and alteration of the countryside has seen trees cleared to make way for fields. Some forest wildlife has adapted to this change and a few of these species have thrived. Other species, however, have declined, along with their traditional woodland habitat.*

Grasslands are areas where the vegetation is dominated by grasses and other herbaceous (non-woody) plants. The vegetation can vary in height from very short, as in chalk downland, to areas of tall rough grazing, which is often composed of many different species of plant that are adapted to survive in poor growing conditions.

Natural grassland has always been a marginal habitat in Britain. The places in the world where grassland dominates as a habitat are generally dry – too dry for many trees to thrive. Surrounded by ocean and with predominantly westerly winds, Britain has never been short of rain. That said, mankind has changed the British countryside immensely, and farmed or managed grassland has been created on a massive scale, to feed cattle, sheep

and other livestock. In places where most fields are filled with crops, native grassland plants sometimes thrive at the margins. Other unlikely but important areas of grassland exist on the verges next to the huge number of highways throughout the country.

Most of Britain's native animals evolved as forest creatures, but some have adapted to live in or make use of the grassland that now exists. Small mammals, such as rodents and shrews, are able to find as much food here as they could in woodland. Some, such as the long-tailed field mouse and the field vole, have made the transition so successfully that they are now more common here than they ever were in the open forest glades and woodland margins that made up their former habitat. Following these creatures have

come their many predators; mammals such as the fox, and birds of prey such as the kestrel. Night hunters, such as the barn owl, also now search for their meals over agricultural land.

Grassland also suits some of Britain's larger creatures, such as roe deer. By day these secretive animals tend to spend their time in areas of woodland, but as dusk approaches they emerge to graze. In places where people rarely venture they can even be seen in open grassland by day. Other animals which are now thought of as native, but which were actually introduced, thrive in British fields because grassland is the natural habitat in which their species evolved. These include the brown hare and the rabbit, both of which were introduced by the Romans as a food source.

# ROCKY SHORES

*The British Isles is a group of islands surrounded by sea. For its size, it has an incredibly long stretch of coastline – 12,429km (7,723 miles), which is more than twice as much as Spain and nearly four times as much as France. A large part of the British coast is rocky, particularly in the north and west. Here, sheer cliffs plunge to shingle beaches or straight into the sea.*

The wildlife of Britain's coasts in some places is truly spectacular. With its many inaccessible cliffs and offshore islands, the shoreline is a breeding centre for huge numbers of Atlantic seabirds. Britain has the world's largest breeding colonies of gannets, for example. Other birds, such as guillemots, razorbills, puffins and kittiwakes, also have internationally important nesting populations on the coasts of Britain.

Rocky cliffs provide ideal nesting sites for birds that feed at sea. The many crags and crevices provide ready-made platforms on which seabirds can lay their eggs, and their vertical or near-vertical faces offer protection from land-based predators. To make sure that their eggs remain where they should, most cliff-nesting seabirds lay eggs which are very rounded at one end and very pointed at the other. This ensures that if they do roll they roll in a circle. Seabird chicks instinctively move very little on the ledge, except to flap their wings in practice for the final plummet towards the sea.

While rocky shores are great places for birds to breed, they offer very few opportunities for feeding. Swept by crashing waves, they often seem almost devoid of life. Some seaweeds cling on here, however, as do some simple animals. Most of the latter are molluscs – gastropods such as limpets, closely related to land slugs and snails, and the more distantly related bivalve molluscs, such as mussels. These creatures provide food for those predators that can break through their protective shells. The master of this art is the oystercatcher, a striking black and white wading bird. It uses its long, heavy orange bill as a hammer to smash its way in, or as a lever to prise them open. Another wading bird found in this habitat is the turnstone. As its name suggests, it uses its much shorter bill to turn over pebbles in search of young crabs and other small prey, as well as hunting for them in seaweed.

Unlike the beaches themselves, the waters which wash the rocky shores are filled with a wealth of wildlife, including many species of fish. Some of these are restricted to the coastal shallows and others have travelled in from deeper waters or are on migration. They provide food not only for the many nesting seabirds but also for seals and other predators, such as porpoises and dolphins.

# HEATHS AND HIGHLANDS

*Britain's heaths, moors and highlands make up some of the most sparsely populated areas in the country. As a consequence, they often feel truly wild, even when they are actually managed through grazing by livestock or by burning, as many are. The large wild animals that live in these places are easy to spot but many smaller species often go unnoticed.*

Much of Britain's wilderness is made up of heaths and moors. In many cases these habitats have been created by the actions of people – Dartmoor, for instance, was once largely covered by oak woodland. This was depleted by centuries of farming, houses and ship-building, leaving a landscape of heather and gorse. In other places heath is entirely natural, such as near the tops of the highest mountains in Scotland and Wales. Here, it is simply too cold and windswept for trees to become established. Instead, upland vegetation is made up of hardy, low-growing shrubs such as heather and crowberry, and slightly larger plants such as juniper in lowland areas.

Britain's heaths, moors and highlands have their own unique wildlife. They are home to birds such as the red grouse, which feeds mainly on heather, and other, rarer species, such as the black grouse and, higher up, the ptarmigan. These plump, rounded game birds are well adapted to cope with the tough conditions they often find themselves in. Both the red grouse and ptarmigan, for instance, have feathered legs and feet. The ptarmigan, which spends the coldest months of the year in a landscape of snow, also changes colour for the winter, changing the mottled brown feathers on its head and upper parts for a plumage of pure white.

Another denizen of high-altitude heath which turns white is the mountain hare. Britain's only truly native lagomorph, it has existed here since before the last Ice Age, a time when it was doubtless much more common and widespread than it is now. Today, like the ptarmigan, it is confined to the tops of mountains and the highest hills. Its camouflage is more than decorative, as it hides it from the sight of its main predator, the golden eagle.

Less lofty moors and heaths, although similar in appearance, are home to different wildlife. In the south of England, for instance, the heath of the New Forest supports all six of Britain's native reptiles: the adder, the grass snake, the smooth snake, the slow-worm and the common and sand lizards. More famous and easily seen, of course, are the New Forest ponies. Like those on Exmoor and Dartmoor, they are owned but are left to their own devices for most of the year and live as if wild.

# RIVERS, LAKES AND WETLANDS

*The British landscape has been shaped by water. During the last Ice Age glaciers ground out valleys between the hills, and since then rivers have shaped the land further as they journey to the sea. The inland rivers and lakes teem with wildlife in and around their shores, while freshwater estuaries, marshes and even garden ponds and urban canals are hosts to both water- and land-based creatures.*

Today, Britain's rivers run through both glacial valleys and valleys they have carved out themselves. The personality of a river changes from its beginning to its end. In its upper reaches a river is relatively small and narrow, but flows quickly as it rushes downhill. Later it slows and widens as it hits flatter ground and is joined by other, smaller tributaries. Finally it pours into lakes or the sea. Most of those which do the latter merge with the waters of the ocean, which rush up their channels with every high tide.

The areas where this merging happens see huge amounts of silt and other sediment dropped from suspension, and are known as estuaries. When the tide goes out their mud flats are exposed, and these areas become a magnet for wading birds, which gorge themselves on the many worms and other invertebrate creatures that live within the mud.

Rivers provide a habitat for a great many fish. Some, such as salmon, migrate into them from the ocean to breed, but the majority of species spend their entire lives in these ribbons of fresh water. Many invertebrates also make their homes in rivers, from insect larvae to crustaceans, such as crayfish. These creatures often provide food for the larger fish, amphibians and mammals in these habitats. In the upper reaches of rivers, dippers dive in search of the insect larvae that live on the bottom, while downstream, otters, kingfishers and herons hunt for fish.

Land-based mammals also make the river banks their home; the otter and the water shrew spend most of their waking hours in water, and beavers are almost entirely water-dwelling. Some rivers flow over such flat ground that they form reed beds and marshes. These habitats also exist on the edges of reservoirs and lakes.

Reed beds have their own distinctive wildlife, including many birds that are not found anywhere else. These creatures range from small species, such as reed warblers and bearded tits, to large predators such as the bittern. They also attract ducks, as do Britain's lakes and other open areas of still water. As well as the familiar birds, amphibians such as the great crested newt and marsh frog can occasionally be spotted in Britain's waterways. While it may be tempting to children to catch tadpoles, they are far better left undisturbed.

# PARKS AND GARDENS

*Wildlife is not only found in the countryside. Seen from the air, British towns and cities are dotted with green oases in the shape of gardens and parks. These man-made habitats are often surprisingly rich in wild creatures. Some, such as garden birds, are easy to spot, but others are more mysterious, particularly those that come out only at night.*

In modern Britian, suburban gardens and city parks have become a haven for many birds.

The popularity of garden bird tables and feeders means that there is often a year-round supply of food, laid on without the need for the birds to search for it. Species which naturally occur in woodlands, such as blue tits and great tits, are now just as likely to be seen in gardens. In some places they are even more common in towns than in the surrounding countryside.

Another factor that has encouraged these birds to take up residence in urban areas is the provision of nest boxes. In the wild these birds nest in holes in trees, but with many woods now being managed, the dead trees which most often offer these natural nest sites are becoming less common,

as they are often removed. Other small birds benefit from the industry of gardeners. Species such as the robin and the dunnock find the open soil of vegetable patches and flower beds to be perfect places to search for the earthworms and other ground-dwelling invertebrates they eat. When the gardener turns over the soil, even more opportunities appear.

As small birds have moved into gardens the creatures that hunt them have followed. One bird of prey now regularly seen in suburbia is the sparrowhawk, a species which evolved to hunt small birds in Britain's forests and woods. Other birds hunt the rodents that live in towns and cities.

In parks, even in the biggest cities, tawny owls are now not uncommon. Some mammals and other creatures

have moved into city parks and gardens to feed on the invertebrates they find there. One such creature is the hedgehog, popular with gardeners because of its predilection for slugs and snails. Other slug and snail predators have been lured in by the provision of breeding sites, notably amphibians. The pond, large or small, has become a lifeline for Britain's frogs, toads and newts.

Mice and rats do well in cities because of the amount of food and waste that is dropped. Another creature which has learned to take advantage of human rubbish is the fox. Many cities now have extremely large populations of foxes. In fact, urban foxes find it so easy to find food that they often live in far greater densities than their cousins in the countryside.

# UNDERSTANDING MAMMALS, AMPHIBIANS AND REPTILES

The evolution of mammals from synapsids (mammal-like 'reptiles') was a gradual process that took approximately 70 million years. Animals are defined in terms of their body organization, their place in evolution and their anatomy.

This part of the book examines how the animals that are defined as either mammal, amphibian or reptile see, hear, smell and taste, how they find food, how they defend their territories, and how they find mates and care for their offspring. It then describes and illustrates each type's body features and some facets of their behaviour. There are also discussions about evolution, survival, reproduction, migration, hibernation, classification and ecology as well as the issues of introduced and endangered species.

*Above: A pair of grey seals basks on the coast of Scotland. Grey seals live across the North Atlantic and can be found on the coasts of northern Europe and the Baltic Sea.*

*Left: Fallow deer buck in the rutting (mating) season. These animals may have been first brought to Britain by the Romans, but were certainly reintroduced by the Normans for hunting in the royal forests of Great Britain and Ireland. The species originated in the Middle East and Mediterranean region.*

# EVOLUTION

*Animals and other forms of life did not just suddenly appear on the Earth. They evolved over billions of years into countless different forms. The mechanism by which they evolved is called natural selection. The process of natural selection was first proposed by British naturalist Charles Darwin.*

Animals dwell in a vast array of habitats, from the waters of the deep oceans to the tops of hills and mountains. The problems faced by animals in these and other habitats on Earth are very different, and so life has evolved in great variety. Each class of animal, whether mammal, amphibian or reptile, needs a body that can cope with its environment. Even in Britain, the diversity of animal life is staggering.

## Darwinian theory

At the turn of the 19th century, geologists began to realize that the world was extremely old. They studied animal fossils and measured the age of the exposed layers of rock found in cliffs and canyons. Today we accept that the Earth is about 4.5 billion years old, but in the early 1800s the idea that the world was unimaginably old was completely new to most people.

### Jumping animals

Many animals can leap into the air, but thanks to natural selection this simple ability has been harnessed by different animals in different ways. For example, click beetles jump in somersaults to frighten off attackers, while blood-sucking fleas can leap enormous heights to move from host to host.

*Above: The hare has muscular hind legs that enable it to leap at high speed – up to 45 miles per hour. Its cousin, the mountain hare, hops like a kangaroo.*

In addition, naturalists had always known that there was a fantastic variety of animals, but now they realized that many could be grouped into families, as if they were related. By the middle of the 19th century, two British biologists had independently formulated an idea that would change the way that people saw themselves and the natural world forever. Charles Darwin and Alfred Wallace thought that the world's different animal species had gradually evolved from extinct relatives, like the ones preserved as fossils.

## Survival of the fittest

Darwin and Wallace came up with the idea of natural selection, suggesting that wild animal species gradually evolved through a system similar to the artificial selection that people used to breed prize cattle, sheep and pedigree dogs.

The theory of natural selection is often described as the survival of the fittest. This is because animals compete with each other for resources including food, water, shelter and mates. Some members of a population of animals will have characteristics that make them better suited to the environment at that time. These 'fitter' animals will be more successful at finding food and avoiding predators. Consequently, they will probably produce more offspring, many of which will also have the same characteristics as their parents. As a result of this, the next generation will contain more individuals with the 'fit' trait. After many generations the whole population may carry the fit trait.

## Variation and time

The environment is not fixed, and does not stay the same for long. Volcanoes, and climate changes, for example, alter the conditions which animals have to confront. Natural selection relies on the way in which different individual animals cope with these changes. Those

*Above: Scientists know about extinct animals from studying fossils such as this fish skeleton. Fossils are the remains of dead plants or animals that have been turned to stone by natural processes over millions of years.*

individuals that were once 'fit' may later die out, as others with a different set of characteristics become more successful in the changed environment.

As the process of natural selection continues for millions of years, so groups of animals can change radically, giving rise to a new species. Life is thought to have been evolving for 3.5 billion years. In that time natural selection has produced a staggering number of species.

New species may gradually arise from a single group of animals. In fact the original species may be replaced by one or more new species. This can happen when two separate groups of one species are kept apart by an impassable geographical feature. Isolated from each other, both groups then evolve in different ways.

## Mammals

Animals of the Mammalia class, including whales, carnivores, rodents, bats and primates, are warm-blooded vertebrates with mammary glands, a thoracic diaphragm, and a four-chambered heart. The largest animal that has ever existed, the blue whale, shares several crucial traits with the tiniest shrew, but these shared characteristics cannot disguise the huge diversity within the mammal class. To add to this great diversity, mammals live in more places on Earth than any other group of animals, from the frozen ice fields of the Arctic to the sandy soil of African deserts, and have each evolved accordingly.

## Amphibians

Cold-blooded vertebrates, typically living on land but breeding in water, belong to the amphibian class, which includes newts, salamanders, frogs, toads, and caecilians. Although amphibians live on every continent, except for Antarctica, none can survive in salt water. Being cold-blooded, most amphibians are found in the warmer regions of the world. Unlike other land vertebrates, amphibians spend the early part of their lives in a different form from that of the adults. As they grow, the young metamorphose into the adult body. Having a larval form means that the adults and their offspring live and feed in different places. In general the larvae are aquatic.

The adults are predatory, feeding on other animals, while the young are generally plant eaters, filtering tiny plants from the water or grazing on aquatic plants lining the bottom of ponds and rivers.

## Reptiles

Cold-blooded vertebrates possessing lungs and an outer covering of horny scales are classified as reptiles, a group of animals consisting of about 6,500 species. Reptiles have a great diversity of body shape and live in a large range of habitats, from the deep ocean to the scorching desert.

Most reptiles lay eggs, but these are different from those of an amphibian because they have a hard, thin shell rather than a soft, jelly-like one. The water-tight shelled egg was an evolutionary breakthrough because it meant that adult reptiles did not have to return to the water to breed. The eggs could be laid in even the driest places.

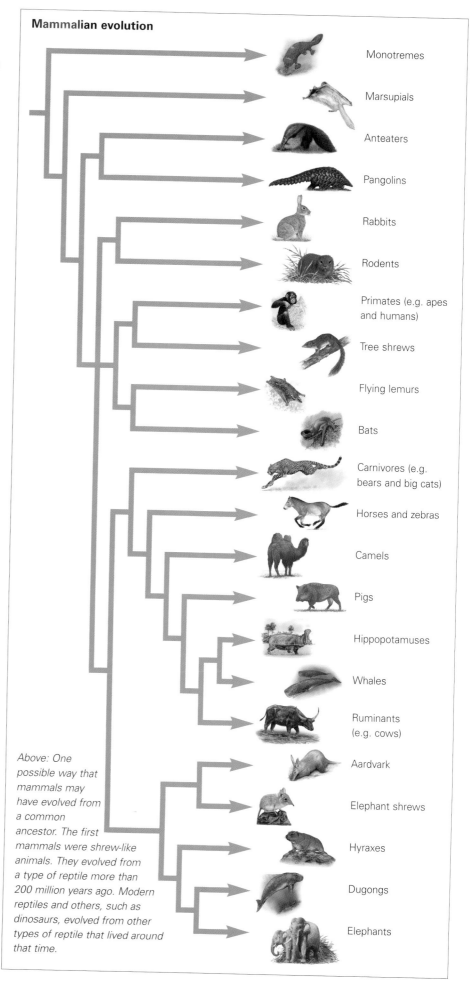

**Mammalian evolution**

Monotremes · Marsupials · Anteaters · Pangolins · Rabbits · Rodents · Primates (e.g. apes and humans) · Tree shrews · Flying lemurs · Bats · Carnivores (e.g. bears and big cats) · Horses and zebras · Camels · Pigs · Hippopotamuses · Whales · Ruminants (e.g. cows) · Aardvark · Elephant shrews · Hyraxes · Dugongs · Elephants

*Above: One possible way that mammals may have evolved from a common ancestor. The first mammals were shrew-like animals. They evolved from a type of reptile more than 200 million years ago. Modern reptiles and others, such as dinosaurs, evolved from other types of reptile that lived around that time.*

# CLASSIFICATION

*Scientists classify all living things into categories. Members of each category share features with each other – traits that set them apart from other animals. Over the years, a tree of categories and subcategories has been pieced together, showing how all living things seem to be related to each other.*

Taxonomy, the scientific discipline of categorizing organisms, aims to classify and order the millions of animals on Earth so that we can better understand them and their relationship to each other. The Greek philosopher Aristotle was among the first people to do this for animals in the 4th century BC. In the 18th century, Swedish naturalist Carolus Linnaeus formulated the system that we use today.

By the end of the 17th century, naturalists had noticed that many animals seemed to have several close relatives that resembled one another. For example lions, lynxes and domestic cats all seemed more similar to each other than they did to dogs, for example, or horses. However, all of these animals – cats, horses and dogs – shared common features that they did not share with frogs, slugs or wasps.

Linnaeus devised a way of classifying these observations. The system he set up – known as the Linnaean system – orders animals in a hierarchy of divisions. From the largest division to the smallest, this system is as follows: kingdom, phylum, class, order, family, genus, species.

## Binomila nomenclature

Each species is given a two-word scientific name, derived from Latin and Greek. For example, *Panthera leo* is the scientific name of the lion. The first word is the genus name, while the second is the species name. Therefore *Panthera leo* means the '*leo*' species in the genus '*Panthera*'. This system of two-word classification is known as binomial nomenclature.

Lions, lynxes and other genera of cats belong to the Felidae family. The Felidae are included in the order

*Above: Within the* Mustelidae *family there are many different characteristics. The pine marten, for example, is the only member with semi-retractable claws.*

Carnivora, along with dogs and similar predators. The Carnivora, in turn, belong to the class Mammalia, which includes horses and all other mammals.

Mammals belong to the phylum Chordata, the major group which contains all vertebrates, including reptiles, amphibians, birds, fish and some other small animals called tunicates and lancelets. In their turn, Chordata belong to the kingdom Animalia, comprising around 31 living phyla, including Mollusca, which contains slugs, and Arthropoda, which contains wasps and other insects.

## Cladistics

Although we still use Linnaean grouping, modern taxonomy is worked out in a different way. Linnaeus classified animals by their outward

*Left: Polecats (*Mustela putorius*) are members of the* Mustelidae *group of carnivorous mammals, and related to pine martens, otters, minks, stoats and weasels.*

## Close relations

Cheetahs, caracals and servals all belong to the cat family Felidae, which also includes lions, tigers, wildcats, lynxes and jaguars. Within this family there are two groups: big and small cats. These can generally be distinguished by their size, with a few exceptions.

For example, the cheetah is often classed as a big cat, but it is actually smaller than the cougar, a small cat. One of the main differences between the two groups is that big cats can roar but not purr continuously, while small cats are able to purr but not roar.

*Above: The cheetah (Acinonyx jubatus) differs from all other cats in possessing nonretractable claws without sheaths. This species is classed in a group of its own, but is often included within the group of big cats.*

*Above: The caracal (Caracal caracal) is included in the group of small cats (subfamily Felinae), but most scientists place it in a genus of its own, Caracal, rather than in the main genus, Felis.*

*Above: The serval (Felis serval) is a medium-sized member of the Felis or small cat genus. This cat has very large ears, which are used to detect the sounds of prey hidden among tall grasses.*

## Distant relations

All vertebrates (backboned animals), including birds, reptiles and mammals such as seals and dolphins, are thought to have evolved from common fish ancestors that swam in the oceans some 400 million years ago. Later, one group of fish developed

limb-like organs and came on to the land, where they slowly evolved into amphibians and later reptiles, which in turn gave rise to mammals. Later, seals and dolphins returned to the oceans and their limbs evolved into paddle-like flippers.

*Above: Fish are an ancient group of aquatic animals that mainly propel themselves by thrashing their vertically aligned caudal fin, or tail, and steer using their fins.*

*Above: In seals, the four limbs have evolved into flippers that make highly effective paddles in water but are less useful on land, where seals are ungainly in their movements.*

*Above: Whales and dolphins never come on land, and their ancestors' hind limbs have all but disappeared. They resemble fish but the tail is horizontally – not vertically – aligned.*

appearance. Although this was usually correct when it came to the large divisions, the method was not foolproof. For example, some early scientists believed that whales and dolphins, with their fins and streamlined

bodies, were types of fish and not mammals at all. Today, accurate classification is achieved through a field of study called cladistics. This uses genetic analysis to check how animals are related by evolutionary change.

Animals are grouped according to how they evolved, with each division sharing a common ancestor somewhere in the past. As the classification of living organisms improves, so does our understanding of life on Earth.

# ANATOMY

*Mammals, reptiles and amphibians come in a mind-boggling array of shapes and sizes. However, all of them – from whales to bats and frogs to snakes – share a basic body plan, both inside and out, down to their internal organs, which vary but again have distinct similarities.*

Vertebrates are animals with a spine, generally made of bone. Bone, the hard tissues of which contain chalky substances, is also the main component of the rest of the vertebrate skeleton. The bones of the skeleton link together to form a rigid frame to protect organs and give the body its shape, while also allowing it to move. Cartilage, a softer, more flexible but tough tissue is found, for example, at the ends of bones in mobile joints, in the ears and the nose (forming the sides and the partition between the two nostrils). Some fish, including sharks and rays, have skeletons that consist entirely of cartilage.

## Nerves and muscles

Vertebrates also have a spinal cord, a thick bundle of nerves extending from the brain through the spine, and down into the tail. The nerves in the spinal cord are used to control walking and other reflex movements by co-ordinating blocks of muscle that work together. A vertebrate's skeleton is on the inside, in contrast to many invertebrates, which have an outer skeleton or exoskeleton. The vertebrate skeleton provides a solid structure which the body's muscles pull against. Muscles are blocks of protein that can contract and relax when they get an electrical impulse from a nerve.

### Invertebrates

The huge majority of animals are invertebrates. They are a much more varied group than the vertebrates and include creatures such as insects, shrimps, slugs, butterflies and starfish. Although some squid are thought to reach the size of a small whale, and octopuses are at least as intelligent as cats and dogs, most invertebrates are much smaller and simpler animals than the vertebrates. Insects thrive in every environment in the world and are essential in the food chain.

*Below: The most successful invertebrates are the insects, including the wasp.*

## Reptile bodies

Reptiles have an internal skeleton made from bone and cartilage. Their skin is covered in scales, which are often toughened by a waxy protein called keratin.

Turtles are quite different from other reptiles. They have a simpler skull and a shell that is joined to the animal's internal skeleton.

*Below: Crocodiles have a very strong body, designed for life in and around shallow water.*

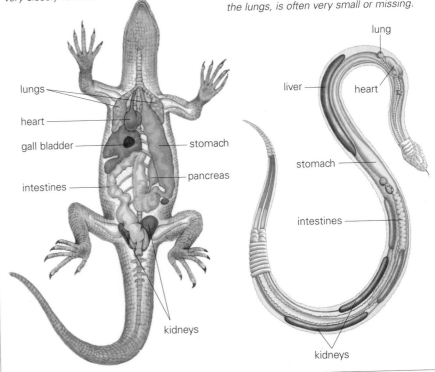

stomach  lungs

windpipe

heart

intestines

*Below: Lizards have a similar body plan to crocodiles, although they are actually not very closely related.*

*Below: Snakes' internal organs are elongated so that they fit into their long, thin body. One of a pair of organs, such as the lungs, is often very small or missing.*

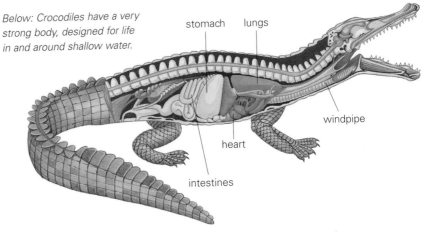

lungs

heart

gall bladder

intestines

stomach

pancreas

kidneys

lung

liver

heart

stomach

intestines

kidneys

When on the move, the vertebrate body works like a system of pulleys, pivots and levers. The muscles are the engines of the body, and are attached to bones – the levers – by strong cables called tendons. The joint between two bones forms a pivot, and the muscles work in pairs to move a bone. For example, when an arm is bent at the elbow to raise the forearm, the bicep muscle on the front of the upper arm has to contract. This pulls the forearm up, while the tricep muscle attached to the back of the upper arm remains relaxed. To straighten the arm again, the tricep contracts and the bicep relaxes. If both muscles contract at the same time, they pull against each other, and the arm remains locked in whatever position it is in.

## Vital organs

Muscles are not only attached to the skeleton. The gut – including the stomach and intestines – is surrounded by muscles. These muscles contract in rhythmic waves to push food and waste products through the body. The heart is a muscular organ made of a very strong muscle which keeps on contracting and relaxing, pumping blood around the body. The heart and other vital organs are found in the thorax, that part of the body which lies between the forelimbs. In reptiles and mammals the thorax is kept well protected, the rib cage surrounding the heart, lungs, liver and kidneys.

Vertebrates have a single liver consisting of a number of lobes. The liver has a varied role, making chemicals required by the body and storing food. Most vertebrates also have two kidneys. Their role is to clean the blood of any impurities and toxins, and to remove excess water. The main toxins that have to be removed are compounds containing nitrogen, the by-products of eating protein. Mammal and amphibian kidneys dissolve these toxins in water to make urine. However, since many reptiles live in very dry habitats, they cannot afford to use water to remove waste, and they instead get rid of it as a solid waste similar to bird excrement.

## Mammalian bodies

Most mammals are four-limbed and have at least some hair on their bodies (exceptions being sea mammals such as whales). The females produce milk. Mammals live in a wide range of habitats and their bodies are adapted in many ways to survive. Their internal organs vary depending on where they live and what they eat.

*Below: Gorillas are knuckle-walkers. Like other apes, they have a large brain for their body size. This allows them to live in complicated social groups.*

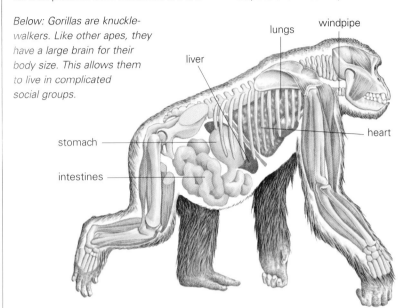

*Below: Cheetahs are built for speed. Their bodies are slender and light, and their claws are nonretractable, allowing them to grip the ground when running.*

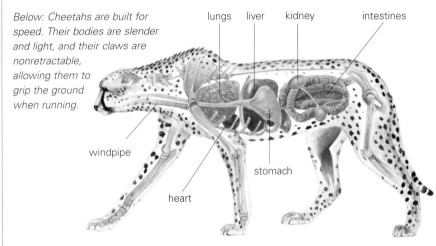

*Below: Elephants have a unique skeleton that can hold the weight of their especially heavy body.*

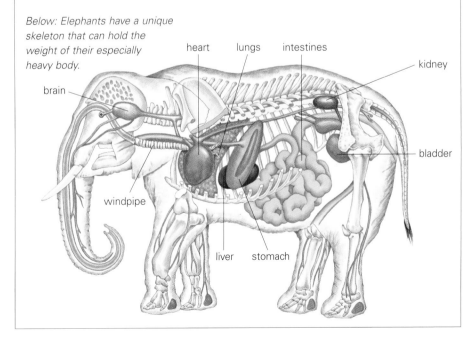

# SENSES

*To stay alive, animals must find food and shelter, and defend themselves against predators. To achieve these things, they are equipped with an array of senses for monitoring their surroundings. Different species have senses adapted to nocturnal or diurnal (day-active) life.*

An animal's senses are its early-warning system. They alert it to changes in its surroundings, which may signal an opportunity to feed or mate, or the need to escape danger. The ability to act quickly and appropriately is made possible because the senses are linked to the brain by a network of nerves which send messages as electric pulses. When the brain receives information from the senses it co-ordinates its response.

In many cases, generally in response to something touching the body, the signal from the sensor does not reach the brain before action is taken. Instead, it produces a reflex response which is hardwired into the nervous system. For example, when you touch a very hot object, your hand automatically recoils; you don't need to think about it.

All animals have to be sensitive to their environment to survive. Even the simplest animals, such as jellyfish and roundworms, react to changes in their surroundings. Simple animals, however, have only a limited ability to move or defend themselves, and have limited senses. Larger animals, such as vertebrates, have a much more complex array of sense organs. Most vertebrates can hear, see, smell, taste and touch.

## Vision

The eyes of invertebrates are generally designed to detect motion. Vertebrates' eyes, however, are better at forming clear images, often in colour. Vertebrates' eyes are balls of clear jelly, which have an inner lining of light-sensitive cells. This lining, called the retina, is made up of one or two types of cell. The rod cells – named after their shape – are very sensitive to all types of light, but are only capable of forming black and white images. Animals which are active at night generally have (and need) only rods in their eyes.

Colour vision is important for just a few animals, such as monkeys, which need, for example, to see the brightest and therefore ripest fruits. Colour images are made by the cone cells – so named because of their shape – in the retina. There are three types of cone, each of which is sensitive to a particular wavelength of light. Low wavelengths appear as reds, high wavelengths as blues, with green colours being detected in between.

The light is focused on the retina by a lens to produce a clear image. Muscles change the shape of the lens so that it

*Above: Frogs have large eyes positioned on the upper side of the head so that the animals can lie mainly submerged in water with just their eyes poking out.*

can focus the light arriving from different distances. While invertebrates may have several eyes, all vertebrates have just two, and they are always positioned on the head. Animals such as rabbits, which are constantly looking out for danger, have eyes on the side of the head to give a wide field of vision. But while they can see in almost all directions, rabbits have difficulty judging distances and speeds. Animals that have eyes pointing forward are better at doing this because each eye's field of vision overlaps with the other. This binocular vision helps hunting animals and others, such as tree-living primates, to judge distances more accurately.

Eyes can also detect radiation in a small band of wavelengths, and some animals detect radiation that is invisible to our eyes. Flying insects and birds can see ultraviolet light, which extends the range of their colour vision. At the other end of the spectrum many snakes can detect radiation with a lower wavelength. They sense infrared, or heat, through pits on the face which enables them to track their warm-blooded prey in pitch darkness.

*Below: The wildcat's eyes are able to reflect light back through the retina, giving the animal excellent night vision because the retina has two chances to catch the light.*

*Below: Like other hunters, a seal has eyes positioned on the front of its head. Forward-looking eyes are useful for judging distances, making it easier to chase down prey.*

## Hearing

An animal's brain interprets waves of pressure travelling through the air, and detected by the ears, as sound. Many animals do not hear these waves with ears but detect them in other ways instead. For example, although snakes can hear, they are much more sensitive to vibrations through the lower jaw, travelling through the ground. Long facial whiskers sported by many mammals, from cats to seals, are very sensitive touch receptors. They can be so sensitive that they will even respond to currents in the air.

In many ways, hearing is a sensitive extension of the sense of touch. The ears of amphibians, reptiles and mammals have an eardrum which is sensitive to tiny changes in pressure. An eardrum is a thin membrane of skin which vibrates as the air waves hit it. A tiny bone (or in the case of mammals, three bones) attached to the drum transmit the vibrations to a shell-shaped structure called a cochlea. The cochlea is filled with a liquid which picks up the vibrations. As the liquid moves inside the cochlea, tiny hair-like structures lining it wave back and forth. Nerves stimulated by this wave motion send the information to the brain, which interprets it as sound.

A mammal's ear is divided into three sections. The cochlea forms the inner ear and the middle ear consists of the bones between the cochlea and eardrum. The outer ear is the tube

joining the outside world and the auricle – the fleshy structure on the side of the head that collects the sound waves – to the middle ear. Amphibians and reptiles do not possess auricles. Instead their eardrums are either on the side of the head – easily visible on many frogs and lizards – or under the skin, as in snakes.

*Below: Rabbits have large outer ears which they use like satellite dishes to pick up sound waves. They can rotate each ear separately to detect sound from all directions.*

*Below: Lizards do not have outer ears at all. Their hearing organs are contained inside the head and joined to the outside world through an eardrum membrane.*

*Above: Snakes, such as this adder, have forked tongues that they use to taste the air. The tips of the fork are slotted into an organ in the roof of the mouth. This organ is linked to the nose, and chemicals picked up by the tongue are identified with great sensitivity.*

## Smell and taste

These two senses are so closely related as to form a single sense. Snakes and lizards, for example, 'smell' the air with their forked tongues. Noses, tongues and other smelling organs are lined with sensitive cells which can analyse a huge range of chemicals that float in the air or exist in food. Animals such as dogs, which are highly dependent on their sense of smell, have long noses packed with odour-sensitive cells. Rabbits' noses have moveable folds to help expose their 100 million scent cells to odours around them and alert them to food or danger. Cats, on the other hand, are less reliant on a sense of smell, and have small nostrils capable only of detecting stronger odours.

# SURVIVAL

*Animals must not only find enough food to sustain life, they must also manage to avoid becoming a predator's meal. To achieve this, animals have evolved many strategies to feed on a wide range of foods, and utilize an array of weapons and defensive tactics to keep safe.*

An animal must keep feeding in order to replace the energy used in staying alive. Substances in the food, such as sugars, are burned by the body, and the subsequent release of energy is used to heat the body and power its movements. Food is also essential for growth. Although most growth takes place during the early period of an animal's life, it never really stops because injuries need to heal and worn-out tissues need replacing. Some animals continue growing throughout life. Proteins in the food are the main building blocks of living bodies.

## Plant food

Some animals will eat just about anything, while others are much more fussy. As a group, vertebrates get their energy from a wide range of sources – as diverse as shellfish, wood, honey and blood. Animals are often classified according to how they feed, forming several large groups filled with many otherwise unrelated animals.

Animals that eat plants are generally grouped together as herbivores. But this term is not very descriptive because there is such a wide range of plant foods. Animals that eat grass are known as grazers. However, this term can also apply to any animal which eats any plant that covers the ground

*Above: Ponies are grazers. They eat grass and plants that grow close to the ground. Because their food is all around them, grazers spend a long time out in the open. They often feed together in herds for safety.*

in large amounts, such as seaweed or sedge. Typical grazers include rabbits and hares; ponies and horses are also grazers. Animals such as roe deer, which pick off the tastiest leaves, buds and fruit from bushes and trees, are called browsers. Many animals have a much broader diet, eating everything

from plants and fungi to invertebrates and larger prey. Animals that eat both plant and animal foods are called omnivores. Badgers are omnivorous, as are humans, but the most catholic of tastes belong to scavenging animals, such as rats and some other rodents, which eat anything they can get their teeth into. Omnivores in general, and scavengers in particular, are very curious animals. They will investigate anything that looks or smells like food, and if it also tastes like food, then it probably is.

## A taste for flesh

The term carnivore is often applied to any animal that eats flesh, but it is more correctly used to refer to an order of mammals which includes cats, dogs, bears and smaller animals, such as weasels. These animals are the kings of killing, armed with sharp claws and teeth. They use their strength and speed to overpower their prey, either by running them down or taking them by surprise with an ambush.

However, land-dwelling carnivores are not the only expert killers. Seals and indeed many fish are highly

*Below: Deer are browsers, not grazers. They will eat some grass but also pick tastier leaves, buds and fruit off trees and shrubs. They often live in herds to stay safe from attack.*

*Below: Stoats are voracious hunters, with a long, lithe, almost serpentine body, which is ideal for pursuing their prey of small mammals through holes and along tunnels.*

Above: Wild boars have few predators,
apart from man. They will charge at humans
if they feel threatened.

**Filter-feeders**
Some animals filter their food from
water. The giant baleen whales do this,
sieving tiny shrimp-like animals called
krill out of great gulps of sea water.
Some tadpoles filter-feed as well,
extracting tiny plant-like animals which
float in fresh water. However, after
becoming adults, all amphibians become
hunters and eat other animals. All snakes
and most lizards are meat-eaters, or
carnivores, as well.

Below: One of the largest animals of all,
humpback whales are filter-feeders. They
do not have teeth. Instead, their gums
are lined with a thick curtain of baleen
that filters out food from the sea water.

effective predators, hunting their prey
underwater. Bats, on the other hand,
eat the insects they catch in the air.

While snakes are much smaller in
comparison, they are just as deadly, if
not more so. They kill in one of two
ways, either suffocating their prey by
wrapping their coils tightly around
them, or by injecting them with a
poison through their fangs. The only
poisonous snake of the British Isles is
the adder. Its venom is used to kill the
lizards and small mammals that it feeds
on. It will only bite humans in defence,
if it is trodden on or provoked.

## Hunter or hunted
Many predators rely on stealth to catch
their prey, and staying hidden is part of
the plan. A camouflaged coat helps
animals blend into their surroundings.
Many species also use this technique to
ensure that they do not get eaten. Most
freeze when danger approaches, and
then scurry to safety as quickly as
possible. Plant-eating animals that live
in the open cannot hide from predators
that are armed with sharp teeth and

Right: The mountain hare's fur begins to
turn white in the autumn. By the time its
Scottish mountain habitat is covered in
snow, it is extremely well camouflaged.

claws. The plant-eaters cannot rely on
such weapons to defend themselves.
They do not possess sharp, pointed
teeth but flattened ones to grind up
their plant food. The best chance they
have of avoiding danger is to run away.
Animals such as deer consequently
have long, hoofed feet that lengthen
their legs considerably; they are, in
fact, standing on their toenails. These
long legs allow them to run faster and
leap high into the air to escape an
attacker's jaws.

Animals that do not flee must stand
and fight. Most large herbivores are
armed with horns or antlers. Although
used chiefly for display, the horns are
the animals' last line of defence when
cornered, and can be very effective.

# REPRODUCTION

*All animals share the urge to produce offspring that will survive after the parents die. The process of heredity is determined by genes, through which characteristics are passed from parents to offspring. Reproduction presents several problems, and animals have adopted different strategies for tackling them.*

Animals have two main goals: to find food and a mate. To achieve these goals, they must survive everything that the environment throws at them, from extremes of the weather, such as floods and droughts, to hungry predators. They have to find sufficient supplies of food, and on top of that locate a mate before their competitors. If they find sufficient food but fail to produce any offspring, their genes will not be passed on.

## One parent or two?

There are two ways in which an animal can reproduce, asexually or sexually. Animals that are produced by asexual reproduction, or parthenogenesis, have only one parent, a mother. The offspring are genetically identical to their mother and to each other. Sexual reproduction involves two parents of opposite sex. The offspring are hybrids of the two parents, with a mixture of their parents' characteristics.

The offspring inherit their parents' traits through their genes. Genes can be defined in various ways. One simple definition is that they are the

*Below: Newts attach their eggs to the leaves of underwater plants, where they stay anchored until they hatch. According to the water temperature this takes 2–3 weeks. The young are born with gills, then metamorphose into air-breathing juveniles.*

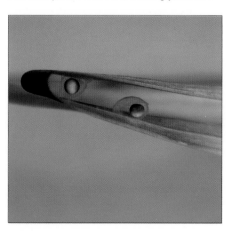

*Above: Many male frogs croak by pumping air into an expandable throat sac. The croak is intended to attract females. The deeper the croak, the more attractive it is. However, some males lurk silently and mate with females as they approach the croaking males.*

unit of inheritance – a single inherited characteristic which cannot be subdivided any further. Genes are also segments of DNA (deoxyribonucleic acid), a complex chemical that forms long chains. DNA is found at the heart of every living cell. Each link in the DNA chain forms part of a code that controls how an animal's body develops and survives. And every cell in the body contains a full set of DNA which could be used to build a whole new body.

Animals which are produced through sexual reproduction receive half their DNA, or half their genes, from each of their parents. The male parent provides his half in the supply of genes contained in the sperm. Each sperm's only role is to find its way to, and fertilize, an egg, its female equivalent. Besides containing the other half of the DNA sequence, the egg also holds a supply of food for the offspring as it develops into a new individual. Animals that are created through parthenogenesis get all their genes from their mother, and all of them are therefore the same sex – female.

*Above: In deer and many other grazing herds, the males fight each other for the right to mate with the females. The deer with the largest antlers often wins without fighting, and real fights only break out if two males appear equally well-endowed.*

## Sexual and asexual reproduction

All mammals reproduce sexually, as do most reptiles and amphibians. However, some amphibians and reptiles reproduce by the asexual process of parthenogenesis. There are benefits and disadvantages to both types of reproduction. Parthenogenesis, where the female grows and develops embryos without fertilization by a male, is quick and convenient. The mother does not need to find a mate, and can devote all her energy to producing huge numbers of young. This strategy is ideal for populating as yet unexploited territory. However, being identical, these animals are vulnerable to attack. If, for example, one is killed by a disease or outwitted by a predator, it is likely that they will all suffer the same fate. Consequently, whole communities of animals produced by parthenogenesis can be wiped out.

Animals produced sexually, on the other hand, are more varied. Each is unique, formed by a mixture of genes from both parents, which means that a group of animals produced by sexual reproduction is more likely to triumph over adversity than a group of asexual ones. However, sexual reproduction takes up a great deal of time and effort.

## Attracting mates

Since females produce only a limited number of eggs, they are keen to make sure that they are fertilized by a male with good genes. If a male is fit and healthy, this is a sign that he has good genes. Good genes will ensure that the offspring will be able to compete with other animals for food and mates of their own. Because the females have the final say in agreeing to mate, the males have to put a lot of effort into getting noticed. Many are brightly coloured, make loud noises, and they are often larger than the females. In many species the males even compete with each other for the right to display to the females. Winning that right is a good sign that they have the best genes.

*Above: A vixen may mate with several males before she settles for one. Males will then supply the female with food until after birth in the spring, but otherwise leave her alone. The kits will leave the litter in the autumn.*

## Parental care

The amount of care that the offspring receive from their parents varies considerably. There is a necessary trade-off between the amount of useful care parents can give to each offspring, the number of offspring they can produce and how regularly they can breed. Mammals invest heavily in parental care, rearing their young after birth, while most young amphibians and reptiles have no contact with parents.

By suckling, mammals ensure that their young grow to a size where they can look after themselves. Generally, the young stay with the mother until it is time for her to give birth to the next litter – at least one or two months. However, in many species, including humans, the young stay with their parents for many years.

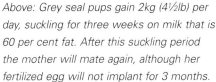

*Above: Grey seal pups gain 2kg (4½lb) per day, suckling for three weeks on milk that is 60 per cent fat. After this suckling period the mother will mate again, although her fertilized egg will not implant for 3 months.*

Other types of animals pursue the opposite strategy, producing large numbers of young that are left to fend for themselves. The vast majority in each batch of eggs – consisting of hundreds or even thousands – die before reaching adulthood, and many never even hatch. The survival rates, for example of tadpoles, the young of frogs, are very low.

Animals that live in complicated societies, such as humans, tend to produce a single offspring every few years. The parents direct their energies into protecting and rearing the young, giving them a good chance of survival. Animals which live for only a short time, such as mice, rabbits, and reptiles and amphibians in general, need to reproduce much more rapidly to make the most of their short lives. They produce high numbers of young, and do not waste time on anything more than the bare minimum of parental care. If successful, these animals can reproduce at an alarming pace.

*Left: A pony on Exmoor with her moulting foal. Most foals are born in May or June. They are herded, registered and sold in the autumn when the foals are just weaned, as the moor has restricted grazing areas.*

# MIGRATION AND HIBERNATION

*The British climate changes throughout the year with the cycle of seasons. Some animals are able to cope with this and are active all year round. Others find their food sources drying up as winter approaches and are forced to either hibernate or migrate until springtime returns.*

Although not harsh, the British winter is a time when certain types of food become very scarce. Leaves fall from the trees, flowers disappear and many ground plants die back. Insects also become far less abundant. For animals that feed on buds, shoots, nuts, fruit or invertebrates, finding enough food to survive becomes harder. Many of those that are able to, such as birds, leave the country. Other creatures, however, go for a different option – they hibernate or spend most of the winter at rest.

How do animals know that it is time to hibernate or migrate? The answer is often that they respond to changing day lengths as the seasons change. All animals are sensitive to daylight, and use it to set their body clocks or circadian rhythms. These rhythms affect all bodily processes, including the build-up to the breeding season. The hibernators begin to put on weight or store food as the days shorten, and

Above: Reptiles that live in cooler parts of the world – adders, for example – spend a long time lying dormant. They do not hibernate like mammals, but because they are cold-blooded and do not need lots of energy to function, they can go for long periods without food.

many migrants start to get restless. Other environmental factors also influence exactly when creatures decide to migrate. If the weather remains warm for longer than usual, summer visitors to Britain may stay longer than usual. By the same token, an unusually cold start to autumn may cause them to set off earlier than normal. The same is true for animals that rest or hibernate through the winter. A mild end to autumn gives more time for fattening up and sees animals delaying the start of hibernation. A longer winter than usual extends the length of hibernation. After all, there is no point in becoming active when it is still freezing cold and there is little or no food about. Hibernation is one way of coping with bad conditions, another is to migrate.

## Migration

In general migrations are two-way trips, with animals returning to where they started once conditions become favourable again. Many people are aware that there are migratory birds in Britain. However, far fewer realize that many British mammals also migrate. Bats may hibernate but they also fly *en masse* in autumn to particular sites where they can spend the winter in

safety. Other mammals, such as Scotland's red deer, make smaller migrations, moving down from the hills to lower altitudes as winter comes.

## Hibernation

True hibernation is a change of state that some animals are able to enter in order to conserve energy. In many ways it is like an extremely deep form of sleep. There is, however, one very important difference: during hibernation body processes slow down immensely – in some bats, for instance, the pulse may drop to just a few beats per minute. This winding down of the metabolism saves a huge amount of energy. A bat in hibernation requires less than 1 per cent of the energy it would need to survive if it were active.

With their heartbeats slowed to the bare minimum and their body functions barely active, hibernating mammals become much colder than they would

---

### Hibernating heart rate

The hibernating animal's heart rate slows to just a few beats per minute. It breathes more slowly and its body temperature drops to just a few degrees above the surrounding air temperature.

*Below: The bodies of true hibernators, such as the dormouse, shut down almost completely during hibernation. Other mammals, such as squirrels, may be out of sight for most of the winter, but they do not become completely dormant and their temperature does not fall drastically.*

normally be. Mammals are commonly thought of as warm-blooded animals – that is to say creatures that are able to generate their own heat in order to keep their body temperatures constant. Those that enter hibernation, however, become more like cold-blooded animals. Their body temperatures plummet until they are close to those of their surroundings. In some cases they may even match the temperature of the air around them. Only when their bodies near 0°C do the metabolisms of hibernating mammals speed up very slightly, just enough to keep them from freezing to death.

Mammals are not the only vertebrates to hibernate. Britain's reptiles and amphibians hibernate too. Like hibernating mammals, their metabolisms slow down and body temperatures drop, and as a consequence they are able to survive for months without feeding. Some amphibians, such as many common frogs, hibernate underwater, burying themselves in the mud at the bottom of ponds. Although air-breathers with lungs, they are also able to 'breathe' through their skin, absorbing oxygen from the water and expelling carbon dioxide into it. When fully active, this skin breathing is not enough to sustain them and they must come to the surface every so often to breathe air. In hibernation, however, their oxygen requirements drop in parallel with the activity of their metabolisms. As long as ponds do not freeze over for too

*Above: Whales make the longest migrations of all mammals. They move from their warm breeding grounds near the Equator to feeding areas in cooler waters near the poles.*

long, and oxygen is able to enter the water through its surface from the air, hibernating frogs at the bottom can last through the winter.

Other amphibians and all reptiles hibernate on land – or under it. They seek out sheltered spots beneath logs, stones or in the burrows of other animals, places where their torpid bodies will be spared from the very worst of the winter weather. Many hibernate alone, but some, such as adders, may gather together, sharing the very small amount of heat their bodies lose through their skin. The ability to hibernate allows these cold-blooded creatures to live much farther north than they would otherwise be able to. Unlike mammals, they rely on their surroundings to warm their bodies up enough to become active, so they could not hunt through the winter even if there were sufficient food. For some, such as the sand lizard, Britain marks the far north of their global range. Others live in even colder countries – both the common frog and common lizard are found inside the Arctic Circle in Scandinavia, for instance.

Hibernation can go on for months, so in order to survive it creatures have to fatten up in autumn. Mammals, reptiles and amphibians all do this. Mammals store most of their fat in

*Above: Bats, like this brown long-eared bat, mate before winter; the females store the sperm inside their body, releasing it on the eggs as spring approaches.*

layers beneath the skin. Reptiles and amphibians store fat in other parts of their bodies – most amphibians, for instance, store it in organs attached to the kidneys.

Not all British mammals that rest through the winter actually hibernate. Both red and grey squirrels, for example, simply spend much of their time asleep. When hungry they set out in search of nuts buried in autumn. For them it is these food parcels, rather than fat reserves, that help them survive.

*Below: Stags will travel down from the uppermost areas of the Scottish Highlands in the winter. They will then spend the coldest months in the more sheltered grazing areas at the fringes of woodland.*

# INTRODUCED SPECIES

*Centuries ago, as people started exploring and conquering new lands, many animals travelled with them. In fact, that's the only way many animals could travel such long distances, often crossing seas. Many of the introduced species then thrived in their new habitats, often at the expense of the native wildlife.*

Looking around the British countryside, you would be forgiven for thinking that cows, sheep and other farm animals are naturally occurring species. In fact, all come from distant parts of the world. Over the centuries, they have been selectively bred to develop desirable characteristics, such as lean meat or high milk production. Despite this, they can be traced back to ancestral species. The sheep, for example, is descended from the mouflon, an animal that still lives wild in a few parts of southern Europe and in central Asia. The cow's ancestry goes back to the aurochs, a huge creature that lived wild in Britain and Europe until a few centuries ago, but is now extinct.

## Animal invaders

Other animals hitched a lift into the British Isles. Some arrived as stowaways on ships. The black rat – also known as the ship rat – is one such species, another is the brown rat. Both of these rodents originated in Asia but now live in Britain. The brown rat is now one of our most common and widespread mammals, having conquered both the countryside and our towns and cities.

There are other introduced creatures in Britain that most people would think of as native. Among those animals is the brown hare, which, it is believed, was brought into Britain by the Romans. The Romans brought other creatures with them too, including the rabbit and, in all probability, the house mouse. The rabbit was brought over and bred for food but the house mouse was almost certainly an accidental introduction. There have been house mice in London for almost as long as there have been people. Excavations of Roman sites in London have found their remains.

Not all of Britain's wild animals are native or introduced. Some, which were once domesticated or kept captive, have escaped and now live in the wild. These creatures are described as feral. Among Britain's many feral animals is the American mink, which was originally brought over to stock fur farms. The American mink is now so common in Britain that it has become a problem in many areas and is blamed for the decline of the native water vole. Other feral animals include livestock that now live as if wild. These include creatures such as the feral goat. Most of Britain's feral

**Cows and sheep**
European cows are believed to be descendants of a now-extinct species of ox called the auroch, while modern sheep are descended from the mouflon. From their beginnings in the Middle East, new breeds were introduced to all corners of the world, where they had a huge effect on the native animals and wildlife.

*Above: Cattle have been bred to look and behave very differently from their wild ancestors. Some breeds lack horns, and they are generally docile animals. Some breeds produce a good supply of milk, while others are bred for their meat.*

*Below: Sheep were among the first domestic animals. They are kept for their meat and sometimes milk, which is used for cheese. The thick coat or fleece that kept their ancestors warm on mountain slopes is now used to make woollen garments.*

*Below: Grey squirrels are one of the most common wild mammals in Europe. They were introduced to Britain in the early 1900s, and in many areas have wiped out the native red squirrel populations.*

*Above: Rabbits and hares have long been seen as native to Britain, but the hare was introduced by the Romans about 2,000 years ago. It is likely that rabbits arrived at the same time, but some evidence suggests that they were introduced later by the Normans.*

goats, particularly those in the Scottish Highlands, are descended from goats that were abandoned when the people who owned them moved away.

## British rarities

Although the countryside might be thought of as wild, Britain is, in reality, a nation largely sculpted and controlled by humankind. Wherever there are farm animals or planted forests we can see the work of our own species. Truly natural habitat in Britain is very scarce and the animals that live there are those that have been able to adapt to the changes humans have wrought on the countryside. Many of the original large mammals have gone, partly due to habitat loss and partly as a result of hunting. During the Dark Ages, Britain was home to wolves, brown bears and aurochs, among other creatures. The countryside may be a less frightening and potentially less dangerous place as

a result but it is also, arguably, impoverished. Other creatures have also suffered and now survive in much smaller populations than in the past.

With many wild animals having declined in numbers over the centuries, Britain has no shortage of rare species. Some, such as the mountain hare, are rare because their habitat has shrunk. Others have declined because of competition from introduced species. The red squirrel, for example, has been ousted from much of its original range by the slightly larger grey squirrel, which was introduced to Britain from North America. More positively, a few of Britain's rarities have 'returned from the dead', having been re-introduced after

becoming extinct in Britain in the past. These include such creatures as the wild boar and the beaver, and birds such as the red kite. Few would disagree that their return has made our nation a more exciting place to live, and enriched the natural habitats of the British Isles. The thought of glimpsing one of these new rarities adds immeasurably to any visit to the places they inhabit.

*Below: With their sharp and ever-growing teeth, rodents are very adaptable animals. Rats and mice have flourished alongside humans, and wherever people go, these little gnawing beasts soon become established, breeding very quickly and spreading into new areas.*

# ENDANGERED SPECIES AND CONSERVATION

*Many animals are threatened with extinction because they cannot survive in a world which is constantly being changed by human intervention. Many species have already become extinct, and if people do nothing to save them, a great many more will follow. The animals of Britain are no exception.*

Surprising though it may sound, there is nothing unusual in extinctions, for they are an important process of the natural world. As the climate and landscape have changed in a given area over millions of years, the animals that live there have also changed. As a new species evolves, so another is forced out of its habitat and becomes extinct. All that remains, if we are lucky, are a few fossilized bones.

## Mass extinction?

Biologists estimate that there are at least several million species alive today, and possibly as many as 30 million. Whatever the figure, there are probably more species on Earth right now than at any other time. Therefore, because of the habitat destruction caused by people, more species are becoming extinct or are being threatened with extinction than ever before.

Geologists and biologists know that every now and then there are mass extinctions, in which great numbers of the world's animals die out forever. For example, it is widely believed that the dinosaurs and many other reptiles were wiped out after a meteorite smashed into Mexico 65 million years ago. We now need to ask: are we witnessing the natural world's latest mass extinction? And are humans to blame?

*Below: A captive breeding programme has recently been set up in the north of Scotland in a bid to save the wildcat.*

*Above: Some natural habitats in the British Isles have been put under pressure by new buildings, but much of Britain's green land is now well protected.*

Most of the world's animal species are insects – especially beetles – and other invertebrates. It is likely that many of these species, especially those living in tropical forests, are becoming extinct. However, since scientists may never had had a chance to describe many of them, nobody knows the true number.

## Life list

With vertebrate animals, it is a different story. Because there are only a few thousand species of animals with backbones, most of which have been recognized for hundreds of years, we know a great deal more about the plight of each species. Many species, for example mice, dogs and horses, thrive in a world dominated by people. However, a great many more species have suffered as people have destroyed their habitats, either deliberately or by upsetting the balance of nature by introducing species from other parts of the world.

The International Union for the Conservation of Nature and Natural Resources (IUCN) produces a Red List of animals which are in danger of extinction. There are currently about 5,500 animals listed in a number of categories, including extinct in the wild, endangered and vulnerable.

Nearly one quarter of all mammals are included on the Red List, up to about four per cent of reptiles, and three per cent of amphibians.

## Endangered British animals

Some animals on the list of endangered species within the British Isles suffer because of loss of habitat, but many are in decline following the introduction of foreign species, which compete or carry disease. The following British mammals are among the most threatened.

*Below: Keeping water vole and mink apart is vital if efforts to reintroduce water voles are to be successful.*

*Above: The hare relies on its speed to escape its natural predators, which include the golden eagle and carnivorous mammals like the red fox and – outside Britain – the wolf.*

*Above: Although not under threat worldwide, the red squirrel has drastically reduced in number in Britain. Fewer than 140,000 individuals are thought to be left.*

The greater horseshoe bat is listed in the government's biodiversity action plan and is one of the rarest mammals in the UK. It has lost many of its roost sites and foraging areas, but it is hoped that intervention will soon increase the current population by 25 per cent.

The wildcat is Britain's last large predator, but it could be extinct within the next decade. Fewer than 400 remain, all in Scotland – the last recorded wildcat in England was shot in 1849. A breeding programme has been set up in a bid to save the species.

*Below: Improved legislation on pesticides and cleaner waters have greatly increased the otter's range in the British Isles.*

Britain's red squirrels are under threat from increasing numbers of grey squirrels, plus disease and traffic. Conservation strategies are focusing on managing conifer forests, the red squirrel's preferred habitat.

The European otter is classed as 'vulnerable to extinction'. Its main threat comes from humans, through habitat destruction, pollution and traffic. It is unclear how many otters still exist in Britain, but numbers are gradually increasing in some areas.

The tiny dormouse is endangered due to the loss of its woodland habitat, and has disappeared from 50 per cent of its former range. Conservation projects are reintroducing them to restored woods.

The water vole is being hunted to near extinction by the American mink, and has suffered an 89 per cent decline. The American mink is not entirely to blame, though; the water vole has seen its natural habitat – wetlands and rivers – eroded through building developments.

The European hare has been declining in Europe due to changes in farming practices, but IUCN states that more research is needed to ascertain whether it should be listed as 'Near Threatened' or not.

## British conservation

There are various bodies, both national and regional, in Britain that campaign on conservation issues. Wildlife Trusts are local organizations of differing size, history and origins, but all share a common interest in wildlife that is rooted in a practical tradition of land management and conservation. Almost all county wildlife trusts are landowners, with many nature reserves. Collectively they are the third largest voluntary-sector landowners in the UK.

The British Trust for Conservation Volunteers, now known as BTCV, was initially set up to organize practical conservation tasks in the countryside for volunteers. Its role has changed considerably and much of the charity's work is now in urban areas. It includes many varied volunteer projects in its work, and also promotes regeneration, recycling and education.

# DIRECTORY OF MAMMALS, AMPHIBIANS AND REPTILES

This chapter focuses on the most significant mammals, amphibians and reptiles that live in Britain. The mammals are organized into related groups: large land mammals; carnivores; rabbits and rodents; insectivores; and bats, followed by a section each on amphibians; reptiles; and large oceanic mammals. Each entry is accompanied by a fact box with a map that shows how far the animal's distribution range extends, together with details on habitat, food, size, weight, maturity, breeding and life span. In addition to the main entries, the directory also contains boxed entries of related animals, with information on their size, distribution, characteristics and behaviour.

*Above: The red fox is one of the most successful carnivores in the British Isles, and is able to thrive in almost any habitat.*

*Left: Common frogs are found all over the British Isles, and have taken full advantage of garden ponds as well as living in wilder areas. They can be difficult to spot as they are able to alter their skin colour to match their surroundings, and sometimes this skin coloration can be quite dramatic – including red, black and blue tones.*

# LARGE LAND MAMMALS

*Deer are a group of hoofed mammals that are found across the Northern Hemisphere. They belong to the Cervidae family of mammals, and are the large land mammals we most commonly associate with the British Isles. Other animals roaming the area include ponies, wild sheep and even wild goats, then there are the wild boar that have recently been successfully re-introduced, albeit accidentally.*

## Red deer
*Cervus elaphus*

Red deer are one of the most widespread of all deer species. In Britain they are most common in the Scottish Highlands, Lake District, East Anglia and the south west. As with species that are spread across the world, the common names used can be confusing. In North America the species is known as elk, while populations of red deer living in the far north of Canada are also known as wapiti, though many biologists argue that wapiti are, in fact, a separate species from red deer. Red deer prefer woodlands, while wapiti are more common in open country. Nevertheless, the two groups of deer very closely resemble each other in most other ways.

Only male red deer have antlers, which reach up to 1.7m (5½ft) across, and a dark shaggy mane. Adult males use their antlers during the rut, which takes place in autumn. The fighting establishes which males will control the harems of females. Antlers fall off in winter and regrow in time for the next year's conquests.

**Distribution**: Northern Africa, Europe, Asia, North America.
**Habitat**: Woodlands.
**Food**: Grass, sedge, forbs, twigs and bark.
**Size**: 1.6–2.6m (5¼–8½ft).
**Weight**: 75–340kg (165–750lb).
**Maturity**: 2 years.
**Breeding**: 1 fawn born in autumn.
**Life span**: 20 years.

**Identification:** Red deer have red coats in summer. In winter, they grow longer and darker fur. Creamy coloured rump; short beige tail. Conspicuous ears.

## Sika deer
*Cervus nippon*

The sika deer is an introduced species. Herds were first brought to Britain from Japan in the 1820s and used to stock deer parks, from which they escaped. Today, the largest populations of this species are to be found in Scotland and Northern Ireland. Smaller populations also occur in England and southern Ireland, but the species is absent from Wales. Sika deer are closely related to red deer and often crossbreed with them where the ranges of the two species overlap. Unlike many other hybrids, the offspring of this crossbreeding tend to be fertile and go on to breed in later life. As a result, many of Britain's sika deer populations are now largely made up of hybrid animals.

In many areas sika deer are solitary, only gathering together in numbers to breed. Where their population is higher, however, they occur in single-sex groups. During autumn and winter, following the rut, these groups often merge.

**Distribution:** Central and Southern China, Japan, Europe, North America, Oceania.
**Habitat:** Woods and heathland.
**Food:** Leaves and other plant matter, both browsed and grazed.
**Size:** 50–95cm (19½–38in).
**Weight:** 30–70kg (66–154lb).
**Maturity:** 1.5–3 years.
**Breeding:** The mating season, or 'rut', occurs between late August and October. A single calf, occasionally twins, is born in May or June.
**Life span:** Up to 15 years.

**Identification**: Purebred sika deer have a thick greyish brown coat in winter. In summer the coat becomes lighter in colour, with pale spots on the back and flanks and a darker stripe along the spine. On the rump there is a white patch bordered by black, which remains unchanged throughout the year. The front spikes of the antlers point forwards. Hybrid animals show characteristics of both purebred sika and red deer.

**Roe deer** (*Capreolus capreolus*) 0.9–1.5m (3–5ft); 15–50kg (33–110lb). This graceful deer is found over large parts of Europe, including Britain, where it lives in forests and on farmland. The smallest type of European deer, the roe deer lives alone or in small groups. When grazing out in the open, the deer form large groups of up to 90 members in order to reduce the risks of attack. In forests, where they are more protected from predators, the deer live in groups of less than 15.

**Chinese water deer** (*Hydropotes inermis*) 50–55cm (19½–21½in); 11–18kg (24–40lb). A small deer, like a cross between a roe and a muntjac. The males have protruding tusks but no antlers. Ears are large and rounded and coat is a uniform brown. Regular sightings are restricted to Bedfordshire, Norfolk and Cambridgeshire. They thrive on diverse plant life, so favour fields, river valleys and woodlands.

**Distribution**: Southern China and Taiwan. Introduced to Britain, established in south and central England and Wales. North of the Humber distribution is patchy, but reaches close to the Scottish border.
**Habitat**: Forest and farmland surrounded by vegetation.
**Food**: Grass, tender leaves and shoots.
**Size**: 60–140cm (23–55in).
**Weight**: 14–33kg (30–73lb).
**Maturity**: Females 1 year; probably older for males.
**Breeding**: 1 fawn each year.
**Life span**: 15 years.

**Identification:** As well as the protruding canine teeth that are also found in a few other species of deer, the lower portions of a male muntjac's antlers are covered in fur. Instead of antlers, females have small bony knobs with a coating of fur.

# Muntjac
*Muntiacus reevesi*

Only the males of these dainty deer carry antlers, and these rarely exceed 15cm (6in) in length. However, the male muntjac's main weapons are its long upper canine teeth, which curve outwards from its lips like tusks. The teeth are usually used in fights to settle territorial disputes with other males, but can also inflict savage injuries on dogs and other attacking animals.

Male muntjacs defend territories of up to 20ha (50 acres) in size, usually close to water, and try to encompass as many of the smaller female territories as possible. When they are nervous, muntjacs make a call that sounds like a dog barking, giving muntjacs their other common name, 'barking deer'. These calls are probably aimed at predators that use ambush tactics to catch their prey. By calling, the muntjacs let the predators know that they have been spotted, and therefore are unlikely to succeed in their ambushes. Muntjacs were introduced into Britain in 1901, and feral populations have established themselves well.

# Fallow deer
*Dama dama*

Fallow deer are easily recognized by their somewhat flattened antlers and spotted summer coats. In some places fallow deer live alone, while in others they come together to form small herds of up to 30 individuals.

The breeding behaviour of this species is variable, and may depend on the way food is distributed. In some places males come together and attempt to attract females with dance-like rituals and bellowing, a behaviour known as a rut. In other places, males attempt to monopolize a group of females by defending good feeding areas from other males. Fallow deer have been introduced to many new places, but their populations are falling because of hunting and climate change.

**Identification:** Golden-brown coat, spotted with white. White and black tail. Male fallow deer sport antlers, which can span 80cm (31½in) from tip to tip. Adults shed and re-grow their antlers every year.

**Distribution**: Originally from the Mediterranean and parts of the Middle East, but introduced to Britain, America and New Zealand.
**Habitat**: Open woodland, grassland and shrubland.
**Food**: Grass, leaves, twigs.
**Size**: 130–170cm (51–67in).
**Weight**: 40–100kg (88–220lb).
**Maturity**: Females at 16 months; males at 17 months.
**Breeding**: A single fawn born annually.
**Life span**: 20 years or more in captivity.

## Feral goat

*Capra hircus*

Britain's feral goats are descended from domesticated animals, but they can now be considered truly wild. In many ways their behaviour mirrors that of the bezoar goats of the Greek Islands, Turkey, Iran and Pakistan, the ancestral species of all of the world's domesticated goats. Like them, they form small, single-sex herds, with males and females only gathering together for the rut. During that time, dominant males join the female herds and do their best to defend them from rivals. Evenly matched males fight for the privilege of mating, charging at one another and clashing together. Younger males at this time of year often wander widely, searching for females that do not have a mate.

Although their behaviour is similar, feral goats differ from bezoar goats in appearance, being smaller and more varied in colour, with longer coats. They tend to feed during the day and spend the night in a cave or similarly sheltered spot, particularly in winter.

Feral goats are often common, but their populations are scattered. They are most numerous in Scotland, where many domesticated goats escaped during the Highland Clearances, when large numbers of people were driven from their homelands.

**Identification:** The coat is usually long and shaggy, particularly in the winter months. For their size, these plant-eaters are extremely nimble and where they occur they can often be seen high up on very steep slopes or precipitous rocky ledges.

**Distribution**: Scotland, Ireland and northern and western England and Wales.
**Habitat**: Rocky areas.
**Food**: Plant matter.
**Size**: 50–60cm (19½–23in).
**Weight**: 25–45kg (55–99lb).
**Maturity**: 9 months–1 year.
**Breeding**: The rut occurs during August and September. Dominant males mate with several females. One or two kids are born in late winter or early spring.
**Life span**: Up to 15 years.

## Soay sheep

*Ovis aries*

The Soay sheep is thought to be the world's most ancient domesticated breed of sheep, having existed wild and in isolation on the island of Soay in the St Kilda archipelago north-west of Scotland for at least 1,000 years. Although no one is absolutely certain when they arrived, genetic and other evidence suggests that the sheep came to Soay with the first human settlers some 4,000 years ago. The island itself is named for these animals, Soay being a corruption of the Viking name Sauda-ey, which means 'island of sheep'.

In 1932, 107 Soays were rounded up and transported to the larger neighbouring island of Hirta, which now supports its own thriving population of these sheep. More recently, Soay sheep were brought to mainland Britain. They are now kept as a rare breed by some farmers and have been released to live semi-wild in a few places, such as Blackpool Pit near St Austell in Cornwall and Somerset's Cheddar Gorge.

Although smaller, Soay sheep are little different in appearance and behaviour from the mouflon, the wild ancestor of all domesticated sheep. Unlike the mouflon, however, they have wool, but this does not need to be sheared as it does in other breeds of sheep. Instead, it is moulted early every summer and a new coat grown later for the winter ahead.

**Distribution**: Soay and Hirta, also introduced elsewhere.
**Habitat**: Islands.
**Food**: Grass and other ground plants.
**Size**: Up to 56cm (22in).
**Weight**: Up to 41kg (90lb).
**Maturity**: 6 months.
**Breeding**: The rut begins in November and continues until mid-December. Ewes give birth, usually to a single lamb, the following March or April.
**Life span**: Up to 20 years.

**Identification:** This small sheep has dark brown or tan coloured wool over most of its body, apart from the belly, which is white, and the face, which has a covering of short hair and lacks wool. The face and legs are brown or tan and there are white marks on the lower jaw and over the eyes. The rams have a single pair of large, backward-curving horns. Ewes also have horns, although smaller and shorter than those of the rams.

# Wild horse

*Equus caballus*

None of Britain's wild horses are truly wild. That said, most do spend the majority of their lives running free, in woods, heaths and moors unbounded by fences. Dartmoor, Exmoor and New Forest ponies are recognized breeds, and all three are rounded up at certain times of the year to be inspected, and some sold at auction. Most of the time, however, they are left to their own devices. Normally they stay together and travel in small herds. These usually consist of several mares with their foals and a stallion. Other stallions remain apart and are driven off by the herd stallion if they stray too close.

One group of horses in Britain is close in appearance and behaviour to the tarpan, the original and now extinct wild horse that once roamed throughout much of Britain and Europe. Those horses, known as Koniks, were reintroduced from the Netherlands in 2002 and now live wild in Kent's Stodmarsh and Ham Fen. Koniks have tarpan blood, having been created in the 19th century by Polish farmers, who captured the last wild tarpans and crossbred them with their own workhorses. Today, much larger herds of Koniks roam wild in Poland in nature reserves and national parks.

**Distribution**: Southern England.
**Habitat**: Woodland, heath and moorland.
**Food**: Grass, heather and other ground plants.
**Size**: Up to 148cm (58in).
**Weight**: Up to 250kg (551lb).
**Maturity**: 2 years.
**Breeding**: Stallions mate with receptive mares between the months of June and September. Foals are born approximately 11 months later.
**Life span**: Up to 30 years.

**Identification:** Dartmoor ponies may be black, brown, grey chestnut or roan in colour. Exmoor ponies are smaller in stature and typically brown. New Forest ponies vary greatly in colour and sometimes have white markings on the head, unlike Exmoor ponies and most Dartmoor ponies. The Koniks of Kent are close in appearance to the tarpan, the original and now-extinct European wild horse. It has a large head, broad body and dun-coloured coat with a thin stripe down the back.

# Wild boar

*Sus scrofa*

Many of the animals that have been accidentally introduced to Britain might be looked upon as invaders, non-native creatures that are now living on our soil. The wild boar, however, is as British as the red squirrel, or at least it was before it was hunted to extinction in the 17th century. Today, the wild boar is back. In England it has been farmed since the 1980s for its meat, and escapees from these farms have set up home in various parts of the country. Populations now roam wild in Kent, Sussex, Gloucestershire and northern Yorkshire.

The wild boar is naturally a creature of woodland. Although large, it is surprisingly nimble and light on its feet. This, combined with its earthy coloration, means that it is far harder to spot than one might imagine. It is this which has enabled the species to live virtually undetected for as long as it has in England. Providing that hunting pressures on the British populations do not increase, it seems likely that the wild boar's range will spread.

This large wild pig is covered with dark brown, bristly hairs. These are especially long in winter, when the large males in particular can have a somewhat shaggy appearance. In common with domestic pigs, which are descended from this species, the body is long and the legs are relatively short. The head and ears are large and it has a prominent snout.

**Distribution**: Southern England, small populations in north Yorkshire and Scotland, also North Africa and Asia.
**Habitat**: Woodland.
**Food**: Fungi, tubers, bulbs, nuts, fruit and other plant matter: also small vertebrates, invertebrates and carrion.
**Size**: Up to 110cm (43in).
**Weight**: Up to 350kg (771kg).
**Maturity**: 8–10 months.
**Breeding**: Mating occurs in late autumn, with the males fighting for access to females. A litter of 1 to 12 piglets is born the following spring.
**Life span**: Up to 27 years.

**Identification:** Some male wild boar have tusks, which protrude from the mouth. Piglets have stripes, which they lose as they mature.

# CARNIVORES

*Some of the small carnivores, the mustelids, are very fast and efficient hunters. They can tackle prey much larger than themselves. Mustelids tend to be solitary animals, defending their territories from all newcomers. Their long, lithe bodies, short legs and sharp claws mean that they are often skilful climbers, capable of reaching the most inaccessible of places and leaving their prey few places to hide.*

## Stoat

*Mustela erminea*

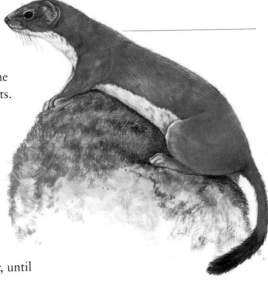

Although rarely seen, stoats are common in the countryside, where they mainly feed on rodents. However, the large males will often prey on rabbits, even though rabbits are considerably larger. Stoats are famed for mesmerizing their prey by dancing around them, before nipping in for the kill. This is not just an old wives' tale. Stoats have been observed leaping around near rabbits in a seemingly deranged fashion. This curious 'dance' seems to have the effect of confusing the rabbits, which just watch the stoat draw slowly closer and closer, until it is too late to escape.

As winter approaches, populations of stoats that live in cooler, northern areas change the colour of their coats. In summer, they are a chestnut colour but, by the time the first snows have fallen, the stoats have changed to pure white. White stoats are known as ermines, and their fur was once prized for its pure colour and soft feel.

**Identification:** In mild climates, stoats have chestnut fur all year round. In colder areas, they moult into white fur in winter. Stoats are distinguished from their smaller cousins, the weasels, by having black tips to their tails.

**Distribution**: Widespread in northern and central Europe extending into Asia and across northern North America. Introduced to New Zealand.
**Habitat**: Anywhere with enough cover.
**Food**: Mammals up to the size of rabbits.
**Size**: 16–31cm (6¼–12¼in).
**Weight**: 140–445g (4oz–1lb).
**Maturity**: 1 year.
**Breeding**: 1 litter per year of 5–12 young.
**Life span**: 10 years.

## Weasel

*Mustela nivalis*

**Distribution**: Arctic to North Carolina; also found in Northern Asia, Africa and Europe.
**Habitat**: Forest, prairie, farmland and semi-desert.
**Food**: Rodents, eggs, nestlings and lizards.
**Size**: 16–20cm (6¼–8in).
**Weight**: 30–55g (1–2oz).
**Maturity**: 8 months.
**Breeding**: Two litters of up to 7 young, born in spring and late summer.
**Life span**: 7 years.

Weasels are common throughout Europe, apart from Ireland, and in North America, Canada and Alaska. They are also found throughout much of the Northern Hemisphere, with the exception of most islands and Arabia. Weasels survive in a wide variety of habitats, but they avoid thick forests, sandy deserts and any exposed spaces. They have a very long body, with a long neck and flat head. This allows them to move with ease over broken ground and inside burrows. The size of this weasel varies with its distribution across the globe. The largest weasels are found in North Africa, while those in North America have the smallest bodies. Weasels live alone outside of the breeding season. Males occupy territories that are home to two or more females. They forage for food at all times of the day or night. They watch carefully for movements caused by prey, before launching an attack and dispatching their victims with a bite to the neck.

**Identification:** In summer, the brown fur is about 1cm (½in) long, but the winter coat is more than double this length. In the far north, the coat turns white in winter.

# Badger
*Meles meles*

Large members of the mustelid family, badgers have a much more diverse diet than most of the small carnivores. Adept at making a meal out of most situations, badgers will eat anything they find, including berries, fungi and carrion. Worms are a particular favourite, and on warm, damp nights badgers can regularly be observed patrolling through pastureland.

One of the badger's greatest assets is its mouth. The way a badger's skull is structured means that it is physically impossible for the animal to dislocate its jaw, allowing badgers to have one of the most powerful bites in the natural world. This trait makes the badger a fearsome foe for any animal that happens to cross its path. Unlike most other mustelids, badgers are very social animals. They live in large family groups centred on communal dens, or setts.

**Distribution**: Throughout Europe (but not north of Arctic Circle) and Asia.
**Habitat**: Favours a mixture of woodland and pastureland, also moving into urban habitats.
**Food**: Omnivorous diet.
**Size**: 65–80cm (25½–31½in).
**Weight**: 8–12kg (17–26lb).
**Maturity**: 1–2 years.
**Breeding**: 1 litter of 1–5 young per year.
**Life span**: 15 years.

**Identification:** The badger's black and white face makes it instantly recognizable. It has silver-grey fur and a stocky body with short legs and white-tipped ears.

# Otter
*Lutra lutra*

**Distribution**: Europe, Asia and North Africa.
**Habitat**: Rivers and lakes.
**Food**: Fish, shellfish, frogs, eggs and insects.
**Size**: 57–70cm (22½–27in).
**Weight**: 13kg (28lb).
**Maturity**: 2 years.
**Breeding**: Pups born mainly in summer.
**Life span**: Unknown.

This species is perhaps more aptly named the Eurasian otter because it is found as far east as Manchuria. It is also found as far north as the tundra line of Siberia and Scandinavia and as far south as the coastal plain of North Africa.

European otters spend most of their waking hours in water, though they build their nests on land. The nests are often made up of a network of tunnels dug into the river bank or running through roots and thick shrubs. Each otter defends a short stretch of river bank, marking its territory with secretions from a scent gland under the base of the tail.

Within the territory an otter has a designated area for entering the water, basking in the sun and playing. Otters are very playful. They are often seen rolling in grass and sliding down muddy slopes into the water. Otters can dive for up to two minutes at a time. Once in the water their whiskers detect the currents produced by the movements of their prey. Air bubbles trapped in the fur keep the skin dry.

**Identification:** The otter has a brown coat, which is paler in Asian populations. Feet are generously webbed to aid with swimming. Each foot has large claws.

## Pine marten

*Martes martes*

The pine marten is our most adept arboreal carnivore, climbing through the trees with a skill only matched by the red squirrel, which it occasionally hunts. Long-bodied and relatively long-legged, it is also surprisingly quick and agile on the ground. Indeed, it is here that it finds the majority of its food, which ranges from mice and other small rodents to beetles, eggs and even fungi. Hunting takes place mainly during dusk and at night. By day, pine martens rest up in their dens, which are usually located in hollow branches or among the exposed roots of fallen trees.

Pine martens were once quite common and widespread through the British Isles. Today, however, they are restricted mainly to Scotland and isolated parts of Wales and northern England. Predators of game birds and poultry, they were persecuted from the 17th to the 19th century as vermin and during that time disappeared from virtually all of their former range. Indeed, by 1926 the only significant population left was confined to a small area of north-west Scotland. In Scotland pine martens have since begun to recover and expand their range, but in England and Wales where they still occur, their numbers remain very low.

Although this carnivore is adapted for a life in the trees, it often descends to the ground and has been seen at bird tables.

**Distribution**: Scotland, north Wales, the far north of England, and Scandinavia.
**Habitat**: Woodlands and forests.
**Food**: Rodents, birds, eggs, carrion, insects, fungi and berries.
**Size**: Up to 78cm (31in).
**Weight**: 1.5–2kg (3–4lb).
**Maturity**: 2–3 years.
**Breeding**: Mating occurs in July and August. Implantation of eggs is delayed, with the result that the 1 to 5 young are born the following spring.
**Life span**: Up to 18 years.

**Identification**: The pine marten has a long, lithe body and a fairly long, slender tail. The fur over most of its body ranges in colour from chestnut to dark brown, although there is a creamy yellow bib. Seen from the front, the face is broad and the head slightly flattened. The ears are quite large and rounded at their tips.

## Red fox

*Vulpes vulpes*

The red fox is a very successful and adaptable species. It is mainly active at night but will forage during the day, particularly when there are hungry cubs to feed. It also enjoys curling up and sunbathing in exposed but private spots, often by railway lines or roadsides.

A pair of foxes shares a home range, often with young from the previous breeding season. Mating takes place from December to February. After a few months, females – also known as vixens – give birth to between 3 and 12 cubs. The availability of food determines whether vixens breed and how many cubs they produce. During the mating season, females and occasionally males give out spine-tingling shrieks.

Red foxes mark their territories with a distinctive scent, which lingers and shows when a fox has been in the area. The scent is left with urine or faeces and is produced by special glands at the base of the tail. There are further scent glands between the pads of foxes' feet and around their lips.

**Distribution**: Europe, Asia and North Africa. Introduced to Australia.
**Habitat**: Able to colonize almost any habitat available.
**Food**: Small vertebrates, invertebrates, kitchen scraps, fruit and carrion.
**Size**: 85–95cm (34–38in).
**Weight**: 4–8kg (9–17½lb).
**Maturity**: 10 months.
**Breeding**: 3–12 pups born in early spring.
**Life span**: 9 years.

**Identification:** The red fox is a large fox with a rusty, red-brown coat and a darker bushy tail with a white tip.

# Wildcat

*Felis sylvestris*

Few animals symbolize the wilderness areas of Britain like the wildcat. Uncommon and elusive, it is rarely seen, a fact which adds to the aura of mystery that surrounds it. The wildcat is actually a very close relative of the domestic cats which share our homes. Their ancestor, the African wildcat, is a smaller and shorter-haired subspecies found throughout much of Africa and the Middle East. As a consequence, domestic cats can interbreed with the wildcat and on occasion this has happened. However, in the core of its range in the Scottish Highlands the wildcat gene pool remains undiluted.

Like domestic cats, wildcats are largely nocturnal (with the exception of mothers with young, which often hunt during daylight). Much of the day is spent sleeping or resting in scrub, with most individuals only stirring as the light begins to fade. Studies have shown that the majority of hunting occurs between the hours of dusk and 2am. A wide variety of small mammal prey is caught, including rodents, rabbits and hares, along with the occasional bird. Carrion is also eaten when it can be found and food is often stockpiled, particularly during the winter months.

**Identification:** The wildcat looks like a large and slightly fluffy domestic tabby cat. Its body is more muscular, however, its head broader, and its tail shorter and much thicker. In colour it is pale brown striped with black: the widest stripes are those on the tail. The eyes are greenish yellow, with vertical, slit-like pupils. The muzzle is paler than the rest of the coat and the whiskers are white. The wildcat has a thick tail with a blunt black tip.

**Distribution**: The Scottish mainland north of Edinburgh and Glasgow.
**Habitat**: Moorland, pasture, scrub and forest.
**Food**: Small mammals and, less often, birds.
**Size**: 95cm (38in)
**Weight**: 3–8kg (6½–17½lb).
**Maturity**: 9–12 months
**Breeding**: Mating usually occurs in March, with the litter of up to 8 kittens born 68 days later.
**Life span**: Up to 11 years

# American mink

*Mustela vison*

American mink are small carnivores that live close to water, where they feed on small aquatic animals. They originally came from North America, but were brought to Asia and Europe, including Britain, to be farmed for their fine fur. They have since escaped into the wild and are now a pest. They are also competition for the very rare European mink.

Mink prefer to live in areas with plenty of cover. Their river-bed dens are generally deserted burrows made by other river mammals, but mink will dig their own when necessary. Mink are active at night and dive into water to snatch their prey. They live alone and will defend their own stretches of riverbank against intruders. A litter of up to 5 young is born two months after mating. They stay inside the dry, underground nests lined with fur, feathers and leaves. In autumn the young begin to fend for themselves.

**Identification:** Mink are known for their luxurious fine fur, which is used for clothing. It has a long slim body and short legs with partially webbed feet. Mainly active at night.

**Distribution**: North America. Introduced to northern Europe.
**Habitat**: Swamps and near streams and lakes.
**Food**: Small mammals, fish, frogs and crayfish.
**Size**: 33–43cm (13–17in).
**Weight**: 0.7–2.5kg (1½–5½lb).
**Maturity**: 1–1.5 years.
**Breeding**: 5 young born in late spring.
**Life span**: 10 years.

# RABBITS AND RODENTS

*Worldwide, there are 54 species of rabbit and hare, all of which belong to the Leporidae family.*
*Some species have been introduced to areas well outside their original range, including our own, familiar*
*rabbit. The Rodentia, with over 2,000 species distributed all around the globe, is by far the largest*
*order of mammals and well represented on the British Isles.*

## Rabbit

*Oryctolagus cuniculus*

The rabbit has had a long association with humans, who have prized it for its soft fur and tasty meat. This species was probably introduced to the Mediterranean from its original home in the Iberian Peninsula more than 3,000 years ago. Rabbits often live in large colonies, inhabiting complex labyrinths of burrows, or warrens, that may have hundreds of entrances. Although rabbits live in close proximity to one another, there is a strong dominance hierarchy within a warren. Each male rabbit – or buck – defends a territory, especially during the breeding season.

Rabbits are famed for their rate of reproduction, and a single female has the potential to produce 30 young per year. Rabbits have been introduced to some areas, such as Australia, where there are no predators capable of controlling their numbers. In these places they have created huge problems, crowding out local species and destroying crops. Ironically, rabbit populations in the species' original range in Spain are too small to support their rare predators such as the Iberian lynx and the imperial eagle.

**Distribution**: Originally the Iberian Peninsula, North Africa and southern France. Introduced to most of Europe, and Australia.
**Habitat**: Farmland, grassland and dry shrubland.
**Food**: Grass, herbaceous plants, bark and twigs.
**Size**: 35–45cm (14–18in).
**Weight**: 1.5–2.5kg (3–5½lb).
**Maturity**: 1 year.
**Breeding**: 1–9 young per litter; up to 7 litters per year.
**Life span**: 9 years.

**Identification:** The rabbit has mottled brown-grey fur and long, upright ears. The tail is white and cotton-like. Sexes are alike.

## Brown hare

*Lepus europaeus*

Unlike rabbits, hares do not live in burrows. They spend most of the time alone, although a few may be seen together at good feeding sites. Hares are mostly active by night. During the day they crouch in small hollows in the grass called forms, sometimes leaving their backs just visible over the vegetation. In Europe, the main breeding season is in spring, and at this time hares can often be seen during the day, with males fighting one another and pursuing females.

A number of predators target hares, and in Europe these include foxes and eagles. If a predator detects a hare, the hare flees, running at speeds of up to 60kph (37mph) and making sharp, evasive turns. Injured or captured hares are known to make high-pitched screams.

In order to reduce the risk of losing all of their young leverets to predators, females hide them in different locations in specially dug forms, and visit them one by one to nurse them. Although brown hares are common, changing farming practices have caused a decline in hare numbers in some countries, such as Britain.

**Identification:** Brown hares are easily distinguishable from European rabbits by their larger size and longer ears and limbs.

**Distribution**: Southern Scandinavia, northern Spain and Britain to Siberia and north-western Iran.
**Habitat**: Grasslands and agricultural land.
**Food**: Grass, herbs, crop plants and occasionally twigs and bark.
**Size**: 60–70cm (23–27in).
**Weight**: 3–5kg (6½–11lb).
**Maturity**: 1 year.
**Breeding**: Litter of 1–8 young; 2 or more litters per year.
**Life span**: 7 years.
**Status**: Common.

# Mountain hare

*Lepus timidus*

**Distribution**: Northern hemisphere, northern Europe and eastern Siberia.
**Habitat**: Tundra, forest and moorland.
**Food**: Leaves, twigs, lichen, grass and heather.
**Size**: 43–61cm (17–24in).
**Weight**: 2–6kg (4½–13lb).
**Maturity**: 1 year.
**Breeding**: End of January to September. Litters of 1–6 young produced twice a year (sometimes more) in spring and summer; gestation varies from 47 to 54 days.
**Life span**: 5 years.

Mountain hares are found at northern latitudes across the globe, from Alaska, northern Canada and Greenland to Scandinavia and Siberia. Small populations also live in Japan, Ireland, Scotland and even the European Alps. They inhabit tundra, conifer forest and moorland in highland regions.

These hares are nocturnal, resting by day in a form (a depression dug into the ground). They do not dig their own burrows, but often take over the burrows of other animals when they need to shelter their young. When not on the move, mountain hares 'hook' before resting. This involves making a final jump to the side so that predators cannot follow its tracks.

Mountain hares are mainly solitary, but in severe weather or at sites where food is plentiful they may congregate in large groups of up to 70. In the breeding season, several males will compete for access to a single female. If a male approaches an unreceptive female too closely, he may be aggressively rebuffed, with the female rising up on her hind legs and batting at him with her paws, claws extended. If the male persists, a longer fight may ensue, with both hares 'boxing' and biting.

**Identification:** These hares moult twice a year. During the winter moult, from October to December, their fur becomes grey or even white, but the animals become brown again in the spring.

# Grey squirrel

*Sciurus carolinensis*

Grey squirrels are native to the open woodlands of eastern North America. They have also been introduced into several parts of northern Europe, including Britain, where they have out-competed the smaller red squirrels for food and breeding sites.

These animals feed primarily on the nuts and buds of many woodland trees. In summer, when they are most active just after dawn and before dusk, grey squirrels also eat insects. In winter, when most animals of their size are hibernating, grey squirrels spend their days eating stores of food that they had buried throughout the previous summer. Grey squirrels may make dens in hollow trees, but are more likely to make nests, or dreys, from twigs and leaves in the boughs of trees.

There are two breeding seasons each year: one beginning in midwinter, the other in midsummer. Males begin to chase a female through the trees a few days before they are receptive to mating. One female may be chased by several males at once. When females are ready, their vulvas become pink and engorged. Litters of three are born six weeks later.

**Identification:** Grey squirrels have, as their name suggests, greyish fur, although many individuals have reddish patches. Their tails, which have many white hairs, are not as bushy as those of the red squirrel.

**Distribution**: South-eastern Canada and eastern United States. Introduced to Britain and northern Europe, and now the most common species in deciduous forests.
**Habitat**: Woodlands, parks and gardens.
**Food**: Nuts, seeds, flowers and buds.
**Size**: 38–52cm (15–20in).
**Weight**: 300–700g (10–24oz).
**Maturity**: 10 months.
**Breeding**: 2 litters each year with 2–4 young per litter after a gestation of 3 months. Mating takes place in late summer and winter. Breeding is later in a cold winter.
**Life span**: 12 years.

# Red squirrel

*Sciurus vulgaris*

**Identification:** Red squirrels can be quite variable in colour, with some individuals being jet black, while others are strawberry blonde. The bushy tail helps them to balance in the treetops. These arboreal rodents are very acrobatic.

The red squirrel has undergone a well-documented decline in Britain due to its not being able to compete with the larger and more robust grey squirrel, which was introduced from North America. The two species actually hardly ever come to blows, and it is thought that the main problem may be that the grey squirrels harbour a viral infection that attacks red squirrels while leaving the greys unaffected.

Red squirrels tend to be most active during early mornings and late afternoons. They rest in the middle of the day. As winter sets in, the squirrels rapidly put on weight, and settle down for a long period of inactivity. Squirrels do not truly hibernate. They never let their body temperatures drop, and they regularly wake up to stretch their legs, drink and feed from food caches made in the autumn.

Red squirrels are mainly solitary animals, and apart from when there is a large concentration of food readily available, the only time they get together in any numbers is when the females become ready to breed. Male squirrels fight over them at this time.

**Distribution**: Europe and Asia.
**Habitat**: Primarily coniferous forests.
**Food**: Seeds and nuts when available, and also fungi, eggs, flowers and tree sap.
**Size**: 25–35cm (10½–14in).
**Weight**: up to 350g (12oz).
**Maturity**: 9–10 months.
**Breeding**: 2 litters of 5–7 young per year.
**Life span**: 4–6 years.

# Water vole

*Arvicola terrestris*

Water voles are also known – confusingly – as water rats. Ratty, of *The Wind in the Willows* fame, was really a water vole, and, like him, these rodents are found living alongside slow-moving rivers, ditches, dykes and lakes. In areas of central Europe, however, water voles do not live by water, preferring dry habitats instead. In some places they are considered to be a serious agricultural pest. Water voles excavate extensive burrow systems in the banks of rivers, with plenty of entrance and exit holes so that they can escape from the various predators they encounter – both in and out of the water. Even so, the average life span of a water vole is a mere five months. Herons, barn owls, brown rats and pike are all known to prey on water voles, but the rodents' most important predators are stoats and mink. Indeed, the introduction of the American mink to Britain has been blamed for the species' rapid decline.

**Distribution**: Widespread across Europe and Asia.
**Habitat**: Banks of slow-flowing rivers and streams.
**Food**: Grasses, rushes and sedges.
**Size**: 14–22cm (5½–8½in).
**Weight**: 150–300g (5–10oz).
**Maturity**: 2 months.
**Breeding**: 3 or 4 litters of 5 through spring and summer.
**Life span**: Up to 3 years.

**Identification:** Water voles have blunter snouts, more rounded bodies and smaller ears than rats; they also have shorter, hairy tails.

## Common dormouse

(*Muscardinus avellanarius*) 65–85mm (2½–3¼in); weight: 15–30g (½–1oz). This protected animal spends 75 per cent of its life asleep in the baskets it weaves for itself out of honeysuckle bark, moss and leaves. It is mainly found in southern England and the Lake District, but habitat loss is a significant problem for the species. It has a bushy tail and orange-brown fur with yellow-white belly and a white throat.

## Orkney vole (*Microtus arvalis orcadensis*) 90–135mm

(3½–5¼in); weight: 14–67g (½–2oz). Only found on the Orkney Islands, where it has existed for at least 4,600 years, this animal is the only vole that is active in daylight. It does not hibernate. The voles are brown in colour; those on the northern islands have paler fur. They favour cultivated farmland and gardens and live in connected burrows.

## Short-tailed vole (*Microtus agrestis*) 8–13cm (3–5in);

weight: 14–50g (½–2oz). Found on grass and marshland, these animals have grey-brown fur, with pale grey belly, small ears and a short tail. They are generally nocturnal. As they run along their trails they emit scent to warn off other voles. Birds of prey pick up the ultra-violet light radiating from the trails.

## Bank vole (*Clethrionomys glareolus*) 8–12cm (3–4½in);

weight: 15–40g (½–1½oz). Typically found in woodland, bank voles have reddish brown fur with cream bellies and small ears. They are only found on the mainland in Britain. They build nests under log piles or among tree roots and bury food stores for the winter.

**Identification:** Dormice look like mice but have furry, not scaly, tails. They accumulate fat in their bodies during the summer ready for the hibernation period.

# Eurasian beaver

*Castor fiber*

Eurasian beavers are the largest rodents in Europe and Asia. They live in or beside woodland waterways. Beavers live in family groups of four or five individuals, with each family defending a small area of river and woodland. A family lives inside a den called a lodge, which is a simple tunnel dug up into the bank from below the water line. In places where this construction is not possible, beavers build a castle of mud, stones and branches. To ensure that the entrance to the lodge is underwater, the beavers build a dam across the river to make a deep pool of calm water. On occasion, the lodge is built into the dam.

Beavers dig canals from the river into the woodland. Using their huge teeth, they fell small trees and cut them into chunks, floating the timber down the canal into the dammed area. The wood is eaten along with water plants, or stored in water for eating later.

**Distribution:** Northern Europe and Siberia.
**Habitat:** Lakes and rivers.
**Food:** Wood and river plants.
**Size:** 80–110cm (31½–43in).
**Weight:** 17–32kg (37½–70lb).
**Maturity:** 3 years.
**Breeding:** Litters of about 3 born early summer.
**Life span:** 14 years.

**Identification:** The Eurasian beaver is similar to the American beaver, but is slightly smaller. It is a powerful swimmer, thanks to a flipper-like tail and webbed feet.

# Edible dormouse

*Glis glis*

Edible dormice are lithe and agile climbers. They spend virtually their entire lives in the treetops, searching for food, and are very reluctant to leave the safety of the branches. They will not cross open areas on the ground. Dormice are one of the few types of mammal to enter a true state of hibernation. Come autumn, they fall into a state of very deep sleep. Their body temperature drops, and heart rate and breathing slow right down. By doing this, they are able to conserve enough energy to last through the winter.

**Distribution:** Central and eastern Europe, north Spain. Introduced into England.
**Habitat:** The canopy of mature deciduous woodland.
**Food:** Nuts, fruit, fungi, bark, insects and occasionally eggs and nestlings.
**Size:** 13–19cm (5–7½in).
**Weight:** 70–300g (2–10oz).
**Maturity:** 2 years.
**Breeding:** 1 litter of 2–9 offspring born in summer.
**Life span:** 7 years.

## Harvest mouse

*Micromys minutus*

The harvest mouse is a little rodent that lives across temperate parts of Europe from northern Spain to Russia. Its range extends into Asia, running through Siberia as far east as Korea. The mouse occupies areas of tall grass and consequently is a common resident of fields of cereal crops, including rice paddies.

Harvest mice each occupy a territory. These overlap, but the mice will avoid coming into contact with each other. When cold weather forces the mice to seek shelter, they congregate in the same place and become more tolerant of each other. Each mouse builds a nest out of grasses, where they sleep for about three hours at a time. Each sleep period is followed by a similar time spent foraging.

**Distribution**: Europe and northern Asia. Northern limit of range is the Arctic Circle.
**Habitat**: Tall grasses.
**Food**: Seeds, fruits and grains.
**Size**: 7cm (3in).
**Weight**: 11g (½oz).
**Maturity**: 35 days.
**Breeding**: Litter of 3–8 young born every 20 days.
**Life span**: 6 months.

**Identification:** Reddish-brown fur with a white underside and large ears. The tail is prehensile and provides extra support while the mouse is climbing. Young are born naked and blind.

## Yellow-necked mouse

*Apodemus flavicollis*

The yellow-necked mouse is naturally a creature of broadleaf woodland. Unlike many mice, which spend most of their time on the ground, it is an expert climber and finds a large proportion of its food in the branches of bushes and trees. In this respect it differs from the wood mouse, which shares its habitat and range. It is also much more likely to be found in houses than the wood mouse, climbing walls to enter open windows and other gaps. The yellow-necked mouse is nocturnal and hence rarely seen by humans. It feeds mainly on fruit, buds, nuts and seeds, and stores excess food in its often extensive tunnel systems to help it survive through the winter month.

Like most other rodents, the yellow-necked mouse is food for many larger animals. While relatively defenceless, it is not incapable of escaping these predators, however. Weasels, owls and other predators are often avoided by impressive leaps off the ground or down from the branches to safety. The yellow-necked mouse can also shed the skin of its tail if gripped by it anywhere other than at the base. Once this part of the tail has been lost and the mouse has escaped, the skinless portion of the tail eventually withers up and falls off.

**Identification:** The yellow-necked mouse is broadly similar to the wood mouse in appearance, although it is usually slightly larger. As its name suggests, it also has a yellowish bib of fur, but this can often be difficult to see. The fur of the back is brown and the underside, apart from the bib, is white. The ears are large and the hairless tail is almost as long as the head and body combined.

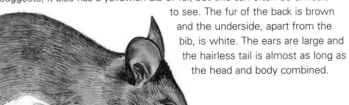

**Distribution**: Central and eastern Wales, the southern half of England, western Europe and Scandinavia.
**Habitat**: Broadleaf woodland, orchards, hedgerows and wooded gardens.
**Food**: Berries, nuts, seeds, fruit and invertebrates.
**Size**: Up to 25cm (10in).
**Weight**: 16–32g (½–1oz).
**Maturity**: 2–3 months.
**Breeding**: Breeding occurs from February until October. Up to three litters are born a year, each containing as many as 11 young. This species sometimes nests in bat or bird boxes.
**Life span**: Up to 1 year.

# House mouse

*Mus musculus*

**Distribution**: Every continent of the world, including Antarctica.
**Habitat**: Generally near human habitation.
**Food**: Waste food, insects plant matter.
**Size**: 15–19cm (6–7½in).
**Weight**: 17–25g (½–1oz).
**Maturity**: 5–7 weeks.
**Breeding**: Usually around 5–10 litters of 3–12 offspring during the year.
**Life span**: 12–18 months.

The key to the house mouse's phenomenal success as a species is its ability to follow humans around the globe, and the way it is able to make use of whatever food sources people provide. By stowing away on ships and, latterly, aeroplanes, house mice have been able to colonize every continent of the world.

Mice were first domesticated, and in some instances worshipped, by the Romans and ancient Greeks. However, these days house mice are considered to be a major pest. They cause billions of dollars' worth of damage to food stores worldwide every year. They also damage buildings, woodwork, furniture and clothing, and are known to carry various dangerous diseases, including typhus and salmonella.

However, house mice are virtually unrivalled by other mammals in their capacity to adapt to new surroundings. Their generalist habits, rapid breeding rate and talent for slipping into places unnoticed have enabled the house mouse to become possibly the most numerous mammal in the world today.

**Identification:** Fur is short and may be light brown to almost black. The belly is pale. Ears, feet and tail are almost hairless.

# Wood mouse

*Apodemus sylvaticus*

The wood mouse, also often referred to as the long-tailed field mouse, is the most common wild mouse in Europe. It lives right across the continent except in the far north of Scandinavia. It is found on the British Isles including the smaller, surrounding islands. The wood mouse also ranges across northern Asia except the cold northern regions and is found south of the Himalayas and as far east as the Altai Mountains of northern China. The mice also live in north-western Africa. With such a wide distribution, it is not surprising that wood mice are able to survive well in several habitats – anywhere with places for the mice to shelter, such as meadows, woodlands, gardens and cultivated fields.

They do occupy houses and other buildings on occasion, especially during cold periods, but generally they dig themselves deep burrows and line them with dried leaves. Newborns are raised in the den for the first three weeks.

Long-tailed field mice are excellent swimmers, climbers and jumpers and can forage successfully almost anywhere. They have typical self-sharpening rodent teeth and so are able to tackle most foods. They are most active in the twilight just before dusk, and at dawn.

**Distribution**: British Isles, mainland Europe, North Africa and northern and eastern Asia.
**Habitat**: Meadows and woodlands. Sometimes homes or other buildings, especially during winter.
**Food**: Roots, fruits, seeds and insects.
**Size**: 8–11cm (3–4¼in).
**Weight**: 16–25g (½–1oz).
**Maturity**: 2 months.
**Breeding**: 4–7 young born in litters produced up to 4 times a year. Gestation period is 25–26 days.
**Life span**: 1 year.

**Identification:** The wood mouse has large eyes so it can see extremely well at night and a long nose that is sensitive enough to smell seeds buried underground. The wood mouse has a long tail but it is not prehensile.

# INSECTIVORES

*The insectivores are a wide-ranging group of small mammals, all with sensitive and highly mobile noses, small eyes and relatively small brains. They are generally solitary, nocturnal animals, the majority of which eat insects, earthworms and other invertebrates. Their teeth are well designed for eating insects, with long incisors for seizing their prey and sharp molars for dealing with their tough bodies.*

## Hedgehog

*Erinaceus europaeus*

Few members of the insectivore family have been able to grow much larger than moles because the food they eat – insects – are so small that they would need to eat a very large quantity. Hedgehogs, however, are more eclectic in their tastes, with a diet that includes earthworms, birds' eggs, frogs, lizards and even snakes. Eating these larger foods has allowed hedgehogs to grow much bigger than is the norm for the group.

Nonetheless, being larger can have its disadvantages, not least being more conspicuous to predators. This is where the hedgehog's famous asset comes in handy. All over its back it has rows of thickened hairs, which narrow into sharp, hard points. Using muscles at the base of the coat, which act like drawstrings, the hedgehog can roll into a ball, becoming a mass of prickles, which is an effective deterrent to predators.

**Distribution**: Western Europe and Northern Russia.
**Habitat**: Woodland, grassland and gardens.
**Food**: Invertebrates.
**Size**: 22–28cm (8½–11in).
**Weight**: 0.4–1.2kg (1–2¼lb).
**Maturity**: 2–3 years.
**Breeding**: 2–6 young born in summer.
**Life span**: 3–4 years.

**Identification:** All over its back are rows of thickened hairs, which narrow at their tips into sharp, prickly points. The muzzle tapers to a blunt, black nose.

---

**Pygmy shrew** (*Sorex minutus*) 6cm (2¼in); 3–6g (under ¼ oz)
Britain's smallest mammal is found on moors, farmland and in forests. It has brown fur with a pointed snout and bulbous head. This creature must eat at least every two hours to survive, and eats the equivalent of its body weight in food each day. It is preyed on by weasels; birds of prey, especially owls; foxes and cats, and is listed as a protected species.

**Identification:** The mole has short but sturdy forelegs and wide claws, which are used for digging tunnels and pulling the animal along. The hind legs are much smaller and there is a short tail. The coat is a velvety black. Eyes are very small. Feet and nose are pink.

## European mole

*Talpa europaea*

The European mole lives across most of Europe, including large parts of Britain, but does not live in southern Europe, which is too dry. However, the species is found across northern Asia as far as China.

Like all moles, this species is a tunneller. It digs using the large claws on its forefeet. Its rounded body and short fur make it easy for the mole to push through loosened soil. The mole needs relatively deep soil to dig in. It pushes the excavated soil out on to the surface, making a molehill.

It is most common in woodlands, where deep soil is held together by tree roots. However, the moles are also found under fields and in gardens. Their tunnels can undermine the structure of the soil, and the molehills ruin lawns.

**Distribution**: Europe and Asia.
**Habitat**: Woodland, fields and meadows.
**Food**: Earthworms.
**Size**: 9–15cm (4–6in).
**Weight**: 70–130g (2–4¼ oz).
**Maturity**: 1 year.
**Breeding**: Single litter of about 3 young born in summer.
**Life span**: 3 years.

# Water shrew

*Neomys fodiens*

The Eurasian water shrew is found across Europe and Asia. The western limit of its range is Britain. It does not live in Ireland. To the east, the species' range extends all the way to the Pacific coast of Siberia.

Most water shrews live close to fresh water, defending a small area of bank in which their burrow is located. Some members of this species live farther away from flowing water, in damp areas such as hedgerows. Shrews live alone. They hunt at all times of the day and night, mostly in water. The tail has a keel of hairs on the underside, which helps with swimming. The shrew's fur traps a blanket of air as the animal submerges, which prevents the little mammal from losing body heat too quickly.

These animals eat about half their own body weight each day. They catch prey in their mouths and stun it with mildly venomous saliva. Only a handful of other mammals deploy venom.

Water shrews breed during the summer. Each female is capable of producing several litters in that time. A typical litter contains about five or six young, although twice this number is possible. The young are weaned after 40 days. Females born early enough can breed in their first year.

**Distribution**: Most of Europe, including Great Britain, and Asia from Turkey to Korea.
**Habitat**: Freshwater streams and ponds.
**Food**: Snails, insects and fish.
**Size**: 10cm (4in).
**Weight**: 18g (½oz).
**Maturity**: 6 months.
**Breeding**: Several litters of between 3 and 12 young produced in summer after a 20-day gestation.
**Life span**: 18 months.

**Identification:** The water shrew has short, very dark fur with a white underbelly and throat. Red-coloured iron compounds coat the tips of its teeth, which makes them more hard-wearing.

# Common shrew

*Sorex araneus*

The Eurasian shrew, known simply as the common shrew in Britain, lives in damp habitats across Europe. Its range stops at the Pyrenees and the shrew does not live in Spain or Portugal or in much of southern France, where it is too dry for them. The range extends to the east as far as Lake Baikal in western Siberia.

The common shrew lives in meadows, woodlands and in broken habitats covered in rocks. It survives on mountainsides as high up as the snow line.

Common shrews live alone and forage for food at dusk and before dawn. They feed on small invertebrates and must consume 90 per cent of their body weight each day. (Being such tiny mammals, they lose body heat very quickly and therefore must eat huge amounts to stay alive.) Hibernating is not an option because the shrews could not build up enough body fat to survive the winter without feeding.

Common shrews produce large litters of about six young. After a couple of weeks, the young emerge from their burrow for the first time and can be seen following their mother in a 'caravan'. The shrews form a train, with each one holding the tail of the shrew in front. The young continue to hold on even when the mother is lifted off the ground.

**Distribution**: Europe from Great Britain and the Pyrenees to Lake Baikal in western Siberia.
**Habitat**: Woodlands, grasslands, rock fields and sand dunes.
**Food**: Woodlice, insects, spiders and worms. Also eats plant foods.
**Size**: 6cm (2¼in).
**Weight**: 9g (¼oz).
**Maturity**: Between 9 and 10 months.
**Breeding**: 2 litters produced in summer after a gestation of 20 days. The young are weaned after 30 days.
**Life span**: 2 years.

**Identification:** The shrew has a tri-coloured fur coat: the back is reddish brown, the underside is pale grey and the flanks and face are brown. Young shrews have paler fur.

# BATS

*With nearly 1,000 species, bats form one of the largest groups among the mammals, living in almost all temperate and tropical parts of the world. They are the only mammals to have truly mastered flight, and more than half of the species use echolocation for navigating and capturing prey at night. Different bats are specialized for eating insects, fruit, flowers, blood, fish and small animals.*

## Pipistrelle bat

*Pipistrellus pipistrellus*

Although common throughout most of Europe, these small bats have declined in some countries due to the loss of roosting sites in trees and the use of toxic chemicals that have been used to treat wood in the buildings where many pipistrelles roost during wintertime. In some parts of Europe, pipistrelles hibernate; however, very cold weather may force over-wintering pipistrelles to move to warmer areas.

Pipistrelles leave their roosts early in the evening to feed, chasing after insects in a characteristically fast and jerky pursuit, using echolocation. A single pipistrelle can eat as many as 3,000 insects in one night. Usually the high-pitched squeaks that pipistrelles make for echolocation are inaudible to humans, but some people can hear the lower-frequency parts of their calls. Mating usually takes place in autumn, when the bats congregate at traditional breeding roosts. Females give birth to their young in summer, when they come together in large maternity colonies to suckle and care for them.

**Identification:** There are two subspecies of pipistrelle bat, distinguished by the pitch of their calls. Most pipistrelles are darker brown on the back, and yellow underneath. They usually have a jet black face mask, black ears and black wing membranes.

**Distribution**: Europe, North Africa, south-western and central Asia, and possibly Korea and Japan.
**Habitat**: Forests, farmland, wetlands and urban habitats, nesting in lofts.
**Food**: Insects.
**Size**: 3–5cm (1–2in); wingspan 19–25cm (7½–10½in).
**Weight**: 4–8g (under ¼oz).
**Maturity**: Females 6 months; males 1 year.
**Breeding**: 1 young or occasionally twins produced per year.
**Life span**: 16 years.

## Greater horseshoe bat

*Rhinolophus ferrumequinum*

The greater horseshoe bat is the largest horseshoe bat in Europe. It is also found in north-western Africa and across most of Asia as far east as Japan. Horseshoe bats belong to the *Rhinolophus* genus, which means 'nose crest'.

The greater horseshoe bat is an insect eater. It hunts at night and specializes in catching large insects such as moths and beetles. They fly close to the ground, scanning for prey with pulses of sound, the echoes of which enable them to locate insects. They catch prey mainly in the air. Horseshoe bats prefer to hunt on warm nights, because most insects cannot fly in cold weather. In the northern parts of its range, where winters are colder, members of this species will not leave their roosts for weeks on end.

These bats roost in caves and smaller holes under rocks. They mate in the autumn, but the females' eggs are not fertilized by the sperm until the following year. Pups are born during the late summer.

**Identification:** The greater horseshoe bat is named after the shape of its nose. The upper nose leaf is pointed but the larger flap below the nose forms a horseshoe shape.

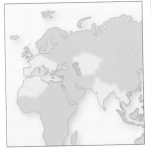

**Distribution**: Europe, north-west Africa and central and south Asia.
**Habitat**: Woodland and shrublands.
**Food**: Large insects.
**Size**: 7cm (3in); wingspan up to 35cm (14in).
**Weight**: 25g (1oz).
**Maturity**: 3 years.
**Breeding**: Single pup born in summer.
**Life span**: 30 years.

# Western barbastelle

*Barbastella barbastellus*

The western barbastelle lives in hill forests, apart from those in cold regions. For example, in Great Britain it survives only in the milder southern regions. The species is more common in southern Europe and the Mediterranean islands. In summer the bats roost in hollow trees and other relatively open spots, where they often squeeze behind patches of loose bark. In winter the barbastelles retreat to more secluded roosts, such as caves, where they hibernate without becoming completely dormant: they will leave the roost every week or two to hunt.

These bats prey on moths and other soft-bodied insects. They do not seem to eat beetles, which have hardened wingcases and tend to have tougher bodies than most insects. The bats snatch prey in mid-air or grab insects as they perch on leaves and branches. Barbastelles hunt along the edges of forests, where there are more flyways for them and their prey.

Across its entire range, this species is under threat. The main reason for this is the loss of its habitat, in particular a lack of hollow trees in which the bats can roost.

**Identification:** Western barbastelles have dark hairs with yellow tips. The neck and chin have long hairs that give the impression of a beard. The feature that distinguishes this species from other bats is the ears, which join across the forehead.

**Distribution**: Great Britain, western and central Europe, Morocco, and the Canary Islands.
**Habitat**: Highland forests in summer but retreat to subterranean caves and mines in winter.
**Food**: Moths and other soft-bodied insects.
**Size**: 6cm (2¼in); wingspan 23cm (9in).
**Weight**: 8g (under ¼ oz).
**Maturity**: 1 year.
**Breeding**: Single pups born in summer. Pups reach full size in about 3 months.
**Life span**: Unknown.

---

### Nathusius's pipistrelle

(*Pipistrellus nathusii*)
Up to 6cm (2¼in), wingspan 25cm (10½in). Nathusius's pipistrelle is a small bat with reddish fur in summer (darker brown in winter) and relatively long wings. It is most common in central and eastern Europe and was not known to breed in Britain until 1997, when the first colonies were found in southern England. Since then, new breeding colonies have been discovered in Lincolnshire and parts of Northern Ireland. Nathusius's pipistrelle is primarily a creature of woodland, with maternity roosts established in hollow trees.

**Identification:** Its fur is soft and fluffy, brownish on the back and light grey, or almost white, underneath. Juveniles are dark grey all over. This species has a horseshoe-shaped nose. When at rest, hanging upside-down from its feet, it wraps its delicate, membranous wings right around its body.

# Lesser horseshoe bat

*Rhinolophus hipposideros*

This is one of the smallest of all British bats. Fewer than 15,000 lesser horseshoe bats are thought to remain in south-west England and Wales. Unlike most bats, it grabs the majority of its prey from the surface of stones and branches rather than catching it in mid-air. By doing this, it is able to feed on spiders and take insects such as moths at rest. This may help it to avoid competition with other bat species.

The bat emerges from its roost towards the end of dusk. It tends to fly quickly and relatively low, rarely more than 5m (16½ ft) above the ground. It is very agile.

The bat hibernates from October until April. Its roosts tend to be in caves or barns. Unlike many other bats, the females give birth in mixed-sex colonies. The young lesser horseshoe bats are independent at seven weeks of age.

**Distribution**: Extinct in the Midlands and south-east England, this species is now restricted to south-west England and Wales.
**Habitat**: Mixed woodland and farmland.
**Food**: Insects, mainly moths.
**Size**: Up to 3–4.5cm (1–1¼in), wingspan 25cm (10½in).
**Weight**: 5–9g (under ¼oz).
**Maturity**: 3–6 months.
**Breeding**: Mating occurs in autumn, with the single pup being born between mid-June and July the following year.
**Life span**: Up to 21 years.

# Grey long-eared bat

*Plecotus austriacus*

**Identification**: Grey long-eared bats have long grey fur and a paler belly than brown long-eared bats. Compared with most other bats, the grey long-eared bat has very large ears. The eyes are also unusually large for a bat. The nose, upper lip, ears and wing membranes are very dark grey to black in colour.

Less common and widespread than the brown long-eared bat (see box opposite), the grey long-eared bat has a similar lifestyle and hunts in a similar way. Like the brown long-eared bat, it emerges after nightfall to search for prey, rather than at dusk, and like most bats the grey long-eared bat hunts and navigates by echolocation, building up a 'sound picture' of its surroundings and prey by listening to the echoes of the high-pitched squeaks it emits. Using this information it plucks moths and other flying insects from the air. Like the brown long-eared bat, it often takes these prey items to a convenient perch before eating.

The breeding behaviour of this species is only poorly understood. What is known is that males become territorial in autumn, defending their area from rivals. It is presumed that males mate with females drawn to their territory, either in response to calls made by the male or in search of food. The grey long-eared bat goes into hibernation in September and only emerges from its long slumber the following April.

**Distribution**: This species is widespread in central and southern Europe, but in Britain it is restricted to the far south of England.
**Habitat**: Farmland and areas near human settlement.
**Food**: Flying insects, mainly moths.
**Size**: Up to 6cm (2¼in), wingspan up to 30cm (12in).
**Weight**: 17–24g (¼–½oz)
**Maturity**: Unknown.
**Breeding**: Mating occurs in autumn. The single pup is born towards the end of the following June.
**Life span**: Up to 15 years.

# Whiskered bat

*Myotis mystacinus*

The whiskered bat emerges from its daytime roost to hunt as dusk begins, spending most of the hours of darkness pursuing moths and other flying insects. Like most bats, it has to eat around half its own body weight to survive. Fortunately moths, in spring and summer at least, are abundant. As autumn draws in, the whiskered bat prepares for a winter of hibernation, surviving on its fat reserves with all of its body processes wound down to the bare minimum. In flight during summer, its body temperature is around 37°C and its heart may beat as many as 400 times per minute. When hibernating, its body temperature drops to just 10°C and its heart rate slows to just 5–20 beats per minute. Whiskered bats go into hibernation in September, but they are among the first bats to emerge the following spring. In some years, they may be seen flying as early as late February. Even in the coldest springs they become active during March.

Whiskered bats tend to hunt over water or between trees, flying close to the ground. Their movement through the air varies greatly. At some times it is swift and weaving: at others it may appear fluttery, direct and quite slow. Prey caught is most often consumed on the wing.

**Identification**: This species is very similar in appearance to Brandt's bat but has darker fur. The back is usually nut-brown or greyish-brown, while the underside ranges from dark to light grey. The relatively long ears are almost black, as are the face and wing membranes. The nose lacks the leaf seen in some other bats.

**Distribution**: Although uncommon, this species is found throughout England, Ireland and Wales, and southern Scotland Also across much of Europe.
**Habitat**: Farmland, parks and areas near human settlement.
**Food**: Flying insects, mainly moths.
**Size**: Up to 4cm (1½in), wingspan up to 25cm (10½in).
**Weight**: 5–9g (under ¼oz).
**Maturity**: 2 years.
**Breeding**: Mating tends to occur in autumn. The single pup is born during the following June or July.
**Life span**: Up to 19 years.

**Brown long-eared bat**
(*Plecotus auritus*) 4–5cm
(1½–2in), wingspan 24–28cm
(9½–11in). One of the most
common bats in the British
Isles, ranging across
woodland, orchards and
parkland. Its fur is a buff-
brown colour, with a pink-
brown face. The ears and
wing membranes are a light
grey-brown.

**Leisler's bat** (*Nyctalus leisleri*)
Up to 9cm (3½in), wingspan
32cm (13in). Leisler's bat can
be found in most parts of
England, Wales and Ireland,
but is absent from Scotland.
It occurs in woodland
habitats, roosting in hollow
trees, as well as bat boxes
and buildings. Leisler's bat is
similar in appearance to the
noctule bat, but is darker in
colour and smaller. The hairs
on its back are dark brown at
the base and reddish towards
the tips, a feature which is
often used to separate it from
the noctule.

**Serotine bat** (*Eptesicus
serotinus*) Up to 8cm (3in),
wingspan up to 38cm (15in).
This bat of mainly lowland
areas seems to prefer
roosting in buildings. It is
confined to southern parts of
Wales and England, being
most abundant in Dorset and
Sussex. It is one of Britain's
largest bats, with long, smoky
brown fur on its back and
lighter, yellowish-brown fur on
the belly. Easily recognized by
its slow wing beat and
tendency to glide.

**Bechstein's bat** (*Myotis
bechsteinii*) Up to 6cm (2¼in),
wingspan up to 30cm (12in).
This rare bat (listed as
Vulnerable) is restricted
mainly to southern England
and parts of southern Wales.
It has long, broad ears with
long projections (tragus). The
fur is pale to reddish brown
on the back and light grey
underneath.

# Noctule bat

*Nyctalus noctula*

The noctule bat is one of the largest and most common
European bats. In winter, noctules roost in hollow trees or
old woodpecker holes, and occasionally in buildings. In
some parts of Europe, groups of 1,000 individuals may
roost together. Noctules hunt insects in flight, and are
capable of flying at speeds of 50kph (30mph) or more.
Usually they forage at dusk, catching insects over woodland
or close to water, and sometimes they are seen hunting
insects that gather around street lamps in towns.

Although noctules are capable of surviving in cold
conditions without food for up to four months, they also
migrate to warmer areas where there is more food. Noctules
have been known to migrate
as far as 2,347km (1,455
miles). In late summer,
solitary male noctules
set up breeding roosts
in tree holes, attracting
up to 20 females with
mating calls and
pheromones. In early
summer, pregnant
females form groups
of related individuals,
then they help one
another nurse their young.

# Brandt's bat

*Myotis brandtii*

Brandt's bat is a relatively new addition to the official list of
British mammals. It was only identified as a separate species
in 1970. Brandt's bat looks so much like the whiskered bat
that its original misidentification is excusable. Like all of
Britain's bats, Brandt's bat is an insect-eater, catching flying
prey while on the wing, and finds its food by
echolocation. The sounds that it makes while
hunting range from 35–80 kilohertz, too high-
pitched for human ears to hear. This, combined
with the fact that it hunts at night, means that it is
rarely noticed, even when very close by.

After emerging during early dusk, it spends
the hours of darkness scouting for moths and
other prey over water or low over the ground.
Before dawn it returns to its roost, more often
than not in a building. As with many other bats,
it chooses different places to roost in summer
from those
where it
hibernates in
winter. Females also form their
own nursery roosts, separate from
males, in early summer.

**Distribution**: Europe to
Japan.
**Habitat**: Forests.
**Food**: Insects, especially
beetles, and also midges
and moths.
**Size**: Up to 8cm (3in),
wingspan 40cm (16in).
**Weight**: 15–40g (½–1½oz).
**Maturity**: Females 3 months;
males 1 year.
**Breeding**: Single litter of 1, 2
or occasionally 3 young born
per year.
**Life span**: 12 years.

**Identification:** The colour of the
noctule bat ranges from a golden
brown to a dark brown on the
back, usually with paler brown
coloration on the belly.

**Distribution**: Northern Euope
and throughout Asia.
**Habitat**: Woodland areas,
particularly near water.
**Food**: Flying insects.
**Size**: Up to 5cm (2in),
wingspan: up to 24cm (9½in).
**Weight**: 4–8g (under ¼oz).
**Maturity**: 2 years.
**Breeding**: Mating takes place
in autumn. The single pup is
born the following year,
between mid-June and July.
**Life span**: Up to 19 years.

**Identification:** Brandt's bat has
light brown shaggy fur with a
golden sheen. The underside is
paler in colour and tinged with
yellow. The nose, ears and wing
membranes are all light brown.

# AMPHIBIANS

*Amphibians spend part of their time in the water and part out of it. When young frogs first hatch out as tadpoles they almost resemble fish. Only as they grow do they start to develop legs and lose their gills, which are replaced by lungs. Then they are able to hunt on land and in the water for food. Young newts breathe through gills, like fish, before becoming dependent on their lungs.*

## Common toad

*Bufo bufo*

The common toad lives away from water for most of the year. Its thick, loose skin and nocturnal habits help to protect it from drying out. Toads protect themselves with foul-tasting chemicals released by warty glands in their skins. If threatened, the common toad also inflates its body and rises up on its legs, to intimidate predators.

Toads use their sticky tongues to catch ants, their favourite prey. They have a good sense of smell, which helps them to find their way to breeding sites each year. They hibernate until February and March – usually a few weeks later than common frogs.

Rather than laying clumps of spawn, as frogs do, common toads release a strand of spawn that hangs on weeds. In warm weather, tadpoles metamorphose in about eight weeks.

**Identification:** Common toads are olive brown and warty. They walk rather than hop like frogs. The males are smaller and have fewer warts than the females. Only the males croak.

**Distribution**: Europe, north-west Africa, and Asia.
**Habitat**: Woodland, gardens, and fields. In the breeding season, they live in ponds and slow-moving rivers.
**Food**: Insects, spiders, slugs and worms.
**Size**: 8–15cm (3–6in).
**Weight**: 250g (9oz).
**Maturity**: 4 years.
**Breeding**: Lays up to 4,000 eggs.
**Life span**: 40 years.

## European common frog

*Rana temporaria*

European common frogs are found in a variety of habitats, including fields and woodland close to water. Their diet is eclectic, including insects, molluscs and worms. Male common frogs have swellings on their first fingers to help them grasp the females when mating. Sometimes two or three males may try to mate with one female. Occasionally she will die in this situation through drowning or being squashed by their combined weight.

Spawning can take place as early as December or January but it is more usual in late February, March or April. Frogs flock to a traditional breeding pond, lake or ditch, where hundreds or thousands may be swimming around. Males emit quiet croaks and can be seen jostling for the best females. While a female is releasing her 1,000–4,000 eggs, the male will spread his sperm directly over them.

After spawning, the ponds become quiet again, as the frogs leave to live on land. They do so until the autumn, when they hibernate under logs and rocks. When it is very cold, they will rest in the water, usually in thick vegetation.

**Identification:** Common frogs are variable in colour, but generally have a greenish-brown body colour with darker blotches and dark masks on their faces.

**Distribution**: Widespread throughout Europe, including Turkey and Russia.
**Habitat**: Live in meadows, gardens and woodland. Breed in puddles, ponds, lakes and canals. Prefer areas of shallow water.
**Food**: Insects, snails, slugs and worms, caught with long, sticky tongues. Tadpoles are herbivores and feed on algae.
**Size**: 6–10cm (2¼–4in).
**Weight**: 25g (1oz)
**Maturity**: 3 years.
**Breeding**: 1,000–4,000 eggs laid.
**Life span**: 12 years.

# Natterjack toad

*Bufo calamita*

**Identification:** The natterjack toad has dark, warty skin and a yellow line all the way from the head to the end of the spine. During the breeding season, the males develop purple-violet throats, while the females' throats remain white. Males have large throat sacs, which are used to make loud calls.

The natterjack toad is found throughout western and central Europe and is the smallest of all the European toads. In northern Europe, including Britain, the toads are restricted to lowland habitats such as heaths and dunes, although they are also often found in broken habitats, such as a quarry. Farther south the toads are able to survive in a wider range of habitats, including the slopes of mountains.

Natterjack toads are nocturnal. They live away from water outside the breeding season and will travel large distances if necessary, using their sense of the Earth's magnetic field as a means of navigating. The toads hibernate under stones and in other sheltered spots during the worst of the winter weather. If alarmed, the toads inflate their bodies and exude an unpleasant-smelling liquid through their skin to scare off predators.

The breeding season lasts for most of the spring and summer. Males position themselves in or near to shallow water and attract mates with their croaks. They are thought to be Europe's noisiest toads because the male's croaking can be heard up to 3km (2 miles) away. Eggs, laid in ponds, hatch in about a week.

**Distribution**: Western and central Europe as far east as the Baltic states, Belarus and western Ukraine.
**Habitat**: Meadows, dunes, quarries and woodlands in the north, and also mountains in the south.
**Food**: Invertebrates.
**Size**: 7cm (3in).
**Weight**: Not known.
**Maturity**: 2 years.
**Breeding**: Single and double strings of eggs laid in shallow water. A female can lay 7,000 eggs in one season.
**Life span**: 10 years in the wild; 17 years in captivity.

# Marsh frog

*Pelophylax ridibundus*

Europe's largest native frog's range extends from eastern France through Europe north of the Alps and into Russia and parts of Asia. In Britain it is confined to south-east England and is most common in Sussex and Kent. The marsh frog was first introduced into Romney Marsh in Kent in 1934 and has slowly spread outwards from there in the decades since. Unlike the common frog, which spends much of its time on land, the marsh frog is highly aquatic and very rarely leaves the water. At the first sign of danger, it disappears beneath the water, and as a consequence, its presence often goes unnoticed.

The marsh frog breeds in May, much later than the common frog, Britain's only native frog species. Its call is a rapid 're...re...re...' and sounds like laughter, hence the species name ridibundus, which means 'laugh in bursts' in Latin. At first the tadpoles feed on plant matter and algae, but they soon turn carnivorous, catching water fleas and other tiny creatures. Some metamorphose before the year is out but others hibernate through the winter. These overwintering tadpoles may be up to 9cm (3½in) long.

**Identification:** The main distinguishing feature of this frog is its size – female marsh frogs have bulky bodies and may grow up to 17cm (6½in) long. Males are smaller and slimmer. The back is green and occasionally has darker spots. The vocal sacs at the side of the male's mouth appear grey – in the closely related pool and edible frogs they are lighter, almost white. The tadpoles are greyish-brown with light, creamy bellies. Their tails are relatively slender and rounded at the tip.

**Distribution**:
South-east England, widespread in central and eastern Europe and the Balkan peninsula to East and Central Asia.
**Habitat**: Ponds, lakes, streams and marshes.
**Food**: Insects and various other invertebrates.
**Size**: Up to 17cm (6½in).
**Weight**: Not known.
**Maturity**: 2–3 years.
**Breeding**: Males start calling in late spring and spawning usually occurs in May. The tadpoles grow much larger than those of the common frog and may overwinter before undergoing metamorphosis.
**Life span**: 11 years.

# Midwife toad

*Alytes obstetricans*

**Distribution**: West and south-west Europe.
**Habitat**: Quarries, scree slopes and uncultivated land. Sand dunes and gardens are inhabited in France.
**Food**: Small insects.
**Size**: 5cm (2in).
**Weight**: Not known.
**Maturity**: 2 years.
**Breeding**: Female lays several batches of 20–60 eggs in strings between April and June, which are carried on the male's back legs. Tadpoles are released into water between 2 and 6 weeks later.
**Life span**: Not known.

The midwife toad looks very similar to the common toad. However, it has vertical pupils instead of horizontal ones, a more pointed snout, and does not have the protective glands behind the head. Midwife toads are night-active and spend the day hidden in crevices in rocks, under logs or in burrows.

In late spring, the males give out short peeping calls to attract females. Mating occurs on land. As the females produce strings of 20–60 eggs, the males catch them with their legs. They then position the strings of spawn between their thighs and waists. The females play no part in looking after the eggs. The eggs remain embedded in a whitish-yellow mass of mucus that keeps them moist.

The male secretes antibiotics over the eggs to protect them from fungus and bacteria. After two to six weeks, the eggs develop into tadpoles. The males travel to ponds where the young release themselves into the water. Some males attract two or more females, and therefore look after a larger number of eggs.

**Identification**: The midwife toad is dull grey, olive or brown in colour, occasionally with green spots and often with darker markings. The belly is whitish with grey blotches. Females sometimes have red spots running down their flanks. This toad is particularly proficient at leaping.

# Common newt

*Triturus vulgaris*

**Distribution**: Northern Europe and western Asia.
**Habitat**: Damp woodlands, gardens and fields.
**Food**: Invertebrates.
**Size**: 11cm (4¼in).
**Weight**: Not known.
**Maturity**: 3 years.
**Breeding**: Up to 300 eggs laid on water plants.
**Life span**: 7 years.

The common newt, or smooth newt as it is sometimes called, lives across northern Europe from the British Isles to Russia and western Asia. It is less reliant on water than most newts and is seen on the ground in damp habitats. Like other newts, however, the common newt must return to water to breed. They prefer ponds and shallow lakes to running water.

The males develop a large crest prior to the spring breeding season. Females are attracted to those males with larger crests. During courtship the males wave their tails at the females before depositing a sperm capsule before her, which she then picks up with her cloaca. Fertilization takes place inside her body. After mating, the female lays up to 300 eggs on water plants. The eggs hatch after about two weeks. The larvae stay close to the bottom of the pool, which keeps them out of the way of the adults, which are more common near to the surface. This divide prevents the two generations competing for food. A larva will metamorphose into the adult form once it reaches 4cm (1½in) long. This might take a year or even longer. In cold waters the larvae may never take the adult form.

**Identification**: The common newt exhibits a variety of colour patterns. The common form is grey-green skin on the upper side and an orange belly with black spots. The male has large spots on the back and grows a jagged crest for the breeding season. Out of season, males and females are very difficult to tell apart, as both are about 10cm (4½ in) in length and light golden-brown in colour.

**Alpine Newt** (*Triturus alpestris*) Up to 6cm (2¼in), tail length up to 5cm (2in). This rather handsome amphibian has been deliberately introduced to parts of Britain. Colonies are known to have become established in Kent, East Surrey, South-east London, Birmingham, Shropshire, Sunderland and parts of central Scotland. The alpine newt is native to central and southern Europe, being most common, as its name suggests, in mountainous and upland areas. In the breeding season the male develops a low yellow crest with black markings. Both sexes have a bright, unspotted red or orange belly.

**Identification:** Male palmate newts have webbed feet, yellow bellies and thin filaments of skin that extend 5mm (¼in) from the tips of their tails. The females are duller and lack the tail filaments.

# Palmate newt

*Triturus helveticus*

The palmate newt lives in western Europe, from Britain to north-west Spain and Portugal and Switzerland. This species is often mistaken for the common newt, but is generally smaller and has fewer spots on the belly, which is also a pale yellow rather than a dark orange. Like the common newt, the palmate newt is regularly found out of water but never strays out of moist habitats.

The newts hibernate under logs and stones from November through to March, when they return to water to breed. The males grow a low smooth crest to attract females and their hind feet become webbed. After mating, the females lay 290–460 eggs on aquatic plants. The eggs hatch within a fortnight. The larvae that emerge have gills for breathing exclusively underwater. Once they reach about 3cm (1¼in) long, their gills are absorbed into the body and they take on the four-legged adult form that can survive out of water. Adults breathe with lungs but can also take oxygen through their skin.

**Distribution**: Western Europe.
**Habitat**: Shallow water and damp land habitats.
**Food**: Invertebrates.
**Size**: 9cm (3½in).
**Weight**: Not known.
**Maturity**: 2 years.
**Breeding**: 400 eggs laid in water.
**Life span**: 12 years.

# Great crested newt

*Triturus cristatus cristatus*

**Distribution**: England, Scotland, central Europe from France to Urals, and southern Scandinavia to Alps.
**Habitat**: Spends most of the year in weedy ponds.
**Food**: Small aquatic invertebrates and vertebrates, including other amphibians.
**Size**: 11–16cm (4¼–6¼in).
**Weight**: 7.5–10.5g (under ¼oz).
**Maturity**: Tadpoles change into newts after 8–16 weeks. Reach adult size after 2 years.
**Breeding**: 200–300 eggs laid between April and mid-July.
**Life span**: 27 years.

During the breeding season, male great crested newts become brightly coloured, particularly on their bellies. They also develop high toothed crests along their backs and white bands along the sides of their tails. The newts hibernate on land during the winter. They return to the water in March, and the males develop their breeding livery two weeks later. Once the breeding season is over, their crests and outer skins are absorbed into their bodies.

Young great crested newts hatch in water as tadpoles. They feed on fish, tadpoles, worms and aquatic insects. The adults feed on larger prey, including newts and frogs. They locate their prey in the mud using smell and sight. Great crested newts are afforded protection by their skins. If threatened, their skins release a white, creamy fluid, which is an irritant to the eyes, nose and mouth of predators.

**Identification:** Great crested newts have dark backs, while their bellies are orange or red with large black blotches or spots. The males are more colourful than the females, with tall crests along their backs during the breeding season.

# REPTILES

*Like amphibians, reptiles are cold-blooded creatures. They rely on the sun or the heat of their surroundings to warm their bodies up. Britain is not far from the northern limit of their range. However, the reptiles that live here are perfectly adapted to survive the conditions they find themselves in. Ireland, famously, has no snakes, supposedly thanks to St Patrick driving them away.*

## Adder

*Vipera berus*

The majority of members of the viper family are venomous, and the adder – or common viper – is no exception. However, adders rarely bite humans, and, even when they do, the consequences are usually no more than a painful swelling. Adders spend most of their day basking in the sunshine, and go out to hunt in the late afternoon. As winter closes in adders hibernate, usually burrowing underground to sleep through the cold weather. The duration of hibernation varies with latitude.

During spring, when they come out of hibernation male adders, having shed their skins, go in search of females, and mating occurs. At the onset of summer, adders migrate along hedgerows and ditches to prime feeding grounds, such as wet meadows. They stay in these areas until summer starts to draw to a close, at which time they head back to drier areas. Female adders give birth to their young, which immediately prepare to hibernate.

**Distribution**: Throughout Europe and northern and western Asia.
**Habitat**: Open places such as heaths, meadows and woodland edges.
**Food**: Lizards, small mammals, nestlings and insects.
**Size**: 65cm (25½in).
**Weight**: Not known.
**Maturity**: Not known.
**Breeding**: 10 young born in late summer.
**Life span**: 15 years.

**Identification:** The adder's predominantly grey-brown colour, with zigzag markings down the back, is very different from the coloration of the grass snake.

## Grass snake

*Natrix natrix*

The grass snake is the most common snake in Britain. It owes its success to its versatility, being able to hunt both on land and in the water. It prefers to prey on frogs, toads and fish, when it can. To acquire enough heat to be able to function properly, the grass snake has to spend much of its time basking in sunlight. However, this does leave it rather exposed to attack. When threatened, a grass snake has a range of defensive tactics including loud hissing, inflating its body with air, biting, producing a foul-smelling secretion from its anus and playing dead. The eggs of the grass snake also need to be kept warm; if they are too cold they will take too long to develop, or not hatch at all. Female grass snakes travel large distances to find suitable places to lay them. Heaps of rotting vegetation, such as compost heaps, are favoured.

**Distribution**: Europe from Scandinavia south to the Mediterranean, North Africa and central Asia east to Lake Baikal, Russia.
**Habitat**: Damp grasslands, ditches and river banks.
**Food**: Amphibians, fish, small mammals and small birds.
**Size**: 0.7–2m (2¼–6½ft).
**Weight**: Not known.
**Maturity**: Not known.
**Breeding**: 8–40 eggs laid in June, July or August depending on the latitude, about 8 weeks after mating.
**Life span**: 20 years.

**Identification:** Dark green body with black flecking and whitish-yellow collars around their necks. They inhabit Britain as far as the Scottish border counties.

# Smooth snake

*Coronella austriaca*

**Distribution**: Widely distributed in Europe, but very restricted range in Britain; found only in Dorset, Hampshire West Sussex and Surrey.
**Habitat**: Heathland and rocky areas.
**Food**: Small mammals, lizards and nestlings.
**Size**: 70cm (27in).
**Weight**:: Not known.
**Maturity**: 3–4 years.
**Breeding**: About 6 babies born in autumn.
**Life span**: 18 years.

Britain's rarest snakes, smooth snakes are restricted to just a handful of sandy heathlands in southern England. Across the Channel, the snakes are found across France and in northern and central parts of the Iberian Peninsula. These snakes are colubrids, sometimes described as typical snakes, largely because they are the most numerous type. Like the great majority of colubrids, they are not venomous at all: they kill their prey by constricting them with their coils. Grass snakes and house snakes are also colubrids.

Smooth snakes hunt during the day. They are secretive reptiles and will slither away into cover if they detect something coming. They are also slow moving. They do not chase prey but stalk it by following its scent and ambushing it as it emerges from a burrow.

These snakes breed in spring. They are the only European species to give birth to their young rather than lay eggs. The young take anywhere between four and five months to develop inside the mother.

**Identification:** Smooth snakes are so called because, unlike grass snakes, which have keel-shaped scales, they have flat, smooth scales. Female smooth snakes are generally larger than the males. The snakes are smaller in the northern parts of their range.

# Slow worm

*Anguis fragilis*

The slow worm has a long, smooth body and lacks legs. Although it is often mistaken for a snake, it is actually a legless lizard. Unlike snakes, it has movable eyelids so that it can blink. It also has a broader, flatter tongue with a notch at the tip rather than a deep fork.

Slow worms hibernate between October and March. The males appear before the females, and when they come out in the spring, they warm themselves up by resting under rocks and logs. Slow worms are secretive creatures and spend most of their time underground. If they are attacked, they can shed their tails, which continue to wriggle for about 15 minutes. This distracts a predator while the slow worm escapes. They eat earthworms, slugs and other garden creatures. Slow worms are thought to be the most common reptile in Europe.

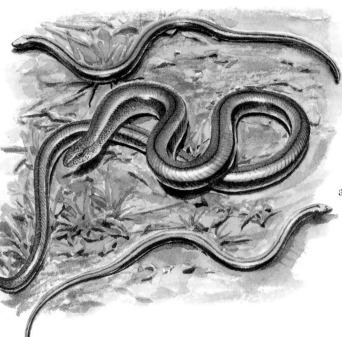

**Distribution**: Widespread throughout Britain, but most common in the south and east of England. Also Europe, South-west Asia and western Siberia.
**Habitat**: Rough grassland, hedgerows, heathland, woodland edges, and moorland. Also found in gardens and along railways.
**Food**: Molluscs and earthworms, and also insects and spiders.
**Size**: 30–50cm (12–19½in).
**Weight**: Not known.
**Maturity**: Females 4–5 years; males 3–4 years.
**Breeding**: Mate in summer; eggs incubated inside body.
**Life span**: 10–15 years.

**Identification:** Females are brown with coppery or reddish-coloured backs, with dark stripes on both sides of the body. Males are brown and lack the stripes. Both sexes have whitish or reddish bellies and throats, often with blue spots, and copper-red eyes.

## Sand lizard

*Lacerta agilis*

**Distribution**: Found naturally in Dorset, Surrey, Hampshire and Merseyside. Introduced to Berkshire, West Sussex, Cornwall, Devon and North Wales. Also in Central and eastern Europe.
**Habitat**: Meadows, steppe, dunes and hedgerows.
**Food**: Insects.
**Size**: 18–19cm (7–7½in).
**Weight**: 12g (under ½oz).
**Maturity**: 2–3 years.
**Breeding**: A dozen eggs buried in a sunny area.
**Life span**: 12 years.

**Identification:** Males are bright green. Females and young are generally brown with darker patterning along their bodies.

The sand lizard is found throughout much of Europe and central Asia. It is one of the few reptiles to live in Britain. It survives in two tiny pockets, one on the south coast and the other in the north-west. In both places, the lizards live in sandy heathlands. Elsewhere in the lizard's range, which extends from southern Sweden to the Middle East, the lizards are found in similar dry habitats.

During courtship, male sand lizards fight over access to the biggest and most fertile females. Both males and females will mate with several partners during a season, as a result of which the eggs laid by a female will have been fertilized by more than one male. Females lay up to 14 eggs in a nest dug in dry, sandy soil close to vegetation. In the northern parts of the lizard's range these nests are located in sunlit areas to ensure that the eggs do not get too cold. In warmer parts, females may be able to produce two clutches in a year.

**Viviparous lizard** (*Lacerta vivipara*) 10–16cm (4–6¼in) One of the most common European reptiles, the viviparous lizard is found across northern and central Europe and into northern parts of Asia. It is the only reptile found in Ireland. Viviparous means 'live birth' – viviparous lizards don't lay eggs, but give birth to fully formed young. These miniatures of their parents are independent from birth, receiving no help from their mothers. Up close they are striking animals, with delicate patterns of coloured scales.

## Leatherback turtle

*Dermochelys coriacea*

The world's largest marine turtle, the leatherback is unique in having a rubbery carapace, or shell, instead of a hard, brittle one. Leatherbacks are the most commonly sighted marine turtle species in British seas. They are usually seen during the summer, and are believed to migrate to the UK to feed on the abundant jellyfish. The largest individuals are true giants, weighing more than 900kg (1,984lb) – as much as 12 average men. Their large size helps them retain some of the heat generated by their metabolism so that, while they remain cold-blooded, their core temperature is usually a few degrees above that of the water, allowing them to exploit higher latitudes than other marine reptiles. They make extensive migration into temperate zones, returning to the tropics to breed. Mating takes place at sea, and the females come ashore to bury their leathery eggs on beaches. This species has undergone a steep decline and is at risk from pollution and disturbance of nesting sites. They feed exclusively on jellyfish and tunicates such as salps and pyrosomes.

**Identification**: The carapace is rubbery, with prominent longitudinal ridges. Very large fore-flippers are characteristic. Dorsal surfaces are black, while the underside is mottled pale pink and black.

**Distribution**: Tropical to cool-temperate waters of oceans worldwide.
**Habitat**: Surface waters from coasts to open ocean, sometimes diving to more than 500m (1,640ft).
**Food**: Jellyfish and other marine invertebrates.
**Size**: 2.8m (9ft).
**Weight**: 100–150kg (220–330lb).
**Breeding**: Mates offshore; eggs laid in batches of 60–100 on sandy beaches; no parental care after laying, although nesting sites are selected with great care.
**Life span**: Not known.

# Loggerhead turtle

*Caretta caretta*

**Identification**: Carapace is reddish brown; scales on front flippers reddish fringed with yellow; yellow ventral surface (plastron).

Considered the most migratory of all sea turtles, loggerheads have been known to make crossings of both the Atlantic and Pacific Oceans. Even young animals spend long periods far out to sea, drifting along with clumps of sargassum weed. Juvenile loggerhead turtles occasionally occur in UK waters. The heavy, powerful jaws and associated muscles that earn the species its name are able to demolish the shells of large crabs and molluscs. Loggerheads commonly live to 30 years but can live far beyond that age. Females lay a clutch of approximately 100 eggs every 1–6 years on the south-eastern beaches of the USA. Thousands of loggerheads are killed annually when accidentally entangled in fishing nets, and since they develop and mature slowly, populations are slow to recover. More damaging however, is the effect of human disturbance at nesting beaches.

**Distribution**: Tropical to warm-temperate waters of oceans worldwide and adjoining seas.
**Habitat**: Surface waters, from coasts to open oceans.
**Food**: Marine invertebrates.
**Size**: 1.2m (4ft).
**Weight**: 680kg (1,500lb).
**Maturity**: Not known.
**Breeding**: Females breed every 2–3 years, and may produce several clutches of eggs, up to 100 at a time, in a single breeding season.
**Life span**: 30–50 years.

# Green turtle

*Larus minutus*

The green turtle is one of the great travellers of the animal kingdom. Unlike most other turtles the adults feed primarily on sea grass, which only grows in shallow coastal waters in certain parts of the world. As a consequence they are tied to these places for feeding, but when the time comes to breed they set off on journeys to the beaches where they themselves hatched. In some cases these may be thousands of kilometres away. Female green turtles only breed once every two to five years, but during a single season can dig as many as nine separate nests. This makes them the most prolific reptiles on the planet – some females can lay well in excess of 1,000 eggs before finally making the return journey to their feeding grounds. The reason green turtles lay so many eggs is simple: hardly any of their offspring survive long enough to breed themselves. Once they have hatched they run the gauntlet of gulls and other predators on the beach. They then enter the sea, where many more predators lurk. The green turtles that occasionally enter British waters are juveniles, too young to breed themselves. Unlike their parents, they are wanderers feeding mainly on jellyfish, which are abundant off British shores, washed along with the Gulf Stream.

**Distribution**: Adults live in tropical and subtropical seas worldwide. Juveniles enter temperate waters and occasionally occur off Britain.
**Habitat**: Adults are normally restricted to coastal waters: juveniles are often found far out to sea.
**Food**: Adults feed on sea grasses and algae; juveniles also eat jellyfish and other marine invertebrates.
**Size**: Up to 1.5m (5ft).
**Weight**: Up to 136kg (300lb).
**Maturity**: 8–13 years.
**Breeding**: Mating occurs just offshore from nesting beaches. Females leave water at night and lay 100–150 eggs. These hatch 45–70 days later.
**Life span**: Unknown, but thought to be at least 50 years.

**Identification**: This huge reptile would be almost impossible to confuse with anything other than another sea turtle. The back is covered with a hard, greenish-brown shell and the four limbs are large flippers, each with obvious, dark scales, clearly separated from one another. The head has a sharp-edged beak and is relatively small. The male has a long tail, which extends far out beyond the rear edge of the carapace.

# OCEANIC MAMMALS

*The cetacean family Delphinidae includes several species that are equally at home in coastal waters or far out to sea. Most are highly social and athletic, and they have a natural curiosity that means they often approach boats, providing a welcome spectacle to break the tedium of long sea voyages.*

## Risso's dolphin

*Grampus griseus*

**Distribution**: Patchy distribution in tropical, subtropical and temperate waters in oceans worldwide and many adjoining seas.
**Habitat**: Open oceans, typically above steeply sloping continental slope.
**Food**: Mainly squid and other cephalopods.
**Size**: 4m (13ft).
**Weight**: 300–400g (660–882lb).
**Maturity**: 5–12 years.
**Breeding**: Virtually unknown
**Life span**: Up to 20 years.

Risso's dolphins are gregarious, typically living in groups of 20 or so individuals. They are often seen from ships and appear curious and playful – apt to leap and breach in a very acrobatic manner. Sightings around Britain are usually around the Hebrides, the Isle of Man, and along the Cornish coast. At times, whole schools seem to disappear completely – presumably migrating in search of food, but the details of these movements and many other aspects of behaviour remain a mystery. Mass strandings occasionally happen. The scars that make the species distinctive are thought to be the result of tussles with other dolphins and with large squid. In older individuals, the scarring may be so dense that the body appears to be almost white.

**Identification**: Blunt head with a square profile and no beak. Body is stout and robust, with long, falcate pectoral fins, a tall falcate dorsal fin and a slender tail. Skin is a variable shade of grey to brown dorsally, pale on the belly. Adults often bear distinctive white scarring to face and body.

## Common bottlenose dolphin

*Tursiops truncatus*

The bottlenose dolphin is known from a wide variety of marine habitats. There are distinct coastal and offshore forms. Popular with people because of their playful nature and apparent 'smile', bottlenoses are also considered to be among the most intelligent of mammals. Groups may number up to several hundred animals. They have been sighted in the Cardigan Bay area of Wales, the Moray Firth in Scotland, and very occasionally off the coast of Cornwall. Aggression is relatively common, especially towards other similar-sized cetaceans. Bottlenoses act co-operatively when hunting or in defence, and they communicate using a highly refined repertoire of body postures and sounds. Prey is detected by echolocation using pulses of sound focused through the melon.

**Identification**: Long, slender body with tall falcate dorsal fin and short falcate pectorals. Head has pronounced melon and short cylindrical beak. Mouth is slightly curved in what appears to be an appealing smile. Skin is fairly uniformly grey, slightly darker on the dorsal surface.

**Distribution**: Tropical and temperate oceans and adjoining seas worldwide, except High Arctic.
**Habitat**: Open and coastal waters.
**Food**: Pelagic and bottom-dwelling fish and invertebrates.
**Size**: 4m (13ft).
**Weight**: 150–200kg (330–440lb).
**Maturity**: 5–10 years.
**Breeding**: Single calves born at intervals of 3 years or more; young are weaned at 18–20 months, but may remain with their mothers for several more years.
**Life span**: Up to 25 years.

# White-beaked dolphin

*Lagenorhynchus albirostris*

Dolphins are notoriously difficult animals to study because they are small and also very wide-ranging. Consequently, not much is known about their habits compared to those of most land-living mammals.

White-beaked dolphins make annual migrations, moving between temperate and subpolar waters, tracking their prey, such as mackerel and herring. They are found only in the shallower waters of the northern North Atlantic and, until the late 1990s, the west coast of Scotland had some of the highest numbers of this species in Europe. However, white-beaked dolphins have almost completely disappeared from the west coast of Scotland in the last few years. Once one of the most commonly seen dolphin species they are now rarely sighted in these waters, and have been replaced with the common dolphin, a species found in warmer waters. The increase in water temperatures around the UK of up to 0.4°C per decade since 1981 is thought to be the cause.

**Distribution**: Ranges widely through the North Atlantic and Arctic Oceans.
**Habitat**: Coastal waters.
**Food**: Medium-sized fish, squid and crustaceans form the bulk of the diet.
**Size**: 2.3–2.8m (7.5–9.25ft).
**Weight**: 180kg (396lb).
**Maturity**: Not known.
**Breeding**: 1 calf born every year.
**Life span**: Not known.

**Identification**: The white-beaked dolphin's counter-shaded coloration helps camouflage it from both above and below. It has a short, thick creamy-white beak and very curved dorsal fin.

**Pantropical spotted dolphin** (*Stenella attenuata*) 2.5m (8¼ft). The pantropical spotted dolphin is probably the most abundant dolphin species, with a population numbering several million worldwide in most tropical and temperate oceans. It is highly gregarious and athletic, and huge schools have been seen performing spectacular displays of leaping, and riding the bow waves of boats.

**Striped dolphin** (*Stenella coeruleoalba*) 2.5m (8¼ft). This is a familiar species of dolphin, common in tropical and temperate waters worldwide. It is a highly gregarious species and individuals are usually to be found in large schools of several dozen animals up to several hundred. They prey on small, schooling fish. It has a white or pink belly and dark blue stripes from the eye to the flipper.

# Common dolphin

*Delphinus delphis*

This dolphin is also called the short-beaked saddleback dolphin. It is especially common in European waters and is typically found in most parts of the North Sea and off the west coast of England, Wales and Scotland. The species also swims in the coastal areas of the Atlantic and Pacific Oceans, including along the coasts of the Americas.

Common dolphins are so-called coastal dolphins because they prefer to swim in warmer water near the surface. However, they are still found far out to sea though seldom dive into deep and colder water. They have many small, curved teeth, which are used for snatching small, slippery fish, such as herrings, from the water.

These mammals are one of the smallest dolphins. There are reports that many schools sometimes group together, forming clans of up to 100,000 individuals. Most of the time they travel at 8kph (5mph) but can hit speeds of 46kph (29mph) in short bursts.

**Distribution**: Mediterranean Sea, Atlantic and Pacific Oceans.
**Habitat**: Ocean waters.
**Food**: Fish, squid and octopus.
**Size**: 1.5–2.4m (5–8ft).
**Weight**: 100–136kg (220–300lb).
**Maturity**: 12–15 years.
**Breeding**: Single young born every 2–3 years.
**Life span**: 35 years.

**Identification**: The common dolphin is one of the smallest dolphin species. They have a distinctive hourglass pattern of pale skin that connects the dark upper skin to the pale lower surface.

## Harbour porpoise

*Phocoena phocoena*

Harbour porpoises are relatively common in British and wider European waters and along the coast of North Africa, where they occupy shallow coastal waters. They are also able to withstand fresh water and often travel in the mouths of large rivers. They are shy, elusive sea mammals. Their numbers are declining primarily because they are frequently caught by accident in commercial fishing nets, as many of the porpoise's prey are also commercially important species.

These porpoises, also known as common porpoises, are social, highly vocal cetaceans. They live in small groups of up to 15 members. They swim more slowly than dolphins and rarely jump out of the water. Instead they rise to the surface to breathe. Harbour porpoises catch fish, such as herrings, sardines and pollack. They also eat squid and shrimp. Like other cetaceans, they use high-pitched clicking sounds to echolocate their prey.

**Distribution**: Mediterranean Sea, Black Sea, North Atlantic and North Pacific.
**Habitat**: Shallow seas and coastal waters. Sometimes venture into estuaries.
**Food**: Fish and squid.
**Size**: 1.3–1.9m (4¼–6¼ft).
**Weight**: 35–90kg (77–198lb).
**Maturity**: 5 years.
**Breeding**: Gives birth mainly in summer.
**Life span**: 20 years.

**Identification:** Unlike their dolphin relatives, porpoises have blunt snouts without a beak. They also have fewer teeth, which tend to be less pointed and have a chisel-like biting edge. These teeth are suited for holding on to large struggling fish.

## Orca

*Orcinus orca*

**Distribution**: Throughout the world's oceans.
**Habitat**: Most common in coastal waters.
**Food**: Seals, other dolphins, fish, squid, penguins and crustaceans.
**Size**: 8.5–10m (28–33ft).
**Weight**: 5.5–9 tonnes (12,000–20,000lb).
**Maturity**: Females 6 years; males 12 years.
**Breeding**: Single young born generally in autumn every 3–4 years.
**Life span**: 60–90 years.

Orcas are also known as killer 'whales', but are actually one of the largest members of the dolphin family. They are commonly found in colder waters and can often be seen in the waters of west Scotland and the Shetland Islands. Orcas are expert hunters, being armed with up to 50 large, pointed teeth, and they catch prey in all areas of the ocean. Although orcas have been detected 1km (0.6 miles) below the surface, they prefer to hunt in shallow waters and often swim into bays and mouths of rivers to snatch food near the shore.

Orcas typically live in pods of five or six individuals. Generally each pod is run by a large male. Females and their young may split off into subgroups. Like other toothed whales and dolphins, orcas produce clicking sounds that are used for echolocation. The whales also communicate with each other using high-pitched screams and whistles. Orcas have several hunting techniques. They break pack ice from beneath, knocking their prey into the water, or they may rush into shallow water to grab prey from the shore or drive prey into the surf, where other members of the pod pick them off.

Orcas breed throughout the year, although most mate in the early summer and give birth in the autumn of the following year. Each pod has a single male, which mates with all the females.

**Identification:** Orcas have black upper bodies and white undersides. They also have grey patches behind their dorsal fins, and white patches along their sides and above the eyes.

# Sperm whale

*Physeter catodon*

The sperm whale is supremely well adapted to life in the deep oceans and can be found around the world; in Britain sightings are most common in Scottish waters. These are the largest hunting predators in the world, with teeth up to 20cm (8in) long and the largest brain of any animal, weighing over 9kg (20lb). They prefer areas of ocean with cold upwellings at least 1km (3,300ft) deep where squid are most abundant. Sperm whales can dive to incredible depths to hunt, occasionally up to 2.5km (1.5 miles). They are social animals and live in groups of 20–40 females, juveniles and young. Sperm whales have been hunted for their oil since the mid-18th century, and, after serious population declines between the 1950s and 1980s, this species is now protected. In the north, sperm whales mate between January and August. In the south, they mate between July and March.

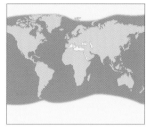

**Distribution**: Ranges throughout oceans and seas worldwide.
**Habitat**: Deep oceans.
**Food**: Mostly squid, including giant deep-sea squid, but also several species of fish and shark.
**Size**: 12–20m (40–66ft);
**Weight**: 12–50 tonnes (26,500–110,000lb).
**Maturity**: Females 7–13 years; males 25 years.
**Breeding**: 1 calf born every 5–7 years.
**Life span**: 77 years.

**Identification:** The sperm whale's distinctive shape comes from its large head, which is typically one-third of the animal's length. The blowhole is located to the front left of the head. This gives rise to a distinctive bushy, forward-angled spray.

# Humpback whale

*Megaptera novaeangliae*

**Identification:** Humpback whales are so called because of their dorsal fins, which may be swelled into humps by deposits of fat. The head and lower jaw are covered in knobbly parts called tubercles, which help streamline the animal by modifiying water flow over its body. Humpbacks have the longest pectoral (arm) fins of any whale – about a third as long as their bodies. These baleen whales have throat grooves, which expand to enlarge the throat size as the feeding whale gulps water. The whale is acrobatic and has often been observed leaping and slapping the water with its fins.

Humpbacks spend their summers feeding far from shore, in the cold waters of the Atlantic, from Iceland and Norway south to south-west Ireland. They feed by taking in huge mouthfuls of sea water, from which their baleen plates then strain out any fish or krill. Pairs of humpbacks also corral fish by blowing curtains of bubbles around them. The fish will not swim through the bubbles and they crowd together as the whales rush up from beneath with their mouths wide open.

In winter, the whales stop feeding and head to warmer, shallow waters near coasts to concentrate on reproduction. During the mating season males sing for days on end to attract receptive females that are not caring for calves that year, and also to help rival males keep away from each other. Pregnant females stay feeding for longer than the other whales, and arrive in the wintering grounds just in time to give birth.

**Distribution**: All oceans.
**Habitat**: Deep ocean water. They come closer to land to mate and calf.
**Food**: Small fish, shrimps and krill.
**Size**: 12–15m (40–50ft);
**Weight**: 30 tonnes (66,000lb).
**Maturity**: 4–5 years.
**Breeding**: Single young born every 2–3 years. Mating takes place in winter. Gestation is 11 months.
**Life span**: 70 years.

# Bowhead whale

*Balaena mysticetus*

**Identification**: There is a ridge on top of the head, in front of the blowholes. The bony head is used to crash through the ice for air in its Arctic home. Dorsal fin is absent, pectorals are broad and triangular and tail flukes form a notched triangle. Males vocalize a haunting and highly varied song in the spring, in order to attract females.

This giant of Arctic waters, which occasionally visits British waters, is a large, deep-bodied whale with a massive head, and enormous, highly arched jaws. It spends its life close to the edge of the sea ice. It can travel considerable distances under ice and, if necessary, can ram air holes in ice almost 2m (6½ft) thick. There is some evidence that this species uses echolocation to help them navigate around ice floes and bergs. Bowheads feed on krill and floating crustaceans.

The huge head and bowed jaw support hundreds of strips, or plates, of a horny material known as baleen. These plates act as strainers, filtering planktonic life from the water as the whale swims. The discovery of 19th-century harpoon tips in individuals alive at the end of the 20th century suggests the species is long-lived, but numbers are small now as a result of hunting.

**Distribution**: Circumpolar waters of the North Atlantic, North Pacific and Arctic Oceans.
**Habitat**: Deep water, close to pack ice.
**Food**: Mainly krill and copepods, as well as other planktonic invertebrates.
**Size**: Up to 20m (66ft).
**Weight**: 50–60 tonnes (110,000–132,000lb).
**Maturity**: 20 years.
**Breeding**: Single calf born every 3–4 years; weaned from about 12 months, may stay with mother several more years.
**Life span**: Unknown, but it is possible up to 100 years.

# Blainville's beaked whale

*Mesoplodon densirostris*

This medium-sized toothed whale occupies a very large distributional range, and is an occasional vagrant in UK waters, but reliable sightings are relatively infrequent outside of the tropical and warm-temperature waters it prefers. Dives are prolonged, up to 20 minutes or more, and probably take the animal into deep water in search of its prey – squid. On surfacing, Blainville's beaked whale breaks the surface beak first, takes a breath, then rolls forward with very little splashing, and is therefore difficult to spot. The bones of this species are among the densest of any mammal and the teeth are bizarre – they erupt from the side of a strangely stepped jaw, and are usually encrusted with tufts of barnacles.

**Identification**: Spindle-shaped body with small falcate dorsal fin and short pectorals. Head has a long, narrow beak and a strongly arched lower jaw with a large emergent tooth on each side. The skin is dark above and paler on the belly, and usually covered with pale scratches and circular scars, the result of attacks by cookiecutter sharks, squid and other whales.

**Distribution**: Patchy distribution in tropical and warm temperate waters of oceans worldwide and some adjoining seas.
**Habitat**: Open waters, particularly those above continental slopes.
**Food**: Squid and small pelagic fish; possibly also bottom-dwelling crustaceans.
**Size**: 4–5m (13–16½ft) and perhaps longer.
**Weight**: 1,090kg (2,400lbs).
**Maturity**: 9 years.
**Breeding**: Not known.
**Life span**: Not known.

# Minke whale

*Balaenoptera acutorostrata*

Distinguished by its pointed snout, the minke is the smallest and most common of the great whales. This whale is apparently migratory, but movements are difficult to follow. It is widely distributed in relatively small numbers along the Atlantic seaboard of Europe mainly from Norway south to France, and in the northern North Sea of Britain. Minkes are found in all oceans, though they are rarely observed in the tropics. They seem to prefer icy waters, and have actually become entrapped in the ice fields on occasion. It seems that pregnant females travel to the tropics in winter to give birth, and the young are independent in time for the return journey. The gestation period is 10 months. Sexual maturity arrives at 6–8 years of age. Minkes tend to be solitary, though sometimes they are seen travelling in pairs or in small groups. They appear to segregate by age and sex more than do other baleen whales. Females remain close to shore, while males are farther out to sea. Minkes are still hunted by Iceland, Norway and Japan in defiance of a whaling ban.

**Identification**: Streamlined with a pointed snout and a ridge along the midline. There are 500–700 short pale plates of baleen and 50–70 pleated furrows on the throat. The skin is black dorsally with a grey chevron on its back; white on the throat and belly, with a white patch on the pectoral fins. The whales do not tend to perform acrobatics for whale watchers, and dive for up to 20 minutes at a time.

**Distribution**: Polar waters of North Atlantic and North Pacific Oceans (dwarf subspecies occurs in Southern Hemisphere).
**Habitat**: Open ocean, often over continental shelves and sometimes coastal waters.
**Food**: Mainly small fish, such as herring, sandlance and capelin, as well as some swarming planktonic crustaceans.
**Size**: 10.5m (34½ft).
**Weight**: 10 tonnes (22,046llb).
**Maturity**: 6–8 years.
**Breeding**: Single calf born every 1 or 2 years. Gestation period of 10 months, weaned at about 6 months and independent soon after.
**Life span**: May live for up to 50 years.

# Northern bottlenose whale

*Hyperoodon ampullatus*

Among the largest-beaked whales, the northern bottlenose was previously subject to intensive hunting, but is now protected. Resident populations appear to inhabit deep water off Nova Scotia and off the Bay of Biscay, while other populations appear to be more nomadic or migratory. They are occasionally seen in coastal north European waters, sometimes as far south as Scotland, from April to September. They live in small groups of fewer than 10 individuals, usually about four. Feeding dives are typically quite short, around 10 minutes, but they can perform extended dives of an hour or more, especially when frightened, and may reach depths of 1,500m (4,920ft). They appear to favour one species of squid (*Gonatus fabricii*) above all other food, but they may also opportunistically take fish and other invertebrates. Despite a history of being hunted, they remain curious animals and will sometimes approach boats.

**Distribution**: North Atlantic Ocean and into Arctic Ocean.
**Habitat**: Deep water, often close to pack ice. Dives to depths of 1,500m (4,920ft).
**Food**: Mostly deep-water squid.
**Size**: 10m (33ft).
**Weight**: 5–7.5 tonnes (11,000–16,535lb).
**Maturity**: 7–11 years.
**Breeding**: Calves born singly in spring after a gestation lasting at least 12 months.
**Life span**: 35–40 years.

**Identification**: Cylindrical body with small pectoral fins and a dorsal fin set two-thirds of the way back. Has a prominent, rounded melon and pronounced beak. Skin is dark grey. The melon and beak are white (grey in females).

# Blue whale

*Balaenoptera musculus*

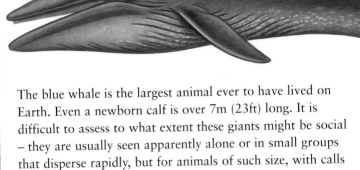

**Distribution**: All oceans, with three major populations in North Pacific, North Atlantic and Southern Hemisphere.
**Habitat**: Open ocean, may also visit coastal waters.
**Food**: Krill.
**Size**: 33m (108ft).
**Weight**: 118 tonnes (260,145lb).
**Maturity**: 10 years.
**Breeding**: Single calf born every 2–3 years after a gestation period of 11 months; development is rapid, young are weaned and independent within 8 months.
**Life span**: Up to 70 years.

The blue whale is the largest animal ever to have lived on Earth. Even a newborn calf is over 7m (23ft) long. It is difficult to assess to what extent these giants might be social – they are usually seen apparently alone or in small groups that disperse rapidly, but for animals of such size, with calls that carry vast distances, several whales spread out over many kilometres might still constitute a cohesive group.

Blue whales may be found in all oceans of the world but are rare visitors to British waters. They migrate to tropical-to-temperate waters during winter months to mate and give birth to calves. They can feed throughout their range, in polar, temperate, or even tropical waters. There appears to be a southerly migration in the austral summer.

The species suffered severely from commercial whaling until the mid-20th century, and doubts remain over its ability to recover.

**Identification**: The largest of the baleen whales. Head broad and flattened. Mouth contains up to 800 baleen plates. Throat folds into about 60 pleated furrows. Dorsal fin is tiny and set well back; pectorals are long and tapering; tail flukes are large and triangular. The skin is mottled grey, appearing blue in water. The underside is often coated in a sulphur-yellow growth of diatoms (single-celled algae).

# Bearded seal

*Erignathus Barbatus*

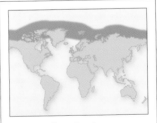

**Distribution**: Arctic coastlines and ice floes, a few individuals travel as far south as Scotland.
**Habitat**: Shallow water covered in thin ice.
**Food**: Shrimps, crabs, clams and fish.
**Size**: 2.4m (8ft)
**Weight**: 340kg (750lb)
**Maturity**: 3–8 years.
**Breeding**: Breeding season takes place in summer on beaches and ice floes.
**Life span**: 25 years.

Bearded seals are solitary animals. They live in the shallow water of the Arctic Ocean but do come on to gravel beaches on islands and the northern coastlines of Eurasia and North America at times, and have even been seen on the coast of Scotland. However, bearded seals prefer areas covered in broken ice. They haul themselves on to the floes to rest and dive between the broken ice to feed; they also ram their heads through thin ice to create breathing holes. Bearded seals find much of their food on the sea bed. Their whiskers detect the tiny water currents produced by the movements of their prey, which include crustaceans such as shrimp and crabs, shellfish such as abalone and clams, and fish. The seals come together in large numbers only during the breeding season, when males sing a warbling song underwater to attract females to their floes.

**Identification**: Bearded seals are named after the long white whiskers that grow on the snout. They have a grey or brown coat that is darker on their back than their underside. Adults are generally the same size, though females may be slightly longer. The large body mass makes their round head and flippers look even smaller in comparison, and their large, wide muzzle contrasts with their small close-set eyes. At the end of each flipper are equal length digits, which gives them a square appearance.

**Hooded Seal** (*Cystophora cristata*) Up to 2.5m (8¼ft), 435kg (960lb). The male has a 'hood' of skin on its head, which is inflated during courtship. Normally, however, this species has short fur, which, in both sexes, is light grey and covered with dark blotches.

**Ringed Seal** (*Pusa hispida*) Up to 1.6m (5¼ft), 140kg (310lb). A small seal, it has a rounded body with silvery to dark grey fur covered with small, pale, ring-like markings.

# Common seal

*Phoca vitulina*

One of the two seal species found commonly in British waters, the common seal has a dog-like face. Its snout is much more rounded than the Roman-style nose which typifies the grey seal, Britain's other common seal. It is difficult to get a good estimate of the common seal's population size because it lives in small, widely distributed groups, and is highly mobile.

Common seals have large, sensitive eyes with specialized retinas, which allow them to see well underwater. However, sometimes the water is too murky for seals to be able to hunt by sight. At these times common seals switch to another sense – touch. Their long whiskers are highly sensitive and allow the seals to feel for prey.

**Distribution**: North Atlantic, Pacific and Arctic coastlines.
**Habitat**: Sheltered coastal waters.
**Food**: Fish, cephalopods and crustaceans.
**Size**: 1.5–2m (5–6½ft).
**Weight**: 45–130kg (99–285lb).
**Maturity**: Females 2 years; males 5 years.
**Breeding**: Single pup produced every year.
**Life span**: 26–32 years.

**Identification**: Common seals vary in colour from black, brown, grey or tan, with darker patches. The pattern is unique to the individual. They have a relatively large head and short flippers.

# Grey seal

*Halichoerus grypus*

The grey seal is found on both sides of the north Atlantic in temperate and sub-arctic waters. Three distinct populations occur; the western Atlantic population, the north-eastern or Baltic population which is endangered, and the eastern Atlantic population, which is centred around British coasts, particularly around Scotland.

Male grey seals are larger than the females. Despite the size difference, males reach their full adult size at 11 years old, which is 4 years earlier than the females.

Grey seals eat a range of fish and also a small amount of aquatic molluscs, such as squid, and crabs and other crustaceans. Grey seals hunt in open water but often return to the shore to rest. Breeding takes place on the coastline. Colonies form in early winter on beaches, rocky shores and in caves. Before breeding, the adults eat a great deal because they will fast while on shore. Females give birth on the beach to the pups conceived the year before, while the males fight for control of the mates. Mating takes place after the calves are weaned.

**Identification**: Both sexes of grey seal are grey, but the males are darker than the females. Females have dark spots on their paler skin, while males have pale spots on their darker bodies.

**Distribution**: Coastlines and islands of northern and western Europe and eastern Canada.
**Habitat**: Rocky coasts.
**Food**: Fish.
**Size**: 1.8–2.2m (6–7¼ft).
**Weight**: 150–220kg (330–485lb).
**Maturity**: 3–6 years.
**Breeding**: Breeding season in winter. The males return to sea after mating. Calves are suckled by their mothers for 17 days. The mothers then leave calves on the beach. The calves follow after a few days.
**Life span**: 25 years.

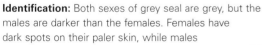

# UNDERSTANDING BIRDS

Birds are winged, bipedal, endothermic (warm-blooded), vertebrate animals that lay eggs. There are around 10,000 living species, making them the most numerous tetrapod vertebrates. The most obvious thing that distinguishes all birds, from the tiny goldcrest (*Regulus regulus*), which is Britain's smallest bird, to the hefty mute swan (*Cygnus olor*), is the presence of feathers on their bodies. The need for birds' bodies to be lightweight so that they can fly has led to evolutionary changes in their anatomy, and yet the basic skeletal structure of all birds is remarkably similar, irrespective of size.

Birdwatching in the British Isles can develop into an absorbing pastime. The pages that follow offer practical tips on observing birds successfully, and present detailed colour illustrations and in-depth profiles of distribution, habitat, food, size, nests and eggs, to help you identify a vast range of species.

*Above: The skylark is renowned for its song flight. The male bird rises vertically from the ground high into the air, where it remains stationary, on fluttering wings, singing its liquid song.*

*Left: Black-headed gulls (*Larus ridibundus*). These noisy and conspicuous birds have highly adaptable and sociable natures, and may be seen in large groups. They have extended their range inland from coastal areas in recent years, thanks to a wider availability of food near to human habitations.*

# EVOLUTION

*Vertebrates – first flying reptiles called pterosaurs, and later birds – took to the air about 190 million years ago. Adapting to an aerial existence marked a very significant step in vertebrate development, because of the need for a new method of locomotion, and a radically different body design.*

## The age of *Archaeopteryx*

Back in 1861, workers in a limestone quarry in Bavaria, southern Germany, unearthed a strange fossil that resembled a bird in appearance and was about the size of a modern crow, but also had teeth. The idea that the fossil was a bird was confirmed by the clear evidence of feathers impressed into the stone, as the presence of plumage is one of the characteristic distinguishing features of all birds. The 1860s were a time when the debate surrounding evolution was becoming fierce, and the discovery created huge interest, partly because it suggested that birds may have evolved from dinosaurs. It confirmed that birds had lived on Earth for at least 145 million years, existing even before the age of the dinosaurs came to a close in the Cretaceous period, about 65 million years ago. As the oldest-known bird, it was given the name *Archaeopteryx*, meaning 'ancient wings'.

## Pterosaurs

A study of the anatomy of *Archaeopteryx*'s wings revealed that these early birds did not just glide but were capable of using their wings for active flight. Yet they were not the first vertebrate creatures to have taken to the skies. Pterosaurs had already successfully developed approximately 190 million years ago, during the Jurassic period, and even co-existed with birds for a time. In fact, the remains of one of the later pterosaurs, called *Rhamphorhynchus*, have been found in the same limestone deposits in southern Germany where *Archaeopteryx* was discovered. The pterosaur's wings more closely resembled those of a bat than a bird, consisting simply of a membrane supported by a bony framework, rather than feathers overlying the skin.

Some types of pterosaurs developed huge wingspans, in excess of 7m (23ft), which enabled them to glide almost effortlessly over the surface of the world's oceans, much like albatrosses do today. It appears that they fed primarily on fish and other marine life, scooping their food out of the water in flight. Changes in climate probably doomed the pterosaurs, however, since increasingly turbulent weather patterns meant that gliding became difficult, and they could no longer fly with ease.

### Avian giants

In the period immediately after the extinction of the dinosaurs, some groups of birds increased rapidly in physical size, and in so doing, lost the ability to fly. Since their increased size meant that they could cover large distances on foot, and as they faced no predators, because large hunting mammals had not yet evolved, these large birds were relatively safe. In New Zealand, home of the large flightless moas, such giants thrived until the start of human settlement about a millennium ago. The exact date of the final extinction of the moas is not recorded, but the group had probably died out entirely by the middle of the 19th century.

*Below: The largest species of moa would have dwarfed a man.*

*Right: An impression of how* Archaeopteryx *may have looked. It is impossible to be sure of its coloration from its fossilized remains.*

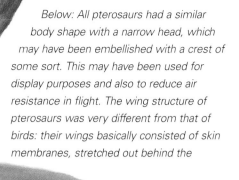

*Below: All pterosaurs had a similar body shape with a narrow head, which may have been embellished with a crest of some sort. This may have been used for display purposes and also to reduce air resistance in flight. The wing structure of pterosaurs was very different from that of birds: their wings basically consisted of skin membranes, stretched out behind the*

*forearms. It was this large surface area that allowed them to glide with little effort, but becoming airborne in the first place required great effort. The lack of body covering over the skin also had the effect of causing greater heat loss from the body. In birds, the feathers provide insulation as well as assisting active flight.*

*Below: Chicks of the South American hoatzin (Opisthocomus hoazin) are unique in possessing claws on their wing tips, which disappear by the time they are old enough to fly.*

## The spread of birds

After the age of *Archaeopteryx*, it is thought that birds continued to radiate out over the globe and became increasingly specialized. Unfortunately, there is very little fossil evidence to help us understand their early history. This lack of fossils is partly due to the fact that the small carcasses of birds would have been eaten whole by scavengers, and partly because their lightweight, fragile skeletons would not have fossilized easily. In addition, most birds would not have been trapped and died under conditions that were favourable for fossilization.

By the end of the age of the dinosaurs, birds had become far more numerous. Many seabirds still possessed teeth in their jaws, reflecting their reptilian origins. These probably assisted them in catching fish and other aquatic creatures. It was at this

stage that the ancestors of contemporary bird groups such as waterfowl and gulls started to emerge. Most of the forerunners of today's birds had evolved by the Oligocene epoch, some 38 million years ago.

Some groups of birds that existed in these times have since disappeared, notably the phororhacids, which ranged widely over South America and even into parts of the southern United States. These birds were fearsome predators, capable of growing to nearly 3m (10ft) in height. They were equipped with deadly beaks and talons, and probably hunted together in groups.

## Recent finds

During the mid-1990s, the discovery of avian fossils in China that were apparently contemporary with those of *Archaeopteryx* aroused considerable interest. Like its German relative, *Confuciusornis* possessed claws on the tips of its wings, which probably helped these early birds to move around. Similar claws are seen today in hoatzin chicks. *Confuciusornis* resembled modern birds more closely than *Archaeopteryx* in one significant respect: it lacked teeth in its jaws. Further study of the recent fossil finds from this part of the world is required, however, as some may not be genuine.

# CLASSIFICATION

*The presence of feathers is one of the main distinguishing characteristics that set birds apart from other groups of creatures on the planet. The number of feathers on a bird's body varies considerably – a swan may have as many as 25,000 feathers, for instance, while a wren has just 11,000 in all.*

Birds (class, Aves) are winged, bipedal, endothermic (warm-blooded), vertebrate animals that lay eggs. There are around 10,000 living species, making them the most numerous tetrapod vertebrates. They inhabit ecosystems across the globe, from the Arctic to the Antarctic. Bird size ranges from the 5cm (2in) bee hummingbird to the 3m (10ft) ostrich. Modern birds are characterized by feathers, a beak with no teeth, the laying of hard-shelled

*Above: Feathering is highly significant for display purposes in some birds, particularly members of the Phasanidae family.*

*Above: A bird's flight feathers are longer and more rigid than the contour feathers that cover the body, or the fluffy down feathers that lie next to the skin. The longest, or primary, flight feathers, which generate most thrust, are located along the outer rear edges of the wings. The tail feathers are often similar in shape to the flight feathers, with the longest being found in the centre. Splaying the tail feathers increases drag and so slows the bird down.*

eggs, a high metabolic rate, a four-chambered heart, and a lightweight but strong skeleton. All birds have forelimbs modified as wings, and most can fly, with some exceptions including ratites, penguins, and a number of diverse native island species. The presence of feathers is their most important distinguishing feature.

## Feathers

Aside from the bill, legs and feet, the entire body of the bird is covered in feathers. The plumage does not grow randomly over the bird's body, but develops along lines of so-called feather tracts, or pterylae. These are separated by bald areas that are known as apteria. The apteria are not conspicuous under normal circumstances, because the contour feathers overlap to cover the entire surface of the body. Plumage may also sometimes extend down over the legs and feet as well, in the case of birds from cold climates, providing extra insulation here.

Feathers are made of a tough protein called keratin, which is also found in our hair and nails. Birds have three main types of feathers: the body,

| | | | |
|---|---|---|---|
| 1 Primaries | 5 Lateral tail feathers | 9 Auricular region | 12 Greater under-wing |
| 2 Secondaries | 6 Central tail feathers | (ear) | coverts |
| 3 Axillaries | 7 Breast | 10 Nape | 13 Lesser under- |
| 4 Rump | 8 Cere | 11 Back | wing coverts |

*Above: The snipe is very hard for predators to spot, due to its camouflaging plumage.*

or contour, feathers; the strong, elongated flight feathers on the wings, and the warm, wispy down feathers next to their skin.

## Plumage

A bird's plumage has a number of functions, not just relating to flight. It provides a barrier that retains warm air close to the bird's body and helps to maintain body temperature, which is higher in birds than mammals – typically between 41 and 43.5°C (106 and 110°F). The down feathering that lies close to the skin, and the overlying contour plumage, are vital for maintaining body warmth. Most birds have a small volume relative to their surface area, which can leave them vulnerable to hypothermia.

A special oil produced by the preen gland, located at the base of the tail, waterproofs the plumage. This oil, which is spread over the feathers as the bird preens itself, prevents water penetrating the feathers, which would cause the bird to become so waterlogged that it could no longer fly. The contour feathers that cover the body are also used for camouflage in many birds. Barring, in particular, breaks up the outline of the bird's body, helping to conceal it in its natural habitat.

The plumage has become modified in some cases, reflecting the individual lifestyle of the species concerned. Woodpeckers, for example, have tail

feathers that are short and rather sharp at their tips, providing additional support for gripping on to the sides of trees. Male ruffs, on the other hand, have elaborate head feathers that they use to impress potential mates.

## Plumage

A bird's plumage can also be important in social interaction. Many species have differences in their feathering that separate males from females, and often juveniles can also be distinguished by their plumage. Cock birds are usually more brightly coloured, which helps them to attract their mates, but this does not apply in every case. The difference between the sexes in terms of their plumage can be quite marked. Cock birds of a number of species have feathers forming crests as well as magnificent tail plumes, which are seen to greatest effect in the galliformes, a species which includes the pheasants and peafowl.

Recent studies have confirmed that the birds that appear relatively dull in colour to our eyes, such as the various species of gull, are seen literally in a different light by other birds. They are able to visually perceive the ultraviolet component of light, which is normally invisible to us, making these seemingly dull birds appear much brighter. Ultraviolet coloration may also be significant in helping birds to choose their mates.

## Moulting

Birds' feathering is maintained by preening, but it becomes frayed and worn over time. It is therefore replaced by new plumage during the process of

moulting, when the old feathers are shed. Moulting is often an annual event, but many young birds shed their nest feathers before they are a year old.

---

### Iridescence

Some birds, such as the starling (below) are not brightly coloured, but their plumage literally sparkles in the light, thanks to its structure, which creates an iridescent effect. One of the particular features of iridescence is that the colour of the plumage alters, depending on the angle at which it is viewed. This phenomenon is particularly common in some groups of birds, notably members of the starling family (Sturnidae), hummingbirds (Trochilidae) and sunbirds (Nectarinidae), which are described as having metallic feathers as a result.

In some cases, the iridescent feathering is localized, while in others, it is widespread over most of the body. Green and blue iridescence is common, with reddish sheens being seen less often. Iridescence is especially common in cock birds, helping them to attract mates. In some cases, therefore, it is seen only in the breeding plumage, notably on the upperparts of the body and the wings rather than the underparts.

---

*Right: The feather shaft holds the feather in place in the skin. The barbs run off the shaft at regular intervals, rather like the branches of a tree, and divide into smaller branches called barbules. These have tiny hooks attached to them that reinforce the structure of the flight feather, making it more rigid.*

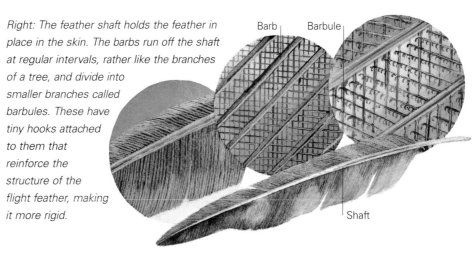

Barb    Barbule

Shaft

# ANATOMY

*The bird's skeleton has evolved to be light yet robust, both characteristics that help with flight. To this end, certain bones, particularly in the skull, have become fused, while others are absent, along with the teeth. The result is that birds' bodies are lightweight compared to those of other vertebrates.*

In order to be able to fly, a bird needs a lightweight body so that it can become airborne with minimal difficulty. It is not just teeth that are missing from the bird's skull, but the associated heavy jaw muscles as well. These have been replaced by a light, horn-covered bill that is adapted in shape to the bird's feeding habits. Some of the limb bones, such as the humerus in the shoulder, are hollow, which also cuts down on weight. At the rear of the body, the bones in the vertebral column have become fused, which gives greater stability as well as support for the tail feathers.

## The avian skeleton

In birds, the most marked evidence of specialization can be seen in the legs. Their location is critical to enable a bird to maintain its balance. The legs are found close to the midline, set slightly back near the bird's centre of gravity. These limbs are powerful, helping to provide lift at take-off and absorb the impact of landing. Strong legs also allow most birds to hop over the ground with relative ease.

There are some differences in the skeleton between different groups of birds. For example, the atlas and axis bones at the start of the vertebral column are fused in the case of hornbills, but in no other family.

## Feet and toes

Birds' feet vary in length, and are noticeably extended in waders, which helps them to distribute their weight more evenly. The four toes may be arranged either in a typical 3:1 perching grip, with three toes gripping the front of the perch and one behind, or in a 2:2 configuration, known as zygodactyl, which gives a surer grip. The zygodactyl grip is seen in relatively few groups of birds, notably parrots and woodpeckers. Touracos have flexible toes so they can swap back and forth between these two options.

The zygodactyl arrangement of their toes helps some parrots to use their feet like hands for holding food. Birds generally have claws at the ends of their toes, which have developed into sharp talons in the case of birds of prey, helping them to catch their quarry even in flight. Many birds also use their claws for preening, and they can provide balance for birds that run or climb.

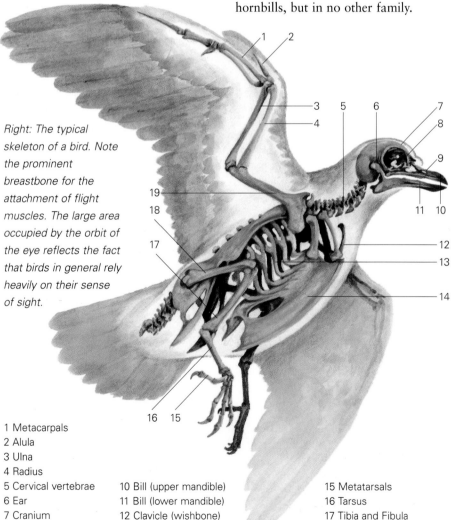

*Right: The typical skeleton of a bird. Note the prominent breastbone for the attachment of flight muscles. The large area occupied by the orbit of the eye reflects the fact that birds in general rely heavily on their sense of sight.*

**Parrot**

*Above: Parrots use their feet for holding food, rather like human hands.*

**Bird of prey**

*Above: In birds of prey, the claws have become talons for grasping prey.*

**Wader**

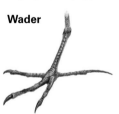

*Above: Long toes make it easier for waders to walk over muddy ground or water plants.*

**Duck**

*Above: The webbed feet of ducks provide propulsion in water.*

1 Metacarpals
2 Alula
3 Ulna
4 Radius
5 Cervical vertebrae
6 Ear
7 Cranium
8 Eye socket
9 Nostril
10 Bill (upper mandible)
11 Bill (lower mandible)
12 Clavicle (wishbone)
13 Ribs
14 Sternum (breastbone)
15 Metatarsals
16 Tarsus
17 Tibia and Fibula
18 Femur
19 Humerus

*Above: The narrow bill of waders such as this curlew (Numenius arquata) enables them to probe for food in sandy or muddy areas.*

*Above: Birds of prey such as the golden eagle (Aquila chrysaetos) rely on a sharp bill with a hooked tip to tear their prey apart.*

*Above: Herons (Ardea) have strong, pointed bills, which they use like scissors to seize and hold slippery prey such as frogs.*

*Above: Shoveler ducks (Anas clypeata) have spatulate bills that they swing from side to side to strain food from the water.*

*Above: The hawfinch (Coccothraustes coccothraustes) has a large bill for cracking seeds, further aided by a pointed tip.*

*Above: The crossbill (Loxia curvirostra) bites between the scales of a pine cone, prises it apart, and dislodges the seed.*

## Bills

The bills of birds vary quite widely in shape and size, and reflect their feeding habits. The design of the bill also has an impact on the force that it can generate. The bills of many larger parrots are especially strong, allowing them to crack hard nut shells. In addition, they can move their upper and lower bill independently, which produces a wider gape and, in turn, allows more pressure to be exerted.

## Wings

A bird's wing is built around just three digits, which correspond to human fingers. In comparison, bats have five digits supporting their fleshy membranes. The three digits of birds provide a robust structure. The power of the wings is further enhanced by the fusion of the wrist bones and the carpals to create the single bone known as the carpometacarpus, which runs along the edge of the wing.

At the front of the chest, the clavicles are joined together to form what in chickens is called the wishbone. The large, keel-shaped breastbone, or sternum, runs along the underside of the body. It is bound by the ribs to the backbone, which provides stability, especially during flight. In addition, the major flight muscles are located in the lower body when the bird is airborne.

## Bizarrely-built birds

Nature has resulted in a number of decidedly odd-looking birds, notably on the offshore islands of vast oceans where they evolved undisturbed by predators. One famous species has captured the human imagination for centuries. First recorded in 1601, the dodo (*Raphus cucullatus*) had been driven to extinction by 1690, although several living examples of this flightless pigeon were brought to Europe, and aroused great curiosity because of their ungainly appearance. Unfortunately, many of today's representations of dodos are the subject of some artistic licence, as there is not a complete surviving specimen in any museum in the world. Those on display at such institutions have been constructed with reference to contemporary accounts and artworks, and it has been noted by ornithologists that, while early European portraits capture the dodo's athleticism, later artworks increasingly depict the famous bird as fat, colourful and ungainly. This may, in part, suggest a preference for the absurd among the artists, but also that the captive dodos were fed an inappropriate diet. These portraits should not be viewed as a measure of strict anatomical accuracy.

*Below: The most striking feature of the dodo was its long, hooked bill. As a flightless bird, its wings were little more than stubs which hung on each side of its plump body. Rather uniquely, it also seems to have possessed a short tail. The legs, by contrast, were thick and strong – a valuable support for its weight, and possibly also an aid to speed and agility when running through woodland.*

# FLIGHT AND LOCOMOTION

*Some birds spend much of their lives in the air, whereas others will only fly as a last resort if threatened.
A few species are too heavy to take off at all. The mechanics of flight are similar in all birds, but flight
patterns vary significantly, which can help to identify the various groups in the air.*

In most cases, the whole structure of a bird's body has evolved to facilitate flight. It is important for a bird to be relatively light, because this lessens the muscular effort required to keep it airborne. The powerful flight muscles, which provide the necessary lift, can account for up to a third of a bird's total body weight. They are attached to the breastbone in the midline of the body, and run along the sides of the body from the clavicle along the breastbone to the top of the legs.

## Weight and flight
There is an upper weight limit of just over 18kg (40lb), above which birds would not be able to take off successfully. The heaviest British birds are the mute swan and the great bustard, both of which closely approach this weight.

## Wing shape and beat
The shape of the wing is important for a bird's flying ability. Birds that soar on rising air currents, such as the buzzard, have relatively long, wide wings. Fast fliers, such as swifts and falcons, have sickle-shaped wings with pointed tips. Those birds that fly in confined habitats, such as woodland,

*Above: Waterfowl such as this mallard (Anas platyrhynchos) find it easy to fly from water, as their plumage does not get waterlogged.*

tend to have shorter wings and a longer tail, which helps with manoeuvrability.

Generally speaking, small birds beat their wings faster than large ones. Birds in flight can often be recognized by the way that they fly. The green woodpecker, for instance, has an undulating flight pattern. It flaps a few times, lifting its body up through the air, then glides a little, dropping down as it does so, before flapping again.

## Lightening the load
Birds have hollow bones with a sort of honeycombed internal structure. However, it is not just the lightness of

a bird's skeleton that helps it to fly. Unlike mammals, birds do not have a bladder. Instead, their urine, in the concentrated form of uric acid, passes out of the body with their faeces.

## Other ways of getting around
All British birds can fly but some prefer instead to run when confronted with danger and only fly as a last resort. This is particularly true of game birds, such as the pheasant, and rails, such as the moorhen. Their short wings and dumpy bodies make flight an effort. Pheasants, in particular, rarely fly far. When they do take to the air, their wing beats are quick and appear laboured. Compared with other birds, however, they are able to run quite fast, their legs and feet being adapted for life on the ground.

Some birds take to the wing if they feel threatened but normally spend most of their time walking around. This is true of Britain's waders, long-legged birds such as plovers and their relatives. Most waders find their food on the ground or in estuary mud, and walk as they search for it. Herons and egrets also move in this way, although their main food is not invertebrates, as it is for most waders, but fish.

*Below: A typical take-off, as shown by a Harris's hawk (Parabuteo unicinctus).*

*1. When resting, a bird typically has a relatively upright stance.*

*2. As it leans forwards for take-off, it raises its wings and starts to lift its legs.*

*3. Leaving its perch, the bird pushes off into the air, and opens its wings.*

*Above: Some gulls (Laridae) spend much of their lives on the wing, scanning the surface of the ocean for a sign of prey.*

## The life aquatic

Almost all of Britain's water birds have webbed feet. Those that swim on the surface use them as paddles to push themselves through the water. Some diving birds use them for propulsion underwater, including cormorants.

Webbed feet can be efficient tools for moving beneath the water's surface, but the ultimate underwater swimmers of the avian world use their wings. The masters of this art in Britain are the auks – sea birds which include the puffin, razorbill and guillemot. Auks effectively fly through the water as they chase after fish. They can also fly in the air, albeit less gracefully than most other birds. Auks hunt fish underwater by diving down from the surface to reach them. Gannets, on the other hand, dive from the air. Unlike auks, gannets are expert fliers

### The aerofoil principle

Once in flight, the shape of the wing is crucial in keeping the bird airborne. Viewed in cross-section from the side, a bird's wing resembles an aeroplane's wing, called an aerofoil, and in fact aeroplanes use the same technique as birds to fly.

The wing is curved across the top, so the movement of air is faster over this part of the wing compared with the lower surface. This produces reduced air pressure on top of the wing, which provides lift and makes it easier for the bird to stay in the air.

The long flight feathers at the rear edge of the wings help to provide the thrust and lift for flight. The tail feathers, too, can help the bird remain airborne. The kestrel (*Falco tinnunculus*), for example, having spotted prey on the ground, spreads its tail feathers to help it remain aloft while it hovers to target its prey.

A bird's wings move in a regular figure-of-eight movement while it is in flight. During the downstroke, the flight feathers join together to push powerfully against the air. The primary flight feathers bend backwards, which propels the bird forwards. As the wing moves upwards, the longer primary flight feathers move apart, which reduces air resistance. The secondary feathers farther along the wing provide some slight propulsion. After that the cycle repeats itself.

*Above: The flow of air over a bird's wing varies according to the wing's position.*
*1. When the wing is stretched out horizontally, an area of low pressure is created above the wing, causing lift.*
*2. As the wing is tilted downwards, the flow of the air is disrupted, causing turbulence and loss of lift.*
*3. When the wing is angled downwards, lift slows, which results in stalling. The bird's speed slows as a consequence.*

and often travel long distances in search of fish. Once they have located a shoal they will gain height, then plummet into the ocean at top speed. Usually many of the birds will dive at once, or in quick succession, for maximum effect before the shoal

moves away. Just before impact with the water the gannet folds its wings back, to make its body shaped like a dart. This enables the bird to travel up to 22m (73ft) below the surface in the quest for its prey.

*4. Powerful upward and downward sweeps of the wings propel the bird forwards.*

*5. When coming in to land, a bird lowers its legs and slows its wing movements.*

*6. Braking is achieved by a vertical landing posture, with the tail feathers spread.*

# SENSES

*The keen senses of birds are vital to their survival, in particular helping them to find food, escape from enemies and find mates in the breeding season. Sight is the primary sense for most birds, but some species rely heavily on other senses to thrive in particular habitats.*

All birds' senses are adapted to their environment, and their body shape can help to reflect which senses are most significant to them.

## Sight and lifestyle

Most birds rely on their sense of sight to avoid danger, hunt for food and locate familiar surroundings. The importance of this sense is reflected by the size of their eyes, with those of starlings (*Sturnus vulgaris*), for

*Above: Scavengers such as this carrion crow have an acute sense of smell and large beak for tearing flesh from a carcass.*

example, making up 15 per cent of the total head weight. The enlargement of the eyeballs and associated structures, notably the eye sockets in the skull, has altered the shape of the brain. In addition, the optic lobes in the brain, which are concerned with vision, are also enlarged, whereas the olfactory counterparts, responsible for smell, are poorly developed.

The structure of the eye also reveals much about a bird's habits. Birds of prey have large eyes in proportion to their head, and have correspondingly keen eyesight. Species that regularly hunt for prey underwater, such as grebes, can see well in the water. They have a muscle in each eye that reduces the diameter of the lens and increases its thickness on entering water, so that their eyes can adjust easily to seeing underwater. In addition, certain diving birds use a lens that forms part of the nictitating membrane, or third eyelid, which is normally hidden. Underwater, when this membrane covers the eye, its convex shape serves as a lens, helping the bird to see in these surroundings.

## Eye position

The positioning of the eyes on the head gives important clues to a bird's lifestyle. Most birds' eyes are set on the sides of the head. Owls, however, have flattened faces and forward-facing eyes that are critical to their hunting ability. These features allow owls to target their prey.

There are disadvantages, though – owls' eyes do not give a rounded view of the world, so they must turn their heads to see around them. It is not just the positioning of owls' eyes that is unusual. They are also able to hunt effectively in almost complete darkness. This is made possible in two ways. First, their pupils are large, which maximizes the amount of light passing through to the retina behind the lens, where the image is formed. Second, the cells here consist mainly of rods rather than cones. While cones give good colour vision, rods function to create images when background illumination is low.

The position of the eyes of game birds such as woodcocks (*Scolopax rusticola*) lets them spot danger from many angles – they can even see a predator behind them. Their only blind spot is just behind the head.

### Field of vision

The positioning of a bird's eyes on its head affects its field of vision. The eyes of owls are positioned to face forwards, producing an overlapping image of the area in front known as binocular vision. This allows the owl to pinpoint its prey exactly, so that it can strike. In contrast, the eyes of birds that are likely to be preyed upon, such as woodcocks, are positioned on the sides of the head. This eye position gives a greatly reduced area of binocular vision, but it does give these birds practically all-round vision, enabling them to spot danger from all sides.

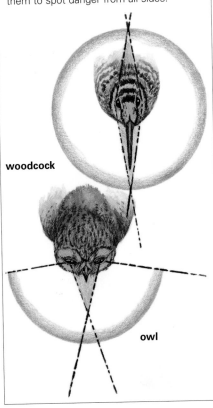

**woodcock**

**owl**

**Echolocation**
This helps tropical mascarene swiftlets (*Collocalia francica*) to navigate inside dark caves. These birds utter a stream of high-frequency clicks, which echo back off surrounding surfaces. The time elapsing between the clicks and echoes indicates the proximity of surrounding objects within range, which helps to prevent collisions.

## Smell
Very few birds have a sense of smell, but kiwis (Apterygidae) and vultures (forming part of the order Falciformes) are notable exceptions. Birds' nostrils are normally located above the bill, opening directly into the skull, but kiwis' nostrils are positioned right at the end of the long bill. They probably help these birds to locate earthworms in the soil. Vultures have very keen eyesight, which helps them to spot dead animals on the ground from the air, but they also have a strong sense of smell, which helps when homing in on a distant carcass.

*Below: Birds have good colour vision. It is this sense that enables bullfinches (*Pyrrhula pyrrhula*) to source food from winter berries.*

## Taste
The senses of smell and taste are linked, and most birds also have correspondingly few taste buds in their mouths. The number of taste buds varies, with significant differences between groups of birds. Pigeons may have as few as 50 taste buds in their mouths, parrots as many as 400.

Birds' taste buds are located all around the mouth, rather than just on the tongue, as in mammals. The close links between smell and taste can lead vultures, which feed only on fresh carcasses, to reject decomposing meat. They may start to eat it, but then spit it out once it is in their mouths, probably because of a combination of bad odour and taste.

## Hearing
Birds generally do not have a highly developed sense of hearing. They lack any external ear flaps that would help to pinpoint sources of sound. The openings to their hearing system are located on the sides of the head, back from the eyes.

Hearing is of particular significance for nocturnal species, such as owls, which find their food in darkness. These birds are highly attuned to the calls made by rodents. The broad shape of their skull has the additional advantage of spacing the ear openings more widely, which helps them to localize the source of the sounds with greater accuracy.

Hearing is also important to birds during the breeding season. Birds show particular sensitivity to sounds falling within the vocal range of their chicks, which helps them to locate their offspring easily in the critical early days after fledging.

## Touch
The sense of touch is more developed in some birds than others. Those such as snipe (*Gallinago*), which have long bills for seeking food, have sensitive nerve endings called corpuscles in their bills that pick up tiny vibrations caused by their prey. Vibrations that could suggest approaching danger can also register via other corpuscles located particularly in the legs, so that the bird has a sensory awareness even when it is resting on a branch.

## Wind-borne sensing
Tubenoses such as albatrosses and petrels (Procellariiformes) have a valve in each nostril that fills with air as the bird flies. These are affected by both the bird's speed and the wind strength. The valves almost certainly act as a type of wind gauge, allowing these birds to detect changes in wind strength and patterns. This information helps to keep them airborne, as they skim over the waves with minimal effort.

*Below: A combination of senses, especially touch, helps oystercatchers (*Haematopus ostralegus*) to detect their prey.*

# SURVIVAL

*All over the world, many birds depend on plant matter as part of their diet, with seeds and nuts in particular providing nourishment. A close relationship between plants and birds exists in many cases. Birds fertilize flowers when feeding on nectar, and help to spread their seeds when eating fruit.*

Many different types of birds are primarily plant-eaters, whether feeding on flowers, fruit, nuts and seeds, or other plant matter. Plant-eating species have to eat a large volume of food compared to meat-eating species, because of the comparatively low nutritional value of plants.

Most British plant-eating birds exist on a varied, seasonal diet. Bullfinches, for example, eat the buds in apple orchards in spring, while later in the year they consume seeds and fruit. Their bills, like those of many other members of the finch family, are stout and relatively conical, which helps them to crack seeds.

## Vegetation
A few British birds survive by feeding mainly on leafy vegetation. The breakdown of such vegetable matter

*Below: Peregrine falcons (*Falco peregrinus*) are adept aerial hunters, with pigeons featuring prominently in their diet. These birds of prey display not just speed, but also superb manoeuvrability when pursuing their quarry.*

presents a considerable level of difficulty, since birds do not possess the necessary enzymes to digest the tough structural cellulose in plants. However, birds such as grouse, which feed regularly on leafy plants such as heather, have evolved long, closed-ended tubes known as caeca, which contain beneficial microbes that break down cellulose.

*Above: Vision is the main sense that allows most birds of prey, such as golden eagles (*Aquila chrysaetos*), to target their victims. These eagles have keen sight.*

## Nuts and seeds
These dry foods are an invaluable resource to many different types of birds. However, cracking the tough outer shell or husk can be a problem. The hawfinch has evolved a particularly strong bill for this purpose. Hawfinches are able to crack open cherry stones to extract the kernel inside.

The most bizarre example of bill adaptation for eating seeds in British birds can be seen in the crossbill. This bird has twisted upper and lower mandibles, the tips of which overlap. The crossbill's beak enables it to extract the pine kernels it eats from inside the tough, woody cones that house them.

## Eating meat
Some British birds are active predators, seeking out and killing their own food. Others prefer to scavenge on carcasses. Some predatory birds are opportunistic feeders, hunting most of the time but

scavenging when the opportunity arises. Both hunters and scavengers have evolved to live in a wide range of environments, and display correspondingly diverse skills to obtain their food.

Birds of prey have sharp beaks that enable them to tear the flesh of their prey into chunks or strips small enough to swallow. Of course many swallow the small mammals and other creatures that they hunt whole. Eating whole animals would cause many creatures problems, because of the bones, skin, feathers and other relatively indigestible body parts that have to be swallowed along with the meat. Owls and birds of prey have evolved a mechanism to overcome this difficulty, however. They regurgitate pellets composed of the indigestible remains of their prey. Other birds that do this include the kingfisher, which produces similar pellets of fish bones and scales.

## Birds of prey

Some avian predators feed mainly on other birds. Among these, some, such as the sparrowhawk (*Accipiter nisus*), catch their victims in fairly level flight. The sparrowhawk uses hedges and similar cover to get close to its prey before it is seen. In this way it is able to take it by surprise. Other predators swoop down on their winged prey from above. The master of this form of attack is the peregrine falcon: it drops from a height with its wings folded to reach incredible speeds, allowing it to both outpace its prey and strike it with sufficient force.

Many British birds of prey catch their prey on the ground. Some, such as the buzzard and golden eagle, hunt mainly over open landscapes, soaring on thermals and other rising air currents and spotting their prey from a height. Others, such as the kestrel, spot their prey from a perch. The kestrel also hovers when searching for food. This enables it to target prey from the air without actually being particularly high above the ground, lessening the time it takes to reach and strike its victims once they have been spotted.

## Hunting techniques

Many predatory birds hunt during the day, but not all, with most owls preferring to seek their prey at night. Mice and other creatures that are caught by owls are killed and eaten immediately. In contrast, shrikes sometimes kill more prey than they can eat at once. These birds, which do hunt by day, store the surplus as a sort of larder, impaling invertebrates such as grasshoppers, and sometimes even very small vertebrates, on to the sharp tips of vegetation.

Of course, not all meat-eating birds hunt land animals – many hunt fish. The osprey, for instance, does this, plunging in feet first to grab its prey from near the surface of the water. Another fish-eating bird that dives from the air is the gannet, although it, like the kingfisher, plunges in head first. Other fish-eating birds catch their prey by diving from the surface and swimming after it underwater. This technique is employed by the cormorant and fish-eating ducks, such as the goosander.

## Scavengers

Although some birds of prey scavenge, in Britain it is the gulls and members of the crow family that find most of their food this way. Gulls, in particular, have learned to scavenge from urban

*Above: Precise judgement allows a kingfisher (Alcedo atthis) to strike with deadly accuracy from a perch. These birds frequent stretches of clear water for this reason.*

areas, with rubbish tips and dustbins acting like magnets for them. This may even help keep other pests, such as rats, away from our city streets on litter collection days. The carrion crow and magpie, on the other hand, are more likely to scavenge on the bodies of animals killed on roads by cars.

*Below: Pink-footed geese (Anser brachyrhynchus) can be a problem in agricultural areas, since they will sometimes descend in large numbers to graze on crops.*

# MATING

*Birds' breeding habits vary greatly. Some birds pair up only fleetingly, while others do so for the whole breeding season, and some species pair for life. For many young cock birds, the priority is to gain a territory as the first step in attracting a partner. Birds use both plumage and their songs to attract a mate.*

A number of factors trigger the onset of the breeding period. In Britain, as the days start to lengthen in spring, the increase in daylight is detected by the pineal gland in the bird's brain, which starts a complex series of hormonal changes in the body. Most birds form a bond with a single partner during the breeding season, which is often preceded by an elaborate display by the cock bird.

## Bird song

Many cock birds announce their presence by their song, which both attracts would-be mates and establishes a claim to a territory. Once pairing has occurred, the male may cease singing, but in some cases he starts to perform a duet with the hen, with each bird singing in turn.

Studies have revealed that young male birds start warbling quite quietly, and then sing more loudly as they mature. This can almost be seen as a reflection of their confidence, both in

*Below: Male and female mallards (*Anas platyrhynchos*) have very different plumage during the mating season. For the rest of the year the two have similar brown coloration.*

*Above: A male ruff (*Philomachus pugnax*) at a lek, where males compete with each other in displays to attract female partners. Ruffs do not form lasting pair bonds, so the hens nest on their own after mating has occurred.*

their ability to sing and to defend a territory from potential rivals. The song is learned, and becomes gradually more complex over time. Finally, when their song pattern becomes fixed, it remains constant throughout the bird's life.

It is obviously possible to identify different species by differences in their song patterns. Experienced birdwatchers may even use their knowledge of songs to lead them to particular birds. However, there are

sometimes marked variations between the songs of individuals of the same species that live in different places. Local dialects have been identified in various parts of a species' distribution, both within Britain and across Europe. In addition, as far as some songbirds are concerned, recent studies have shown that over the course of several generations, the pattern of song can alter markedly. Unlike other characteristics, such as plumage, it seems that birdsong is far from fixed.

Birds produce their sounds – even those species capable of mimicking human speech – without the benefit of a larynx and vocal cords like humans. The song is created in a voice organ called the syrinx, which is located in the bird's throat, at the bottom of the windpipe, or trachea.

The structure of the syrinx is very variable, being at its most highly developed in songbirds, which possess

*Above: Mute swans (*Cygnus olor*) are one of the species that pair for life. They become highly territorial when breeding, but outside the nesting period they often form flocks on large stretches of water. In spite of their common name, they can vocalize to a limited extent, by hissing and even grunting.*

as many as nine pairs of separate muscles to control the vocal output. As in the human larynx, it is the flow of air through the syrinx that enables the membranes here to vibrate, creating sound. An organ called the interclavicular air sac also plays an important role, and birds cannot sing without it. The depth of song is not always proportional to size. The small Cetti's warbler (*Cettia cetti*) is an occasional visitor to British shores. It will emit a sudden burst of clear, penetrating notes over a few seconds, which ceases as abruptly as it began. When breeding, males will even sing during the night to attract potential female mates.

## Breeding behaviour

Many birds rely on their breeding finery to attract their mates. Some groups assemble in communal display areas known as leks, where hens witness the males' displays and select a mate. A number of different British species establish leks, including the ruff, the capercaillie and the black grouse. Males on these display grounds pose and strut about, but in the end it

is up to the females who gets to mate and who does not. Unlike most other birds, the males take no part in nest-building, incubation or raising the young – those duties are left entirely to the females. As a consequence, successful males may father dozens of chicks. Others may never get to breed at all.

Some birds sing and some pose to attract a mate or seal a partnership. A few species exhibit another form of behaviour – the courtship dance. British birds that do this include the great crested grebe. In this species partners approaching one another with gifts of weed in their bills before rising up breast to breast on the water. The common crane also dances, and pairs call in unison to strengthen the bond between them.

Other species use a combination of factors to attract a mate. Male weaver birds (Ploceidae), for example, moult at the onset of the breeding season to display brightly coloured plumage, which is intended to lure the female bird to their elaborate nest. These complex constructions are made from densely packed grass and twigs, and may even boast a long and complex entrance tunnel. The successful pairing of the weavers will depend finally on the female's approval of the nest. Hens often assent to breed with older cocks, whose nest-building abilities show more sophistication than those of the younger birds.

## Life partners

Many male and female birds form no lasting mating relationship, although the pair bond may be strong during the nesting period. It is usually only in long-lived species, such as swans (Anatidae), that a lifelong bond between pairs is formed.

Pair bonding in long-lived species has certain advantages. The young of such birds are slow to mature, and are often unlikely to nest for five years or more. By remaining for a time in a family group, and sheltering the developing birds until they are strong enough to fend for themselves, adults can improve the survival prospects of their young.

*Below: Greenfinches (*Carduelis chloris*) are very sociable birds that will commonly be seen gathered on a feeder or table, often selecting only the sunflower seeds and discarding the others. The female greenfinch is responsible for building the nest, which is made from twigs and grass and lined with soft roots and hair. The nesting site is usually a dense thicket or bush. The hen incubates the eggs alone, but when the chicks hatch they are looked after by both parents.*

# NESTING

*All birds reproduce by laying eggs, which are covered with a hard, calcareous shell. The number of eggs laid at a time – known as the clutch size – varies significantly between species, as does egg coloration. Nesting habits also vary, with some birds constructing very elaborate nests.*

Birds incubate their eggs to keep them sufficiently warm for the chicks to develop inside. The incubation period often does not start until more than one egg has been laid, and sometimes not until the entire clutch has been completed. The interval between the laying of one egg and the next varies. If incubation does not start until egg-laying has finished, the chicks will all be of a similar size when they hatch, increasing their survival rate. Birds that start incubating before they have finished laying have clutches with chicks of different sizes.

The male and female may share incubation duties, as in the case of most pigeons and doves, or just one member of the pair may incubate the eggs, usually the female.

The eggshell may appear to be a solid barrier but in fact contains pores, which allow water vapour and carbon dioxide to escape from the egg, and oxygen to enter it to reach the embryo. Before hatching, each chick uses the egg tooth on the tip of its upper bill to cut through the inner membrane into the air space at the blunt end of the shell, which forms as water evaporates from the egg. Here, the chick starts to

*Below: A chicken's egg showing the embryo's development. 1. The fertilized egg forms a ball of cells that will gradually develop into an embryo. 2 and 3. The embryo develops. 4. The chick is almost fully developed. 5. The fully grown chick cuts its way out of the egg.*

*Above: Blue tits (*Parus caeruleus*) are typical of many birds that leave the nest before they are able to fly effectively. The young remain hidden in vegetation and are fed by their parents in these critical early days after leaving the nest.*

breathe atmospheric air for the first time. About 48 hours later, it emerges from the egg.

The colour and marking of an egg is directly linked to the nesting site. Birds that breed in hollow trees produce white eggs, because these are hidden from predators and do not need to be camouflaged. The pale coloration may also help the adult birds to locate the eggs as they return to the nest,

lessening the chances of damaging them. Birds that build more open, cup-shaped nests tend to lay coloured eggs, often with a mottled pattern – this acts as a useful camouflage, making them less obvious to potential nest thieves.

## Nest styles
Different types of birds build nests of various shapes and sizes, which are characteristic of their species. Groups such as finches build nests in the form of an open cup, often concealed in vegetation. Most pigeons and doves construct a loose platform of twigs. Swallows are among the birds that use mud to construct their nests. They scoop muddy water up from the

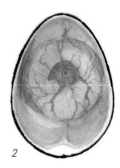
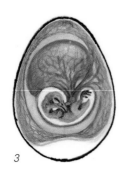

1          2          3          4          5

*Above: Foster parents such as this reed warbler continue to feed the young cuckoo even when the impostor dwarfs them in size.*

*Above: A pair of fulmars (*Fulmarus glacialis*) at their nest. Choosing a location close to the sea means they can obtain food easily.*

*Above: The broad and often colourful gape of chicks allows parent birds such as this blackcap (*Sylvia atricapilla*) to feed their offspring quickly and efficiently. Weak chicks that are unable to raise their heads and gape at the approach of a parent will quickly die from starvation.*

surface of a pond or puddle, mould it into shape on a suitable wall, and then allow it to dry and harden like cement.

Cup-shaped nests are more elaborate than platform nests, being usually made by weaving grasses and twigs together. The inside is often lined with soft feathers. The raised sides of the cup nest lessen the likelihood of losing eggs and chicks, and also offer greater protection from the elements to the adults during incubation. The hollow in the nest's centre is created by the birds compressing the material here before egg-laying begins.

Suspended nests enclosed by a domed roof offer even greater security, less accessible to predators because of their design and also their position, often hanging from slender branches. Waxbills build a particularly elaborate nest, comprising two chambers. There is an obvious upper opening, which is always empty, suggesting to would-be predators that the nest is unoccupied. The birds occupy the chamber beneath, which has a separate opening.

Some birds, such as plovers and many ducks, nest on the ground. These species rarely build elaborate nests but instead usually create a small hollow, which they may then line with feathers or other material. Ground-nesting birds are especially vulnerable to predators. Most rely on camouflage for survival, and their eggs and chicks are usually well camouflaged too.

## Hatching out

The chicks of different bird species hatch out at various stages of development. Species that remain in the nest for some time after hatching, including tits and finches, hatch in a blind and helpless state and are entirely dependent on their parents at first. If not closely brooded, they are likely to become fatally chilled. In contrast, some species have chicks that leave the nest soon after hatching. These tend to be ground-dwelling birds. Although unable to fly, the

*Below: Most eggs have a generally rounded shape, but seabirds such as guillemots (*Uria aalge*) breeding on rocky outcrops lay eggs that are more pointed. This shape helps to prevent the eggs from rolling over the cliff.*

chicks can run sometimes just hours after hatching. Ducks and many other water birds also have chicks that leave the nest early.

Many adult birds offer food to their offspring. This can be a particularly demanding period, especially for small birds that have relatively large broods. Great tits, for example, have up to 15 eggs in a clutch and when the chicks have hatched they must supply their offspring with huge quantities of insects. The parents typically feed their chicks up to 60 times an hour, as well as eating themselves and keeping the nest clean.

# MIGRATION

*Some birds live in a particular place all year round, but many are only temporary visitors. Typically, species fly to temperate latitudes in spring, and return to warmer climates at the end of summer. They have a wide distribution, but are seen only in specific parts of their range at certain times of the year.*

Seasonal migration is a major factor in the life of many birds. In some cases this migration is very obvious and involves huge distances but at other times it is much more subtle. In Britain swallows, swifts and many small passerines such as wood warblers and redstarts are migratory birds. They are present in the summer, but fly south along with many other species to warmer climes for winter. Similarly, many ducks and geese are only present in Britain during winter, returning north in summer to breed. Birds that are sighted in the UK all year round such as robins and starlings are often joined by birds migrating from further north.

The routes that birds follow on their journeys are often well defined. Land birds try to avoid flying over large stretches of water, preferring instead to follow coastal routes and cross the sea

*Right: Various routes between Europe and Africa are chosen by migrant birds. Crossings are not usually direct, if this would involve a potentially hazardous ocean journey. Even when crossing small areas of water such as the Mediterranean, birds will follow routes where the land masses are close together.*

*Below: Some southern European populations of Canada geese (*Branta canadensis*) are now losing their migratory instincts, as the winters here are less harsh and food is quite plentiful.*

at the shortest point. For instance, many birds migrating from Britain to Africa fly over the Straits of Gibraltar. Frequently, birds fly at high altitudes when migrating. Some do this to take advantage of tail winds. Others, such as many birds of prey, rise on thermals (columns of hot air) then, effectively, glide to save energy, losing height very gradually until they hit the next thermal or other pocket of rising air.

Most migrating birds fly at greater speeds than usual, which helps to make their journey time as short as possible. The difference can be significant – migrating swallows travel at speeds between 3 and 14km/h (1.8–8.7mph) faster than usual, and are assisted by the greater altitude, where the air is thinner and resistance from friction is consequently less.

---

### Banding birds

Much of what we know about migration and the lifespan of birds comes from banding studies carried out by ornithologists. Bands placed on the birds' legs allow experts to track their movements when the ringed birds are recovered again. The rings are made of lightweight aluminium, and have details of the banding organization and when banding was carried out. Unfortunately, only a very small proportion of ringed birds are ever recovered, so the data gathered is incomplete. Now other methods of tracking, such as radar, are also used to follow the routes taken by flocks of birds, which supplements the information from banding studies.

*Below: A mute swan (Cygnus olor) wearing a band. Coloured bands can help to identify individual birds from some distance away.*

---

*Right: The swallow migrates from Africa and arrives in Britain from April to May for its breeding season.*

Some birds travel huge distances on migration. Arctic terns, for example, cover distances of more than 15,000km (9,300 miles) in total, as they shuttle between the Arctic and Antarctic. They fly an average distance of 160km (100 miles) every day. Size does not preclude birds from migrating long distances, either. For instance, large numbers of goldcrests – Britain's smallest bird – fly in from Scandinavia, the Baltic states and Russia for winter.

### Preparing for migration

The migratory habits of birds have long been the subject of scientific curiosity. As late as the 1800s, it was thought that swallows hibernated in the bottom of ponds because they were seen skimming over the surface in groups before disappearing until the following spring. Now we know that they were probably feeding on insects to build up energy supplies for their long journey ahead.

Even today, the precise mechanisms involved in migratory behaviour are not understood. Feeding opportunities are limited when birds are migrating, although their energy requirements are higher. We do know that birds feed up before setting out, and that hormonal changes enable them to store more fat in their bodies to sustain them. In addition, birds usually moult just before migrating, so that their plumage is in the best condition to withstand the buffeting that lies ahead.

### Navigation

Birds use both learned and visual cues to orientate themselves when migrating. Young birds of many

*Right: The starling is a partial migrant, which means that it migrates in some places but not in others. In October and November flocks of migrant starlings start arriving along the east coast of Britain. Most have flown across the North Sea from Belgium or the Netherlands, after travelling across northern Europe.*

species, such as swans, learn the route by flying in the company of their elders. However, some young birds set out on their own and reach their destinations sucessfully without the benefit of experienced companions, navigating by instinct alone. Birds such as swifts (Apopidae) fly mainly during daytime, whereas others, including ducks (Antidae), migrate at night. Many birds fly direct to their destination but some detour, breaking their journey to obtain food and water.

Experiments have shown that birds orientate themselves using the position of the sun and stars, as well as by following familiar landmarks. They also use the Earth's magnetic field to find their position. The way in which these various factors work together, however, is not yet fully understood.

# ENDANGERED SPECIES AND CONSERVATION

*It has been estimated that three-quarters of the world's birds may come under threat in the 21st century. Habitat destruction poses the most serious danger, so conservationists are striving to preserve bird habitats worldwide. Direct intervention of various kinds is also used to ensure the survival of particular species.*

For many birds, life is short and hazardous. Quite apart from the risk of predation, birds can face a whole range of other dangers, from starvation and disease through to inadvertent interference or persecution by humans. The reproductive rate is higher and the age of maturity earlier in species that have particularly hazardous lifestyles, such as blue tits. These species often breed twice or more each year in rapid succession.

## Rising and falling numbers

Some birds will travel long distances from their native habitat when living conditions become unfavourable. Pallas's sandgrouse (*Syrrhaptes paradoxus*), for instance, a species normally found in central and eastern parts of Asia, has occasionally invaded the more temperate habitats of western Europe to breed. Large-scale irruptions (irregular movements) of this type were recorded in 1863, 1868 and 1908, involving thousands of birds, and

*Below: The white-tailed sea eagle (*Haliaeetus albicilla*) died out in Scotland in 1918. Captivity-reared birds were introduced to the region and eventually established a colony.*

*Above: The population of the Dartford warbler (*Sylvia undata*) nearly disappeared from the British Isles in the early 1960s because of harsh winters. Since then milder winters, teamed with careful conservation of its heathland environment, has meant that the number of birds in the British Isles has now soared.*

sightings were made from the Faeroe Islands in the far North Atlantic, southwards to Spain, with numerous identifications in the British Isles. Despite these often protracted relocations to ensure survival, the range of the grouse has never extended permanently into Europe. Similar fluctuations affect other bird colonies when food runs into short supply. Waxwings, for instance, often irrupt to find food when supplies become scarce in their habitat. Many of the waxwings that are sometimes seen in the Britain Isles in the autumn and winter fly in to find food.

## Group living

Safety in numbers is a major benefit of group living, as it can bring increased protection to birds both in the air and on the ground. For example, the way in which flocks manage to co-ordinate their flight, by weaving, dipping and rising together as a group, makes it far more difficult for an aerial predator to focus on an individual.

Coloration can also disguise the number of individuals within a flock, and it serves to protect more vulnerable lone birds too. The mottled colouring on the head and upperparts of many shore and game birds, for instance, breaks up their outline so that, while on the ground, they merge more effectively against the land and are less conspicuous to birds of prey circling above.

*Above: This guillemot (Uria aalge) killed in Scottish waters is just one of the countless avian victims claimed by oil spillages each year. Large spills of oil can have devastating effects on whole populations.*

## Effects of humans

It is generally assumed that human interference in the landscape is likely to have harmful effects on avian populations. However, this is not always the case. For instance, the common pheasant, a native of Asia, is now found across much of Britain, thanks to human interest in these game birds, which are bred in large numbers for sport shooting. Many more survive than would naturally be the case, thanks to the attention of gamekeepers who not only provide food, but also help to curb possible predators in areas where the birds are released.

Game birds, however, are a rare exception to the general rule. Human interference does generally have a negative impact on bird numbers. Many parts of Britain today are far less rich in birds than they once were. The worst affected regions are those dominated by arable farming. Here, natural forest habitat has been replaced by endless acres of crops. These provide food for a few species, such as the wood pigeon, but are effectively deserts for most others. The pesticides sprayed on these crops ensure that insects in these fields are sparse and the birds that would feed on them do not visit these areas. The up-side of arable farming is the planting of species-rich hedgerows.

## Conservation

Preserving what natural habitat remains in Britain is the best and most cost-effective way to ensure the survival of our wild birds. In addition, conservationists may take a variety of direct measures to safeguard the future of particular species, such as breeding in captivity, or translocation. The latter method sees conservation officials remove the youngest chicks from wild nests; these are subsequently reared to independence and released into a new location, where it is hoped they will thrive. Using this approach, golden eagles have been translocated to Ireland from their native home in the Scottish Highlands.

Some previously extinct birds in Britain have now been re-introduced. Perhaps the best-known example is the white-tailed sea eagle, which was first re-introduced into Scotland in the 1970s. Other birds that have become locally extinct have also benefited from re-introduction programmes. The red kite, for example, was confined to Wales until quite recently. Now it lives in many locations across England, places where it thrived before being hunted and poisoned to extinction.

## Climate change

Previously, the main threats to British birds have been habitat loss, egg collectors and persecution by farmers and gamekeepers. In the near future, global warming will almost certainly

*Above: Glove puppets resembling the parent bird's head are often used when hand-rearing chicks such as this peregrine falcon (Falco peregrinus), to encourage the birds to bond with their own kind when eventually released.*

become the greatest threat to the survival of some species. It is likely that rising temperatures will cause some habitats, such as montane heath (which occurs above the tree line), to shrink and alter the distribution of plant species in Britain, affecting many birds. The melting of the polar ice caps will threaten seabird populations by destroying their nesting areas. Rising sea levels will also threaten low-lying wetlands favoured by wading birds.

*Below: Conservation groups around Britain work to keep reed beds and other important bird habitats functional. For example, they will root out invasive foreign plants that tend to overrun diverse native species.*

# DIRECTORY OF BIRDS

Birds are a scientific class of vertebrates that, millions of years ago, evolved the power of flight. Most species, including all of those found wild in Britain today, still have that ability. As a group they form the most visible component of British animal life. Few journeys outdoors, even in cities, are completed without seeing birds of one species or another at some point along the way.

Many British birds are resident, staying here all year round, but others are migratory. Some of these arrive in spring and stay here to breed. Others fly in during autumn and leave again the following spring. The following directory groups the birds by type, beginning with the many seabirds that live on the coast and shoreline of the British Isles, and finishing with the warblers and other small birds, which make their homes in the gardens and city parks all over the country.

*Above: The great tit is one of the British Isles' most recognizable birds, being a regular visitor to gardens, particularly those with a supply of seed or peanuts. Its natural diet is insects and caterpillars, and it can be useful in reducing garden pests.*

*Left: The common buzzard is one of the most common raptors in Europe, thanks largely to its adaptable feeding habits.*

# GULLS

*Gulls are linked in many people's minds with the seaside, but some species have proved very adept
at adjusting to living alongside people, and generally profiting from the association. A number of gulls
have now spread to various locations inland. Shades of white and grey generally predominate in the
plumage of these birds, making them quite easy to recognize.*

## Herring gull

*Larus argentatus*

These large gulls are often seen on fishing jetties and
around harbours, searching for scraps. They have also
moved inland and can be seen in areas such as rubbish
dumps, where they scavenge for food, often in quite
large groups. Herring gulls are noisy by nature,
especially when breeding. They frequently nest on
rooftops in coastal towns and cities, a trend that began
in Britain as recently as the 1940s. Pairs can become
very aggressive at breeding time, swooping
menacingly on people who venture too
close to the nest site (and even including
the chicks once they have fledged).

**Identification:**
White head and
underparts, with
grey on the back
and wings. Prominent
large, white spots on the black
flight feathers. Distinctive pink
feet. Reddish spot towards the tip
of the lower bill. Some dark
streaking on the head and neck in
winter. Sexes are alike. Young
birds are mainly brown, with dark
bills and prominent barring on
their wings.

**Distribution**: The northern
Atlantic north of Iceland and
south to northern Africa and
the Mediterranean. Also the
North Sea and Baltic areas to
northern Scandinavia and
Arctic Russia.
**Habitat**: Coasts and inland.
**Food**: Fish and carrion.
**Size**: 60cm (23in), wingspan
137–146cm (54–57½in).
**Nest**: Small pile of vegetation.
**Eggs**: 2–3, pale blue to
brown with darker markings.

## Black-headed gull

*Larus ridibundus*

These gulls are a common sight not only in coastal areas but
also in town parks with lakes. They move inland during the
winter, where they can often be seen following ploughing
tractors searching for worms and grubs disturbed in the soil.
Black-headed gulls nest close to water in what can be quite
large colonies. Like many gulls, they are noisy birds, even
calling at night. On warm, summer evenings they can
sometimes be seen hawking flying ants and similar insects
in flight, demonstrating
their airborne agility.

**Identification:** Throughout the
summer, distinctive black head
with a white collar beneath and
white underparts. The wings
are grey and the flight feathers
mainly black. In the winter, the
head is mainly white except for
black ear coverts and a
black smudge above
each eye, while
the bill is red
at its base
and dark at the tip.

*Above: The black feathering on the head
is a transient characteristic, appearing only
in the summer (above right).*

**Distribution**: Greenland,
Europe, the coast of north-
western Africa and into Asia.
**Habitat**: Coastal areas.
**Food**: Typically molluscs,
crustaceans and small fish.
**Size**: 39cm (15½in),
wingspan 100–110cm
(39½–43in).
**Nest**: Scrape on the ground
lined with plant matter.
**Eggs**: 2–3, pale blue to
brown with darker markings.

# Great black-backed gull

*Larus marinus*

These large gulls can be extremely disruptive when close to other nesting seabird colonies. Not only will they harry returning birds for their catches, but they will also take eggs and chicks on occasion. In winter, great black-backed gulls move inland to scavenge on rubbish tips, although they are generally wary of people and are unlikely to be seen in urban areas. Banding studies have revealed that many of those that overwinter in Britain are actually birds of Norwegian origin, which return to Scandinavia to breed the following spring. Pairs are often quite solitary at this time, especially when nesting near people, though they are more likely to nest in colonies on uninhabited islands.

**Identification:** Very large gull. White head and underparts with black on the back and wings. White-spotted black tail. Large area of white is apparent at the wing tips in flight. Bill is yellow with a red tip to the lower side. Pale pinkish legs. Sexes are alike.

**Distribution**: From northern Spain north to Iceland and eastwards through the North Sea and Baltic to Scandinavia. Also present on the eastern side of North America.
**Habitat**: Coastal areas.
**Food**: Fish and carrion.
**Size**: 74cm (29in), wingspan 152–170cm (60–67in).
**Nest**: Pile of vegetation.
**Eggs**: 2–3, brownish with dark markings.

---

**Lesser black-backed gull** (*Larus fuscus*) 56cm (22in), wingspan 127–148cm (50–58in). Breeds around the shores of the extreme north of Europe, moving as far south as parts of northern Africa in winter. Similar to the great black-backed gull, but smaller, and lacks the prominent white markings on the flight feathers. Legs are yellow. Sexes are alike.

**Glaucous gull** (*Larus hyperboreus*) 68cm (27in), wingspan 130–140cm (51–55in). Coastal areas of northern Europe. Very pale bluish-grey wings with white edges. Head and underparts white in summer, developing grey streaks in winter. Sexes are alike.

**Yellow-legged gull** (*Larus cachinnans*) 58cm (23in), wingspan 137–145cm (54–57in). Found in coastal areas of southern England. It has a white head and underparts, grey back and wings, and small white spots on the black flight feathers. The wings are black towards the tips. The bill and legs are yellow, and there is a red spot on the lower bill.

# Common gull

Mew gull *Larus canus*

Common gulls often range inland over considerable distances, searching for earthworms and other invertebrates to feed on. In sandy coastal areas they will seek out shellfish as well.

There is a distinct seasonal variation in the range of these gulls. At the end of the summer they leave their Scandinavian and Russian breeding grounds and head farther south in Europe, to France and various other locations in the Mediterranean. Here they overwinter before migrating north again in the spring.

In spite of its rather meek appearance, this species will bully smaller gulls such as the black-headed gull and take food from them. Common and black-headed gulls are often found in the same kind of inland environment, both showing a preference for agricultural areas and grassland.

**Distribution**: Iceland and throughout Europe, with the main breeding grounds in Scandinavia and Russia. Also extends across Asia to western North America.
**Habitat**: Coasts and inland areas close to water.
**Food**: Shellfish, small fish and invertebrates.
**Size**: 45cm (18in), wingspan 110–125cm (43–49½in).
**Nest**: Raised nest of twigs and other debris.
**Eggs**: 2–3, pale blue to brownish-olive in colour, with dark markings.

**Identification:** White head and underparts with yellow bill and yellowish-green legs. Wings are greyish with white markings at the tips, which are most visible in flight. Flight feathers are black with white spots. Tail is white. Dark eyes. Greyish streaking on the head in winter plumage. Sexes are alike. Young birds have brown mottled plumage, and it takes them more than two years to obtain adult coloration.

# Kittiwake

*Rissa tridactyla*

The largest kittiwake breeding colonies are in the Arctic. They also breed in the UK during spring and summer, but spend the winter on the wing over the Atlantic. They seek out steep-sided cliffs, with so many birds packing on to ledges that both adults may encounter difficulty in landing at the same time. These sites are defended from takeover for most of the year, not just during the nesting period. The nest is made from scraps of vegetation, especially seaweed, combined with feathers and bound together with mud. The narrow, shelf-like nature of the site makes it difficult for aerial predators to attack the kittiwakes. Away from the nest, these birds remain largely on the wing, swooping down to gather food from the surface of the ocean. Global warming is thought to be behind food chain changes and the subsequent swift decline in the Scottish population.

**Identification:** Head whitish with a black marking on the back. Back and wings greyish. Flight feathers black, with white spots on the tips. Bill yellow, legs are black. Sexes alike. Young birds have a black bill, plus a black band across the neck, wings and tail tip.

**Distribution**: Circumpolar range. Present beyond Iceland and northern Scandinavia in the summer, and around the British Isles and western Europe throughout the year. Winters up to southern Scandinavia. The commonest gull in the Arctic region.
**Habitat**: Ocean and shore.
**Food**: Fish and invertebrates.
**Size**: 40cm (16in), wingspan 90–100cm (35½–39½in).
**Nest**: Made from vegetation and mud, built on cliff ledge.
**Eggs**: 2, buff-olive, blotched.

# Iceland gull

*Larus glaucoides*

The name of this gull is misleading, since it is only present on Iceland (and in Europe) outside the breeding season. The gulls found in the British Isles are those that breed in north-eastern Greenland; birds farther south on Greenland are resident there throughout the year. Young birds travel farther afield, and are often seen with other gulls, frequently scavenging for food in coastal waters and inland at reservoirs and rubbish dumps. Iceland gulls will consume almost anything edible. At sea they prefer to feed on the surface, although they may dive to catch fish or invertebrates. Breeding typically starts on Greenland around the middle of May, with pairs nesting on steep, inaccessible cliffs, often in the company of other seabirds, whose eggs and chicks may be preyed upon by the Iceland gulls. The gull winters as far south as Britain, and is often seen on Shetland.

**Identification:** Predominantly white, with pale grey coloration on the wings. Bill is yellowish, with a red spot near the tip of the lower bill. Legs and feet pink. Sexes are alike. Out of breeding condition, adult birds display brownish markings on the head, extending on to the breast. Young birds are very pale in colour, with a brownish bill.

**Distribution**: The Greenland population overwinters on Iceland, around the British Isles and in parts of Scandinavia. North-eastern Canadian population overwinters south to Virginia in the US and inland to the Great Lakes.
**Habitat**: Typically near cliffs adjoining sea coasts.
**Food**: Fish and other edible items.
**Size**: 63cm (25in), wingspan 115–137cm (45–54in).
**Nest**: Made from seaweed and other vegetation.
**Eggs**: 2–3, olive-brownish in colour.

# Ring-billed gull

*Larus delawarensis*

**Identification:** A black ring encircles the yellow bill, close to its tip. Typical gull patterning, with white head showing mottling in winter. Wings are greyish, with white markings on the black wing tips. Legs are yellow. Sexes are alike. Young birds are lightly mottled.

These gulls are originally visitors from North America, but seem to have taken up residence in many coastal areas of Britain. Most move to the more southerly parts of their range, although some wander north as far as Alaska. Over recent years they have become relatively common in Florida, where they were first recorded in 1930. On the west coast their distribution extended from California in 1940 up to British Columbia by 1974. Even more remarkably, since the 1970s they have been crossing the Atlantic in large numbers, and are no longer considered rare vagrants in the UK. Ring-billed gulls are adaptable feeders, and on the prairies will congregate in flocks to pick up grubs from the soil as the land is ploughed. They also catch fish by diving underwater when hunting at sea.

**Distribution**: Originates from North America, down the Atlantic seaboard and elsewhere, but observed annually in western Europe, especially in the British Isles.
**Habitat**: Coasts and inland, including agricultural areas.
**Food**: Omnivorous.
**Size**: 53cm (21in), wingspan 124cm (49in).
**Nest**: Made of vegetation.
**Eggs**: 3, usually buff-coloured with blotches.

# Little gull

*Larus minutus*

The little gull could hardly be better named. The world's smallest species of gull, it is about the size of a fieldfare or mistle thrush, but is even more dainty in its appearance. Its small, delicate bill betrays its preference for relatively tiny items of food, compared with other gulls. Its plumage is roughly similar to that of the black-headed gull or the slightly larger Mediterranean gull, but on the wing it is just as likely to be confused for a tern. Like terns, the little gull has a light, buoyant flight, and sometimes descends to pick objects of food from the water, fluttering over the surface without landing on it.

The little gull breeds in large colonies around estuaries and in freshwater marshes in northern Europe and parts of Asia (it also breeds in Canada). Most British sightings tend to be of passage migrants, around autumn and spring, although in some years as many as 800 birds spend the winter here. Young little gulls have distinctive black marks on the upper side of each wing, forming a W shape. These marks disappear as the birds enter their second year, but instead they now appear on the underwing.

**Distribution**: This bird occurs in British coastal regions during migration from the Firth of Forth southwards. Also found in Asia and North America.
**Habitat**: Coastal regions, particularly estuaries and sandy or muddy beaches.
**Food**: Insects and other invertebrates, occasionally small fish.
**Size**: 26cm (10¼in), wingspan 65cm (25½in).
**Nest**: Lined, on the ground among vegetation.
**Eggs**: Olive to buff, marked with numerous small spots.

**Identification**: This bird looks like a smaller and more dainty version of the black-headed gull. The main difference, apart from size, is the beak, which is much shorter. The blackish-brown feathers on the head, in summer plumage, also extend farther back – in the black-headed gull the nape of the neck is white. In winter plumage, a dark grey cap remains; this is missing from the winter plumage of the black-headed gull.

# TERNS

*Terns are easily distinguished, even from gulls, by their relatively elongated shape. Their long, pointed wings are an indication of their aerial ability. Some terns regularly fly great distances on migration, farther than most other birds. Not surprisingly, their flight appears to be almost effortless. When breeding, terns prefer to nest in colonies.*

## Common tern

*Sterna hirundo*

These graceful birds are only likely to be encountered in northern parts of their range between April and October, after which time they head south to warmer climes for the duration of the winter period. Travelling such long distances means that they are powerful in flight, and yet are also very agile. Their strongly-forked tail helps them to hover effectively, allowing them to adjust their position before diving into the water in search of quarry. They are very versatile feeders and may also hawk food on the wing. Common terns are represented on all the continents, their long bills providing a simple way of distinguishing them from gulls.

**Identification:** Long body shape, with black on the top of the head extending down the back of the neck. Rest of the face and underparts whitish-grey. Back and wings greyish, with long flight feathers. Narrow white streamers on the tail. Bill is red with a dark tip, which becomes completely black in the winter. The plumage in front of the eyes becomes white during winter. Legs and feet are red. Sexes are alike.

**Distribution**: Great Britain, Scandinavia and central Europe in summer. Migrates to Africa for the winter.
**Habitat**: Near water.
**Food**: Mainly fish, but also eats crustaceans.
**Size**: 36cm (14¼in), wingspan 70–80cm (27–31½in).
**Nest**: Scrape on the ground.
**Eggs**: 3, pale brown with dark spots.

## Sandwich tern

Cabot's tern *Sterna sandvicensis*

A summer visitor to northern Europe, this species is often sighted slightly earlier than the common tern, and also leaves just before its relative. The sandwich tern is significantly larger and is surprisingly noisy, with the sounds of its calls having been likened to a grating cartwheel. Although these terns will skim over the water surface seeking food, they can also dive spectacularly from heights of up to 10m (33ft). Sandwich terns usually breed in high-density colonies in the open on sand bars and similarly exposed coastal sites, although they may sometimes nest on islands in lakes.

**Identification:** Shaggy black crest evident at the back of the head. The entire top of the head is black during the summer, while a white forehead is characteristic of the winter plumage. The bill is long and black with a yellow tip. Rest of the head and underparts are white, and the wings are grey. Sexes are alike.

**Distribution**: Around the shores of Great Britain and northern Europe, as well as the Caspian and Black seas. Winters farther south in the Mediterranean region and northern Africa. Also found in South-east Asia, the Caribbean and South America.
**Habitat**: Coastal areas.
**Food**: Fish and sand eels.
**Size**: 43cm (17in), wingspan 88–97cm (34½–38½in).
**Nest**: Scrape on the ground.
**Eggs**: 1–2, brownish-white with darker markings.

**Little tern** (*Sterna albifrons*)
21–25cm (8–10in), wingspan
40–48cm (16–19in). Little
terns are adaptable breeders,
nesting both on the coast and
inland. They prefer mainland
breeding sites, and will
associate in small groups.
Their diet is varied, with land
invertebrates featuring
significantly when breeding
inland. Little terns undertake
long migrations, with western
European populations
overwintering on the western
coast of Africa, and eastern
European birds heading to
the opposite coast. They
hover when hunting over
water. On land they take
invertebrates from branches.

# Roseate tern

*Sterna dougallii*

In northern parts of their range these terns are brief summer
visitors, only likely to be present from about the middle of
May until the end of August. Their distribution is quite
localized. They are most likely to be seen where the shore is
shallow and sandy, providing them with better fishing
opportunities. They dive into the water to catch their prey
from heights of no more than 2m (7ft), and may also take
fish from other terns. Their shorter wings and quicker wing
beats make them incredibly agile in flight. Roseate terns
avoid open areas when nesting, preferring sites that are
concealed among rocks or vegetation.

**Identification:** This tern gets its name from the slight pinkish suffusion
on its whitish underparts. Compared to other terns, it has relatively long
tail streamers and quite short wings. The bill is primarily blackish with a
red base in the summer. Entire top of the head is black in summer, and
the forehead turns white in winter. Sexes are alike. Subspecies differ in
both wing and bill length.

**Distribution**: From the British
Isles south to Spain and west
Africa. Winters along the
west African coast.
**Habitat**: Coastal areas.
**Food:** Mainly fish.
**Size**: 36cm (14¼in),
wingspan 74–84cm (29–33in).
**Nest**: Scrape on the ground.
**Eggs**: 1–2, cream or buff with
reddish-brown markings.

# Arctic tern

*Sterna paradisaea*

It can be very difficult to distinguish this species from the common tern, but the Arctic tern's
bill is shorter and does not have a black tip in the summer. The tail too is longer, and the tail
streamers are very evident in flight. Arctic terns undertake the most extensive migration of
all birds, flying virtually from one end of the globe to the other. After breeding in the
vicinity of the Arctic Circle the birds head south, often beyond Africa to Antarctica, before
repeating the journey the following year, though it appears that at least some of the young
birds stay in the Antarctic for their first full year. Arctic terns nest communally, often
choosing islands on which to breed.

They will react aggressively to
any potential predators in their
midst, with a number of
individuals turning on and
mobbing an intruder.
Most birds arrive in
England from Antarctica
in May and June. They
breed and depart in August.

**Identification:** Black area covering the
entire top of the head, with white chest
and underparts. Wings grey. Bill is dark red,
becoming black in the winter, when the
forehead is white. They have long, swallow-like tail
streamers. Sexes are alike.

**Distribution**: Breeds in the
Arctic and northern Europe.
Migrates south to overwinter
in southern Africa.
**Habitat**: Sea and fresh water.
**Food:** Fish; invertebrates.
**Size**: 38cm (15in), wingspan
74–84cm (29–33in).
**Nest**: Hollow on the ground,
lined with vegetation.
**Eggs**: 2, can be brownish,
bluish or greenish in colour,
with dark markings.

# OTHER SEABIRDS

*Keen eyesight, possibly assisted by a sense of smell, helps seabirds find food in the oceans. Marine invertebrates feature prominently in their diet, and they will often congregate in areas where krill are to be found, along with other predatory creatures such as whales. They seek out inconspicuous places to nest, such as underground burrows or the crevices in a rocky cliff face.*

## Storm petrel

*Hydrobates pelagicus*

Like others of its kind, the storm petrel prefers to nest on islands, its traditional nesting grounds including the Balearics and similar localities in the Mediterranean region. Unfortunately, however, coastal development is having an adverse effect on breeding populations in some areas. The storm petrel breeds on islands west of the UK and on the Northern Isles from May to September. In the winter it moves south and is seen off Namibia and South Africa. As with other storm petrels, this species is only able to feed on smaller items of food due to its restricted gape. It is thought that they are able to locate food not only by sight but also by smell, which is rare in birds. Their usual diet is comprised of planktonic creatures such as krill, but they have learned to scavenge for edible items thrown overboard from ships, especially trawlers. If threatened at close quarters, they regurgitate their foul-smelling stomach contents as a deterrent.

**Identification:** Slightly larger than a sparrow. Dark brownish-grey in colour overall, with a pale whitish area on the undersides of the wings, and on the sides of the rump. Square-shaped tail, with the legs not extending beyond the tip when in flight.

**Distribution**: Ranges from Norway and southern Iceland via the western side of Great Britain right down to the Cape of Good Hope. Also present through much of the Mediterranean Sea.
**Habitat**: Over the ocean.
**Food**: Small fish, crustaceans and squid.
**Size**: 18cm (7in), wingspan 43–48cm (17–19in).
**Nest**: Rocky crevice.
**Eggs**: 1, white.

## Leach's storm petrel

*Oceanodroma leucorhoa*

With an extensive distribution and a population comprised of more than 10 million individuals worldwide, Leach's storm petrel is regarded as a very common species. However, these birds are vulnerable to predators when breeding, even in the isolated locations that they frequent. Their relatively small size means they can suffer attacks by larger seabirds such as gulls, which prey especially on newly fledged chicks. Should they survive this critical early period of their development, the young Leach's storm petrels have a life expectancy of nearly a quarter of a century. Soon after the breeding period has ended, the North Atlantic population moves southwards for the duration of the winter, extending to the coast of South Africa with occasional reports also from the Indian Ocean. As with other storm petrels, they may follow pods of whales, feeding on the food churned up by these cetaceans, and also scavenging on their faeces.

**Identification:** Starling-sized, with brownish head and back. Rump is predominantly white, with a brown stripe running down its centre. Broad, forked tail feathers. Sexes are alike.

**Distribution**: Atlantic population extends from Norway south to both coasts of Great Britain, present in the North Sea and the Baltic Sea. Extends right down to the tip of Africa. There is also a separate, widespread population in the Pacific.
**Habitat**: Over the ocean.
**Food**: Mostly small fish, crustaceans and squid.
**Size**: 22cm (8½in), wingspan 43–48cm (17–19in).
**Nest**: Underground burrow or rocky crevice.
**Eggs**: 1, white.

# Gannet

Northern gannet *Morus bassana*

**Distribution:** Along the eastern seaboard of North America, extending across the Atlantic via southern Greenland and Iceland to eastern Scandinavia, and southwards through the Mediterranean and down the western coast of Africa.
**Habitat**: Sea.
**Food**: Fish.
**Size**: 88–100cm (34½–39½in), wingspan 180cm (71in).
**Nest**: Usually on a cliff, built from seaweed and other marine debris held together by droppings.
**Eggs**: 1, whitish.

The largest of all gannets, this species can weigh up to 3.6kg (8lb). It is the only member of this group found around the North Atlantic. These gannets are powerful in the air, and their keen eyesight allows them to detect shoals of fish such as herring and mackerel in the sea below. When feeding, gannets dive down into a shoal, often from a considerable height, seizing fish from under the water. Their streamlined shape also enables them to swim.

Breeding occurs in the spring, when the birds form large colonies in which there is often a lot of squabbling. Gannets start to arrive in Britain in January and migrate south in late summer. The biggest colony is at Bempton Cliffs in Yorkshire. They are also seen in Scotland and Wales.

**Identification:** A large bird with a pointed beak. Plumage is mainly white, pale yellow plumage on the head extends down the neck. Black flight feathers. Tail feathers are white, and the feet are dark grey. Sexes are alike. Young birds are dark brown in colour.

**Great skua** (*Catharacta skua*) 50cm (19½in), wingspan 124–140cm (49–55in). These large, powerfully built birds hover in an unusual way before touching down on the water. Predominantly brown with lighter streaking and barring. Strong hooked bill. Feeds on fish and carrion.

# Arctic skua

Parasitic jaeger *Stercorarius parasiticus*

Arctic skuas are very adept at stealing fish from other seabirds, preferring this method of feeding more than any related species. Yet they are also effective hunters, easily catching lemmings and other small rodents in their northern breeding grounds. Their diet alters dramatically through the year, and they will feed on insects and even berries during the brief Arctic summer. In the summer these birds are spotted in Shetland and Orkney, but they are best seen when migrating in the autumn off the coasts of north-west Scotland. Once the chicks have migrated southwards they may stay in the southern hemisphere for their first year. Unlike many seabirds, these skuas often migrate over land, possibly because they will stay close to the coasts on arrival, rather than ranging over the ocean.

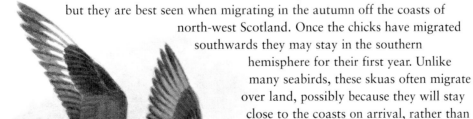

**Distribution**: Overwinters south of the equator, mainly on Africa's southern Atlantic seaboard but also on the south-eastern coast. Breeds in the far north of Europe, including parts of Scotland and Scandinavia.
**Habitat**: Open ocean.
**Food**: Fish and rodents.
**Size**: 44cm (17¼in), wingspan 110–125cm (43–49½in).
**Nest**: Scrape on the ground.
**Eggs**: 1–2, olive with dark spots.

**Identification:** Sleek, gull-like appearance with long, narrow tail extensions averaging nearly 9cm (3½in) in the summer. Dark crown, with brownish-grey wings and tail, and white underparts at this stage too. The dark colour morph displays no white plumage, while youngsters have a barred appearance. Sexes are alike. Young birds have blue legs.

# Manx shearwater

*Puffinus puffinus*

In March, large numbers of Manx shearwaters gather to breed in remote coastal areas, typically on islands through their range. Incubation is shared, with both members of a pair sitting individually for up to six days. The eggs hatch after a period of about eight weeks, and the young birds emerge from the nesting chamber at 11 weeks. They mature slowly, and may not start breeding themselves until they are about six years old. Despite their arduous migration they are long-lived birds, surviving for at least 30 years in the wild. While the majority of Manx shearwaters cross the Atlantic to overwinter off South America, a small number head directly south, being recorded along the coasts of Namibia and the Cape. In the British Isles they breed on offshore islands from January, then migrate to South America in July.

**Identification:** Long, straight wings with a stiff-winged flap then glide flight pattern. Sooty-black upperparts, with white plumage beneath, including the undertail coverts. Sexes are alike.

**Distribution**: Widely distributed from north of Norway and Iceland to the coast of northern Africa during the summer breeding period. Migrates south along the eastern seaboard of South America and across the Atlantic to South Africa.
**Habitat**: Over the ocean.
**Food**: Small fish, also squid.
**Size**: 35cm (14in), wingspan 76–89cm (30–35in).
**Nest**: Underground burrow.
**Eggs**: 1, white.

# Northern fulmar

*Fulmarus glacialis*

These birds are versatile feeders, tracking trawlers or congregating in large groups in the wake of boats. These seabirds will scoop up fish during the day and hunt squid at night, as these invertebrates rise up from the ocean depths. If necessary, they will dive into the water to catch food. They are also adept scavengers, feeding on the remains of whales and other marine mammals washed up on to beaches. They nest communally, usually on sheer cliff faces, where they can colonize inaccessible ledges. In some parts of their range they may even build nests inland on buildings, but they generally favour islands and other remote sites rather than the mainland. Northern fulmars are thought to have a life expectancy of around 34 years, but it may be more than a decade after fledging before the birds are ready to breed.

**Distribution**: Present in much of the Northern Hemisphere, in the Arctic region and much of the North Atlantic. Reaches the Iberian Peninsula at the most southerly tip of its range.
**Habitat**: Open ocean.
**Food**: Fish, squid and sometimes carrion.
**Size**: 50cm (19½in), wingspan 101–117cm (40–44in).
**Nest**: Bare cliff ledge.
**Eggs**: 1, white.

**Identification:** Varies in colour throughout its range, with both light and dark morphs: light form has a whitish head and underparts with grey above; dark morphs are greyish-brown overall. Sexes are alike, but males are larger.

# Yelkouan shearwater

*Puffinus yelkouan*

The Yelkouan shearwater was long considered a subspecies of the Manx shearwater, and the two do have a great many features in common. Physically, they are almost impossible to tell apart – their coloration and size are very similar, as are their movements in flight. The main difference between them is their calls: the call of the Yelkouan shearwater is much higher pitched and more drawn out than that of the Manx shearwater. Unfortunately for the average birdwatcher, the Yelkouan shearwater is usually silent at sea. During night-time around its breeding colonies, however, it is highly vocal.

The Yelkouan shearwater breeds around the central and eastern parts of the Mediterranean Sea. After breeding, the birds head out on to the water. Most spend the winter on the Mediterranean Sea itself, but a small number head out into the Atlantic. It is these birds which very occasionally make their way into British waters. As with other shearwaters during winter, this species is most likely to spotted with binoculars or a telescope from high headlands or from a boat out at sea.

**Identification**: This bird is normally seen in flight, when the blackish-brown upperparts contrast strongly with the white belly and undersides of the wings. Seen from below, the front and rear edges of the wings are brown. The feet are large and extend slightly beyond the tail in flight, which, from a distance, has the effect of making the tail appear longer than it actually is.

**Distribution**: This species breeds in the Mediterranean basin but is sometimes spotted off British shores, most often around the south-west of England.
**Habitat**: Open ocean.
**Food**: Fish and squid.
**Size**: Up to 38cm (15in), wingspan: 76–89cm (30–35in).
**Breeding**: Breeding begins in early spring. A single egg is laid, which hatches around seven weeks later. Like most other shearwaters, this species nests in burrows.
**Nest**: In burrows.
**Eggs**: 1, chalky white.

# Great shearwater

*Puffinus gravis*

The great shearwater is an uncommon visitor to British waters. It breeds during our winter (summer in the Southern Hemisphere) on Gough Island and Tristan da Cunha in the South Atlantic. Once breeding is over it heads across the Equator towards the coastal waters of eastern North America, with most individuals ending up off New England and Canada. Some, however, spend the non-breeding months farther out at sea and a small portion of these are very occasionally blown towards Britain by intense gales.

The great shearwater may be spotted from high cliffs along the shore but is more often seen from the decks of ships out at sea. The two white bands, one behind the head and the other at the base of the tail, are a clear distinguishing feature, making it relatively easy to identify in flight. Like other shearwaters it usually flies close to the surface, sometimes appearing to almost walk on the waves with its outstretched webbed feet. Birds in British waters may be seen on their own, but by nature the great shearwater is a sociable species. It often associates with gulls, sitting with them in rafts on the surface of the sea.

**Identification**: This bird is much larger and has a slower flapping flight than most shearwaters. Seen from above, the wings and back are pale brown and the tail and cap of the head are black, with a band of white separating them from the brown of the back. The bill is also black. From below, this bird appears largely white, with the wings edged in black. Again, the black tail and bill are clearly visible.

**Distribution**: Outside the breeding season, this species feeds in the North Atlantic. In Britain it is most often seen from July to September off south-west England and the north and west coasts of Scotland.
**Habitat**: Open ocean.
**Food**: Fish and squid.
**Size**: Up to 52cm (20in), wingspan: 105–122cm (41½–48in).
**Nest**: At the end of a small burrow or in the open on grass.
**Eggs**: 1, white.

# COASTAL AND ISLAND BIRDS

*Most seabirds are not brightly coloured, with white and black as well as hues of grey predominating in their plumage. They are often highly social, especially when breeding, nesting in large colonies on rocky stacks or inaccessible cliffs, which afford them some protection from predators. Food for their offspring is gathered often some distance from the nest site.*

## Guillemot

Common murre *Uria aalge*

**Distribution**: From north of Iceland and Scandinavia southwards to the Atlantic coast of the Iberian Peninsula, and west across the Atlantic to North America. Also present throughout the northern Pacific.
**Habitat**: Ocean and shore.
**Food**: Fish and invertebrates.
**Size**: 43cm (17in), wingspan 49–58cm (19¼–23in).
**Nest**: Cliff ledges.
**Eggs**: 1, bluish-green with dark spots.

The upright resting stance of the guillemot and its ability to hop, together with its black and white coloration and fish-eating habits, have led to these birds being described as the penguins of the north. However, unlike penguins they can fly. This enables them to reach their rocky and inhospitable nesting sites, where large numbers pack on to the cliff ledges to breed; as many as 20 breeding pairs can crowd in every 1m² (11 sq ft). The sheer density of numbers here offers protection against raiding gulls since there is little space for the predators to land, and they will be met with a fearsome barrier of sharp, pointed bills if they try to swoop down. Fall-offs in fish stocks can have an adverse effect on guillemot numbers, as will oil pollution.

**Identification:** Black head, neck and upperparts, with white edges to the wing coverts. Slight mottling on the flanks, otherwise underparts white. Throat and sides of the neck are white in non-breeding plumage. Sexes are alike. Dark sides to the neck in young birds.

## Black guillemot

*Cepphus grylle*

This bird of icy northern waters can also be seen as far south as Shetland and Orkney, and down the west coast of Scotland. Small numbers can also be found on the Cumbrian coast, along the northern Irish coast, and on the Isle of Man. They seek food on the sea floor, typically diving to depths of 20m (66ft). Pairs generally stay together, breeding each year in the same location. In the far north, colonies may consist of as many as 1,000 pairs, but elsewhere pairs may nest on their own. Both sexes share the incubation, which takes about 30 days. Fish is the preferred food for the chicks, which may be fed up to 15 times a day, though during the winter crustaceans feature more prominently in their diet. Black guillemots are common in their range: the Icelandic population is estimated at 50,000 pairs.

**Identification:** Jet black coloration, with prominent white patches on wings. Long, pointed black bill and red feet. In winter, has white underparts and white barring on the back, while retaining its black-and-white wing pattern. Young birds have darker upperparts, with spotting rather than barring on their wings in winter. Sexes are alike.

**Distribution**: Occurs from Iceland around the northern coast of Great Britain, although not typically encountered in the English Channel, via Scandinavia and the Baltic Sea up to the coast of Russia. Circumpolar range continues via Asia to North America.
**Habitat**: Sea and rocky cliffs.
**Food**: Fish and invertebrates.
**Size**: 32cm (12½in), wingspan 50–55cm (19½–21½in).
**Nest**: Scrape on cliff.
**Eggs**: 1–2, whitish-coloured with dark markings.

# Razorbill

*Alca torda*

The distinctive broad, flattened shape of the bill, resembling a cut-throat razor, explains the common name of these auks. They can often be observed swimming with their tails held vertically, rather than flat, enabling them to be distinguished from seabirds of similar size and coloration. Razorbills are adaptable feeders, and their diet varys according to location. Pairs display a strong bond and return to their traditional breeding sites, which may sometimes be no more than steep, inaccessible rocky stacks off the coast. They show no tendency to construct a nest of any kind, and the hen will lay her single egg on a narrow ledge directly above the ocean. The pear-like shape of the razorbill's egg helps to prevent it from rolling over the edge if accidentally dislodged. Even so, losses of eggs are fairly high, with predators such as gulls swooping down on unguarded sites. The bird breeds around the coast of Britain, with the largest colonies in northern Scotland, and none between the Humber river and the Isle of Wight. They only come to shore to breed.

**Identification:** Black upperparts, with white edging along the back of the wings and a vertical white stripe across the bill. Black coloration more strongly defined in breeding birds, with a white horizontal stripe reaching from the eyes to the bill. Sexes are alike. Young birds have smaller bills with no white markings.

**Distribution**: From north of Iceland and Scandinavia south to the Iberian Peninsula and northern Africa, extending into the eastern Mediterranean. Also present throughout the North Atlantic to the American coast.
**Habitat**: Ocean and shore.
**Food**: Fish and crustaceans.
**Size**: 39cm (15½in), wingspan 63–68cm (25–27in).
**Nest**: Cliff-face crevices.
**Eggs**: 1, whitish-coloured with brown spots.

# Puffin

*Fratercula arctica*

These auks occur throughout the northern Atlantic but breed south to the British Isles and the coast of France. They have unmistakable bills, rather akin to those of parrots. Young puffins have narrower and less brightly coloured bills than the adults. Puffins come ashore to nest in burrows on cliffs and coastal areas where they can breed largely hidden from predators. Sand eels figure prominently in their diet at this time, and adult birds often fly quite long distances to obtain food. When underwater, puffins use their wings like flippers, enabling them to swim faster. Adult birds fly back to their young with up to ten sand eels hanging in their bills at a time.

**Identification:** Whitish sides to the face. Black plumage extends back from the top of the bill over the crown and around to the neck. The back and wings are also black. Underparts are white, with a grey area on the flanks. Distinctive broad, flattened bill with a red area running down its length and across the tip. Greyish base with yellow area intervening. Bill is less brightly coloured and the sides of the face are greyish during the winter. Sexes are alike.

*Left: The puffin's bill varies depending on the bird's age and the time of year.*

**Distribution**: Throughout the northern Atlantic, including the west coast of Africa. Breeds south in Britain and northern Europe.
**Habitat**: Sea, coastal areas.
**Food**: Fish.
**Size**: 32cm (12½in), wingspan 50–60cm (19½–23in).
**Nest**: Underground burrow.
**Eggs**: 1, white.

*Right: Puffins excavate nesting tunnels underground or use existing holes.*

# Little auk

*Alle alle*

Despite its relatively restricted distribution, the little auk is considered to be one of the most numerous seabird species in the world. These birds form huge nesting colonies in the Arctic region during the brief summer, before heading south at the approach of winter as the sea begins to freeze. Little auks are often more likely to be spotted at this time of year, frequently flying very low over the waves or even through them on occasion. They have a distinctive flight with whirring, quick wingbeats. Sometimes, however, fierce storms make feeding virtually impossible, and in a weakened state little auks are driven into coastal areas, a phenomenon often described as a 'wreck'. Many starling-sized little auks are seen in the autumn off the east coasts of Scotland and England. In the winter they are spotted off the northerly coasts of the British Isles.

**Identification:** In summer plumage, the head and upper part of the chest are black. The back, wings and upper surface of the tail feathers are also black, aside from white streaks apparent over the wings. During the winter, the black on the face is broken by white, leaving a black band across the throat. The bill is small and black. Sexes are alike.

**Distribution**: Entire coastline of Greenland and Iceland to northern Scandinavia, across the North Sea to the coast of eastern England.
**Habitat**: Sea, coastal areas.
**Food**: Microscopic plankton.
**Size**: 20cm (8in), wingspan 34–38cm (13½–15in).
**Nest**: Cliff or crevice.
**Eggs**: 1, pale blue.

# Cormorant

Great cormorant *Phalacrocorax carbo*

This is the most common species, although there are disagreements about certain races. The isolated South African form *P. c. lucidus* ('white-breasted cormorant') is often regarded as a distinct species since it differs markedly in appearance, with a more extensive white throat extending on to the upper chest, and dark, greenish-black wing plumage. Cormorants can be seen in habitats ranging from the open sea to inland freshwater lakes, where they are the bane of fishermen, as the birds prey on boats' quarry, diving and chasing the fish underwater.

   Although they nest colonially in a wide variety of sites, it is not uncommon to see odd individuals perched on groynes and similar places. While human persecution and oil spillages represent dangers, these cormorants can have a life-expectancy approaching 20 years. Britain has ecologically important colonies of overwintering birds around the coast, in lagoons and even at inland gravel pits and reservoirs.

**Identification:** Predominantly black once full-grown adult, with a white throat area. A white patch is present at the top of each leg in birds in breeding condition. There are some regional variations. Bluish skin around the eyes. Bill is horn-coloured at its base and dark at the tip. Young birds are brownish with paler underparts. Sexes are alike.

**Distribution**: Scandinavia and the British Isles southwards via the Iberian Peninsula, through the Mediterranean, and on to north-western Africa. May occur in southern Africa. Range also extends to North America, southern Asia and Australia.
**Habitat**: Mainly coastal, sometimes inland.
**Food**: Largely fish.
**Size**: 94cm (37in), wingspan 121–160cm (47½–63in).
**Nest**: Made of seaweed and other flotsam.
**Eggs**: 3-4, chalky white.

# Common shag

Green cormorant *Phalacrocorax aristotelis*

These shorebirds range over a wide area, but in contrast to the more common cormorant they very rarely venture into reservoirs or other freshwater areas. They also shy away from artificial structures such as harbour piers, roosting instead on cliffs and rocky stacks. Young birds may disperse far from where they hatched, especially those of the more northerly populations, but are likely to return in due course to breed in the same area. However, younger birds command only the less favourable sites, often around the perimeter of the nesting colony. The common shag's breeding season varies according to latitude, typically not commencing until March in the far north of its range, by which time the northern African population will have almost ceased nesting. The number and size of colonies fluctuates quite significantly, depending on the availability of food. Common shags catch fish underwater, diving to pursue their quarry, but unlike some cormorants never appear to hunt co-operatively.

**Identification:** Black with a slight greenish suffusion to the plumage, and an upturned crest on the head. Iris is blue. The bill is dark grey with a bare yellowish area of skin at its base. Legs dark grey. Non-breeding adults lose their crest and display mottled brown coloration on the throat. Young birds are entirely brown. Sexes are alike.

**Distribution**: Ranges around much of coastal Iceland and the north Scandinavian coast, south around the British Isles and the North Sea, around coastal Europe and through the Mediterranean to the Black Sea and north Africa.
**Habitat**: Coastal areas.
**Food**: Mainly fish.
**Size**: 80cm (31½in), wingspan 95–110cm (38–43in).
**Nest**: Made of seaweed with a grass lining.
**Eggs**: 3–5, a chalky, bluish-white colour.

# King eider

*Somateria spectabilis*

Like most birds from the far north, the king eider has a circumpolar distribution that reaches right around the top of the globe. Seasonal movements of these sea ducks tend to be more widespread than in other eiders. They are remarkably common, with the North American population estimated at two million individuals. Huge groups of up to 100,000 birds congregate when moulting, although for the breeding season they split up and pairs nest individually across the Arctic tundra. The king eider breeds along the north-eastern Arctic coasts of Europe, North America and Asia, and is spotted off the north-eastern coast of Scotland. King eiders are very powerful swimmers and generally dive to obtain their food. They are smaller than the British common eider duck.

**Identification:** Drakes in breeding condition have an orange area edged with black above a reddish bill. Light grey head plumage extends down the neck. Chest is pale pinkish-white, with black wings and underparts. Ducks are mainly a speckled shade of brown, with the pale underside of their wings visible in flight. In eclipse plumage, drakes are a darker shade of brown, with an orangish-yellow bill and white plumage on the back.

**Distribution**: From the coast of Iceland westwards around the British Isles and along northern Scandinavia. Also present in northern latitudes of eastern Asia and on both coasts of North America, as well as Greenland.
**Habitat**: Tundra and ocean.
**Food**: Mainly crustaceans and marine invertebrates.
**Size**: 63cm (25in), wingspan 90–94cm (35½–37in).
**Nest**: Hollow on the ground lined with down.
**Eggs**: 4–7, olive-buff.

## Common eider

*Somateria mollissima*

This is the most common European sea duck. Eiders are seen off the Northumberland coast up to the west coast of Scotland, off the Yorkshire coast and off Cornwall and Wales. Belfast Lough is a stronghold. Common eiders occur in large flocks and nest in colonies on islands, where they are safe from predators. The start of the breeding period depends on latitude, often not commencing until June in the far north. The nest is lined with their dense down, which safeguards the eggs from being chilled. While the ducks are incubating, drakes congregate to moult out of their breeding plumage. Outside the nesting period, common eiders are most likely to be observed close to shore. They do not generally migrate far, although ducks and young birds disperse farther than drakes. They usually forage for food underwater.

**Distribution**: Northern and north-western parts of Europe extending to Siberia. Also from eastern Asia to both Pacific and Atlantic coasts of North America.
**Habitat**: Coastal areas.
**Food**: Mainly invertebrates.
**Size**: 70cm (27in), wingspan 90–106cm (35½–42in).
**Nest**: Hollow on the ground lined with down.
**Eggs**: 1–8, yellowish-olive.

**Identification:** Drake in colour has a black cap to the head, with black underparts and flight feathers. Rest of the body is white, and the bill is greyish. Out of colour, drakes are blackish-brown, lacking the barring seen in ducks, and have white upperwing coverts. Ducks are predominantly a combination of black and brown in colour, with a dark bill and legs.

## Long-tailed duck

Oldsquaw *Clangula hyemalis*

These sea ducks often congregate in large numbers, although in winter females and young birds tend to migrate farther south in flocks than do adult drakes. They spend most of their time on the water, obtaining food by diving under the waves. They come ashore to nest on the tundra, where the ducks lay their eggs directly on to the ground under cover. The drakes soon return to the ocean to moult. When migrating, oldsquaws fly low in lines, rather than in any more organized formation. The long-tailed duck is a winter visitor to the British Isles, generally seen in migratory passage from Northumberland up to northern Scotland.

**Distribution**: Circumpolar, breeding in northern Europe and the Arctic. Winters farther south.
**Habitat**: Coasts and bays.
**Food**: Mainly crustaceans and marine invertebrates.
**Size**: 47cm (18½in), wingspan 65–80cm (25½–31½in).
**Nest**: Hidden in vegetation or under a rock.
**Eggs**: 5–7, olive-buff.

**Identification:** Black head, neck and chest, with white around the eyes and white underparts. Head becomes white across the top outside the breeding season, with patches of black evident on the sides. Grey rather than brown predominates on the wings. Long tail plumes present throughout the year. The smaller ducks undergo a similar change in appearance, with the sides of the face becoming white rather than black.

# Brent goose

Brant goose *Branta bernicla*

Brent geese start breeding in June. A site close to the tundra shoreline is favoured, with pairs lining the scrape with plant matter and down. It takes nine weeks from egg-laying to the young geese leaving the nest, after which they head south with their parents. Goslings may not breed until they are three years old. On the tundra, brent geese graze on lichens, moss and other terrestrial vegetation, while in winter they feed mainly on aquatic plants like seaweed, which is plucked from under the water as the geese up-end their bodies. On land, they graze by nibbling the shoots of plants. From October to March, brent geese can be seen on British estuaries and saltmarshes, particularly the Wash, North Norfolk, the Thames estuary and in the harbours of Chichester and Langshore. Populations are also seen in Northern Ireland and on Lindisfarne.

**Distribution**: Breeds in the Arctic, overwintering in Ireland and parts of north-western Europe. Other populations overwinter in eastern Asia and along both coasts of North America.
**Habitat**: Bays and estuaries.
**Food**: Plant matter.
**Size**: 66cm (26in), wingspan 110–120cm (43–47in).
**Nest**: Scrape on the ground.
**Eggs**: 1–10, whitish.

**Identification:** Black head and neck, with trace of white on lower neck. Wings are grey-black. Flanks are white, with barring. Abdomen is white in the American brant (*B. b. hrota*) from the east, but often dark in its western relative, the black brant (*B. b. nigricans*). Sexes are alike. The young geese may lack white neck patches.

# Barnacle goose

*Branta leucopsis*

Every October, more than 65,000 barnacle geese fly in from their summer breeding grounds in Svalbard and Greenland to spend the winter in Scotland, Ireland or the Solway Firth. These beautiful birds migrate here to avoid the Arctic snows and feed through the winter in their large flocks before finally returning in the spring. In medieval times, the appearance of barnacle geese in autumn was a mystery no one understood. It was then believed that these birds developed from goose barnacles, creatures we now know to be crustaceans. The goose barnacle bears a vague resemblance to the head of a barnacle goose and it was thought that the birds – which had never been seen nesting – grew from them and emerged fully feathered before flying to shore.

Today, through radio tracking and other scientific methods, we know the true story of the barnacle goose to be almost as remarkable. Those which winter in Ireland fly across the North Atlantic to get there, while those seen in the Solway Firth arrive from Svalbard, having nested not much more than 1,000km from the actual North Pole. During their migrations barnacle geese can reach great speeds. In 2007, one goose travelling from Svalbard and carrying a satellite transmitter clocked up 127km h (78mph), with the help of a 60km h (37mph) tail wind.

**Distribution**: This species can be seen from October to March in the north-west of Scotland, Northern Ireland and around the Solway Firth. Also through much of Northern and eastern Europe.
**Habitat**: Estuaries, marshes and fields.
**Food**: Plant matter.
**Size**: Up to 63cm (25in), wingspan up to 137cm (54in).
**Nest**: Inland cliff edge.
**Eggs**: 4–5, white.

**Identification**: As British geese go, the barnacle goose is quite small – somewhere between a greylag or Canada goose and a duck in size. The creamy white face and black neck make it unmistakable, however. The belly is white, the back barred with blue and grey stripes and the tail black. In flight, it often forms long lines, with individuals within these constantly communicating with a chorus of loud yapping or barking sounds.

# WADERS

*Wading birds generally are tall, sleek birds with long beaks which they use to hunt in shallow waters. Some wading birds undertake regular migrations from Europe to Africa, usually following the land rather than flying across the ocean. Others, referred to as vagrants, occasionally crop up unexpectedly, typically having crossed the Atlantic from North America, perhaps having been blown off course.*

## Red-necked phalarope

Northern phalarope *Phalaropus lobatus*

**Distribution**: Circumpolar, breeding throughout the Arctic, with the European population overwintering in the Arabian Sea region.
**Habitat**: Tundra and shore.
**Food**: Mostly plankton and invertebrates.
**Size**: 20cm (8in), wingspan 31–36cm (12¼–14¼in).
**Nest**: Scrape on the ground.
**Eggs**: 3-4, buff-coloured with brown spots.

These long-distance migrants fly north to breed in the Arctic region from late May onwards, frequently choosing sites well away from the coast. The ground here is boggy at this time of year, since only the top layer of soil thaws out and the meltwater is unable to drain away. Insects provide a ready source of food for the phalaropes on which they can rear their chicks. Unusually, both incubation and rearing are undertaken by the male alone. Having laid their eggs, the hens depart the breeding grounds soon afterwards, followed by the males about a month later, once the chicks are independent. The young will be the last to leave. Red-necked phalaropes head south across Europe to their wintering grounds, breaking their journey by stopping off in Kazakhstan and around the Caspian Sea, where they can be observed feeding on lakes, before flying on through the Gulf of Oman to the Arabian Sea. Small numbers breed on the Western and Northern Isles of Scotland from May to June.

**Identification**: Cocks duller than hens, with reduced chestnut-orange to the chest and whiter throat. Underparts whitish, grey barring on the flanks. Dark wings (less streaked in cocks). Long, pointed bill. Blackish legs and feet. Young birds have brown rather than black crowns.

## Curlew

Eurasian curlew *Numenius arquata*

The distinctive call-note of the curlew, which gives rise to its name, is audible from some distance away. This wader's large size and its long, narrow bill also help to distinguish it from other shorebirds, and its legs are so long that the toes protrude beyond the tip of the tail in flight. Curlews are most likely to be seen in coastal areas outside the breeding season, where they feed by probing in the sand with their bills. They return to the same wintering grounds each year, and can live for more than 30 years. They are seen all around the UK, especially in estuaries.

**Distribution**: Present throughout the year in the British Isles and adjacent areas of northern Europe. Breeds widely elsewhere in Europe and Asia, migrating south in winter.
**Habitat**: Marshland, moorland and coastal areas.
**Food**: Omnivorous.
**Size**: 57cm (22½in), wingspan 78–88cm (31–34½in).
**Nest**: Scrape on the ground concealed by vegetation.
**Eggs**: 4, greenish-brown with darker spots.

**Identification**: Streaked plumage, with lighter ground colour on the throat and buff chest. Larger dark patterning on the wings. Underparts and rump are white. Cocks have plain-coloured heads, but hens' heads usually show a trace of a white stripe running down over the crown. Hens are also distinguished by their longer bills, which can be up to 15cm (6in) in length. When not breeding, the curlew has grey rather than buff plumage.

# Ringed plover

Greater ringed plover *Charadrius hiaticula*

In spite of their relatively small size, these waders have strong migratory instincts. They are most likely to be seen in Europe during May, en route to their breeding grounds in the far north, and then again from the middle of August for about a month, before finally leaving European shores to make their way south to Africa for the winter. Ringed plovers typically breed on beaches and on the tundra, the mottled appearance of their eggs and the absence of an elaborate nest providing camouflage. They can be seen in large flocks outside the nesting season, often seeking food in tidal areas. Many UK birds are resident all year round, while European birds winter here and those from Greenland and Canada pass through on migration.

**Identification:** Black mask extends over the forehead and down across the eyes. There is a white patch above the bill and just behind the eyes. A broad black band extends across the chest. The underparts are otherwise white. The wings are greyish-brown and the bill is orange with a black tip. In winter plumage the black areas are reduced, apart from the bill, which becomes entirely blackish. White areas extend from the forehead to above the eyes. Cheek patches are greyish-brown, and there is a similar band on the upper chest. Sexes are alike.

**Distribution**: Along most of western and northern coastal Europe, and North America. Winters around continental Africa. Also recorded in Asia.
**Habitat**: Coasts and tundra.
**Food**: Freshwater and marine invertebrates.
**Size**: 19cm (7½in), wingspan 35–40cm (14–16in).
**Nest**: Scrape on the ground.
**Eggs**: 4, stone-buff with black markings.

**Lesser yellowlegs** (*Tringa flavipes*) 27cm (10½in), wingspan 58–64cm (23–25¼in). Typically breeds in the far north of North America, wintering in Florida and farther south in Central America, but vagrants are recorded annually off the British Isles. Narrow black bill, with dark streaking on the chest and white underparts. The back and wings are mottled and the flight feathers are dark. Characteristic yellow legs. Young birds have buff spotting on brown upperparts. Sexes are alike.

**Greater yellowlegs** (*Tringa melanoleuca*) 36cm (14in), wingspan 58–64cm (23–25¼in). Another northern American vagrant sighted around the British Isles, usually during the winter. Larger than the lesser yellowlegs, with a longer, darker bill that curves slightly upwards towards its tip. More barring also evident on the underparts in breeding plumage. Young birds have darker backs. Sexes are alike.

# Whimbrel

*Numenius phaeopus*

The whimbrel is larger than most waders. Although it may probe for food, it often snatches crabs scampering across the sand. In their tundra nesting grounds whimbrels have a more varied diet, eating berries and insects too. Both adults help to incubate and raise the young. They begin their migration journey south in July, when they can often be seen flying over land, seeking out inland grassy areas, such as golf courses, in search of food. Unusually, some whimbrels may avoid land, flying directly from Iceland to Africa over the Atlantic Ocean. It is not uncommon for young birds to remain here for their first year, before returning north again. The whimbrel is increasingly breeding in Shetland and Orkney.

**Distribution**: Breeds in Iceland, Scandinavia and Scotland. Overwinters from western Mediterranean and around the coast of Africa, including Madagascar, and islands in the Indian Ocean.
**Habitat**: Tundra and shore.
**Food**: Mostly invertebrates and berries.
**Size**: 45cm (18in), wingspan 76–84cm (30–33in).
**Nest**: Grass-lined scrape.
**Eggs**: 4, olive-coloured with dark blotches.

**Identification:** Brown crown with lighter central stripe. Fainter brown line through eyes. Brown streaks on silvery background on rest of body. Back and wings darker brown. Long, down-curving bill. Sexes are alike. Young have a shorter, straighter bill.

## Oystercatcher

*Haematopus ostralegus*

Their large size and noisy nature ensure these waders are quite conspicuous. The oystercatcher's powerful bill is a surprisingly adaptable tool, enabling the birds not only to force mussel shells apart but also to hammer limpets off groynes and even prey on crabs. When feeding inland, the oystercatchers use their bills to catch earthworms in the soil without any difficulty. Individuals will defend favoured feeding sites such as mussel beds from others of their own kind, although they sometimes form large flocks numbering thousands of birds, especially during the winter.

**Identification:** Head, upper chest and wings are black. Underparts are white. There is a white stripe on the wings. It has a straight orangish-red bill, which may be shorter and thicker in cock birds. Legs are reddish. In winter plumage, adults have a white throat and collar, and pale pink legs.

**Distribution**: Shores of Europe, especially Great Britain, extending to Asia and down the north-western and Red Sea coasts of Africa.
**Habitat**: Tidal mudflats, sometimes in fields.
**Food**: Cockles, mussels and similar prey.
**Size**: 44cm (17¼in), wingspan 76–89cm (30–35in).
**Nest**: Scrape on the ground.
**Eggs**: 2–4, light buff with blackish-brown markings.

---

**Purple sandpiper** (*Calidris maritima*) 22cm (8½in), wingspan 42–46cm (16½–18¼in). This bird winters around the British Isles. It has a whitish stripe above each eye, with a dark brown area behind; chestnut and brown markings on the dark wings; brown streaking down the neck and over the underparts; down-curving, dark bill and yellowish legs. Young birds have brownish-grey breast with spots. In non-breeding, there is a purplish blush over the back. Hens are larger.

**Stone curlew** (*Burhinus oedicnemus*) 42cm (16½in), wingspan 80cm (31½in). *Oedicnemus* derives from the Greek for 'swollen-shinned', and this bird is also known as 'thick knees' due to its large heavy-looking legs. It has adapted to a relatively dry environment, and its mottled plumage enables it to blend in well against a stony background. When frightened, it drops to the ground in an attempt to hide. These birds are more active after dark. However, their call-notes, which sound rather like 'curlee', are audible over distances of 2.5km (1.5 miles) when the surroundings are quiet.

**Common redshank** (*Tringa totanus*) 27cm (10½in), wingspan 58–67cm (23–26in). The redshank has a greyish head and wings, with striations and mottling on the chest, back and wings and a white area in front of each eye. The bill is red with a dark tip; legs are bright red. Young birds have yellow-orange legs and feet.

**Turnstone** (*Arenaria interpres*) 23cm (9in), wingspan 54cm (21in). Similar to the redshank but smaller, more chestnut coloured on their back with white underparts. Legs are orange.

## Avocet

Pied avocet *Recurvirostra avosetta*

The unique shape of the avocet's long, thin, upward-curving bill enables these birds to feed by sweeping the bill from side to side in the water, locating their prey predominantly by touch. Pairs can display very aggressive behaviour when breeding, and in some areas may gather in very large numbers, nesting at high densities. Although they usually move about by wading, avocets can swim well and will place their heads underwater when seeking food. On migration, avocets fly quite low in loose lines.

The avocet is one of the Royal Society for the Protection of Birds' most successful conservation stories.

**Distribution**: Europe (except in the far north) and northern Africa, often close to the coast. Extends into western Asia. Some winter in Africa.
**Habitat**: Mostly lagoons and mudflats.
**Food**: Small crustaceans and other invertebrates.
**Size**: 46cm (18¼in), wingspan 78cm (31in).
**Nest**: Scrape on the ground lined with vegetation.
**Eggs**: 4, pale brown with faint markings.

**Identification:** Slender, with long, pale blue legs. White overall, with black plumage on the top of the head extending down the neck. Black stripes over the shoulder area and the sides of the wings. Flight feathers are black. Long, thin black bill curves upwards at the tip. Hens often have shorter bills and a brownish tinge to their black markings.

# Black-tailed godwit

*Limosa limosa*

This bird is wide-ranging and spends the winter in places as far flung as Australia, western Europe and West Africa, and breeds from Asiatic Russia to central Europe and central Asia. Its breeding grounds are typically boggy grassland, and it is more likely to be found on freshwater than the bar-tailed godwit. Egg-laying begins in April, with pairs returning to the same nesting sites, which are out in the open rather than concealed in tall grass. The adults share incubation, which lasts about three weeks, but the chicks are largely brooded by the female. They fledge within five weeks, after which the godwits migrate to their winter quarters, where the young may remain until their second year. Black-tailed godwits can adapt to habitat change, and in the 20th century returned to breed in Britain, where they were formerly extinct. When feeding in water they may vibrate their feet to disturb aquatic invertebrates, including larvae, and in muddy water snails may be found by touch. In Africa they often feed mainly on vegetation.

**Distribution**: Breeding range extends from Iceland and southern Scandinavia through much of western and central Europe into Asia. Western population overwinters in parts of the British Isles and the Iberian Peninsula. Others move further south into Africa, Asia and Australia.
**Habitat**: Coast and marshes.
**Food**: Mainly invertebrates.
**Size**: 44cm (17¼in), wingspan 70–80cm (27–31½in).
**Nest**: Pad of vegetation.
**Eggs**: 3–5, greenish-brown with dark blotches.

**Identification:** Dark stripe runs through each eye, with a white streak above. Pale sides to the face. Chestnut on the neck and upper breast, becoming mottled with black streaks on the lower chest. Underparts white, but some regional variation. Wings brownish-grey with individual blackish markings. Long, narrow bill, pinkish at the base and dark at the tip. Legs are black. Chestnut is missing from both sexes in non-breeding plumage. Young birds have no barring across their underparts. Hens are less brightly coloured than cocks.

# Bar-tailed godwit

*Limosa lapponica*

These godwits fly long distances to and from their breeding grounds. Studies have shown that birds observed in western Europe during the winter are most likely to have come from as far east as the Yamal peninsula. Those overwintering in southern Africa will have originated from farther into Asia, their journey entailing crossing the Caspian sea. It is estimated that nearly three-quarters of a million bar-tailed godwits undertake this annual journey to Africa, after the end of the breeding season in late July or August.

It is possible to gain an insight into the gender of individual birds by watching a flock feeding on an outgoing tide, as hens, with their longer bills, are better equipped to feed in deeper water. The godwits favour estuarine rather than freshwater areas. Young birds remain on the wintering grounds for their first year, while the adult birds head back north again in May. They pass through the UK, or stop for winter in the eastern estuaries.

**Distribution**: Scandinavia and northern Asia to Alaska. Winters in British Isles and western Europe to Africa.
**Habitat**: Tundra and coasts.
**Food**: Mainly invertebrates.
**Size**: 16cm (6¼in), wingspan 70–80cm (27–31½in).
**Nest**: Lined scrape.
**Eggs**: 2–5, greenish-brown with dark blotches.

**Identification:** Chestnut. Back has shades of brown with pale edging. Dark stripe runs through each eye; crown is dark. Long, up-curved bill, paler at base. Legs and feet grey. Hens have whitish underparts, with fine brownish striations on chest and flanks. Both have barred tail and greyer underparts in non-breeding. Females are larger. Young have buff neck and upper breast.

# DUCKS, SWANS AND GEESE

*Waterfowl are generally conspicuous birds on water, but their appearance and distribution can differ markedly through the year. Drakes often resemble hens outside the breeding season, when their plumage is much plainer. Some species are migratory, heading south to escape freezing conditions, while others are to be found on stretches of water that may at times be covered in ice.*

## Mallard

*Anas platyrhynchos*

**Distribution**: Throughout the northern hemisphere, resident through western Europe. Also occurs in north Africa.
**Habitat**: Open areas of water.
**Food:** Mostly plant matter, but some invertebrates.
**Size**: 60cm (23in), wingspan 80–97cm (31½–38½in).
**Nest**: Usually a scrape lined with down feathers.
**Eggs**: 7–16, buff to greyish-green in colour.

These ducks are a common sight, even on stretches of water in towns and cities, such as rivers and canals. They may congregate in quite large flocks, especially outside the breeding season, but they are most evident in the spring, when groups of unpaired males chase potential mates. The nest is often constructed close to water and is frequently hidden under vegetation, especially in urban areas. These birds feed both on water, upending themselves or dabbling at the surface, and on land.

**Identification:** Metallic green head with a white ring around the neck. Chest is brownish, underparts are grey, and a blackish area surrounds the vent. Bluish speculum in the wing, most evident in flight, bordered by black-and-white stripes. Hen is brownish-buff overall with darker patterning, and displays the same wing markings as drake. Hen's bill is orange, whereas that of male in eclipse plumage (outside the breeding season) is yellow, with a rufous tinge to the breast.

## Teal

*Anas crecca*

The teal is both a British resident and a winter visitor. Small numbers (1,600–2,800 pairs) nest in the north-west of Scotland every year, with the female making a shallow nest, lined with dried leaves and down plucked from her own breast. Far larger flocks arrive in the autumn from the Baltic region and north-west Europe and Siberia. Britain's winter population is mainly found on the Mersey estuary and Somerset Levels.

The male teal's courtship display is something to behold. After dipping the tip of his bill beneath the water, the drake whistles, then arches his back and tips back his head, while simultaneously raising his wings over his back and cocking his tail.

**Identification**: The male has a chestnut-coloured head with broad green eye patches. His flanks are grey, his chest spotted and his tail yellow, edged with black. As with most ducks, the female is duller, being a plain mottled brown. Both sexes have distinctive bright green wing patches, which can be used to distinguish them from other ducks in flight.

**Distribution**: This species is found throughout the British Isles. Also across northern Europe, migrating to southern Europe and Africa for the winter.
**Habitat**: Ponds, lakes and coastal bays.
**Food**: Plant matter and aquatic invertebrates.
**Size**: Up to 38cm (15in), wingspan 52–58cm (20–23in).
**Nest**: Built on dry ground, usually in an upland area.
**Eggs**: 8–10, pale buff, sometimes with a greenish tinge.

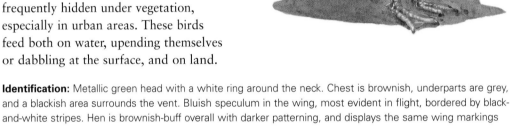

# Shoveler

Northern shoveler *Anas clypeata*

The broad bills of these waterfowl enable them to feed more easily in shallow water. They typically swim with their bill open, trailing it through the water to catch invertebrates, although they also forage both by upending and catching insects on reeds. Shovelers choose wet ground, often some distance from open water, as a nesting site, where the female retreats from the attention of other drakes. Like the young of other waterfowl, young shovelers take to the water soon after hatching.

**Identification:** Dark metallic green head and orange eyes. White chest and chestnut-brown flanks and belly, with a black area around the tail. Both back and wings are black and white. The remainder of the body is predominantly white. Broad blue wing stripe, which enables drakes to be recognized even in eclipse plumage, when they resemble hens. Very broad black bill. Hens are predominantly brownish but have darker blotching, yellowish edges to the bill and paler area of plumage on the sides of the tail feathers.

**Distribution**: Widely distributed throughout the northern hemisphere, overwintering as far south as central Africa.
**Habitat**: Shallow coastal and freshwater areas.
**Food**: Aquatic invertebrates and plant matter.
**Size**: 52cm (20in), wingspan 70–84cm (27–33in).
**Nest**: Down-lined scrape.
**Eggs**: 8–12, green to buff-white in colour.

**Garganey** (*Anas querquedula*) 41cm (16¼in), wingspan 63–68cm (25–27in). Ranges from England and France eastwards across Europe, overwintering south of the Sahara. Present in Asia. Prominent white stripe from the eyes down along the neck. Remainder of the face and breast area are brown with black barring. Greyish area on the body. Wings are greyish-black. Brown mottling over the hindquarters. Hens have mottled plumage with a distinctive buff-white area under the chin. Drakes in eclipse plumage resemble hens but with grey areas on the wings.

**Ferruginous duck** (*Aythya nyroca*) 42cm (16½in), wingspan 76–89cm (30–35in). Occurs throughout much of eastern Europe and into Asia, overwintering around the Mediterranean and farther south in Africa, as well as in parts of South-east Asia. Chestnut plumage, lighter on the flanks than the back, with white eyes. Very obvious white wing stripe. Whitish belly, underwing and undertail area. Greyish bill, black at the tip. Hens have a pale band across the bill and brown eyes (which distinguishes them from drakes in eclipse plumage).

**Pintail** (northern pintail, *Anas acuta*) 62cm (24½in), wingspan 90cm (35½in). Found throughout the Northern Hemisphere, the pintail migrates south for the winter to central Africa. It has a long, narrow black tail. The head is blackish, with white stripes on the neck down to the breast and underparts. It has grey flanks, while the wings are greyish with prominent wing stripes. Hens are brown, with darker patterning on the plumage and a long, pointed tail with a white edge to the wings in flight.

# Pochard

*Aythya ferina*

These ducks are most likely to be found on open water, where they can often be seen diving for food. Islands are favoured as breeding grounds since they provide relatively secure nesting sites, particularly where there is overhanging vegetation. Pairs will stay together for the duration of the nesting period. Subsequently the pochards form large flocks, sometimes moving away from the lakes and other still-water areas to nearby rivers, especially in winter when ice is likely to form on the water's surface. In Britain, the pochard is most likely to be seen on open lakes and gravel pits in lowland areas of eastern England and Scotland. The birds that breed here will often disperse to Europe in the winter.

**Distribution**: Resident in parts of western Europe, extending eastwards into Asia. Overwinters farther south, in parts of western and central Africa.
**Habitat**: Marshland, lakes.
**Food**: Aquatic creatures and plant matter.
**Size**: 49cm (19¼in), wingspan 70–80cm (27–31½in).
**Nest**: Under cover, lined with down feathers.
**Eggs**: 6–14, greenish-grey.

**Identification:** Chestnut-brown head and neck, with black chest and a broad grey band encircling the wings and body. Black feathering surrounds the hindquarters. Eyes are reddish. Black is replaced by a greyish tone in eclipse plumage. Hens are significantly duller in coloration, having a brownish head with buff areas and a noticeable stripe extending back from the eyes. Brown also replaces the drake's black plumage.

## Goosander

Common merganser *Mergus merganser*

Like many waterfowl of the far north, the goosander occurs at similar latitudes in Europe and Asia. Diving rather than dabbling ducks, they are also called sawbills because of the small, sharp projections running down the sides of their bills, which help them to grab fish more easily. Seen in wooded areas close to water, pairs will nest in a hollow tree or even a nest box, lining it with down to insulate the eggs and prevent them rolling around. Outside the breeding period, goosanders form large flocks numbering thousands of birds on lakes and similar stretches of fresh water. They may, however, prefer to fish in nearby rivers, returning to the lake at dusk. Goosanders tend to remain in their nesting location until the water starts to freeze over, whereupon they head south. They pair up mainly over winter, returning north to breed the following spring.

**Distribution**: Ranges from Iceland and Scandinavia south through northern Europe, including the British Isles, but does not extend to the Iberian Peninsula.
**Habitat**: Lakes and rivers.
**Food**: Predominantly fish.
**Size**: 64cm (25¼in), wingspan 78–94cm (31–37in).
**Nest**: Hole in a tree.
**Eggs**: 6–17, ivory or pale buff in colour.

**Identification:** Narrow body. Drake has dark green head and neck, with green on the primary flight feathers. Underparts white, back is greyish. Ducks have chestnut-brown head and white under the throat. Bill and legs red. Drakes in eclipse plumage have a white front to the wings.

## Canada goose

*Branta canadensis*

There are a number of different races of Canada goose which all vary in plumage and size. This species has proved to be highly adaptable. Its numbers have grown considerably in Europe, especially in farming areas, where the geese descend in flocks to feed on crops during the winter once other food has become more scarce. When migrating, flocks fly in a clear V-shaped formation. In common with many waterfowl, Canada geese are not able to fly when moulting, but they will readily take to the water at this time and can dive if necessary to escape danger. These geese prefer to graze on land, returning to the relative safety of the water during the hours of darkness.

Canada geese are now widely viewed as a pest because they are so widespread and can be noisy and confrontational, as well as scaring away other species. They were first introduced to Britain in the late 17th century as an addition to King James II's waterfowl collection in St James' Park in London.

**Identification:** Distinctive black head and neck. A small area of white plumage runs in a stripe from behind the eyes to under the throat. A whitish area of feathering at the base of the neck merges into brown on the chest. The wings are dark brown and there is white on the abdomen. The legs and feet are blackish. Sexes are alike.

**Distribution**: Present in the British Isles and southern Scandinavia, and other parts of north-western Europe. Also throughout the far north of North America, wintering in the southern USA.
**Habitat**: Very variable, but usually near water.
**Food**: Vegetation.
**Size**: 55–110cm (22–43in), wingspan 127–173cm (50–68in).
**Nest**: Made from vegetation, on the ground.
**Eggs**: 4–7, whitish.

## Snow goose

*Anser caerulescens*

Although considered a vagrant rather than a regular visitor to north-western parts of Europe, snow geese are a relatively common sight in some areas during the winter months. They are especially attracted to farmland, where grazing opportunities are plentiful, and this appears to be helping the birds to extend their range. As with all waterfowl, however, there is always the possibility that sightings of snow geese are in fact escapees from waterfowl collections rather than wild individuals. The calls of snow geese have been likened to the bark of a dog.

*Above: There are three types of snow goose, one of which is actually a dark, grey-coloured bird known as the blue snow goose. Blue snow geese are much less common than their white counterparts.*

**Identification:** Blue-phase birds (above) are dark and blackish, with white heads and white borders to some wing feathers. Young birds of this colour phase have dark heads. White-phase birds (left) are almost entirely white, with dark primary wing feathers. Young of this colour phase have greyish markings on their heads. Sexes are alike.

**Distribution:** The far north of North America, Greenland and north-eastern Siberia. Frequently overwinters in Great Britain and nearby coastal areas of north-western Europe.
**Habitat:** Tundra and coastal lowland agricultural areas.
**Food:** Vegetation.
**Size:** 84cm (33in), wingspan 137–170cm (54–67in).
**Nest:** Depression on the ground lined with vegetation.
**Eggs:** 4–10, whitish.

## Mute swan

*Cygnus olor*

These graceful birds can be seen in a wide range of habitats and may occasionally even venture out on to the sea, although they will not stray very far from the shore. They prefer to feed on aquatic vegetation, but can sometimes be found grazing on short grass. In town and city parks, mute swans often eat a greater variety of foods, such as grain and bread provided for them by people. They rarely dive, but instead use their long necks to dabble under the surface of the water to obtain food. Pairs are very territorial when breeding and the male swan, known as a cob, will actively try to drive away people with fierce movements of its wings if they venture too close.

**Identification:** Mainly white, with a black area extending from the eyes to the base of the orange bill. A swollen knob protrudes over the upper part of the bill. The legs and feet are blackish. Hens are smaller with a smaller knob on the bill. Young birds are browner.

**Distribution:** Resident throughout the British Isles and adjacent areas of western Europe, often living in a semi-domesticated state. Also occurs in the north-west Black Sea area and in parts of Asia. Localized introduced populations also found in other areas including South Africa, the eastern USA, Australia and New Zealand.
**Habitat:** Larger stretches of fresh water and estuaries.
**Food:** Mainly vegetation.
**Size:** 160cm (63in), wingspan 200–240cm (79–94½in).
**Nest:** Large pile of heaped-up aquatic vegetation.
**Eggs:** 5–7, pale green.

# Whooper swan

*Cygnus cygnus*

Although some Icelandic whooper swans are sedentary throughout the year, the majority of these birds undertake regular migrations, so they are likely to be observed in southern Europe only during the winter months. At this time they often frequent areas around inland waterways, such as the Black and Caspian seas. Pairs nest on their own, and the young chicks fly alongside their parents on the journey south. In the winter, whooper swans may sometimes invade agricultural areas, where they eat a range of foods varying from potatoes to acorns, although generally they prefer to feed on aquatic vegetation.

**Identification:** Body plumage is white, although sometimes it may be stained. The base of the bill is yellow, extending as far as the nostrils, and the tip is black. Legs and feet are grey. Hens are a little smaller, while young birds have pinkish rather than yellow bases to their bills.

**Distribution**: Iceland and north-western parts of Europe. Northern Scandinavia eastwards to Siberia. Overwinters farther south.
**Habitat**: Wooded ponds and lakes. Winters near the coast.
**Food**: Vegetation.
**Size**: 165cm (65in), wingspan 200–235cm (79–92½in).
**Nest**: Mounds of plant matter, often moss.
**Eggs**: 3–7, pale green.

---

**Greylag goose** (*Anser anser*) 74–84cm (29–33in), wingspan 149–168cm (59½–66in). Greylag geese are often seen in flocks, often alongside Canada geese, all around southern England. These tend to be populations that have been built upon birds released in certain areas, whereas the flocks seen in Scotland from September to April are the 'truly wild' native and overwintering birds. The greylag is large and solid in build, weighing from 2.3–5.5kg (5–12lb). Feet and legs are pink, bill is triangular and orange, head and neck are light brown and breast is soft grey leading to a very pale undercarriage. Wings are darker grey with white feather tips. They prefer lowland areas, water meadows and river valleys and graze on grasses, seeds and roots.

**The Egyptian goose** (*Alopochen aegyptiacus*) 63–73cm (25–28½in), wingspan 134–154cm (52½–60½in). A striking bird with a dark patch around the eye, a pink bill and pale head. The back of the neck has dark reddish brown plumage that extends to form a slim ring around the throat. The wing feathers are colourful, with dark green, russet red and soft brown parts. The belly and breast plumage is a soft beige-brown and the legs are pink. The bird breeds in Africa and is mainly found in the Nile Valley. It is thought that the ancient Egyptians kept the geese as 'guard dogs'. It was introduced to Britain and other northern European countries, where feral populations have since built up. In Britain, it is generally seen on lakes in East Anglia. It grazes on seeds and grass.

# Bewick's swan

Tundra swan *Cygnus columbianus bewickii*

Bewick's swan is one of two species of tundra swan (*C. columbianus*), the other being the whistling swan. They differ most noticeably on the bill – Bewick's has more yellow coloration – but share identical lifestyles. Both breed in the Arctic during the brief summer. Breeding starts in May, with the life-long pairs heaping up vegetation to form their bulky nests. The eggs hatch after about a month, and the young cygnets are able to fly when six weeks old. They travel with their parents on the southward migration during September, but it may be four years before they are ready to nest themselves. If they can avoid the hunters, Bewick's swans may live for over 20 years.

**Distribution**: Breeds along the north Russian coast to Siberia. Overwinters in southern British Isles, parts of north-western Europe, and in Asia south of the Caspian Sea across to Japan.
**Habitat**: Pools, marshland.
**Food**: Mainly vegetation.
**Size**: 127cm (50in), wingspan 183–224cm (72–88in).
**Nest**: A heaped-up pile of aquatic vegetation.
**Eggs**: 3–5, pale greenish.

**Identification:** White overall with a restricted area of yellow on the bill that does not extend as far as the nostrils. Cobs (male swans) are larger than females (known as pens). Young birds are greyish with a pinkish bill.

# Pink-footed goose

*Anser brachyrhynchus*

The pink-footed goose is a winter visitor to Britain with large flocks arriving in October and remaining here until April. It is estimated that around 240,000 of these birds spend the winter here and numbers appear to have increased almost tenfold over the last 50 years, perhaps due to the increased protection of their winter roosts by organizations such as the Royal Society for the Protection of Birds (RSPB). Britain's pink-footed geese actually make up a large chunk of the species' global population. They migrate to Britain from Iceland and eastern Greenland, where they breed. Like other geese, they feed mainly on grass and are often seen in fields. Their small, stubby bills and rounded heads give them a distinctive profile and make them relatively easy to tell apart from the otherwise similar greylag and white-fronted geese that also winter here. From a distance, their heads also look darker, sometimes almost black. Pink-footed geese form huge flocks but individual families appear to have strong ties. Young geese migrate into Britain with their parents and spend the whole autumn and winter with them, before making the return journey alongside them in the spring.

**Identification**: Although similar in size to the greylag and white-fronted goose, the pink-footed goose appears daintier, mainly as a consequence of its smaller bill. Like its legs and feet, this is pink in colour. Most of the body is covered with brown to pinkish-grey feathers, although the head and neck are darker and the rump is white. As with most other geese, it is usually seen in large flocks.

**Distribution**: Greenland and Icelandic populations have their main wintering grounds in east coast of Scotland, the Wash, Ribble and Solway estuaries. Birds from Svalbard migrate via the Norwegian coast to Denmark and North Sea coasts.
**Habitat**: Large estuaries and surrounding farmland.
**Food**: Grass and other ground plants.
**Size**: 76cm (30in), wingspan 137–170cm (54–67in).
**Nest**: On open ground or cliff edges.
**Eggs**: 4–5, white, but often become a dirty yellow-brown during incubation.

# Bar-headed goose

*Anser indicus*

This goose is a native of central Asia, with most nesting on the shores of high mountain lakes in Tibet and other parts of western China. After the short summer, its flocks escape the snows to spend the winter in northern India and Burma. They reach these places by migrating over the Himalayas and every year, some bar-headed geese pass directly over Mount Everest. Although most bar-headed geese migrate at somewhat lower altitudes, a few have been recorded flying at heights of more than 9,000m (29,520ft).

An attractive bird, the bar-headed goose has become a common addition to wildfowl collections, both large and small. Perhaps inevitably, some have escaped from these and now live wild in Britain. A very small number of pairs have even been recorded as breeding. On the continent, feral bar-headed geese are much more common than they are here and some have been known to cross the Channel. As a consequence, this bird is often spotted in the east of England. Farther north and west, sightings are much more rare.

**Distribution**: Native to central Asia. In Britain its distribution is scattered.
**Habitat**: High mountain lakes.
**Food**: Plant matter.
**Size**: 76cm (30in), wingspan 168cm (66in).
**Nest**: Unknown.
**Eggs**: 3–6, white.

**Identification**: The bar-headed goose is sometimes seen in the company of other geese but is striking enough to stand out from the crowd. Its most obvious feature is the one that gives it its name – its white head with two horseshoe-shaped dark brown bars across it, the front one reaching to the corners of the eyes. Other notable features include the pale orange to yellow legs, feet and bill.

# OTHER WETLAND BIRDS

*The wetlands of the British Isles have long been havens for birds. Unfortunately, the number of natural wetland habitats has dwindled as farming has increased and the land has become drier. Populations of birds such as redshanks and snipes have declined. However, British nature reserves do provide breeding grounds and sustain smaller populations of the birds that thrive in these rich habitats.*

## Red-throated diver

Red-throated loon *Gavia stellata*

**Distribution**: Breeds Iceland, Scandinavia and northern Europe and Asia. Overwinters around British Isles, southern Scandinavia and Iberian Peninsula. Present in the Black and Caspian seas. Also North America and Asia.
**Habitat**: Pools, open country.
**Food**: Mainly fish.
**Size**: 64cm (25¼in), wingspan 90–110 (35½–43in).
**Nest**: Pile of vegetation.
**Eggs**: 1–3, olive-brown with dark spots.

Red-throated divers pair up for life and stay together throughout the year. In May they return to their northern nesting grounds, revisiting the same location each year. Their nest, usually located among vegetation and surrounded by water, is simply a loose pile of plant matter. This is added to during the incubation period, potentially developing into a large mound. Both parents share incubation duties, although the female normally sits for longer than the male. Young red-throated divers can take to the water almost immediately after hatching, but usually remain at the nest for the first few days. Even once the chicks have entered the water they may still occasionally be carried on their parents' backs. Survival rates can be low, but if they make it through the critical early months of life these divers may live for up to 23 years.

**Identification:** Distinctive red throat patch present in adults of both sexes during the breeding period. The head is grey and the back of the neck is streaked black and white. Upperparts are brown, underparts white. During winter it has a pale grey crown, with speckling down the back of the neck and white spotting on the back; remaining underparts are white. Yellowish-grey bill. Young birds can be identified by their greyish-brown heads.

## Black-throated diver

Black-throated loon *Gavia arctica*

This species occurs in slightly more southerly locations than its red-throated relative, preferring the taiga (forested) area of northern Europe rather than the treeless tundra zone. However, it still has a circumpolar distribution, and is present in North America, but absent from Iceland and Greenland. The British Isles marks the southerly extent of the black-throated diver's breeding range. An estimated 150 pairs nest here during the summer, and numbers can rise significantly when they are joined by overwintering birds that have bred further north in Scandinavia. Solitary by nature, these divers seem especially vulnerable to any disturbance on their breeding grounds. As their name suggests, they seek their food largely underwater, diving to depths of up to 6m (20ft) in search of fish, including freshwater species such as sticklebacks and marine species such as herring.

**Identification:** In breeding condition, has a distinctive grey head and neck, and a black throat with conspicuous white stripes running down the sides of the neck. Underparts are white, with finer black striping on the sides of the upper breast. Back and wings are predominantly black, with prominent areas of white barring and spotting. Bill, legs and feet black. Remaining upperparts are brownish-grey with a white area on the flanks. Young birds resemble adults out of colour. Sexes are alike.

**Distribution**: Scandinavia and the far north of Europe and Asia. Overwinters in northern Scandinavia, British Isles and northern Spain. Also in the northern Mediterranean, and the Black and Caspian seas.
**Habitat**: Freshwater lakes and sheltered coastal areas.
**Food**: Fish, some invertebrates and vegetation.
**Size**: 65cm (25½in), wingspan 100–122cm (39½–48in).
**Nest**: Plant matter by water.
**Eggs**: 1–3, olive-brown with darker spots.

# Red-necked grebe

*Podiceps grisegena*

This bird is found in the temperate regions of the northern hemisphere. Its winter habitat is usually calm coastal waters, although some birds may winter on large lakes. The red-necked grebe will dive at any sign of danger and is able to swim with only its heads above the water. The birds prefer shallow lakes and marshes for breeding sites. They have a striking mating dance and, once paired, make a nest from water plants on top of floating matter. The birds are protected in the UK, and are rarely seen, although more appear for the winter months.

In common with other grebes, they eat their own feathers, possibly because these help to protect the stomach from damage by sharp fish bones. Feathers may also delay the bones on their passage through the gut, giving the stomach acids more time to dissolve them. After breeding, the adults moult their flight feathers to become flightless. Migration occurs when they regrow.

**Distribution**: Breeds in eastern Europe and as far west as parts of Scandinavia. Overwinters in coastal areas around the North Sea and eastern Mediterranean.
**Habitat**: Shallow freshwater lakes and marshes.
**Food**: Fish, crustaceans, insects and and invertebrates.
**Size**: 40–50cm (16–19½in), wingspan 61–88cm (24–34½in).
**Nest**: Plant matter anchored to submerged plants.
**Eggs**: 4–5, white or pale blue.

**Identification**: Dull grey winter plumage, changing in the breeding season to a red neck, black cap and pale face. Young birds are dull greyish brown. It has a thicker neck than the great crested grebe and a short, pointed dark beak with yellow underside. Feet and legs are black.

# Great crested grebe

*Podiceps cristatus*

**Distribution**: Eastern parts of Europe, overwintering farther south. Generally resident in western Europe. Occurs in parts of northern, eastern and southern Africa, and into Asia.
**Habitat**: Extensive reedy stretches of water.
**Food**: Fish and invertebrates.
**Size**: 52cm (20in),wingspan 58–74cm (23–29in).
**Nest**: Mound of reeds.
**Eggs**: 3–6, chalky-white.

Great crested grebes are primarily aquatic birds, and their flying ability is compromised by their short wings. They can dive very effectively, however, and often disappear underwater when they feel threatened. Rarely observed on land, these grebes are relatively cumbersome since their legs are located far back on the body, limiting their ability to move fast across open ground. Their toes are not fully webbed, unlike those of waterfowl, but they can swim quickly due to their streamlined body shape. They use their ruff-type facial feathers during display.

**Identification**: Black from top of the head to the back. Brownish sides to the body in winter. Extensive black crest, with a chestnut ruff at rear of head in summer. Bill reddish pink.

**Little grebe** (*Tachybaptus ruficollis*) 28cm (11in), wingspan 43cm (17in). The little grebe, or dabchick, is a charming small bird of slow rivers, canals and lake margins. It is present in Britain and Ireland all year round. Just over 10,000 pairs are estimated to breed in the UK. In October, their numbers are boosted by the arrival of as many as 36,000 visiting birds from the continent, who head for inland waters, estuaries and coastal bays.

Like its larger cousins, the little grebe is a fish-eater, diving from the surface to catch its prey. As its size would suggest, it hunts small fish and invertebrates. This fact, combined with its relatively small food requirements, means that it is able to live on large ponds, streams and other freshwater habitats too small to support larger birds. As a consequence, it is not only the most widespread but also the most numerous grebe in Britain. However, its shy nature and tendency to lurk near reeds or similar cover mean that it can be difficult to spot, and consequently it often seems to be less common than it actually is.

Like most grebes, the little grebe is an excellent parent. Adult birds often carry their chicks on their backs and pass them small fish, crustaceans and molluscs to eat. The chicks are also given feathers to swallow. These form a protective lining in the stomach to guard against fish bones.

# Great bittern

Eurasian bittern *Botaurus stellaris*

Bitterns are shy by nature, more likely to be heard than seen, thanks to the loud booming calls of cock birds at night as they try to attract mates. They are very patient hunters, relying on stealth to avoid detection before striking fast once their quarry is within reach. Great bitterns are largely solitary by nature and form no strong pair bond, only coming together to mate. The female is solely responsible for incubating the eggs and rearing the chicks. Hatching takes 26 days, with the chicks fledging after eight weeks. In freezing weather northern bitterns will head to warmer latitudes, where they may be more conspicuous. The isolated South African race (*B. s. capensis*) is slightly darker in colour than its northern relative.

**Identification:** Relatively light, yellowish-brown colour overall, with variable black markings. A white streak is present under the throat, with dark areas on the top of the head and along the sides of the bill, which is yellowish, as are the legs and feet. Markings of young birds are less defined on the upperparts. Adult hens are paler than cocks.

**Distribution:** Breeds widely in eastern Europe, and is present in various parts of western Europe where suitable habitat exists. Also found in north-east and central Africa, with a separate population in southern Africa.
**Habitat:** Reedbeds.
**Food:** Fish and other aquatic creatures.
**Size:** 80cm (31½in), wingspan 100–130cm (39½–51in).
**Nest:** Mat of vegetation in the reeds.
**Eggs:** 4–5, pale blue.

# Grey heron

*Ardea cinerea*

These large, opportunistic hunters are often shy on the ground and can be difficult to spot. They are usually seen in flight, with their long necks tucked back on to their shoulders and their legs held out behind their bodies. They fly with relatively slow, quite noisy wing beats. Grey herons are very patient predators. They stand motionless, looking closely for any sign of movement in the water around them, then lunge quickly with their powerful bills to grab any fish or frog that swims within reach. During the winter, when their freshwater habitats are frozen, grey herons will often move to river estuaries in search of food. These birds frequently nest in colonies, and some breeding sites may be used for centuries by successive generations. In Britain the grey heron is often seen standing silently at the water's edge waiting for prey, at estuaries, wetland marshes, gravel pits, reservoirs, lakes and rivers. It will also take stock from garden ponds and fish farms. There are just over 14,000 breeding pairs of heron in Great Britain.

**Identification:** Powerful yellow bill. White head, with black above the eyes extending to long plumes off the back of the head. Long neck and chest are whitish with a black stripe running down the centre. Grey wings and black shoulders. Underparts are lighter grey. Long yellowish legs. Sexes are alike.

**Distribution:** Throughout most of Europe into Asia, except for the far north. Also in Africa, but absent from the Sahara and the Horn.
**Habitat:** Water with reeds.
**Food:** Fish and any other aquatic vertebrates.
**Size:** 100cm (39½in), wingspan 173–195cm (68–77in).
**Nest:** Platform of sticks built off the ground.
**Eggs:** 3–5, chalky-blue.

# Great northern diver

*Gavia immer*

**Distribution**: Coastal waters around most of Britain and western Europe, ranging to Alaska, Canada, Greenland and Iceland.
**Habitat**: Lakes, estuaries and coastal waters.
**Food**: Fish.
**Size**: 100cm (39½in), wingspan 122–152cm (48–60in)
**Nest**: Near the water's edge.
**Eggs**: 1–3, white.

A winter visitor to Britain, the great northern diver has an enormous range, encompassing Alaska, Canada, Greenland and Iceland, as well as the coastal waters of western Europe. Most of Britain's 3,000 or so wintering birds fly in from Greenland and Iceland, with the first arrivals appearing in August. The majority spend their time off Scottish shores or the coast of Cornwall, but some fly inland to winter on lochs, reservoirs and lakes. During the following April and May they return to their breeding grounds, although some younger birds remain here throughout the summer.

The great northern diver searches for its food underwater and is a powerful swimmer. Its body is supremely adapted for this lifestyle. It swims not with its wings but its feet, which are located just beneath the front edge of the tail. Indeed, its feet are set so far back that it is unable to lift its body off the ground. As a result, it is forced to nest right by the water's edge, where it is able to slide its body out like a boat riding up on a beach.

**Identification**: This is the largest of the divers to be found in British waters. Not only is its body bigger but its bill is also much thicker and heavier in appearance. The summer plumage is quite striking, with a black head and neck, the latter with two half collars of white striped with black. In winter plumage the bill is paler, and the bottom half of the head and the front of the neck are white. When swimming, the body sits low in the water.

# Common crane

*Grus grus*

The common crane was once widespread in Britain, but during the Middle Ages it was hunted to extinction for food. Today it is back and breeding in small numbers in the fens of Suffolk. At the time of writing, young cranes are being raised by the Wildfowl & Wetlands Trust in Gloucestershire. Once they reach adulthood they will be released into selected sites and to form new breeding populations.

When nesting, pairs like to have their own space, but at other times this species is sociable and usually seen in numbers. At the start of the breeding season in spring, common cranes perform their courtship dance. Individuals leap vertically into the air with wings spread and legs dangling. Once one bird has started others around it join in. It is thought that the dance may help birds to select a partner. Once pairs have formed they regularly reinforce the bonds between them with another behaviour, known as unison calling. This is initiated by the male and involves both birds calling with their heads thrown back and beaks pointed skyward.

**Identification:** With its black head, white nape and drooping plume of tail feathers, the common crane is hard to confuse with any other bird. Unlike the grey heron, which is similar in size, it is normally seen in flocks. In flight the neck is held outstretched, unlike that of the grey heron. Flocks fly in 'V' formation and often make trumpeting calls. The long, trailing legs can be used to distinguish them from geese.

**Distribution**: UK migrants confined to south and east England. Breeds in small numbers in Suffolk. Wide range across northern parts of Europe and western Asia. Long distance migrant wintering in Africa and southern Europe. Accidental vagrant in North America, Alaska and western Canada.
**Habitat**: Marshland (breeding) and open agricultural land.
**Food**: Invertebrates, small vertebrates and seeds and other plant matter.
**Size**: 130cm (51in), wingspan 200–230cm (79–90½in).
**Nest**: A mound of vegetation located in wetland.
**Eggs**: 2, brownish or olive spotted with red brown.

# Water rail

*Rallus aquaticus*

Being naturally very adaptable, these rails have an extensive distribution, and are even recorded as foraging in tidal areas surrounded by seaweed in the Isles of Scilly off south-west England. In some parts of their range they migrate to warmer climates for the winter. Water rails survive in Iceland during the winter thanks to the hot thermal springs, which never freeze. They are very territorial when breeding and, as in other related species, their chicks hatch in a precocial state. They are found across the UK, but not in huge numbers. They are most common in the east and south.

**Identification:** Long, reddish bill with bluish-grey breast and sides to the head. Narrow brownish line extending over the top of the head down the back and wings, which have black markings. Black-and-white barring on the flanks and underparts. Short tail with pale buff underparts. Sexes are alike.

**Distribution**: Extensive, from Iceland throughout most of Europe, south to northern Africa and east across Asia to Siberia, China and Japan.
**Habitat**: Usually reedbeds and sedge.
**Food**: Mainly animal matter, but also some vegetation.
**Size**: 26cm (10¼in) wingspan 40–45cm (16–18in).
**Nest**: Cup-shaped, made from vegetation.
**Eggs**: 5–16, whitish with reddish-brown spotting.

# Coot

Eurasian coot *Fulica atra*

**Distribution**: From Great Britain eastwards throughout Europe, except the far north, south into northern Africa and east to Asia. Also present in Australia and New Zealand.
**Habitat**: Slow-flowing and still stretches of water.
**Food**: Various kinds of plant and animal matter.
**Size**: 42cm (16½in), wingspan 70–80cm (27–31½in).
**Nest**: Pile of reeds at the water's edge.
**Eggs**: 1–14, buff to brown with dark markings.

Open stretches of water are important to coots, enabling them to dive in search of food. During the winter, these birds may sometimes assemble in flocks on larger stretches of waters that are unlikely to freeze over. Coots may find their food on land or in the water, although they will dive only briefly in relatively shallow water. Pairs are very territorial during the breeding season, attacking the chicks of other coots that venture too close and even their own chicks, which they grab by the neck. Such behaviour is often described as 'tousling'. The young usually respond by feigning death, which results in them being left alone.

**Identification:** Plump, sooty-grey body with a black neck and head. Bill is white with a white frontal plate. The iris is a dark brownish colour. White trailing edges of the wings evident in flight. Long toes have no webbing. Sexes are alike.

# Moorhen

Common moorhen *Gallinula chloropus*

Although usually found in areas of fresh water, moorhens are occasionally seen in brackish areas – for example, on the Namibian coast in south-western Africa. Their long toes enable them to walk over aquatic vegetation. These birds feed on the water or on land and their diet varies according to the season, although seeds of various types make up the bulk of their food. If danger threatens, moorhens will either dive or swim underwater. They are adept divers, remaining submerged by grasping on to underwater vegetation with their bills. Moorhens are resident in lowland areas of the British Isles. In public parks, moorhens can become quite tame, darting in to obtain food provided for ducks.

**Distribution**: From Great Britain east through Europe except for the far north. Occurs through Africa, especially southern parts, also much of South-east Asia and parts of the Americas.
**Habitat**: Ponds and other areas of water edged by dense vegetation.
**Food**: Omnivorous.
**Size**: 30cm (12in), wingspan 50–58cm (19½–23in).
**Nest**: Domed structure hidden in reeds.
**Eggs**: 2–17, buff to light green with dark markings.

**Identification:** Slate-grey head, back and underparts. Greyish-black wings. A prominent white line runs down the sides of the body. The area under the tail is white and has a black central stripe. Greenish-yellow legs have a small red area at the top. The bill is red apart from a yellow tip. Sexes are alike.

# Water pipit

*Anthus spinoletta*

These pipits undertake regular seasonal movements, nesting at higher altitudes in the spring, where they often frequent fast-flowing streams. Pairs nest nearby, choosing a well-concealed location. Subsequently they will retreat to lower altitudes for the winter months, and are not averse to moving into areas of cultivation, such as watercress beds in southern Britain. The birds breed in the Alps and mountainous regions of central and southern Europe, and will only be seen in Britain from October to April. Most pipits head south, rather than north, of their breeding sites for the winter and are found in Mediterranean regions. There are about 100 overwintering individuals recorded. These aquatic pipits are lively birds, and are sometimes encountered in small flocks. They can often be observed on the ground, searching for invertebrates, and will readily make use of cover to conceal their presence should there be any hint of danger. Their song is attractive, and rather similar to that of the closely related rock pipit (*A. petrosus*), with studies of their song pattern revealing regional variations between different populations. Water pipits, like others of their kind, often utter their song in flight, and this is most likely to be heard at the start of the nesting period.

**Distribution**: Southern England and western Europe, extending to the northern African coast and into South-east Asia.
**Habitat**: Marshes, still water areas. Nests by streams.
**Size**: 17cm (7in), wingspan 22–28cm (8½–11in).
**Food**: Largely insectivorous.
**Nest**: Made of vegetation.
**Eggs**: 3–5, greenish with darker markings.

**Identification:** In breeding plumage, has a white stripe above the eye, a white throat with a distinctly pinkish tone to the breast, and a white abdomen. Slight streaking evident on the flanks. The head is greyish and the back and wings are brownish. During winter, the breast becomes whitish with very obvious streaking. Wings are lighter brown overall. Regional variations apply. Sexes are alike.

# Dipper

*Cinclus cinclus*

The dipper's name comes from the way in which it bows, or 'dips' its body, often on a boulder in the middle of a stream, rather than describing the way it dives into the water. It will bob up and down, cocking its tail. Dippers are very adept at steering underwater with their wings, and can even elude birds of prey by plunging in and disappearing from view, before surfacing again further downstream. They feed mainly on aquatic invertebrates caught underwater, sometimes emerging with caddisfly larvae and hammering them out of their protective casings on land. Pairs work together to construct their nest, which may be concealed in a bridge or a hole in a rock. The hen usually sits alone, and the youngsters will fledge after about three weeks. Norway's dipper population is increasing as streams in the southern mountains remain free of ice, possibly due to global warming. The population of dippers in Great Britain and Ireland is mainly resident, and up to 20,000 breeding pairs are recorded.

**Identification:** Prominent white throat and chest. Brown on head extends below the eyes, rest of the plumage is dark. Young birds are greyish with mottling on their underparts. Some regional variation, usually relating to the extent of chestnut below the white of the chest. Dark bill, legs and feet. Sexes are alike.

**Distribution**: Present in much of Scandinavia but only irregularly through the rest of Europe. Absent from central and eastern England and much of north-west Europe. Range extends south to parts of northern Africa. Also present in Asia.
**Habitat**: Stretches of fast-flowing water.
**Food**: Aquatic invertebrates and small fish.
**Size**: 20cm (8in), wingspan 25–30cm (10–12in).
**Nest**: Domed mass made from vegetation.
**Eggs**: 1–7, white.

# Aquatic warbler

*Acrocephalus paludicola*

**Distribution**: Mainland Europe. Few remaining strongholds in eastern Europe, notably in Poland, ranging into Asia. Migrates south to western Africa.
**Habitat**: Waterlogged areas, with sedge.
**Food**: Invertebrates.
**Size**: 13cm (5in), wingspan 17–19cm (6½–7½in).
**Nest**: In tussocks of sedge.
**Eggs**: 4–6, greenish-coloured with dark markings.

The aquatic warbler's range has contracted significantly over recent years, as the sedgeland areas that these birds favour have been increasingly drained for agriculture. However, they are seen more widely on migration, when they take a westerly route down over the Strait of Gibraltar. During the autumn in particular, they can even be seen in southern parts of England. They remain in Africa from November through to April, before heading north again, where they occur in a number of scattered locations in areas of suitable habitat, including flooded grassland. Aquatic warblers may be difficult to observe since they tend not to utter any calls away from their breeding grounds. When nesting, they will usually sing most frequently towards dusk, from a suitable perch rather than in flight. They are shy birds by nature, and prefer to search for food near the base of reedbeds. They are also very agile, often perching on two adjacent reeds rather than grasping the same stem with both feet.

**Identification:** Black areas on the head, with a central yellow-buff streak and broader areas above the eyes. Similar markings also at the top of the wings. The remaining wing plumage is brownish with black markings, with marked streaking over the lower back. Underparts are paler and have variable fine streaking. Young birds less brightly coloured. Sexes are similar.

# Great reed warbler

*Acrocephalus arundinaceus*

Great reed warblers return to their northern breeding grounds from April onwards, with their distinctive and sometimes harsh calls betraying their presence in the reedbeds. However, they are notoriously difficult to spot, due to the colour of their plumage. They sing from the tops of reed stems, and this provides the best opportunity to spot them. They are very agile, able to clamber between the reed stems with ease. In flight, great reed warblers stay close to the water's surface, with their tail feathers held out. The female constructs the nest in May, which is suspended from several adjacent reed stems, about half-way up their length. Incubation lasts around two weeks and is shared by both members of the pair, as is the rearing of the young. They leave the nest after about 12 days. Both young and adult birds migrate south as early as September.

**Distribution**: Most of Europe, but restricted to the extreme south in both Scandinavia and the British Isles. Overwinters in Africa south of the Sahara, except the far south and the Horn of Africa. Resident population in northern Africa.
**Habitat**: Reedbeds.
**Food**: Invertebrates.
**Size**: 20cm (8in), wingspan 25–30cm (10–12in).
**Nest**: Vegetation woven into a basket shape.
**Eggs**: 4–6, bluish-green with dark markings.

**Identification:** Upperparts are dark brown, with darker areas on the wings and a pale stripe running through the eyes. Whitish underparts, becoming more buff in colour on the flanks. Some greyish streaking evident across the breast. Bill is blackish, lighter below, while the legs and feet are typically greyish. Young birds are rusty-brown above, with buff underparts. Sexes are alike.

# Reed warbler

*Acrocephalus scirpaceus*

The reed warbler is a summer visitor to our shores, arriving in mid-April and leaving in October. It spends the winter in sub-Saharan Africa, with some flying as far south as Zambia. As many as 120,000 pairs are thought to nest in Britain, the vast majority in East Anglia and the more southerly counties of England. Despite their abundance, these birds are rarely seen, a testament to their excellent camouflage and tendency to remain in the reed beds where they nest and raise their young. When it is spotted, the reed warbler can be extremely difficult to identify with certainty. Its tail is narrower and its eye stripes less obvious than those of either Savi's or Cetti's warblers, which share its habitat, and its smaller size can be used to differentiate it from the great reed warbler, a much rarer visitor to Britain. However, the marsh warbler and Blyth's warbler both look almost identical to the reed warbler. Neither are as common in reed beds but both do occur in them at the same time of the year. The main distinguishing feature of the reed warbler is its song (see below). Fortunately, singing birds tend to perch high up on reeds, making the chances of spotting one singing more likely.

**Distribution**: British Isles except Scotland and Northern Ireland, Central Africa, Mediterranean, Europe.
**Habitat**: Reed beds
**Food**: Insects and berries
**Size**: 13cm (5in), wingspan 17–19cm (6½–7½in).
**Nest**: A deep cup of dried grass, attached to reed stems.
**Eggs**: 4–5, greenish to white.

**Identification**: This small, inconspicuous bird is a typical warbler, warm brown above and buff coloured beneath. It lacks any real distinguishing features, having no spots, streaks or other obvious markings. The reed warbler is perhaps most easily identified by its song – a flow of 'churr-churr-churr . . . chirruc-chirruc-chirruc' notes, which is often described as sounding like two pebbles being chinked together.

## Kingfisher

Common kingfisher *Alcedo atthis*

These birds are difficult to spot, as they perch motionlessly while scanning the water for fish. Once its prey has been identified, the kingfisher dives down in a flash of colour. A protective membrane covers its eyes as it enters the water. Its wings provide propulsion, and having seized the fish in its bill the bird darts out of the water and back onto its perch with its catch. The whole sequence happens incredibly fast, in just a few seconds. The kingfisher then stuns the fish by hitting it against the perch, before swallowing it. It regurgitates the bones and indigestible parts of its meal later.

*Left: Kingfishers dive at speed into the water, aiming to catch their intended quarry unawares.*

**Identification:** Bluish-green extending over the head and wings. The back is pale blue, a blue flash is also present on the cheeks. The throat area is white, and there are white areas below orange cheek patches. Underparts are also orange, the bill is black. In hens, the bill is reddish at the base.

**Distribution**: Occurs across most of Europe, but absent from much of Scandinavia. Also present in northern Africa, ranging eastwards through the Arabian peninsula and South-east Asia as far as the Solomon Islands.
**Habitat**: Slow-flowing water.
**Food**: Small fish. Also preys on aquatic insects, molluscs and crustaceans.
**Size**: 18cm (7in), wingspan 24–25cm (9½–10¼in).
**Nest**: Tunnel excavated in a sandy bank.
**Eggs**: 6–10, white.

---

### Marsh warbler

(*Acrocephalus palustris*) 13cm (5in), wingspan 20cm (8in). This bird is generally found in central Europe into Asia, north to south Scandinavia, and rarely in the British Isles. It winters through much of East Africa. It is similar to the reed warbler, but with a slightly greyer tone to the brown upperparts. Its underparts are whitish, with brownish suffusion on the chest and flanks. It can be identified by its shorter bill and longer wings, the tips of which clearly extend behind the rump when the bird is perched. Sexes are alike.

### Snipe

(*Gallinago gallinago*) 28cm (11in), wingspan 45cm (18in). These waders are shy by nature, and may even be nocturnal feeders. In some parts of their range, such as the British Isles, they remain sedentary. They have dark mottled plumage on the chest and wings. Underparts are white. The long bill may be larger in hens, otherwise sexes alike.

## Bearded tit

Bearded reedling *Panurus biarmicus*

This species' distribution is directly affected by the availability of marshland with extensive reedbeds. Contrary to their name they are members of the babbler family, rather than tits, although their lively nature and jerky tail movements, coupled with their overall appearance, are more suggestive of the latter group. In addition to providing a source of insects, the reeds also produce seeds which the bearded tits eat over the winter. Nevertheless, these small birds can suffer a high mortality rate when the weather is harsh. Pairs breed alone, and the male is largely responsible for nest-building. Both birds incubate and care for the chicks, which may fledge at just nine days old. Pairs may rear up to three broods in a year. Up to 560 bearded tit pairs are recorded as breeding in Britain, but harsh winters have caused a decline in the population. They are found mainly on the east coast, but also on the central south coast and coastal areas of the north-west of England.

**Distribution**: Localised distribution from southern parts of Scandinavia and England through areas of Europe and parts of Asia.
**Habitat**: Reedbeds.
**Food**: Invertebrates, seeds.
**Size**: 15cm (6in), wingspan 16–17cm (6¼–6½in).
**Nest**: Made of vegetation.
**Eggs**: 5–7, white with dark markings.

**Identification:** Reddish-brown overall, with a relatively long tail which tapers to its tip and white patches on the wings. Cocks have a grey head, with a prominent black area beneath each eye, and a white throat. Hens have a brownish head, with a grey-white throat. Young birds are similar to hens, but with a black area on their backs. Bill is yellowish-orange, legs and feet are black.

# WOODLAND BIRDS

*Woodland birds are often heard long before they can be seen, partly because they are difficult to spot, but also because they are easily disturbed and will freeze or take flight at the slightest noise. There is much concern at the moment that many of the woodland bird species in the British Isles are in serious decline, either because of noise pollution in Britain, or changes in land use in West Africa, where many of them migrate from.*

## Cuckoo

Common cuckoo *Cuculus canorus*

The distinctive call of the cuckoo, heard when these birds return from their African wintering grounds, has traditionally been regarded in Europe as one of the earliest signs of spring. Typically, they are only resident in Europe between April and September. Adult cuckoos have an unusual ability to feed on hairy caterpillars, which are plentiful in woodlands throughout much of the summer.

Common cuckoos are parasitic breeders – the hens lay single eggs in the nests of smaller birds such as hedge sparrows (*Prunella modularis*), meadow pipits (*Anthus pratensis*) and wagtails (*Motacilla* species). The unsuspecting hosts hatch a cuckoo chick who ejects other eggs or potential rivals from the nest in order to monopolize the food supply.

*Right: The young cuckoo lifts eggs on its back to eject them from the nest.*

**Identification:** Grey head, upper chest, wings and tail, and black edging to the white feathers of the underparts. In hens this barring extends almost to the throat, offset against a more yellowish background. Some hens belong to a brown colour morph, with rufous feathering replacing the grey, and black barring apparent on the upperparts.

**Distribution**: Throughout the whole of Europe, ranging eastwards into Asia. Also present in northern Africa. Populations in northern Europe overwinter in eastern and southern parts of Africa, while Asiatic birds migrate as far as the Philippines.
**Habitat**: Various.
**Food**: Mainly invertebrates, including caterpillars.
**Size**: 36cm (14¼in), wingspan 70–76cm (27–30in).
**Nest**: None – lays directly in other birds' nests.
**Eggs**: 1 per nest, resembling those of its host.

## Green woodpecker

*Picus viridis*

**Distribution**: Range extends across most of Europe, absent from much of Scandinavia, Ireland, Scotland and various islands in the Mediterranean. Present in parts of north-western Africa.
**Habitat**: Open woodland.
**Food**: Mainly invertebrates.
**Size**: 33cm (13in), wingspan 45–52cm (18–20in).
**Nest**: Tree hole.
**Eggs**: 5–8, white.

Unlike many of its kind, green woodpeckers hunt for food mainly on the ground, using their powerful bills and long tongues to break open ants' nests. They are equally equipped to prey on earthworms, which are drawn to the surface of lawns after rain, and may catch small creatures such as lizards. In the autumn, fruit forms a more significant part of their diet, but they avoid seeds, and so are not drawn to bird feeders. Pairing begins during the winter, with excavation of the nesting chamber taking two weeks to a month to complete. Unlike many woodpeckers they do not drum loudly with their bills to advertise their presence, but pairs can be quite vocal. Incubation is shared, with the hen sitting during the day. Hatching takes just over a fortnight, with the young fledging when a month old.

**Identification:** Red crown, with red below the eyes and blackish in between. Regional variations. Underparts greyish to green. Back and wings darker green, with yellow spotting. Yellowish rump. Hens often have black rather than red stripes below the eyes. Young are heavily spotted and barred, with a greyer crown.

# Great spotted woodpecker

*Picoides major*

Great spotted woodpeckers can be found in coniferous and deciduous woodland, especially in areas where the trees are mature enough for the birds to excavate nesting chambers. Their powerful bills enable them to extract grubs hidden under bark and to wrest the seeds from pine cones – the birds use so-called 'anvils', which may be existing tree holes, as vices to hold the cones fast, so as to gain more leverage for their bills.

**Identification:** Black top to the head. Black areas also from the sides of the bill around the neck, linking with a red area at the back of the head. Wings and upperside of the tail are predominantly black, although there is a white area on the wings and white barring on the flight feathers. Underside of the tail mostly white. Deep red around the vent. Hens are similar but lack the red on the hindcrown.

**Distribution:** Throughout most of Europe except for Ireland, the far north of Scandinavia and much of south-eastern Europe. Also found in North Africa. Ranges eastwards into Asia.
**Habitat:** Woodland.
**Food:** Invertebrates, eggs and seeds.
**Size:** 25cm (10in), wingspan 38–44cm (15–17¼in).
**Nest:** Tree hollow.
**Eggs:** 5–7, white.

# Lesser spotted woodpecker

*Dendrocopos minor*

The lesser spotted woodpecker is the smallest of the three woodpeckers native to Britain. It is also the least common. Although broadly similar in colour to the great spotted woodpecker it is a much more compact and diminutive bird, about the same size as a greenfinch. The lesser spotted woodpecker is a resident and does not migrate. It is found throughout Wales and most of England but is absent from Ireland and rare in Scotland, only ever occurring in the far south. The greatest numbers are to be found in south-east England, the only place in Britain where it is locally common.

The lesser spotted woodpecker feeds mainly on wood boring insect larvae, breaking into their tunnels by hammering away with its strong, pointed bill. Like all woodpeckers it has an extremely long, slender tongue. Once it has exposed part of a tunnel it uses this to probe inside, skewering the soft-bodied larvae with the hard, pointed tip. Backward facing barbs hold the prey in place as the tongue is pulled back into the beak. In spring and summer this species supplements its diet with insects plucked from leaves and the surface of the bark. These often smaller prey items make up the bulk of food fed to the chicks.

**Identification:** The body is boldly patterned with black and white feathers. The male has a red crown bordered with black; the crown of the female is white. A series of black and white horizontal bars runs across the back of the body. Two-thirds the size of the great spotted, it shares its cousin's pied plumage, with even more extensive barring on the wings and back. However, the barring is somewhat blurred. It produces a weaker drumming sound than the great spotted, and its high-pitched, peevish-sounding call is also weaker. The flight pattern is undulating.

**Distribution:** Range extends throughout most of Europe except for Iceland, Ireland, northern Britain and much of Spain and Portugal. Also present south into Algeria and Tunisia, and eastward into Asia.
**Habitat:** Woods, parkland, gardens and orchards.
**Food:** Invertebrates.
**Size:** 15cm (6in), wingspan 23–26cm (9–10½in).
**Nest:** Excavated nest hole.
**Eggs:** 3–8, glossy white.

# Golden oriole

*Oriolus oriolus*

Golden orioles are difficult to spot, preferring to hide away in the upper reaches of woodland, although they will sometimes descend to the ground in search of food and water. Their diet varies, consisting mainly of invertebrates from spring onwards, with fruits and berries more significant later in the year. Migrants arrive at the southern tip of Africa by November, and by March will have set off on the long journey back to Europe. Sightings in Britain are rare, but 5–17 pairs are recorded in the south-east. It is unclear where the small north-west African population disperses to after breeding, but they head south also, returning by mid-April. Males establish territories on arrival at their breeding grounds.

**Identification:** Yellow. Black wings with a yellow patch. Red bill. Hens have greenish-yellow upperparts, streaked underparts mainly white, yellow flanks and blackish wings. Young are more greyish-green, white underparts only slight yellow.

**Distribution**: Breeds right across mainland Europe, to the southernmost parts of Scandinavia, extending east into Asia. In the British Isles, restricted to eastern England. Also present in north-west Africa, overwintering throughout the continent.
**Habitat**: Prefers deciduous woodland areas.
**Food**: Invertebrates, berries and fruits.
**Size**: 25cm (10in), wingspan 44–48cm (17¼–19in).
**Nest**: Cup-shaped.
**Eggs**: 3–4, creamy-buff with dark spotting.

# Woodcock

*Scolopax rusticola*

Outside large towns and cities, most people have woodcocks as relatively close neighbours, but despite this fact they are rarely seen. Woodcocks are largely nocturnal and they are incredibly well camouflaged. For most of the year during the hours of daylight they sit tight in dense cover, their bodies hidden from view by their cryptic plumage. The exception to this rule occurs during the breeding season, when males make so-called roding flights over woodland at dusk. The purpose of these flights is uncertain – it may be that the males are visually advertising their ownership of a territory, or it may be that they are simply seeking out females with which to mate. Woodcocks disturbed from their resting places escape by taking flight and zigzagging through the trees before dropping down into cover again.

The woodcock feeds mainly on earthworms, which it finds in damp ground. In this respect it has a lot in common with the snipe, the only other bird which shares part of its habitat and with which it might be confused. Unlike the snipe, however, the woodcock has brown rather than pale underparts. It is also has a more rounded, dumpy appearance. Like the snipe, the woodcock is absent from Devon and Cornwall except in the winter, when a small number of birds fly in from the continent.

**Distribution**: From Russia to western Europe, and throughout the British Isles, with the exception of the Outer Hebrides and Shetland.
**Habitat**: Low-lying woodland.
**Food**: Earthworms and other invertebrates.
**Size**: 38cm (15in), wingspan 55–65cm (21½–25½in).
**Nest**: A lined cup, or a slight hollow, lined with dead leaves, on the ground in low cover in woodland or heather.
**Eggs**: 4, pale brown with darker speckles.

**Identification**: The woodcock is a stout, somewhat dumpy wading bird with relatively short legs. Its bill is long, tapering and perfectly straight, and its eyes are set quite high up on its head. The woodcock's mottled brown plumage camouflages it perfectly among the leaf litter of the woodlands it inhabits. As a consequence it is very rarely spotted on the ground and is much more likely to be seen in flight.

# Hawfinch

*Coccothraustes coccothraustes*

With their characteristic stocky, powerful bills, hawfinches are able to crack open cherry stones and the hard kernels of similar fruits to feed on the seeds within. They usually feed off the ground, but may sometimes descend to pick up fallen fruits. In the spring they will also eat emerging buds, as well as feeding on invertebrates, with their bill strength enabling them to prey on even hard-bodied beetles without difficulty. Pairs are formed during the spring, with the cock bird harrying the female for a period beforehand. She will then start to build the nest, which can be located in the fork of a tree more than 22m (72ft) above the ground. The incubation period lasts approximately 12 days, and the young leave the nest after a similar interval. Hawfinches are most likely to be observed in small flocks over the winter period, with populations occurring in more northern areas usually moving southwards at this time.

This bird is Great Britain's largest finch, but is a shy bird so experts have found it hard to quantify the numbers living there. It appears that the population is in decline, and is now restricted to South-east England, the Welsh Borders and the home counties. Hawfinches are easier to see in the winter, when they feed on the ground.

**Identification:** Adult male in breeding condition has a black area around the bill and eyes, with a brown crown and grey around the neck. Whitish area on the wings and black flight feathers. Underparts are brownish. Bill is black, paler in non-breeding, as is the head. Hens have paler and greyer heads, and greyer secondary flight feathers. Young birds have streaking on their underparts.

**Distribution**: Resident in most of Europe, although absent from Ireland. Breeds in the south of Scandinavia and farther east into Asia, where these populations are only summer visitors. Some reported sightings on various Mediterranean islands and parts of north-western Africa.
**Habitat**: Mixed woodland.
**Food**: Large seeds, buds, shoots, fruit and fruit stones.
**Size**: 16cm (6¼in), wingspan 29–33cm (11–13in).
**Nest**: Cup-shaped, made of plant matter.
**Eggs**: 3–6, bluish-white to green, with dark markings.

# Long-tailed tit

*Aegithalos caudatus*

The tail feathers of these tits can account for nearly half their total length. Those birds occurring in northern Europe have a completely white head and underparts. The Turkish race (*A. c. tephronotus*) in contrast displays more black feathering, including a bib, with evident streaking on its cheeks. Long-tailed tits are lively birds, usually seen in small parties, and frequently in the company of other tits. They are often most conspicuous during the winter, when the branches are without leaves.

Long-tailed tits will roost together, which helps to conserve their body heat – sometimes as many as 50 birds may be clustered together. Groups can be quite noisy when foraging during the day. Their breeding period starts early, in late February, and may extend right through until June.

**Identification:** Dumpy and long-tailed. Black stripe above each eye extends back to form a collar. Head and upper breast otherwise whitish. Underparts rose-pink. Reddish-brown shoulders, white edges to the flight feathers. Young birds are duller, with brown on their heads. Sexes are alike.

*Right: Long-tailed tits build a large nest with a side entrance.*

**Distribution**: Resident throughout virtually the whole of Europe, but absent from central and northern parts of Scandinavia. Extends into Asia, but not found in Africa.
**Habitat**: Deciduous and mixed woodland.
**Food**: Invertebrates, seeds.
**Size**: 15cm (6in), wingspan 16–19cm (6¼–7½in).
**Nest**: Ball-shaped, usually incorporating moss.
**Eggs**: 7–12, white with reddish speckling.

# Crested tit

*Parus cristatus*

Although these tits can lower their crest feathers slightly, the crest itself is always visible. This makes crested tits easy to distinguish, even when they are foraging with other groups of tits, which happens especially during the winter period. They rarely venture high up, preferring to seek food on or near the ground. Invertebrates such as spiders are preferred, although they often resort to eating conifer seeds during the winter. Crested tits frequently create food stores, particularly during the autumn, to help them survive through the harsher months when the ground may be blanketed with snow. Seeds are gathered and secreted in holes in the bark, and among lichens, while invertebrates are decapitated and stored on a shorter-term basis. Nesting begins in March, with a pair choosing a hole, usually in rotten wood, which they can enlarge before constructing a cup-shaped lining for their eggs. In more southerly areas, two broods of chicks may be reared in succession.

The most common sightings in the British Isles are in Caledonian pine forests and Scottish pine plantations.

**Identification:** Triangular-shaped, blackish-white crest. Sides of the face are also blackish-white, with a blackish line running through each eye and curling round the hind cheeks. Black collar joins to a bib under the bill. Upperparts brownish. Underparts paler buff, more rufous on the flanks. Young as adults but have brown rather than reddish irides. Sexes are alike.

**Distribution:** Resident from Spain across to Scandinavia (although not the far north) and Russia. Present in the British Isles only in northern Scotland. Absent from Italy.
**Habitat:** Conifer woodland.
**Food:** Mainly invertebrates, seeds in winter.
**Size:** 12cm (4½in), wingspan 17–20cm (6½–8in).
**Nest:** In a rotten tree stump.
**Eggs:** 5–8, white with reddish markings.

# Common redstart

*Phoenicurus phoenicurus*

This member of the thrush family seeks cover when building its nest. It is often constructed inside a tree hollow, but sometimes an abandoned building or even an underground tunnel is chosen. The hen incubates alone for two weeks until the eggs hatch, with both parents subsequently providing food for their growing brood. Fledging takes place around two weeks later. The pair may sometimes nest again, if food is plentiful. When migrating south, birds from much of Europe take a westerly route through the Iberian Peninsula. Those passing farther east through Libya and Egypt are believed to come from Russia. Males generally leave first, enabling them to establish their breeding territories by the time they are joined by the hens.

**Identification:** Cock birds have a prominent white area above the bill extending back above the eyes. Remainder of the face is black, and the head and back are grey. Chest is rufous, becoming paler on the underparts. Hens are duller, with a greyish-brown head and buff-white underparts. Young birds have brown heads and rufous tails.

**Distribution:** Breeding range extends across virtually the whole of Europe, including Scandinavia, and eastwards into Asia. Absent from Ireland. Also occurs in parts of north-west Africa, and overwinters in a band south of the Sahara.
**Habitat:** Woodland.
**Food:** Mainly invertebrates and berries.
**Size:** 15cm (6in), wingspan 20–24cm (8–9½in).
**Nest:** Built in a suitable hole.
**Eggs:** 5–7, bluish with slight red spotting.

**Wood warbler**
(*Phylloscopus sibilatrix*) 14cm (5½in), wingspan 24cm (9½in). This summer visitor to Britain arrives in April to pair, mate and nest. It is most common in the west of England, Wales and Scotland, with the largest populations occurring in the oak woods of western Wales. The wood warbler is absent from much of eastern England north of London and it is also scarce in Ireland. The bird has a distinctive eye bar and yellow upper chest and throat. The back is leafy green and the belly white.

**Willow tit** (*Poecile montanus*) 12cm (5in), wingspan 7cm (3in). Most often seen in willow thickets on damp ground, this bird has a black cap and bib, white cheeks and belly. It has a rounded head, so appears to lack a neck. It looks very similar to the marsh tit but has a pale wing panel.

# Common crossbill

*Loxia curvirostra*

The crossbill's highly distinctive bill can crack the hard casing of conifer seeds, enabling the bird to extract the inner kernel with its tongue. These finches also eat the pips of various fruits, and will prey on invertebrates, particularly when they have young to feed. The breeding season varies through their wide range, starting later in the north. Both members of the pair build the nest, which is constructed in a conifer, sometimes more than 18m (60ft) high. Common crossbills only rarely descend to the ground, usually to drink, unless the pine crop is very poor. When faced with a shortage of food, they move to areas far outside their normal range. This phenomenon, known as an irruption, occurs once a decade in Europe. In Great Britain, an estimated 20,000 pairs of crossbills breed in the Scottish Highlands, on the north coast of Norfolk, in the New Forest and the Forest of Dean.

**Identification:** Males are reddish with darker blackish feathering on the top of the head, more evident on the wings. Underparts reddish, paler towards the vent. Upper and lower parts of the distinctive blackish bill are curved at the tip. Hens are olive-green, darker over the back and wings, and have a paler rump. Young birds resemble hens, but have evident streaking on their bodies.

**Distribution**: Resident throughout much of Scandinavia and northern Europe, extending into Asia. Found elsewhere in Europe, usually in areas of coniferous forest, extending as far as northern Africa.
**Habitat**: Coniferous forests.
**Food**: Mainly the seeds of pine cones.
**Size**: 15cm (6in), wingspan 25–28cm (10–11in).
**Nest**: Cup-shaped, made from vegetation.
**Eggs**: 3–4, whitish-blue with reddish-brown markings.

# Brambling

*Fringilla montifringilla*

After breeding in northern parts of Europe, the harsh winter weather forces bramblings to migrate to more southerly latitudes in search of food. Here they can be seen in fields and other open areas of countryside. These finches feed largely on beech nuts, relying heavily on the forests of central Europe to sustain them over the winter period. Although normally occurring in small flocks, millions of individuals may occasionally congregate in the forests. They are often seen amid flocks of chaffinches from September until March or April in the British Isles, generally on wooded farmland but occasionally visiting gardens. Bramblings have a rather jerky walk when on the ground, sometimes hopping as well when searching for food. Their diet is much more varied during the summer months, when they are nesting. Caterpillars of moths in particular are eagerly devoured at this time and used as a rearing food for their young. Bramblings have a relatively rapid breeding cycle. The hen incubates the eggs on her own, and they will hatch after about a fortnight. The young birds leave the nest after a similar interval.

**Identification:** Black head and bill. Orange underparts, white rump and white wing bars. Underparts whitish, blackish markings on the orange flanks. Duller in winter, with pale head markings and yellowish bill. Hens as winter males, but have greyer sides to the face and duller scapulars. Young birds as hens but brown, with a yellowish rump.

**Distribution**: Breeds in the far north of Europe, through most of Scandinavia into Russia, extending eastwards into Asia. Overwinters farther south throughout Europe, extending to parts of north-western Africa.
**Habitat**: Woodland.
**Food**: Beech nuts, seeds and berries. Insects in summer.
**Size**: 18cm (7in), wingspan 24–26cm (9½–10½in).
**Nest**: Cup-shaped, made from vegetation.
**Eggs**: 5–7, a dark greenish-blue colour.

# Treecreeper

Eurasian creeper *Certhia familiaris*

The treecreeper's long hind toes assist them in climbing vertically up tree trunks. Having reached the top of the trunk, the treecreeper flies down to the base of a neighbouring tree and begins again, circling the bark, probing likely nooks and crannies with its fine, curved bill, looking for the insects that make up its sole diet. The pointed tips of the tail feathers provide extra support. Pairs start nesting in the spring, with the cock bird chasing after his intended mate. They seek out a small, hidden cavity where a cup-shaped nest can be constructed. The hen incubates mainly on her own for two weeks, and the young fledge after a similar interval. It is not uncommon, especially in southern parts of their range, for pairs to breed twice in succession. The birds are usually spotted one at a time, as they are quite solitary creatures, although they will roost together in very cold weather.

*Above: Small crevices in a trunk may be used as a nesting site.*

**Identification:** Mottled brownish upperparts, with a variable white stripe above the eyes, depending on race. Underparts whitish. Narrow, slightly curved bill. Young birds similar to adults. Sexes are alike.

**Distribution**: Much of northern Europe, except for the far north of Scandinavia. Sporadic distribution through France and northern Spain, not occurring farther south on the Iberian Peninsula. Not present in northern Africa, but extends into Asia.
**Habitat**: Dense woodland.
**Food**: Assorted invertebrates.
**Size**: 14cm (5½in), wingspan 17–20cm (6½–8in).
**Nest**: Small hollow.
**Eggs**: 5–7, white with reddish-brown markings.

# Tree pipit

*Anthus trivialis*

Tree pipits sing with increasing frequency at the start of the breeding period. Their nest is constructed close to the ground in open countryside, well hidden from predators. This need for camouflage may explain the variable coloration of their eggs. These long-distance migrants overwinter in Africa, reaching southern parts towards the end of October. Tree pipits feed on the ground, moving jauntily and pausing to flick their tails up and down, flying to the safety of a nearby branch at any hint of danger. As well as invertebrates they may also eat seeds and berries. Solitary and quiet, these pipits are not easily observed away from their breeding grounds. They begin returning to Europe in April.

In the British Isles tree pipits are widespread from April through to September, but occur in greatest numbers in the western uplands. They favour young conifer woodlands and open heath. Their numbers in more southerly regions of England have fallen enough to cause concern in the last 25 years, perhaps due to decline in suitable habitats.

**Distribution**: Occurs widely through much of Europe up into Scandinavia and eastwards into Asia. Overwinters across Africa south of the Sahara, continuing down the eastern side of the continent, with isolated populations in Namibia and South Africa.
**Habitat**: Woodland.
**Food**: Mainly invertebrates.
**Size**: 15cm (6in), wingspan 25–28cm (10–11in).
**Nest**: Made of grass.
**Eggs**: 4–6, greyish with variable markings.

**Identification:** Brownish upperparts with dark streaking. White edging to the wing feathers. Buff stripe above each eye, darker brown stripes through and below them. Throat whitish. Underparts pale yellowish with brownish streaking. Bill dark, especially at the tip. Legs and feet pinkish. Young birds are more buff overall. Sexes are alike.

# Woodlark

*Lullula arborea*

The attractive whistling call of these larks, characterized by a distinctive yodelling tone, is mainly heard at sunrise or even on a starry night, rather than during the daytime. They are not easy birds to spot, since their plumage provides them with excellent camouflage. Woodlarks spend long periods on the ground, but sometimes fly up to perch, and this is when they are most conspicuous. Nesting also often occurs on the ground, with both members of the pair building the nest in a suitable hollow, although they may prefer to utilize a shrub or young sapling. The hen sits alone, and the chicks hatch about two weeks later. The young woodlarks develop quickly, and may leave the nest at only 10 days old, emerging on foot since they are not able to fly well at this stage. In the autumn, those birds occurring in more easterly parts head to south-west Europe to overwinter. Some fly farther afield, over the Strait of Gibraltar to north-western Africa. Southern and eastern England have the biggest populations in Britain.

**Identification:** A white stripe above each eye. Top of the head streaked black and brown, ear coverts brownish. Streaked back, white tip to short tail. Underparts streaked, white on the abdomen. Yellowish-brown bill, yellowish legs and feet. Young have blacker crown, more spotted underparts. Sexes are alike.

**Distribution**: Range extends throughout much of Europe, but resident only in more westerly areas. Restricted to the south in England. Breeds right across the continent as far as southern parts of Scandinavia. Also extends to north-west Africa.
**Habitat**: Open woodland.
**Food**: Mostly invertebrates, seeds in winter.
**Size**: 15cm (6in), wingspan 26–30cm (10¼–12in).
**Nest**: Deep and cup-shaped, made of vegetation.
**Eggs**: 1–6, white with some brown speckling.

# Yellowhammer

*Emberiza citrinella*

**Distribution**: Resident in Britain and breeds through much of Europe except for Iceland and parts of Portugal and Spain. Widespread in southern and western Europe in winter. Range also extends eastward into central Asia.
**Habitat**: Farmland with hedges, grasslands, heaths, also coasts.
**Food**: Seeds, berries, invertebrates.
**Size**: 16cm (6¼in), wingspan 23–29cm (9–11in).
**Nest**: Cup-shape of grass and moss.
**Eggs**: 3–5, white to purplish with reddish markings.

This colourful, distinctive bunting is best known for its song – a rapid, rhythmic series of notes ending with a flourish, often likened to the phrase 'a little bit of bread and no cheese'. The males sing their song in summer near the nest, which is built low along a hedge. Yellowhammers are seed- and grain-eaters, and like many similar birds their populations have declined in recent years. Formerly found throughout much of rural Britain except the far north and west, they no longer frequent much of their old range, but they are now more often seen in gardens, especially in winter, when they form feeding flocks with other buntings, finches or sparrows. Yellowhammers pair up in spring and raise two or three broods in a season. The eggs are incubated for 12–14 days with chicks fledging 11–13 days after hatching. The male helps the female to feed the young on insects, and takes over feeding altogether when his mate lays a new clutch.

**Identification:** A long, slender bunting with a long tail. The adult male in breeding plumage has a bright-yellow head and underparts, streaked with light-brown markings. The chest is light brown. Upperparts and rump are chestnut-brown with dark streaks on the back. Males are less brightly coloured in winter. Hens generally duller, having brownish-yellow plumage with darker streaks. Juveniles even browner.

# SWIFTS, SWALLOWS AND MARTINS

*With their short beaks and pointed wings, these airborne insect-eaters are among Britain's most accomplished fliers. All are summer visitors to our shores, coming here to breed but leaving for warmer climes as autumn approaches. They build characteristic mud nests, often quite near to human thoroughfares, and will 'dive-bomb' any perceived invaders.*

## Swift

Common swift *Apus apus*

**Distribution**: Found across virtually the whole of Europe, extending to northern Africa and Asia. Overwinters in southern Africa.
**Habitat**: In the air.
**Food**: Flying invertebrates, such as midges and moths.
**Size**: 17cm (6$^1$/2in), wingspan 40–48cm (16–19in).
**Nest**: Cup-shaped, built under cover.
**Eggs**: 2–3, white.

Flocks of swifts are most noticeable when uttering their distinctive, screaming calls, flying low overhead in search of winged insects. At other times they may appear little more than distant specks in the sky, wheeling around at heights of 1,000m (3,300ft) or more. Their flight pattern is quite distinctive, consisting of a series of rapid wingbeats followed by gliding into the wind. Their tiny feet do not allow them to perch, although they can cling to vertical surfaces. Except when breeding, swifts spend their entire lives in the air, and are apparently able to sleep and mate in flight too. If hunting conditions are unfavourable, such as during a cool summer, nestling swifts respond by growing more slowly, while the adults can undergo short periods of torpidity to avoid starvation.

**Identification:** Dark overall, with relatively long, pointed wings and a forked tail. Pale whitish throat. Sexes are alike.

## Swallow

Barn swallow *Hirundo rustica*

The swallows' return to their European breeding grounds is one of the most welcome signs of spring. Pairs return to the same nest site every year. Cock birds arrive back before their partners and jealously guard the site from would-be rivals. As well as aiding its flight, longer forked tails may also help attract females. Although swallows may use traditional nesting sites such as caves or hollow trees, they more commonly build their nests inside buildings such as barns, choosing a site close to the eaves. It can take up to a thousand trips to collect enough mud to complete a new nest.

**Distribution**: Throughout almost all of northern hemisphere. European populations winter in Africa.
**Habitat**: Open country, close to water.
**Food**: Flying invertebrates.
**Size**: 19cm (7$^1$/2in), wingspan 31–34cm (12$^1$/4–13$^1$/2in).
**Nest**: Made of mud, built off the ground.
**Eggs**: 4–5, white with reddish-and-grey spotting.

**Identification:** Chestnut forehead and throat, dark blue head and back, and a narrow dark blue band across the chest. The wings are blackish and the underparts are white. Long tail streamers. Sexes are alike.

## House martin

*Delichon urbica*

The house martin's breeding habits have changed significantly due to an increase in the number of buildings in rural areas. They traditionally nested on cliff faces, but over the past century began to prefer the walls of houses and farm structures as sites, as well as beneath bridges and even on street lamps, where a ready supply of nocturnal insects are attracted to the light. The nest is usually spherical and normally made of mud. The base is built first, followed by the sides. On average, the whole process can take up to two weeks to complete. House martins are highly social by nature, nesting in huge colonies made up of thousands of pairs where conditions are suitable. Even outside the breeding period, they will associate in large flocks comprising hundreds of individuals. They are generally seen near agricultural, wooded or watery areas rich in insect life.

**Distribution**: Throughout the whole of Europe, extending eastwards across much of Asia. Overwinters in Africa south of the Sahara.
**Habitat**: Open country, close to water.
**Food**: Flying invertebrates.
**Size**: 13cm (5in), wingspan 25–29cm (10–11in).
**Nest**: Cup made of mud.
**Eggs**: 4–5, white.

**Identification:** Dark bluish head and back. Black wings with white underwing coverts. The underparts and rump are also white. Forked tail is dark blue. Sexes are alike.

## Sand martin

African sand martin, bank swallow *Riparia riparia*

Europe's smallest member of the hirundine family of swallows and martins can usually be observed near lakes and other stretches of water in the summer, frequently swooping down over the surface to catch invertebrates. They are most likely to be nesting in colonies nearby, in tunnels excavated in suitable sandy banks. Sometimes conservationists provide artificial homes for them in gravel pits. Their burrows can extend up to 1m (3ft) into the bank, and the nesting chamber at the end is lined with grass, seaweed and similar material. The eggs are laid on a soft bed of feathers. Once the young martins leave the nest, they stay in groups with other chicks, waiting for their parents to return and feed them. The adults typically bring around 60 invertebrates back from each visit. Parents recognize their offspring by their distinctive chattering calls. If danger threatens, the repetitive alarm calls of the adult sand martins cause the young to rush back into the nesting tunnels.

Populations have crashed twice in the past 50 years because of drought in their winter habitat in Africa.

**Identification:** Brown on the head, back, wings and tail, with a brown band across the breast. Throat area and underparts are white. Long flight feathers. Small black bill. Sexes are alike. Young birds have shorter flight feathers, and are browner overall.

**Distribution**: Ranges across virtually the whole of Europe and parts of northern Africa into Asia. Overwinters in sub-Saharan Africa.
**Habitat**: Open country, close to water.
**Food**: Flying invertebrates.
**Size**: 11cm (4¼in), wingspan 29–32cm (11–13in).
**Nest**: Hole in a sandbank.
**Eggs**: 3–4, white.

# GAME BIRDS, PIGEONS AND DOVES

*A number of pheasant and partridge species have been selectively bred and released for sport, so that sightings far outside their usual areas of distribution are not unusual. In Europe, these game birds are most likely to be observed during the winter months, when there is less natural cover available and groups may be forced to forage more widely.*

## Common pheasant

Ring-necked pheasant *Phasianus colchicus*

Common pheasants show considerable individual variation in appearance throughout their European range. This is due to hybridization between races, resulting in the loss of distinguishing characteristics. Even odd black-feathered (melanistic) examples are not uncommon. This situation has arisen because of widespread breeding and subsequent release into the wild for shooting. They occur naturally in Asia. Common pheasants usually live in groups of a cock bird with several hens. They forage on the ground, flying noisily and somewhat clumsily when disturbed, and may roost off the ground.

**Identification**: Cock bird has prominent areas of bare red skin on each side of the face, surrounded by metallic dark greenish plumage. Variable white area at the base of the neck. The remainder of the plumage is predominantly brown, with the underparts a more chestnut shade with dark blotching. Hens are lighter brown overall, with darker mottling, especially on the back and wings.

**Distribution**: Range extends through western Europe, except for the Iberian Peninsula, and in a band eastwards through central Asia as far as Japan. Has also been introduced to the United States, Australia, Tasmania and New Zealand.
**Habitat**: Light woodland.
**Food**: Seeds, berries, young shoots, also invertebrates.
**Size**: 62–89cm (24½–35in), wingspan 80–90cm (31½–35½in).
**Nest**: Scrape on the ground.
**Eggs**: 7–15, olive-brown.

---

**Chukar partridge** (*Alectoris chukar*) 35cm (14in), wingspan 48cm (19in). Introduced to the British Isles. Similar colouring to red-legged partridge, but with cream area on the sides of the face and chest, a broad white stripe above the eyes and black on the side of the lower mandible. Hens lack tarsal swelling of males.

**Grey partridge** (*Perdix perdix*) 32cm (13in), wingspan 56cm (22in). Occurs in a broad band across central Europe from Ireland to Asia, sightings are rare in Britain. It has a mottled plumage of grey and brown, highlighted by a red face and throat and a horseshoe-shaped black belly patch. Browner than a red-legged partridge, and flank markings are less bold.

## Red-legged partridge

*Alectoris rufa*

The red-legged partridge was brought to England for shooting as long ago as the late 1600s, and its adaptable nature ensured that its range steadily expanded. However, during the 20th century the chukar partridge, which hybridizes with the red-legged variety, was also introduced to the British Isles. Today it can be difficult to determine whether partridges are pure or cross-bred red-legged individuals, even in their natural range.

Red-legged partridges form individual pairs when breeding. The cock bird chooses and then prepares the nest site.

**Distribution**: Found naturally from the Iberian Peninsula to Italy. Introduced to Britain.
**Habitat**: Open countryside.
**Food:** Mainly plant matter, some invertebrates.
**Size**: 38cm (15in), wingspan 30–45cm (12–18in).
**Nest**: Scrape on the ground.
**Eggs**: 9–12, pale yellowish-brown with dark spotting.

**Identification:** Prominent black collar with distinctive black streaks extending around the sides of the neck to the eye. Black stripe continues through the eye to the bill, with white above and below the throat. Bluish-grey above the bill, and on the breast and barred flanks. Brownish abdomen. Hens lack the tarsal spurs on the legs.

## Collared dove

*Streptopelia decaocto*

The westerly spread of these doves during the second half of the 20th century was one of the most dramatic examples of the changing patterns of distribution among bird species. In this case, the triggers for the distribution change are unclear. Collared doves had been recorded in Hungary in the 1930s, and they moved rapidly over the next decade across Germany and Austria to France, and also headed north to Denmark and the Netherlands. The species was first sighted in eastern England during 1952, and a pair bred there three years later. The earliest Irish record was reported in 1959, and by the mid-1960s the collared dove had colonized almost all of the UK. No other bird species has spread naturally so far and so rapidly in recent times, to the extent that the collared dove's range now extends right across Europe and Asia.

*Above: The collared dove's nest is almost incredible; a flimsy platform of twigs in a tree, or sometimes on a building.*

**Identification:** Pale greyish-fawn with a narrow black half-collar around the back of the neck. Dark flight feathers with white edging along the leading edge of the wing. White tips to tail feathers visible when spread. Depth of individual coloration can vary. Sexes are alike.

**Distribution:** Across Europe, apart from the far north of Scandinavia and the Alps, eastwards to Asia. More localized on the Iberian Peninsula and in North Africa particularly.
**Habitat:** Parks and gardens.
**Food:** Seeds and some plant matter.
**Size:** 34cm (13½in), wingspan (48–55cm (19–21½in).
**Nest:** Platform of twigs.
**Eggs:** 2, white.

## Golden pheasant

*Chrysolophus pictus*

Adult cock golden pheasants are naturally polygamous, living with two or three hens, but very little else has been documented about the habits of these birds in the wild. They occur in areas where there is dense vegetative cover, and because they live on the ground, observing them in these surroundings is difficult. They are very shy birds, and roost in trees at night. They feed mainly on the leaves and shoots of a variety of plants, as well as eating the flowers of rhododendrons. In the British Isles they are confined to the areas they were introduced to for game in Scotland, England and Wales. The golden pheasant is smaller than the common pheasant.

**Identification:** Golden-yellow feathering on head, lower back and rump. The underparts are vibrant scarlet, merging into chestnut. The ruff or tippet on the neck is golden with black edging to the plumage and the upper back is green. Has long, mottled tail feathers. Hens in comparison are smaller and a duller colour, being essentially brown with mottling or barring on the feathers. Their tail feathers are pointed at the tips. Young birds resemble hens but have less pronounced markings.

**Distribution:** Occurs naturally in central China. Introduced to a few localities elsewhere, most notably in Norfolk, eastern England.
**Habitat:** Wooded areas with shrubs and bamboo.
**Food:** Vegetation and invertebrates.
**Size:** 70–115cm (27–45in), wingspan 70–90cm (27–35½in).
**Nest:** A scrape on the ground.
**Eggs:** 5–12, buff.

**Red grouse** (*Lagopus lagopus*) 33–38cm (13–15in), wingspan 56cm (22in). Also known as Willow grouse. Found in the uplands of the north and west British Isles. Mainly reddish-brown, a plump body and short tail and slightly hooked beak. Its legs have a covering of pale feathers. It feeds on heather, berries, seeds and insects. Females and young birds do not have such showy red combs above the eyes as the males. When a bird is disturbed it will fly up from the grass with a whirring wing beat.

**Black grouse** (Eurasian black grouse, *Tetrao tetrix*) Cock 58cm (23in); hen 45cm (18in), wingspan 80cm (31½in). Present in Scotland and northern England. Mainly black, with scarlet combs above the eyes. White wing bar, white undertail coverts and a white spot at the shoulder area. The tail feathers are curved. The hen is brown, speckled with black barring, and has a white wing bar.

**Stock dove** (*Columba oenas*) 33cm (13in), wingspan 70cm (27in). This bird is sometimes confused with feral pigeons and wood pigeons. Grey head with green iridescence on the neck. Wings are dark grey with black markings and a black band across the tips of the tail feathers. Pale grey rump and lower underparts. Pinkish grey chest.

**European turtle dove** (*Streptopelia turtur*) 27cm (10½in), wingspan 55cm (21½in). Found in much of Europe but not common in Ireland, Scotland or Scandinavia. More brightly coloured on the wings than its East Asian cousin, having orange-brown feathers with darker centres. Black-and-white barring on the sides of the neck. The head is greyish, and the underparts are pale with a slight pinkish hue. White edge to the tail feathers.

*Right: Male capercaillies fan their tail feathers when displaying to hens at sites known as leks.*

# Capercaillie

Western capercaillie *Tetrao urogallus*

Like New World turkeys (*Meleagris* species), male capercaillies adopt a display pose with tail feathers fanned out in a circle. They display communally to hens at sites known as 'leks'. After mating with her chosen partner, the hen nests and rears the young alone. The weather in the critical post-hatching period has a major impact on the survival rate of chicks – in wet springs, many become fatally chilled. Hens are about a third of the weight of cocks. Both sexes have strong, hooked bills, which enable them to easily nip off pieces of tough vegetation such as Scots pine (*Pinus sylvestris*) shoots. This helps them to survive when the ground is covered by snow.

**Distribution**: Present in Scotland and other mountainous regions in western Europe. Range extends through much of Scandinavia and eastwards through northern Asia.
**Habitat**: Coniferous and deciduous areas.
**Food**: Buds and shoots.
**Size**: 80–115cm (31½–45in), wingspan 90–125cm (35½–49½in).
**Nest**: A shallow scrape on the ground.
**Eggs**: 6–10, yellow with light brown blotches.

**Identification**: Greyish-black head with an obvious red stripe above each eye. Green area on the chest. Wings are chestnut, the rump and tail blackish. Underparts are variable, ranging from predominantly white to black. Legs are covered with brown feathers, toes are exposed. Hens have an orangish patch on the sides of the face and chest, brown mottled upperparts and whiter underparts.

# Rock ptarmigan

*Lagopus mutus*

These grouse live in a region where natural cover is very scarce, and undergo a stunning transformation in appearance through the year. Their summer plumage is mottled brown and their winter plumage is white, except for the eye patch and tail, enabling them to merge into the snowy landscape. When snow is on the ground, rock ptarmigans feed on buds and twigs of shrubs such as willow, which manage to grow in this treeless region. Adult males with large combs appear to have more success in finding a mate, and those with magnificent combs are more likely to be bigamous.

Pairs nest in the brief Arctic summer, often choosing a site protected by shrubs. The cock stays nearby while the hen incubates alone. The chicks are covered in down and can move easily, but are not able to fly until their flight feathers have emerged fully, at about ten days old. There are 10,000 breeding pairs recorded in Scotland. They are only seen in the highlands, although in extremely cold weather they may move down to the edge of woodland for shelter. Ptarmigan do not migrate and are a very sedentary species.

**Distribution**: Circumpolar. Present in Iceland, Scotland, northern Scandinavia and in the Alps and Pyrenees. Also in the far north of Asia, North America and Greenland.
**Habitat**: Tundra.
**Food**: Buds, leaves, berries and other plant matter.
**Size**: 38cm (15in), wingspan 43–50cm (17–19½in).
**Nest**: Scrape on the ground, lined with vegetation.
**Eggs**: 6–9, creamy-buff, heavily blotched and spotted with blackish-brown.

**Identification:** Head is mottled and brownish, with red above each eye. Similar patterning across the body, which becomes white in the winter. Males have blackish stripes on the face.

# Quail

Eurasian migratory quail *Coturnix coturnix*

Although these relatively small quails often inhabit agricultural areas, they are hard to spot thanks to their shy natures and the effective camouflage provided by their plumage. Common quails prefer to remain concealed, but take to the wing if necessary, when they are both agile and fast. Their wings appear relatively large when flying, reflecting the fact that these small birds may fly long distances each year.

There is a distinction between the resident African population and migratory birds, with the latter being slightly larger in size and not as rufous in coloration. Throughout their range, these quails tend to occur in areas of grassland, as this vegetation provides them with natural cover.

**Identification:** A pale stripe runs above the eye and a thinner, narrower black stripe runs beneath. There is a small white area faintly bordered by black on the upper chest. The top of the head and back are dark brown. The remainder of the underparts are fawn, becoming paler on the abdomen. Hens lack the white patch, have mottled plumage and are duller in their overall coloration. Young common quail look very similar to the adult hens, but can be distinguished by the absence of stripes on the lower part of their cheeks and the absence of barring on their flanks.

**Distribution**: Occurs in Europe in summer, wintering in Africa south of the Sahara. Also resident in North Africa.
**Habitat**: Open country.
**Food**: Seeds and some invertebrates.
**Size**: 18cm (7in), wingspan 30–35cm (12–14in).
**Nest**: Grass-lined scrape on the ground.
**Eggs**: 5–13, buff with darker markings.

# Rock dove

*Columba livia*

True rock doves have a localized range and favour cliffs and ruined buildings on which to breed. In the past, rock doves were kept and bred by monastic communities, where the young doves (known as squabs) were highly valued as a source of meat. Inevitably, some birds escaped from their dovecotes and reverted to the wild, and their offspring gave rise to today's feral pigeons, which are a common sight in almost every town and city, scavenging whatever they can from our leftovers. Colour mutations have also occurred, and as well as the so-called 'blue' form there are now red and even mainly white individuals today.

**Identification:** Dark bluish-grey head, slight green iridescence on the neck. Light grey wings with two characteristic black bars across each wing. Feral pigeons often have longer wings than rock doves. Reddish-purple coloration on the sides of the upper chest. Remainder of the plumage is grey with a black band at the tip of the tail feathers. Sexes are alike.

*Below: Rock doves' nests are often constructed on a ledge and are made out of twigs or straw.*

**Distribution:** Rock dove occurs naturally in northern areas of Scotland and nearby islands, and in western Ireland. Also found around the Mediterranean. The feral pigeon's range extends throughout Europe and southern Africa, as well as to other continents.
**Habitat:** Originally cliffs and mountainous areas.
**Food:** Mainly seeds.
**Size:** 35cm (14in), wingspan 63–70cm (25–27in).
**Nest:** Loose pile of twigs or similar material.
**Eggs:** 2, white.

# Wood pigeon

*Columba palumbus*

Wood pigeons can be significant agricultural pests in arable farming areas. In towns they will often frequent parks with established stands of trees, descending into nearby gardens and allotments to raid growing crops. However, they also occasionally eat potential crop pests such as snails. Pairs sometimes nest on buildings, although they usually prefer a suitable tree fork. Their calls are surprisingly loud and are often uttered soon after dawn. Outside the breeding season these birds will often congregate in large numbers. If danger threatens, they can appear quite clumsy when taking off.

**Distribution:** Throughout most of Europe except for northern Scandinavia and Iceland, ranging eastwards into Asia. Also present in north-western Africa.
**Habitat:** Areas with tall trees.
**Food:** Seeds, plant matter and invertebrates.
**Size:** 43cm (17in), wingspan 75–80cm (29½–31½in).
**Nest:** Platform of twigs.
**Eggs:** 2, white.

**Identification:** Grey head, with a reflective metallic-green area at the nape of the neck and characteristic white patches on the sides. Bill is reddish at the base, becoming yellow towards the top. Purplish breast becoming paler on the underparts. Tip of tail is black. White edging to the wings most evident in flight, forming a distinct band. Sexes alike.

# CORVIDS

*Studies suggest that corvids rank among the most intelligent avian species. Many of these birds display an instinctive desire to hoard food, such as acorns, to help sustain them through the winter months. Their plumage is often predominantly black, sometimes with grey and white areas. Corvids are generally noisy and quite aggressive by nature.*

## Magpie

Common magpie *Pica pica*

Bold and garrulous, magpies are a common sight throughout much of their range. They are often blamed for the decline of song-birds because of their habit of raiding the nests of other birds. They are usually seen in small groups, although pairs will nest on their own. If a predator such as a cat ventures close to the nest, there will be a considerable commotion, resulting in the nesting magpies being joined by others in the neighbourhood to harry the unfortunate feline. Magpies sometimes take an equally direct approach when seeking food, chasing other birds, gulls in particular, to make them drop their food. Magpies are quite agile when walking, holding their long tails up as they move.

**Identification:** Black head, upper breast, back, rump and tail, with a broad white patch around the abdomen. Broad white wing stripe and dark blue areas evident below on folded wings. Depending on the light, there may be a green gloss apparent on the black plumage. Sexes alike, but the cock may have a longer tail.

**Distribution**: Much of Europe and south to North Africa. Represented in parts of Asia and North America.
**Habitat**: Trees with surrounding open areas.
**Food**: Omnivorous.
**Size**: 52cm (20in), wingspan 56–61cm (22–24in).
**Nest**: Dome-shaped stick pile.
**Eggs**: 2–8, bluish green with darker markings.

---

**Jackdaw** (western jackdaw, *Corvus monedula*): 34cm (13in), wingspan 50cm (9½ in). Ranges throughout western Europe and North Africa. Present in southern Scandinavia and east Asia. Dark grey, lighter on the neck. Eye is pale blue. Short bill. Sexes alike.

**Carrion crow** (*Corvus corone*): 51cm (20in), wingspan 100cm (39½ in). Found in western and south-western parts of Europe. Black plumage. The broad, blunt bill is curved on its upper surface, with no bare skin at the base and feathering around the nostrils. Sexes are alike.

**Red-billed chough** (*Pyrrhocorax pyrrhocorax*): 40cm (16in) wingspan 80cm (31in). Small populations are found on cliffs of south-western and western parts of Britain. Also found in Ireland and around the Mediterranean. Glossy black plumage with a distinctive, curved, narrow red bill. Pink legs and feet. Sexes alike.

## Jay

Eurasian jay *Garrulus glandarius*

Throughout their wide range, there is some local variation in the appearance of these jays, both in the depth of colour and the amount of black on the top of the head. However, their harsh call, which resembles a hoarse scream, coupled with a flash of colour, help identify them. Jays are shy by nature and rarely allow a close approach. They store acorns and other seeds in the autumn, and such caches help to sustain them through the winter when the ground may be covered in snow, restricting their opportunities to find other food. During the summer, these jays may raid the nests of other birds, taking both eggs and chicks.

**Identification:** Pinkish brown with a greyer shade on the wings. Streaking on the head. Broad, black moustachial stripe with whitish throat. White rump and undertail area. Tail is dark. White stripe on the wings with black and blue markings on the sides of the wings. Sexes alike.

**Distribution**: Throughout most of Europe (except Scotland and the extreme north of Scandinavia). Also present in North Africa and Asia.
**Habitat**: Woodland.
**Food**: Omnivorous.
**Size**: 35cm (14in), wingspan 52–58cm (20–23in).
**Nest**: Platform of twigs.
**Eggs**: 3–7, bluish green with dense speckling.

# Rook

*Corvus frugilegus*

These highly social corvids nest in colonies, partly because they inhabit areas of open countryside where there are few trees available. There is, nevertheless, a strong bond between the members of a pair. The rookery serves as the group's centre, which makes them vulnerable to human persecution, but although they eat corn, they are valued for consuming invertebrates as well. The rook's bill is adapted to digging in the ground to extract invertebrates, especially cranefly ('daddy-long-legs') larvae. Outside the breeding season, it is not uncommon for rooks to associate with other corvids, such as jackdaws, crows and ravens, as an alternative to the rookery may be used as a roosting site at this time.

**Distribution**: Throughout Europe east to Asia. Some move south in the winter to the north Mediterranean.
**Habitat**: Close to farmland.
**Food**: Omnivorous, but mainly invertebrates.
**Size**: 49cm (19¼in), wingspan 78–89cm (31–35in).
**Nest**: Made of sticks built in trees.
**Eggs**: 2–7, bluish green with dark markings.

**Identification:** Black plumage, pointed bill with bare, pinkish skin at its base. The nostrils of rooks are unfeathered, distinguishing them from carrion crows. Rooks also have a flatter forehead and a peak to the crown. Sexes alike.

# Raven

Common raven *Corvus corax*

**Distribution**: Mainly south-western Europe and North Africa north to Scandinavia and east throughout most of northern Asia. Also present in North America, Greenland, Iceland and the British Isles.
**Habitat**: Relatively open country.
**Food**: Carrion.
**Size**: 67cm (26in), wingspan 120–160cm (47–63in).
**Nest**: Bulky, made of sticks.
**Eggs**: 3–7, bluish with darker spots.

**Identification:** Very large in size with a powerful, curved bill. Entirely black plumage. Wedge-shaped tail in flight, when the flight feathers stand out, creating a fingered appearance at the tips. Males often larger than females.

The croaking calls of the raven are a foolproof way of identifying this bird, and its size is also a good indicator. Ravens are the largest members of the crow family occurring in the Northern Hemisphere. The impression of bulk conveyed by these birds is reinforced by their shaggy throat feathers, which do not lie sleekly. There is a recognized decline in size across their range, with ravens found in the far north larger than those occurring farther south. Pairs occupy relatively large territories, and even outside the breeding season they tend not to associate in large flocks. When searching for food, ravens are able to fly quite effortlessly over long distances, flapping their wings slowly.

# OWLS

*Most owls become more active after dark, and so are more likely to be heard than seen. They are predatory birds, and it is possible to determine their diet by examining their pellets, which are the indigestible remains of their prey regurgitated after a meal. These pellets are often found near their nests or at favoured roosting sites, indicating their presence.*

## Tawny owl

*Strix aluco*

The distinctive double call notes of these owls reveal their presence, even though their dark coloration makes them difficult to spot. Tawny owls prefer ancient woodland, where trees are large enough to provide hollow nesting cavities. They will, however, adapt to using nest boxes, which has helped to increase their numbers in some areas. Nocturnal by nature, these owls may nevertheless occasionally hunt during the daytime, especially when they have chicks in the nest. They usually sit quietly on a perch, waiting to swoop down on their quarry. Young tawny owls are unable to fly when they first leave the nest, and at this time the adults can become very aggressive in protecting their offspring.

**Identification:** Tawny-brown, with white markings across the wings and darker striations over the wings and body. Slight barring on the tail. Distinctive white stripes above the facial disc, which is almost plain brown. Some individuals have a greyer tone to their plumage, while others are more rufous. The bill is yellowish-brown. Sexes are similar, although females are generally larger and heavier. Females are also distinguished by their higher-pitched song.

**Distribution**: Across Europe (not Ireland) to Scandinavia and eastwards into Asia. Also occurs in North Africa.
**Habitat**: Favours ancient temperate woodland.
**Food**: Small mammals, birds and invertebrates.
**Size**: 43cm (17in), wingspan 95–105cm (38–41½in).
**Nest**: Tree hole.
**Eggs**: 2–9, white.

## Barn owl

*Tyto alba*

Barn owls seek out dark places in which to roost, using buildings in various parts of their range. They may be seen in open country, swooping over farmland, with some individuals choosing to pursue bats. Males in particular will often utter harsh screeches when in flight, which serve as territorial markers, while females make a distinctive snoring sound for food at the nest site. They pair for life, which can be for more than 20 years. Barn owls have adapted to hunting along roadside verges, but here they are in real danger of being hit by vehicles.

**Distribution**: Worldwide. Throughout western Europe, Africa (except the Sahara) and the Middle East.
**Habitat**: Prefers relatively open countryside.
**Food**: Voles and amphibians, also invertebrates.
**Size**: 39cm (15½in), wingspan up to 106cm (42in).
**Nest**: Hollow tree or inside a building.
**Eggs**: 4–7, white.

**Identification:** Whitish, heart-shaped face and underparts. In much of Europe, underparts more yellowish-orange. Top of the head and wings greyish-orange with spots. Eyes black. Males often paler than females.

**Long-eared owl** (*Asio otus*) 37cm (14½in), wingspan 98cm (38½in). The long-eared owl is resident throughout much of northern England, northern Wales and Ireland, and occurs in summer through much of northern Scotland. Despite being widespread, however, it is rarely seen. Not only is it nocturnal, it is also exceedingly well camouflaged and tends to choose areas of dense cover in which to roost. The long-eared owl is named for the two ear-like tufts of feathers which protrude from the top of its head. These are actually nothing to do with its true ears, which are hidden beneath the plumage on the sides of its head.

**Short-eared owl** (*Asio flammeus*) 42cm (16½in) wingspan 110cm (43in). The short-eared owl is found throughout Great Britain, being resident in southern and eastern Scotland, most of north and parts of eastern England and much of western Wales. Elsewhere in Scotland it is a summer visitor, while it is a winter visitor to eastern Wales and most of southern England. It also occurs during the winter in parts of eastern and southern Ireland. Compared with the long-eared owl, the short-eared owl is frequently seen, being occasionally active by day and preferring to hunt over open habitats. It can be most easily distinguished from other British owls by its piercing yellow eyes.

# Eagle owl

Eurasian eagle owl *Bubo bubo*

The eagle owl's scientific name reflects the sound of its loud calls, which are clearly audible on still nights even from quite a distance. Pairs will call alternately before mating, and the call notes of the female are higher-pitched than the male's. In spite of their large size, these owls fly quietly and may sometimes be seen soaring. Formidable hunters, they will occasionally take large, potentially dangerous quarry such as buzzards and herons. Eagle owls are adaptable in their feeding habits, and may sometimes resort to catching earthworms and fish, as well as eating carrion when hunting opportunities are limited.

**Distribution**: Throughout southern Europe, Scandinavia and eastwards across Asia. Small populations in parts of western Europe and western North Africa.
**Habitat**: Rocky areas and relatively open country.
**Food**: Mammals and birds.
**Size**: 73cm (29in), wingspan 140–200cm (55–79in).
**Nest**: Cliff ledges, or occasionally on the ground.
**Eggs**: 1–4, white.

**Identification:** Brownish with dark markings on the wings. Underparts are buff-brown with streaking, most evident on the breast. Prominent ear tufts. Black bill, orange irides. Hens are often slightly larger. There may be great variation in appearance, and at least 13 different races are recognized.

# Little owl

*Athene noctua*

Little owls can be seen resting during the daytime, on telegraph poles and similar perches in the open. Introduced to Britain in the 1800s, they have since spread right across southern England. They hover in flight, but are rather ungainly when walking on the ground. One factor which has assisted their spread is their adaptability in choosing a nest site – disused factories and even rabbit warrens may be used. The hen sits alone for the incubation, which lasts 24 days. Both adults feed the young, who fledge after five weeks. The young owls will be independent within a further two months.

**Identification:** White spotting on the head, white above the eyes and a whitish moustache. Heavy brown streaking on a white chest. Larger whiter spots on the wings, barring on the flight feathers and banding across the tail. Whitish legs and feet. Bill yellowish, irides yellow. Young lack white spotting on the forehead. Sexes are alike, but hens usually larger.

**Distribution**: Range extends from southern Britain and throughout most of Europe at a similar latitude (not as far as Scandinavia) eastwards into Asia. Also present in northern parts of Africa, extending to parts of the Middle East.
**Habitat**: Prefers relatively open country.
**Food**: Invertebrates and small vertebrates.
**Size**: 25cm (10in), wingspan 50–56cm (19½–22in).
**Nest**: Tree hole or a cliff hole.
**Eggs**: 3–5, white.

# BIRDS OF PREY

*Aerial agility is a feature associated with birds of prey, particularly those that hunt other birds. Some are equally adept at pursuing terrestrial prey. Many species have developed specialized hunting techniques, and the young of these birds have to remain with the adults for some time after fledging in order to learn the skills they will need to feed themselves.*

## Red kite

*Milvus milvus*

**Distribution**: Range includes Wales, the Midlands, northern England and south-west Scotland. Also in the Iberian Peninsula and North Africa, and across Europe to south Sweden, and Russia.
**Habitat**: Light woodland.
**Food**: Small birds, mammals and carrion.
**Size**: 66cm (26in), wingspan 145–170cm (57–67in).
**Nest**: Platform of sticks, built in a tree.
**Eggs**: 1–4, white with reddish-brown markings.

Although very agile hunters, red kites also seek carrion such as dead sheep. This behaviour has resulted in their persecution in some areas because of misplaced fears that the kites actually kill lambs. When seeking prey, red kites circle repeatedly overhead, relying on their keen eyesight to spot any movement on the ground. They will then drop and sweep low, homing in on their target. Up until the 1700s, flocks of red kites were common scavengers on the streets of London, where they were sufficiently tame to swoop down and steal food from children. It was their willingness to scavenge, however, that led to a dramatic reduction in their numbers, since they were easily killed using carcasses laced with poison.

**Identification**: Predominantly reddish-brown, with a greyish head streaked with darker markings. Darker mottling over the wings, with some variable streaking on the underparts as well. Feet are yellowish with black talons. White areas under the wings and forked tail can be clearly seen in flight. Sexes are alike.

## Hen harrier

Northern harrier *Circus cyaneus*

Hen harriers are very distinctive hunters, flying low over moorland, seeking not only small mammals but also birds. Their preference for hunting grouse has led to persecution by gamekeepers in various parts of their range. However, over the winter months these harriers may be forced to feed largely on carrion. Their range extends farther north than those of related species, into the tundra region, but they are not resident in far northern areas throughout the year, and will head farther south before the start of winter. Hen harriers are unusual in not only roosting on the ground but also breeding on the ground. Once the breeding season is over they will often congregate at communal sites, which may be used for several generations.

**Identification**: Mainly chestnut overall, streaked with white. Darker over the wings. Narrow white band around each eye, with a solid brown area beneath. Tail is barred. The bill is dark, and the legs are yellow. Hens are larger.

**Distribution**: Throughout much of the northern Hemisphere. Extends across most of Europe, including Scandinavia, east to Asia. Often moves south for the winter as far as North Africa.
**Habitat**: Moorland.
**Food**: Mainly small mammals and birds.
**Size**: 52cm (20in), wingspan 97–110cm (38½–43in).
**Nest**: On the ground, hidden in vegetation.
**Eggs**: 3–5, whitish.

BIRDS OF PREY **155**

**Black kite** (*Milvus migrans*) 60cm (23in), wingspan 130–170cm (51–67in). Present on much of mainland Europe to Asia and Australia. Also occurs in North Africa and overwinters south of the Sahara. Mainly brown but darker on the wings. The underparts are decidedly rufous. Barring on the tail. Some grey markings on the head. Sexes are alike.

**Montagu's harrier** (*Circus pygargus*) 52cm (20in), wingspan 97–115cm (38½–45in). Found in Europe, North Africa and Asia. Overwinters in central and eastern Africa south of the Sahara. Predominantly grey, with barring on the lower underparts. Narrow white rump. Hens are larger, with brown plumage. In dark morph, males are blackish and hens are a dark chocolate-brown.

**Rough-legged buzzard** (*Buteo lagopu*) 52–60cm (20–23in), wingspan 110–130cm (43–51in). These buzzards hunt rodents, but take birds including snow buntings, grouse and wood pigeons in the winter. Insects and spiders may also be caught, along with fish, and carrion may be scavenged. Pairs return to their Scandinavian breeding grounds in mid-April, reusing a nest. In Britain they are seen along the east coast.

**Honey buzzard** (*Pernis apivorus*) 52–60cm (21–24in), wingspan 135–150cm (52–59in). This migrant from Africa is actually a kite. It feeds on the larvae and nests of wasps and hornets. It has pale plumage under its wings and belly with brown bars. The male's head is blue-grey, while the female's is brown. Tail and wings are longer than the common buzzard's.

# Sparrowhawk

Eurasian sparrowhawk *Accipiter nisus*

These hawks favour preying on groundfeeding birds, and males generally take smaller quarry than females, reflecting the difference in their respective sizes. Even females rarely take birds much larger than pigeons, although they will prey on thrushes. Pairs nest later in the year than many songbirds, so there are plenty of nestlings to prey on and feed to their own chicks. Sparrowhawks have short wings and are very agile in flight, able to manoeuvre easily in wooded areas. They approach quietly with the aim of catching their target unawares, seizing their prey using their powerful feet.

**Identification:** Grey head, back and wings, with darker barring on the grey tail. Barred underparts. Bare yellow legs and feet, with long toes. Cock birds are smaller than hens and have pale rufous areas on the lower sides of the face, extending to the chest, while the barring on their underparts is browner.

*Left: Young male sparrowhawks fledge several days before their heavier female siblings.*

**Distribution**: Resident in most of Europe (except the far north of Scandinavia), North Africa and the Canary Islands. Migratory birds overwinter around the Red Sea. Extends east to Asia.
**Habitat**: Light woodland.
**Size**: 28–38cm (11–15in), wingspan 60–75cm (23–29½in).
**Food**: Mainly birds.
**Nest**: Made of sticks.
**Eggs**: 4–6, pale blue with reddish-brown markings.

# Common buzzard

Eurasian buzzard *Buteo buteo*

With its rather broad and stocky appearance, the common buzzard's silhouette in flight helps to confirm its identity. Buzzards are capable of soaring for long periods, before suddenly swooping down to seize a rabbit – their traditional prey, particularly in many parts of Europe. On the other hand, buzzards can sometimes be observed hunting invertebrates, walking purposefully on the ground in search of their quarry. They may occasionally be spotted on roads too, feeding on roadkill, even placing themselves in danger from the passing traffic. However, buzzards remain one of the most common raptors in Europe, thanks largely to their adaptable feeding habits.

**Identification:** Mainly dark brown, with a variable amount of white plumage around the bill and on the underparts. The tail is barred, with paler plumage around the vent. Legs and feet are yellow, and the bill is yellow with a dark tip. White predominates in the pale morph. Hens are often larger.

**Distribution**: Resident in western Europe. Summer visitor Scandinavia and Asia. Migratory European birds overwinter in Africa.
**Habitat**: Areas with trees.
**Food**: Small mammals and other prey.
**Size**: 57cm (22½in), wingspan 110–130cm (43–51in).
**Nest**: Platform of sticks, usually in a tree.
**Eggs**: 2–4, white.

# Golden eagle

*Aquila chrysaetos*

**Identification:** Brown overall, with yellowish-brown plumage on the back of the head extending down the nape of the neck. Those eagles inhabiting desert areas, such as the Middle East, are slightly paler overall. The bill is yellow with a dark tip. Feet are also yellow, with black talons. Hens are larger in size than cocks.

These majestic eagles generally inhabit remote areas away from people, where they are likely to be left undisturbed. When seen in flight, the golden eagle's head looks relatively small compared to its broad tail and large, square-ended wings. It has some yapping call notes not unlike those of a dog, but generally its calls are quite shrill. Golden eagles have adapted their hunting skills to suit their environment. For instance, in some areas they take tortoises, dropping the reptiles from a great height in order to smash their shells before eating them; in other areas, they may prey on cats. They prefer to capture their quarry on the ground, swooping down low, rather than catching birds in the air.

**Distribution**: Ranges sporadically through the Mediterranean region and eastwards into Asia. Present in Scotland and Scandinavia. Also occurs in parts of northern Africa.
**Habitat**: Mountainous areas.
**Food**: Birds and mammals.
**Size**: 90cm (35½in), wingspan 180–220cm (71–87in).
**Nest**: Massive cliff nest made of sticks.
**Eggs**: 2, white with some dark markings.

# White-tailed sea eagle

*Haliaeetus albicilla*

The white-tailed sea eagle is one of the great success stories of conservation and reintroduction in Britain. The fourth largest eagle in the world, this spectacular creature was hunted, trapped and poisoned to extinction in Britain in the early 19th century. In 1975, a reintroduction programme began on the island of Rhum off the west coast of Scotland, using birds brought in from Scandinavia. In 1985, the species first successfully bred and today there are an estimated 42 breeding territories along Scotland's north-west coast. Sadly, the white-tailed sea eagle continues to face threats, mainly from egg collectors and individuals laying out poisoned bait, ostensibly to kill crows and foxes.

The white-tailed sea eagle is a territorial bird. In Britain, pairs remain in the same territory for the whole of their lives (farther north, some migrate to escape the worst hardships of winter). Young birds are eventually forced to leave and look for territories of their own. The size of the average territory required to support a pair – between 50 and 130 square kilometres – means that this bird is always destined to be uncommon in Britain, even if it manages to extend its range.

**Identification**: This enormous bird is almost unmistakable. The only other British species it might be confused with is the golden eagle, but the white-tailed sea eagle has much broader, club-ended wings and a bright white tail, as its name suggests. Apart from its tail, the white-tailed sea eagle is covered with feathers of mottled shades of brown. There are also pale areas on both the upper and lower sides of the wings.

**Distribution**: Largest populations are in Norway and Russia, also found in south-west Greenland, Denmark, Sweden, Poland and Germany. In the UK is mainly confined to the islands and rocky coasts of western Scotland, although a reintroduction programme in eastern Scotland has begun.
**Habitat**: Coastal regions and islands.
**Food**: Fish, birds, small mammals and carrion.
**Size**: 68–92cm (27–36in), wingspan 180–244cm (71–96in).
**Nest**: Built with twigs and branches, lined with rushes and grasses.
**Eggs**: 1–3, dull white.

## Kestrel

Common kestrel *Falco tinnunculus*

These common birds of prey can frequently be seen hovering at the side of busy roads, largely undisturbed by the traffic thundering close by. Roadsides provide them with good hunting opportunities, and their keen eyesight enables them to spot even quite small quarry such as grasshoppers on the ground. In the winter, they may resort to hunting earthworms drawn to the surface by heavy rainfall. Kestrels also venture into towns, hunting in parks.

**Identification:** Bluish-grey head, with a black stripe under each eye and a whitish throat. Dense black spotting on the pale brownish chest, extending to the abdomen. Wings are chestnut-brown with black markings. Rump and tail feathers are grey with black tips. Hens are similar but have browner heads and distinct barring across the tail feathers.

**Distribution**: Range extends throughout western Europe across to South-east Asia and North Africa. Also breeds in Scandinavia.
**Habitat**: Open countryside.
**Food**: Invertebrates and small mammals.
**Size**: 37cm (14½in), wingspan 65–80cm (25½–31½in).
**Nest**: Platform of sticks in a tree or farm building.
**Eggs**: 3–7, pale pink with dark brown markings.

## Peregrine falcon

*Falco peregrinus*

Peregrine falcons are powerful aerial predators, swooping down incredibly quickly on unsuspecting birds from above. Indeed, it is thought that they can dive at speeds of up to 350km/h (217mph). The impact made by their feet when they strike is so great that their quarry is frequently killed instantaneously. Pigeons are generally favoured as prey, although they may also hunt waterfowl. Peregrine falcons are highly adaptable hunters and can very occasionally be sighted in cities, where apartment blocks replace the crags from which they would normally fly on hunting excursions.

**Hobby** (*Falco subbuteo*) 35cm (14in), wingspan 82–92cm (32–36in). This beautiful bird of prey is similar in size to a kestrel. However, in its general appearance it has more in common with a peregrine falcon, with a dark blue back, barred underside and facial mask, complete with 'moustache'. Like the peregrine, the hobby is an expert flier, catching winged prey. Unlike that larger bird, however, which dives from a height, the hobby pursues and grabs its victims in level flight. Its prey varies from large insects such as dragonflies to small birds like swallows and martins.

**Distribution**: Resident in most of western Europe and much of Africa. One of the most adaptable and widely distributed birds of prey, occurring on all continents.
**Habitat**: Usually near cliffs, sometimes open ground.
**Food**: Birds.
**Size**: 38–52cm (15–20in), wingspan 95–115cm (38–45in)
**Nest**: Cliff ledges.
**Eggs**: 3–4, whitish with red-brown markings.

**Identification:** Dark grey upperparts. A broad blackish stripe extends down below each eye, and the surrounding white area extends right around the throat. The barring on the chest is lighter than on the abdomen. Darker markings are apparent on the grey feathers of the back and wings. The tail is barred, with paler grey feathering at the base. The legs and feet are yellow. Wings appear relatively narrow when seen in flight. Hens are much larger than male birds.

## Osprey

*Pandion haliaetus*

The distribution of the osprey extends to all inhabited continents, making it one of the most wide-ranging of all birds. It has adapted to feeding on stretches of fresh water as well as on estuaries and even the open sea, swooping down to grab fish from just below the water's surface using its powerful talons. Ospreys are capable of carrying fish weighing up to 300g (11oz) without difficulty. In many areas, especially in Europe, ospreys are migratory, and the birds will head south to Africa for the duration of the northern winter. Populations occurring in Scotland and Scandinavia will fly south of the Sahara, rather than joining the resident osprey population in north Africa. The main UK stronghold of nesting sites is Scotland, and Cumbria is also significant. Birds leave for Africa again in September.

**Distribution**: Around the globe. European ospreys range from the British Isles to the Iberian Peninsula and other areas, and from parts of Scandinavia eastwards into Asia. Widely distributed throughout Africa south of the Sahara during the winter.
**Habitat**: Close to stretches of water.
**Food**: Fish.
**Size**: 58cm (23in), wingspan 145–170cm (57–67in).
**Nest**: Platform of sticks built in a tree.
**Eggs**: 3, white in colour with darker markings.

**Identification:** Brown stripes running through the eyes and down over the back and wings. The eyes are yellow. Top of the head and underparts are white. Brown striations across the breast, most marked in hens. Tall, upright stance, powerful grey legs and talons. Hens are significantly heavier than cocks.

## Goshawk

*Accipiter gentilis*

Goshawks are opportunistic hunters. In the far north, birds such as grouse (*Tetraonidae*) are significant in their diet, but in central Europe they prey more on pigeons and rabbits. The Spanish population hunts lizards, although larger quarry is preferred. Appearance is equally variable through their range, with birds from the far north paler than those farther south. Breeding starts in April, with pairs seeking out tall trees as nesting sites, each occupying a large territory. The bulky nest is made from sticks with a softer lining of leaves. Incubation lasts five weeks. Young cock goshawks leave the nest after a similar interval, about a week before their female siblings.

**Distribution**: Throughout mainland Europe, except for the far north of Scandinavia and southern parts of the Iberian Peninsula. Localized in British Isles (absent from Ireland). Small population present in north-west Africa, opposite the Strait of Gibraltar. Extends across Asia. Also found in North America down to Mexico.
**Habitat**: Forested areas.
**Food**: Mammals and birds.
**Size**: 68cm (27in), wingspan 98–115cm (38½–45in).
**Nest**: Platform made from sticks and leaves.
**Eggs**: 1–5, bluish-white.

**Identification:** Dark cap, pale around the eyes. Grey ear coverts, lighter wings. White underparts finely barred with grey. Broad, light-and-dark grey tail banding. Iris orange. Yellow cere, dark tip to the bill. Hens slaty-grey, cocks bluish-grey. Young brownish above, with brownish streaking on buff-coloured underparts.

# Red-footed falcon

*Falco vespertinus*

A rare visitor to Britain, the red-footed falcon is an unusual bird of prey as it usually arrives alone, blown off course during its annual migration. In its wintering and breeding grounds, however, it is a very social bird. Roosts are colonial and can sometimes contain several thousand individuals. Nesting is also a social affair, with birds taking over rookeries after their original corvid builders and occupants have left.

While it breeds and roosts in large numbers, the red-footed falcon hunts alone. Much of its insect prey is caught in flight – crickets, grasshoppers and locusts are particularly favoured. Small vertebrates, such as mice and lizards, are sought both from the air and on the ground. This falcon will often hover, kestrel-like, as it scans the ground below for prey, dropping down suddenly on its victims. Alternatively, it may land and chase after prey on foot. Lizards and insects in particular are often caught in this way. Most of its hunting is done around the hours of dawn and dusk, when it can often be spotted flying low, particularly over rivers. Its flight is usually graceful, with quick wing beats and occasional periods of gliding, but it becomes more erratic and jerky as it chases after prey.

**Identification**: Compared with most falcons this bird is small and relatively slender. The two sexes differ markedly in appearance: the male has mostly slate-grey plumage, but with the lower belly, undertail and thighs a warm chestnut colour. The legs are red, as are the eye-rings and a patch of skin at the base of the bill. The female is larger and has blue-grey upper parts with black bands, a pale head and a rusty orange to pale yellow belly.

**Distribution**: This species breeds in eastern Europe and is a rare visitor to Britain where most sightings occur in eastern England from May to July.
**Habitat**: Open country
**Food**: Small mammals, lizards and insects
**Size**: 28–31cm (11–12¼in), wingspan 65–75cm (25½–29½in).
**Nest**: Nest communally in the nests of other birds, particularly rooks, after their young have fledged.
**Eggs**: 3–5, red-brown with darker speckles.

# Merlin

Pigeon hawk *Falco columbarius*

These highly adaptable hawks can be observed in a wide range of environments. They tend to breed in the far north where there is little cover, swooping low and fast above the ground in search of prey. Pairs may sometimes seek out and pursue their quarry together, increasing their chances of making a kill. Indeed, merlins have even been seen hunting in the company of other birds of prey. The merlin prefers to tackle birds in flight rather than seizing individual birds when they are perching.

**Identification**: Orange-brown underparts and collar with dark streaking. Crown and wings are bluish-grey with dark streaking. Streaking also on the whitish cheeks. A broad dark band on the tail with a white tip. Hens have brownish-grey upperparts with a series of four or five narrow light bands extending down the tail. Upperparts are whitish with brown markings. Males usually smaller than females.

**Distribution**: Present in the British Isles throughout the year. Occurs in Scandinavia, moving south in the winter down to North Africa. Occurs in Asia and the Americas also.
**Habitat**: Lightly wooded and open countryside.
**Food**: Mostly birds.
**Size**: 33cm (13in), wingspan 52–68cm (20–27in).
**Nest**: In trees or sometimes on the ground.
**Eggs**: 3–6, buff with variable reddish speckling.

**Gyr falcon** (*Falco rusticolus*) 63cm (25in), wingspan 110–130cm (43–51in). These light bluish-grey falcons can be sighted in coastal regions, where they prey on seabirds. They fly low in open countryside, taking birds and small rodents, preferring to catch their quarry on the ground rather than in flight. The birds are present in Scotland, Ireland and Cornwall.

**Marsh harrier** (*Circus aeruginosus*) 48–56cm (19–22in), wingspan 115–130cm (45–51in). The marsh harrier is a varied hunter. It raids nests as well as catching birds and mammals. It has a varied diet, dependent on its range, that may change throughout the year. The bird is rare in Britain, and does not breed at all in Ireland or Wales.

# MIGRATORY INSECTIVORES, LARKS AND WAGTAILS

*In temperate areas, obtaining sufficient invertebrate prey throughout the year can be difficult. During the winter, winged insects such as butterflies, bees and flies either hibernate or die. Not surprisingly, many birds migrate south in the autumn in search of a more dependable food supply.*

## Nightjar

European nightjar *Caprimulgus europaeus*

Nightjars are regular summertime visitors to Europe. These birds are nocturnal by nature, which makes them relatively difficult to observe. However, they have very distinctive calls, likened both to the croaking of a frog and the noise of a machine, which are uttered for long periods and carry over a distance of 1km (⁵⁄₈ mile). During the daytime, nightjars spend much of their time resting on the ground, where their mottled, cryptic plumage provides them with excellent camouflage, especially in woodland. Additionally, they narrow their eyes to slits, which makes them even less conspicuous. Nightjars are sufficiently agile in flight to catch moths and other nocturnal invertebrates, flying silently and trawling with their large gapes open. If food is plentiful, pairs may rear two broods in succession, before beginning the long journey south to their African wintering grounds.

**Identification:** Very small bill and long wings. Greyish-brown and mottled in overall appearance, with some black areas, especially near the shoulders. There are white areas below the eyes and on the wings, although the white spots on the wings are seen only in cock birds.

**Distribution**: Most of Europe and north-west Africa, east to Asia. Northern European birds overwinter in south-eastern parts of Africa, while southern European birds migrate to western Africa.
**Habitat**: Heathland and relatively open country.
**Food**: Invertebrates.
**Size**: 28cm (11in), wingspan 56–63cm (22–25in).
**Nest**: Scrape on the ground.
**Eggs**: 2, buff-coloured, with darker markings.

## Pied flycatcher

*Ficedula hypoleuca*

These flycatchers hawk invertebrates in flight, and will also catch slower-moving prey such as caterpillars. They can frequently be seen in oak woodlands in Europe during the summer, though may range north to the taiga, where mosquitoes hatching in pools during the Arctic summer provide an almost constant supply of food. The breeding grounds in the British Isles are restricted to north-west England, mainly in woodlands, and Wales.

**Distribution**: Summer visitor to Europe. Breeding range extends throughout Europe, although not the far north. Overwinters in Africa north of coastal Nigeria to Djibouti.
**Habitat**: Most areas where insects are common.
**Food**: Invertebrates.
**Size**: 13cm (5in), wingspan 20–24cm (8–9½in).
**Nest**: Hole in a tree.
**Eggs**: 5–9, pale blue.

**Spotted flycatcher**
(*Muscicapa striata*) 15cm (6in), wingspan 23–25cm (9–10in). From May to August spotted flycatchers can be seen throughout the UK, although they are scarce in the far north and west. More sightings occur in Devon and Kent. Best looked for along woodland edges and in parks and gardens. Greyish-brown upperparts, with darker streaking on the head extending to the whitish underparts. Area above the bill is also white. Relatively long wings and long, distinctive, square-tipped tail that can be spread to aid hovering. Bill, legs and feet are blackish. Young birds have dull yellowish markings extending from the head down over the wings, rump and tail. Sexes are alike.

**Identification:** Summer plumage is a combination of black and white. White patches are present above the bill and on the wings. The underparts are white, and the remainder of the plumage is black. Hens also have whitish underparts and white areas on the wings, while their upperparts are brownish. Cocks in non-breeding plumage resemble adult hens, but retain the blackish wings and uppertail coverts.

# Lapwing

Northern lapwing *Vanellus vanellus*

These birds are also known as peewits in some areas due to the sound of their calls. Flocks of lapwings are a common sight in farmland and wetland areas, where they comb the ploughed soil for invertebrates. They are easily recognized even from a distance by their distinctive crests. Lapwings may breed in loose groups, and their scrapes are lined with what often becomes quite a substantial pile of vegetation. Lapwings may move long distances during prolonged spells of severe winter weather, sometimes congregating in huge flocks in estuaries when freshwater areas become frozen.

**Identification**: Long, narrow, backward-curving black crest, with black on the face which is separated by a white streak in hens. Underparts are white, except for the chestnut undertail coverts. Wings are dark green, with a greyer green area on the neck. White cheek patches behind the eyes are broken by a black line. Outside the breeding period facial plumage is buff, and white areas are restricted to the chin and throat.

**Distribution**: Occurs from southern Scandinavia south across the whole of Europe to the Mediterranean. Migrates eastwards across Asia as far as Japan. Also occurs in North Africa, and may even be seen in areas farther south.
**Habitat**: Marshland, farmland.
**Food**: Mainly invertebrates.
**Size**: 30cm (12in), wingspan 67–72cm (26–28in).
**Nest**: Scrape on the ground.
**Eggs**: 4, light brown with dark markings.

# Dartford warbler

*Sylvia undata*

These small warblers have been recorded from Sweden, but their most northerly breeding outpost is in southern Britain, where they maintain a tenuous foothold – numbers become severely depleted in harsh winters. They roost in groups, which helps conserve body heat. Dartford warblers forage low down in shrubbery, sometimes venturing to the ground, where they can run surprisingly quickly. Berries feature more significantly in their diet during the winter, certainly in northern areas. Males establish breeding territories in the autumn. They sing more loudly and frequently during the spring, raising the grey feathers on the sides of their faces as part of the courtship ritual. The nest is built by both adults, hidden in a shrub. The hen incubates mainly on her own, for two weeks, and the chicks fledge after a similar interval.

**Identification**: Cock bird has a greyish head, back and wings. White spots on the throat, reddish chest and a grey central area to the underparts. Red area of skin encircles each eye. The bill is yellowish with a dark tip, and the legs and feet are yellowish-brown. Hens are paler with white throats. Young birds have grey-buff underparts, with no orbital skin and dark irises.

**Distribution**: Range extends through western parts of Europe, including the Iberian Peninsula, the western Mediterranean region and western parts of North Africa. Also present in southern parts of England.
**Habitat**: Heathland.
**Food**: Mostly invertebrates, but some berries.
**Size**: 14cm (5¹/₂in), wingspan 13–18cm (5–7in).
**Nest**: Cup-shaped, made from vegetation.
**Eggs**: 3–5, whitish with darker markings.

## Wryneck

*Jynx torquilla*

Wrynecks return to their breeding grounds by April, when pairs are very territorial. They seek a suitable hollow, which may be in a tree, on the ground or in a bank. When displaying, pairs face each other and shake their heads, opening their bills to reveal pink gapes. The two-week incubation is shared, and both adults care for their young, who fledge after three weeks. They are independent in a further two weeks. Two broods may be reared. If disturbed on the nest, a sitting adult will stretch out its head and neck, before suddenly withdrawing it, hissing like a snake. Wrynecks use their long, sticky tongues to rapidly pick up ants, and will eat other invertebrates such as spiders. The best time to spot wrynecks in Britain is in May on the south and east coasts, although they may be seen on migration in August and September.

**Distribution**: Breeds through most of mainland Europe, extending eastwards into northern Asia. Absent from Ireland, and the only British breeding population is in Scotland. Overwinters in Africa in a broad band south of the Sahara, with a resident population also in the north-west.
**Habitat**: Open country.
**Food**: Mainly ants.
**Size**: 17cm (6¹/₂in), wingspan 28–30cm (11–12in).
**Nest**: Suitable hole.
**Eggs**: 7–10, white.

**Identification:** Mottled grey on the upperparts, browner over the wings. Broad, tapering tail. Dark stripe through each eye, narrower adjacent white stripe above. Throat and chest are buff with streaking. Abdomen barred, mainly white with buff near the vent. Young birds are duller. Sexes are alike.

## Pied wagtail

*Motacilla alba*

These lively birds have adapted to changes in their environment, moving from coastal areas and marshland into farmland, and can even be observed hunting on and beside roads. Pied wagtails are not especially shy birds, and the movements of their tail feathers, which give them their common name, strike an unmistakeable jaunty pose.

The race that breeds in the British Isles is different from that observed elsewhere in Europe as cocks have black plumage on their backs during the summer. This area turns to grey for the rest of the year. The mainland European form is often described as the white wagtail as these birds have a greyish back for the whole year.

**Distribution**: Resident throughout western Europe, British Isles and western North Africa, with the winter distribution there more widespread. Seen in Scandinavia and Iceland only during the summer.
**Habitat**: Open areas.
**Food**: Invertebrates.
**Size**: 20cm (8in), wingspan 28cm (11in).
**Nest**: Concealed, sometimes in walls.
**Eggs**: 5–6, whitish with grey markings.

**Grey wagtail** (*Motacilla cinerea*) 20cm (8in), wingspan 28cm (11in). A marginal wetland bird, grey wagtails are most likely to be observed near fast-flowing streams darting across rocks in search of invertebrates. They live in pairs and construct their cup-shaped nests close to water or among the roots of a tree. Resident in most of western Europe. Grey head and wings, yellow underparts.

**Meadow pipit** (*Anthus pratensis*) 15cm (6in), wingspan 23cm (9in). Resident in the British Isles and neighbouring parts of western Europe east to Denmark. Individuals from more northerly and easterly areas overwinter around the Mediterranean. Brownish head and wings with darker markings. Dark streaking on the breast and flanks, which are a darker shade of buff. Underparts become whiter in summer. Sexes are alike.

**Identification:** Variable through range. Prominent white area on the head with a black crown and nape. A black area extends from the throat down on to the chest. The rest of the underparts are white. The back is grey or black depending on where the wagtail is from.

# Skylark

*Alauda arvensis*

The coloration and patterning of the skylark help it to remain hidden on the ground, where it sometimes freezes to escape detection. If disturbed at close quarters, however, it takes off almost vertically. Skylarks are unusual in that they reveal their presence readily by singing. They engage in what are described as song flights – fluttering their wings, they rise slowly through the air to a height of typically 100m (330ft) or so. The distinctive rounded song of the skylark can be heard through most of the year, even in the depths of winter. During the breeding period in the spring and summer, a sitting hen may draw attention away from her nest site by feigning injury, dragging one wing along the ground and taking off only as a last resort.

**Distribution**: Resident throughout much of western Europe from Denmark southwards. Also occurs in North Africa. Breeding range extends farther north to Scandanavia and eastwards to Asia.
**Habitat**: Open countryside, especially farmland.
**Food**: Plant matter and invertebrates.
**Size**: 18cm (7in), wingspan 30cm (12in).
**Nest**: On the ground.
**Eggs**: 2–3, grey-white and thickly spotted.

**Identification:** Greyish-brown plumage over the back and wings, with speckling becoming paler on the flanks. Underparts are mainly white. Whitish stripe extends back from the eyes, and ear coverts are greyish. Short crest on the crown, although it is not always visible. Hens are similar but lack the crest.

# Greater short-toed lark

*Calandrella brachydactyla*

The greater short-toed lark breeds in southern Europe, northern Africa and central and southern Asia. It winters even farther south, so a sighting in Britain is a rare occurrence indeed. In many ways, the greater short-toed lark is a southerly equivalent of our own skylark. Like the skylark, it lives and nests on open ground, and the males, lacking natural perches, instead sing in flight to advertise their ownership of a territory, attract females and deter potential rivals. The greater short-toed lark differs in the way that it sings: males often stop singing suddenly, almost as if they have fallen asleep, and drop from the air, only to 'reawaken' and regain height while singing before suddenly stopping again. In its appearance, the greater short-toed lark is only broadly similar to the skylark. Unlike that bird it lacks a crest on its head and its underside is a much brighter white – dazzling almost, when seen in bright sunlight. In truth, it is much more likely to be confused with the lesser short-toed lark, with which it shares parts of its breeding range. The lesser short-toed lark, however, has clear streaks across its chest and a much plainer and less elaborate pattern on its face.

**Distribution**: Southern Europe, northern Africa, central and souther Asia. A rare visitor to Britain: most sightings occur in the Isles of Scilly.
**Habitat**: Dry open grassland
**Food**: Seeds and insects
**Size**: 13–14cm (5–5½in), wingspan 24–32cm (9½–14in).
**Nest**: On the ground.
**Eggs**: 2–3, dull white, spotted.

**Identification:** At first sight this bird might appear like any other lark. However, its belly is almost pure white and completely lacks streaks, spots or other markings, a feature which sets it apart from its relatives. The neck is also very plain and only marked near the edges, with a few streaks or neat, black, horizontal stripes. Unlike those of the skylark, the wings lack a white trailing edge, a feature which can be used to separate the two species when in flight.

# GARDEN FINCHES

*Finches are small songbirds with short stout bills adapted for crushing seeds; to perform this activity they have adopted various different feeding strategies to exploit a wide variety of food sources without competing with each other. Goldfinches, for example, probe for and eat small seeds such as teasel, whereas the stout-billed hawfinch (see woodland birds) can crack tougher seeds such as cherry.*

## Chaffinch

*Fringilla coelebs*

The behaviour of the chaffinch changes significantly during the year. These birds can be seen in groups during the winter, but at the onset of spring, and the breeding season, cock birds become very territorial, driving away any rivals. While resident chaffinches remain in gardens and similar settings throughout the year, large groups of migrants seeking refuge from harsh winter weather associate in large flocks in farmland areas. Chaffinches usually prefer to feed on the ground, hopping and walking along in search of seeds. They seek invertebrates almost exclusively for rearing their chicks.

**Identification:** Black band above the bill, with grey over the head and neck. Pinkish cheeks and underparts. The back is brown, with two white wing bars. Cocks are less brightly coloured in winter plumage. Hens have dull grey cheek patches and dark greyish-green upperparts. Underparts are a buff shade of greyish-white.

**Distribution**: Resident in the British Isles and western Europe, and a summer visitor to Scandinavia and eastern Europe. Also resident in the west of northern Africa and at the south-western tip.
**Habitat**: Woodland, parks and gardens.
**Food**: Mostly seeds, but some invertebrates.
**Size**: 16cm (6¼in), wingspan 14–18cm (5½–7in).
**Nest**: Cup-shaped, usually in a tree fork.
**Eggs**: 4–5, light brown or blue with dark, very often smudgy, markings.

## European goldfinch

*Carduelis carduelis*

The long, narrow bill of the goldfinch enables it to prise kernels out of seeds, and these birds often congregate in the winter to feed on stands of thistle heads and teasel. Alder cones are also a favoured food at this time of year. Goldfinches are very agile birds, capable of clinging on to narrow stems when feeding. They are social by nature, usually mixing in small flocks in areas where food is plentiful, although they are usually shy when feeding on the ground. They have a relatively loud, attractive, twittering song. Pairs usually prefer to build their nest in the fork of a tree rather than concealing it in a hedge.

**Identification:** Bright red face with black lores. Black area across the top of the crown that broadens to a collar on the neck. White extends around the throat, and a brown necklace separates the white on the throat from the paler underparts. Brown back and flanks; otherwise underparts are white. Bill is narrow and pointed. Wings are black with white spotting and yellow barring. Tail is black with white markings. Hens display duller coloration with less yellow.

**Distribution**: Occurs throughout much of the British Isles and mainland Europe, but confined to the south of Scandinavia. Also in North Africa.
**Habitat**: Woodland and more open areas.
**Food**: Seeds and invertebrates.
**Size**: 13cm (5in), wingspan 20–25cm (8–10in).
**Nest**: Cup-shaped, made of vegetation.
**Eggs**: 5–6, bluish white with darker markings.

**Common linnet** (*Carduelis cannabina*) 14cm (5¹/₂in), wingspan 20–25cm (8–10in). Resident throughout western Europe. Grey head with a red crown. Back and wings are brown. The sides of the chest are red, becoming paler on the flanks with a white area on the breast. Hens are much duller with a short grey bill.

**Common redpoll** (*Carduelis flammea*) 14cm (5¹/₂in), wingspan 22cm (8in). Occurs in northern Europe, moving farther south in the winter. Crimson-red cap and black lores contrast with the yellowish bill. The brown upperparts are streaked. Red chest fades to white on the steaked abdomen. White wing bar. Hens are similar but lack the red on the chest.

**Common rosefinch** (*Carpodacus erythrinus*) 15cm (6in), wingspan 23–25cm (9–10in). Cock has a deep pinkish-red head, breast and rump. Lower underparts are whitish. Wings and tail are brown. Dark stocky bill, pinkish-brown legs and feet. Hens are brownish overall.

**Siskin** (*Carduelis spinus*) 12cm (5in), wingspan 20–23cm (8–9in). This little finch has a forked tail and narrow bill, with a black cap and bib and bright yellow-green body plumage. Birds are particularly common in Wales and Scotland in conifer, alder and birch woods.

**Snow bunting** (*Plectrophenax nivalis*) 17cm (6½in), wingspan 38cm (15in). Best looked for in winter on coastal sites in Scotland and eastern England. Males in summer have white heads and underparts contrasting with a black mantle and wing tips. Females are more mottled above.

# Greenfinch

*Carduelis chloris*

Greenfinches have quite stout bills that enable them to easily crack open tough seed casings to reach the edible kernels inside. These birds are most likely to be observed in areas where there are trees and bushes, which provide nesting cover. In the winter, greenfinches visit bird tables, readily taking peanuts as well as foraging in gardens. Groups of greenfinches are also sighted in more open areas of countryside, such as farmland, searching for weed seeds and grains that may have been dropped during harvesting. Pairs will often nest two or three times in succession during the summer, and when there are chicks in the nest the birds consume invertebrates in much larger quantities. The females incubate the eggs by themselves, but the chicks are fed by both partners.

**Distribution**: Throughout Europe and much of northern Africa, but absent from more northern parts of Scandinavia.
**Habitat**: Edges of woodland and more open areas.
**Food**: Largely seeds and some invertebrates.
**Size**: 16cm (6¼in), wingspan 16–18cm (6¼–7in).
**Nest**: Bulky, cup-shaped.
**Eggs**: 4–6, whitish to pale blue with darker markings.

**Identification:** Greenish head, with greyer areas on the sides of the face and wings. Yellowish-green breast, with yellow also evident on the flight feathers. Relatively large, conical bill. Male becomes duller in the wintertime. Hen is duller, with greyer tone overall, brownish mantle and less yellow on the wings. Forked tail.

# Bullfinch

*Pyrrhula pyrrhula*

These birds are unmistakable thanks to their stocky appearance and the bright pink coloration of the males. Often seen in gardens, they may also be seen in woodland. Bullfinches are regarded as a potential pest by fruit farmers as they eat emerging buds in early spring, but are also beneficial, by eating invertebrates.

Breeding starts from mid-April onwards, with a pair constructing their nest using twigs and lining the interior with softer material. The hen sits alone, with incubation lasting 14 days, after which both adults feed their growing brood. The chicks leave the nest when about 2¹/₂ weeks old.

**Identification:** Cock has a black face and top to the head, with deep rosy-pink underparts, lighter around the vent. Grey back, black wings and tail with a white area on the rump. The bill, legs and feet are all black. Hen is similar but with brownish underparts. Young birds lack the black cap seen in hens, and show brownish coloration on the wing coverts.

**Distribution**: Ranges widely across Europe, except the far north of Scandinavia and the southern half of the Iberian Peninsula, and extending eastwards through Asia. Also present on the Azores.
**Habitat**: Woodland areas.
**Food**: Seeds, invertebrates
**Size**: 16cm (6¼in), wingspan 16–25cm (6¼–10in).
**Nest**: Cup-shaped, made from vegetation.
**Eggs**: 4–6, greenish-blue with dark brownish markings.

# WARBLERS AND OTHER SMALL BIRDS

*Spotting these birds in a garden is not always easy since their neutral coloration merges in well against the foliage. Supplying food on a bird table, and perhaps a nesting box, may encourage them. They generally favour overgrown areas where there will be a good supply of invertebrates. Some are resident in northern latitudes throughout the year, while others migrate to Africa for the winter.*

## Wren

*Troglodytes troglodytes*

Although often difficult to spot due to their size and drab coloration, these tiny birds have a remarkably loud song which usually betrays their presence. Wrens can be found in areas where there is plenty of cover, such as ivy-clad walls, scurrying under the vegetation in search of spiders and similar prey. During the winter, when their small size could make them vulnerable to hypothermia, the wrens huddle together in roosts overnight to keep warm. However, populations are often badly affected by prolonged spells of severe weather. In the spring, the hen chooses one of several nests that the male has constructed, lining it with feathers to form a soft base for her eggs.

Wrens are surprisingly common, although not always conspicuous, with the British population alone made up of an estimated ten million birds.

**Identification:** Reddish-brown back and wings with visible barring. Lighter brown underparts and a narrow eye stripe. Short tail, often held vertically, which is greyish on its underside. Bill is long and relatively narrow. Sexes are alike.

**Distribution**: Resident throughout Europe, except in Scandinavia and neighbouring parts of Russia during the winter. European wrens move south in the winter. Present in northern Africa.
**Habitat**: Overgrown gardens and woodland.
**Food**: Mainly invertebrates.
**Size**: 10cm (4in), 13–17cm (5–6½in).
**Nest**: Ball-shaped.
**Eggs**: 5–6, white with reddish-brown markings.

**Distribution**: Found throughout most of Europe, except for Ireland, northern England and Scotland. Also restricted to southern parts of Scandinavia. Occurs in northern Africa opposite the Strait of Gibraltar.
**Habitat**: Gardens and parks with mature trees.
**Food**: Invertebrates, nuts and seeds.
**Size**: 14cm (5½in), wingspan 22–28cm (8½–11in).
**Nest**: In a secluded spot.
**Eggs**: 6–9, white with heavy reddish-brown speckling.

## Nuthatch

*Sitta europaea*

With relatively large, strong feet and very powerful claws, nuthatches are adept at scampering up and down tree trunks. They hunt for invertebrates, which they extract from the bark with their narrow bills, but their compact and powerful beak also enables them to feed easily on nuts. The nuthatches first wedge the nut into a suitable crevice in the bark, then hammer at the shell, breaking it open so they can extract the kernel. They will also store nuts, which they will eat when other food is in short supply. The bill is also useful as a tool for plastering over the entrance hole of their nest in the spring. The opening, just small enough to allow the adult birds to squeeze in and out, helps to protect them from predators. nuthatches are most likely to be encountered in areas with broadleaved trees, as these provide food such as acorns and hazelnuts.

**Identification:** Bluish-grey upperparts from head to tail. Distinctive black stripes running from the base of the bill down the sides of the head, encompassing the eyes. Underparts vary in colour from white through to a rusty shade of buff, depending on the race. Dark reddish-brown vent area, more brightly coloured in cocks.

# Willow warbler

*Phylloscopus trochilus*

**Distribution**: Occurs in the summer from the British Isles right across most of Europe. Overwinters in Africa.
**Habitat**: Wooded areas.
**Food**: Small invertebrates.
**Size**: 12cm (5in), wingspan 16–22cm (6¼–8½in).
**Nest**: Dome-shaped, built on the ground.
**Eggs**: 6–7, pale pink with reddish spotting.

**Identification**: Greyish-green upperparts, with a pale yellowish streak running across each eye. Pale yellow throat and chest, with whitish underparts. The yellow plumage is much whiter in birds from more northern areas. Willow warblers are very similar to chiffchaffs, but usually have paler legs and have longer wings and no eye ring.

The subdued coloration of these small birds is so effective that, despite being one of Europe's most common species, willow warblers are very inconspicuous. Difficult to observe in their wooded habitat, it is their song, which heralds their arrival in woodland areas in early spring, that usually betrays their presence. In the British Isles, the willow species is the most numerous of all warblers, with a population estimated at around three million pairs. These warblers are typically resident in Europe between April and September. Their nest is hidden among the vegetation and features a low entry point.

In late summer, willow warblers can often be seen in loose association with various tits, before they head off to their African wintering grounds. Although willow warblers will not visit bird tables, they may be seen in gardens with lots of shrubbery, where they will flutter at the edge of branches searching for aphids and other insects underneath the leaves. The management of woodland fringes as well as a decline in their African habitats has led to a reduction in numbers of willow warblers. The bird's song is melodic and rippling, and fades rather than stopping abruptly.

**Blackcap** (*Sylvia atricapilla*) 15cm (6in), wingspan 20–23cm (8–9in). Resident population is restricted to southern parts of the British Isles (including Ireland), France, the Iberian Peninsula and Italy; also north-western Africa. Jet black area on the crown, extending just above the eye and bordered by grey above the bill. Remainder of the head and breast is greyish. White plumage under the throat. Back, wings and underparts are olive-grey. Sexes are alike. Young birds have a reddish-brown cap.

# Garden warbler

*Sylvia borin*

Rather dull coloration, coupled with their small size, ensures these warblers are relatively inconspicuous, particularly when darting among foliage. However, their attractive song and call notes may help identify them in the undergrowth. Garden warblers arrive on their breeding grounds from middle of April onwards, and construct a fairly large nest using a variety of plant matter, usually including stems of grass, and lining it with softer material. The hen sits alone through the incubation period, which lasts approximately 12 days, but subsequently both parents will seek food for their rapidly growing brood. The young quickly leave the nest, sometimes when just nine days old, and may be forced to scrabble among the vegetation to escape would-be predators until they are able to fly from danger. In more southern parts of their breeding range, pairs of garden warblers may produce two successive broods of chicks. They return to Africa in September.

**Identification**: Olive-brown head and upperparts, with a greyish area present at each side of the neck. Underparts are greyish-white, buffer along the flanks. Bill and legs are dark greyish. Young birds similar to adults. Sexes are alike.

**Distribution**: Summer range extends from Scandinavia southwards across virtually all of Europe. Migrates south for the winter to much of Africa.
**Habitat**: Gardens with trees, also parks.
**Food**: Mainly invertebrates.
**Size**: 14cm (5½in), wingspan 20–22cm (8–8½in).
**Nest**: Made of vegetation.
**Eggs**: 4–5, buff with brown spots.

# Chiffchaff

*Phylloscopus collybita*

The chiffchaff is a lively warbler, generally common through its range and often seen in gardens, particularly those with trees nearby. There are regional differences in appearance, with individuals found in western and central areas having brighter yellow coloration than those birds occurring farther north and east. Its unusual name reflects its common two-note song pattern. Pairs are likely to start nesting from April onwards, with the female building the nest on her own. This is positioned relatively close to the ground in a suitable bush or shrub that provides good cover, typically an evergreen such as rhododendron, or sometimes in among brambles, offering protection against predators. The chiffchaffs slip in and out of the nest itself via a side entrance. The hen undertakes the incubation on her own, and this lasts for about 13 days, with the young chicks subsequently fledging after a similar interval. Chiffchaffs may rear two broods during the summer.

The chiffchaff arrives in Britain in March and departs again in August and September.

**Identification:** Yellowish stripe above each eye, with a black stripe passing through the centre. Underparts whitish, with variable yellow on the sides of the face and flanks. Rest of the upperparts dark brownish-green. Pointed bill is dark. Legs and feet are black. Sexes are alike.

**Distribution**: Occurs through most of Europe during the summer but absent from parts of northern Scandinavia and Scotland. Resident in parts of southern Britain and Ireland and farther south, near the Mediterranean. Overwinters in northern Africa and south of the Sahara. Also found in Asia.
**Habitat**: Wooded areas.
**Food**: Invertebrates.
**Size**: 12cm (4½in), wingspan 15–20cm (6–8in).
**Nest**: Dome-shaped, made from vegetation.
**Eggs**: 6, white in colour with brownish spotting.

# Goldcrest

*Regulus regulus*

These warblers are the smallest birds in Europe and are surprisingly bold, drawing attention to themselves with their high-pitched calls and the way they jerkily flit from branch to branch. They can be easily distinguished from the slightly larger firecrest (*R. ignicapillus*) by the absence of a white streak above the eyes. Goldcrests associate in groups both of their own kind and also with other small birds such as tits, seeking food relatively high up in the branches rather than at ground level. Pairs split off to breed in the early spring, with both sexes collecting moss and other material to construct their nest. This may be hung off a conifer branch, up to 12m (40ft) off the ground, although it may also be concealed among ivy or similar vegetation. Cobwebs act as thread to anchor the nest together, and the interior is lined with feathers. The young will have fledged by three weeks old, and the adults may nest again soon afterwards and rear a second brood. The bird is widespread throughout the UK apart from northern Scotland and in treeless areas such as the Norfolk fens.

**Identification:** Dumpy appearance, with cock birds having an orange streak (yellow in hens) running down the centre of the head, bordered by black stripes on each side. Prominent area of white encircling the eyes, with much of the rest of the head pale grey. White wing bars. The plumage on the back is greyish-green. Underparts are paler in colour. Bill is black, legs and feet greyish. Young birds have greyish heads and pale bills.

**Distribution**: Resident through much of Europe, where pairs spend the summer. Northern pairs often move south to the Mediterranean for the winter. Range also extends eastwards into Asia.
**Habitat**: Wooded areas.
**Food**: Mainly invertebrates.
**Size**: 9cm (3½in), wingspan 14–15cm (5½–6in).
**Nest**: Suspended basket made of moss.
**Eggs**: 7–8, buff-white with brown markings.

# House sparrow

*Passer domesticus*

A common sight on garden bird tables and in city parks, house sparrows have adapted well to living so closely alongside people, even to the extent of nesting under roofs of buildings. These sparrows form loose flocks, with larger numbers congregating where food is readily available. They spend much of their time on the ground, hopping along but ever watchful for passing predators such as cats. It is not uncommon for them to construct nests during the winter, which serve as communal roosts rather than being used for breeding. During the nesting period, when the cock birds' bill turns black, several males will often court a single female in what has become known as a 'sparrows' wedding'.

**Distribution**: Very common, throughout Europe, and eastwards across Asia. Also present in northern and south-east Africa.
**Habitat**: Urban and more rural areas.
**Food**: Invertebrates and seeds, but very adaptable.
**Size**: 15cm (6in), wingspan 19–23cm (7½–9in).
**Nest**: Tree hollows and under roofs of buildings.
**Eggs**: 3–6, whitish with darker markings.

**Tree sparrow** (*Passer montanus*) 13cm (5in), wingspan 20cm (8in). Smaller than a house sparrow and more active, with its tail almost permanently cocked. It has a chestnut brown head and nape (rather than grey), and white cheeks and collar with a contrasting black cheek-spot. The tree sparrow can be seen all year round but is scarcer in the British uplands, and the far north and west. The main populations are now found across the Midlands, southern and eastern England. It is almost absent from the south-west, Wales and the north-west. Best looked for in hedgerows and woodland edges.

**Identification**: Rufous-brown head with a grey area on top. A black stripe runs across the eyes and a broad black bib runs down over the chest. The ear coverts and the entire underparts are greyish, and there is a whitish area under the tail. Hens are a duller shade of brown, with a pale stripe behind each eye and a fawn bar on each wing.

# Grasshopper warbler

*Locustella naevia*

Difficult to observe, these warblers are very adept at clambering through grass and low vegetation. They may be spotted running across open ground, flying low if disturbed and seeking vegetation as cover. Their song, which is usually heard at dusk, may also betray their presence. They sing in bursts of up to a minute in duration, and their calls incorporate ringing notes that have been likened to the sound of a muffled alarm clock. Grasshopper warblers migrate largely without stopping, and have been observed in West Africa from August onwards. They undertake the return journey to their breeding grounds in Europe and Asia between March and May, flying in a more easterly direction, often crossing the Mediterranean from Algeria. They can be found throughout Britain, although they are rarely seen in Scotland. The breeding period extends from May until July, with the bulky nest built close to the ground. The chicks hatch after two weeks, and are reared by both adults before leaving the nest as early as 10 days old.

**Distribution**: Breeds through central and northern parts of Europe as far as southern Scandinavia. Present in much of the British Isles. Absent from the Mediterranean region. Overwinters in parts of Africa, especially on the western side.
**Habitat**: Marshland and grassland areas.
**Food**: Invertebrates.
**Size**: 13cm (5in), wingspan 15–19cm (6–7½in).
**Nest**: Made of vegetation.
**Eggs**: 6, creamy with brownish-red spotting.

**Identification**: Olive-brown upperparts. Streaked head, back and undertail coverts. Faint eye stripe. Underparts whitish, more yellowish-green on the breast. Variable chest markings. Narrow, pointed bill. Pink legs and feet. Sexes are alike. Young birds have yellowish underparts.

## Coal tit

*Parus ater*

These tits are often to be seen in gardens feeding on bird tables, sometimes taking food which they will then store in a variety of locations, ranging from caches on the ground to suitable hollows in trees. The urge to store food in this way becomes strongest in the late summer and during the autumn, and helps the birds to maintain a food supply through the coldest months of the year. This hoarding strategy appears to be very successful, since coal tit populations rarely crash like many other small birds following a particularly harsh winter. In fact, these tits have increased their breeding range significantly over recent years, with their distribution now extending to various islands off the British coast, including the Isles of Scilly.

During the winter, in their natural habitat of coniferous forest, they may form flocks comprised of many thousands of individuals, yet in gardens they are only usually seen in quite small numbers.

**Identification:** Jet black head, with white patches on the sides of the face and a similar area on the nape. Greyish-olive upperparts, with white wing bars, and brownish-white underparts, although some marked regional variations. Young birds have pale yellowish cheek patches. Sexes very similar, but the female's head markings may be duller. The bill is black. Legs are greyish.

**Distribution**: Resident throughout the whole of Europe, although absent from northern parts of Scandinavia. Range extends south to north-western parts of Africa, and spreads right across Asia to Japan.
**Habitat**: Wooded areas.
**Food**: Mostly invertebrates and seeds.
**Size**: 11cm (4¼in), wingspan 17–20cm (6½–8in).
**Nest**: Cup-shaped, made from vegetation.
**Eggs**: 8–11, white with reddish markings.

## Great tit

*Parus major*

**Distribution**: Found through all of Europe except in parts of northern Scandinavia, and ranges south as far as northern Africa. Also extends widely across much of Asia.
**Habitat**: Woodland.
**Food**: Invertebrates, seeds.
**Size**: 14cm (5½in), wingspan 22–25cm (8½–10in).
**Nest**: Cup-shaped, made from vegetation.
**Eggs**: 5–12, white with reddish spotting.

There is a marked difference in appearance between great tits throughout their wide range. They form groups after the breeding season, often associating with other small birds, foraging for food through woodland as well as visiting bird tables, where their bold, jaunty nature makes them conspicuous. Although they do not hoard food like some tits, they are able to lower their body temperature significant overnight when roosting, effectively lessening the amount of energy they need. Great tits become much more territorial at the start of the breeding season, which in Europe typically starts during March. They build their nest in a tree hollow, but readily use garden nestboxes where provided. Studies have shown that the male seeks out potential nesting sites within the pair's territory, but it is the female who has the final choice. Pairs may nest twice during the breeding period, which lasts until July.

**Identification:** Cock has a black head with white cheek patches. Broad band of black feathering extends down the centre of the body, with yellow plumage on either side. Wings are olive-green at the top, becoming bluish on the sides and on the flight feathers and tail. Hens are similar but display a narrower, uneven vertical black band. Young birds significantly paler overall, with yellowish cheeks and little of the vertical band seen in adults.

# Blue tit

*Parus caeruleus*

**Distribution**: Throughout Europe except the far north of Scandinavia. Also present in north-western Africa.
**Habitat**: Wooded areas, parks and gardens.
**Food**: Invertebrates, seeds and nuts.
**Size**: 12cm (4½in), wingspan 11–14cm (4¼–5½in).
**Nest**: Tree holes.
**Eggs**: 7–16, white with reddish-brown markings.

A common visitor to British bird tables, blue tits are lively, active birds by nature, and are welcomed by gardeners because they eat aphids. Their small size allows them to hop up the stems of thin plants and, hanging upside down, seek these pests under leaves. Blue tits are well-adapted to garden life and readily adopt nest boxes supplied for them, as well as feeding on peanuts. Their young leave the nest before they are able to fly properly, and are therefore vulnerable to predators such as cats. Those that do survive the critical early weeks can be easily distinguished by the presence of yellow rather than white cheek patches.

**Identification:** Has a distinctive blue crown edged with white, and a narrow black stripe running back through each eye. White cheeks. Underparts are yellowish, and the back is greyish-green. There is a whitish bar across the top of the blue wings. The tail is also blue. Sexes are similar but hens are duller.

---

**Marsh tit** (*Parus palustris*) 13cm (5in), wingspan 18–19cm (7–7½in).The black cap extends over the top of the head, and there is usually a small area of black below the bill. Broad whitish area on the cheeks; the back and wings are brown. The underparts are paler; bill black; legs greyish. Young birds have whiter underparts.

**Redwing** (*Turdus iliacus*) 21cm (8in), wingspan 33–36cm (13–14¼in). The UK's smallest thrush, generally only seen in the winter, has plumage similar to the song thrush but with distinctive red patches on its flanks and a cream strip above the eye. It eats berries and worms and is often seen among flocks of fieldfares.

**Dunnock** (*Prunella modularis*) 14–15cm (5½-6in), wingspan 19–20cm (7½–8in). This bird looks like a sparrow, but has a finer, black bill and a blue-grey head and breast. It tends to creep through vegetation after insects.

# Robin

*Erithacus rubecula*

The robin's cheery appearance belies its strong aggressive streak, for these birds are highly territorial. In the garden, robins can become very tame, regularly hopping down alongside the gardener's fork or spade to snatch invertebrates such as earthworms that come to the surface. Young, recently fledged robins look very different from mature individuals – they are almost entirely brown, with dense spotting on the head and chest. Robins sing year-round, especially during the breeding season. The autumn song sounds rather melancholy, and the spring one is upbeat. They also have a harsh, tick-like warning note which is often drawn out and repeated, particularly when they are alarmed by the presence of a nearby predator such as a cat. Since robins usually feed on the ground, they can be very vulnerable to these predators.

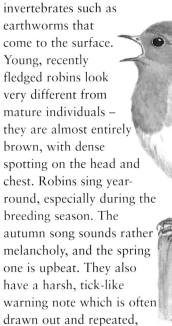

**Distribution**: Resident in the British Isles, western Europe and parts of northern Africa. Scandinavian and eastern European populations winter farther south.
**Habitat**: Gardens, parks and woodland areas.
**Food**: Invertebrates, berries, fruit and seeds.
**Size**: 14cm (5½in), wingspan 12–16cm (4½–6¼cm).
**Nest**: Under cover, often near the ground.
**Eggs**: 5–7, bluish-white with red markings.

**Identification:** Bright orange extends from just above the bill, around the eyes and down over virtually the entire breast. The lower underparts are whitish-grey, becoming browner on the flanks. Top of the head and the wings are brown. Pale wing bar. Sexes are alike.

# Song thrush

*Turdus philomelos*

**Identification:** Brown back and wings, with some black areas evident, and a yellow-buff area across the chest. Dark markings that extend over the chest and abdomen are shaped like arrows, rather than circular. Sexes are alike. Young birds have smaller spots, which are likely to be less numerous on their underparts.

The song of these thrushes is both powerful and musical. It can be heard particularly in the spring at the start of the breeding season, and is usually uttered from a relatively high branch. Song thrushes are welcomed by gardeners as they readily hunt and eat snails and other pests on the ground. Having grabbed a snail, the birds choose a special site known as an anvil where they smash it against a rock to break the shell and dislodge the mollusc within. These thrushes are excellent runners, and this allows them to pursue quarry such as leatherjackets (the larvae of certain species of crane fly, *Tipula* species). When breeding, song thrushes build a typical cup-shaped nest, which the hen is mainly or even solely responsible for constructing.

**Distribution:** Ranges widely throughout the whole of Europe. Eastern populations head to the Mediterranean region for the winter. Also present in northern Africa, even as far south as the Sudan.
**Habitat:** Woodland areas, parks and gardens.
**Food:** Invertebrates, berries.
**Size:** 22cm (8½in), wingspan 33–36cm (13–14¼in).
**Nest:** Cup-shaped.
**Eggs:** 5–6, greenish-blue with reddish-brown markings.

# Blackbird

*Turdus merula*

Blackbirds frequently descend on lawns to search for invertebrates. Earthworms, which feature prominently in their diet, are most likely to be drawn to the surface after rain, and slugs and snails also emerge in wet conditions. In the 19th century, blackbirds were rarely seen in gardens, but today they have become commonplace. They are quite vocal and have a variety of calls. Cocks are talented songsters, and both sexes will utter an urgent, harsh alarm call. Although blackbirds do not associate in flocks, pairs can be seen foraging together. As with other thrushes, their tails are surprisingly flexible and can be raised or lowered at will. It is not unusual to see pied blackbirds, with variable amounts of white among the black plumage. The majority of these birds, especially those with the most extensive white areas, are cock birds.

**Identification:** Jet black plumage contrasts with the bright yellow bill, which becomes a deeper yellow during the winter. Hens are drab in comparison, brownish overall with some streaking, notably on the breast, and have a darker bill.

*Left: The hen usually incubates eggs, although occasionally the cock may share the task.*

**Distribution:** Resident throughout virtually the whole of Europe, except the far north of Scandinavia. Also present in northern Africa. The majority of Scandinavian and eastern European populations are migratory.
**Habitat:** Woodland, gardens and parkland.
**Food:** Invertebrates, fruit and berries.
**Size:** 29cm (11½in), wingspan 34–38cm (13½–15in).
**Nest:** Cup-shaped, hidden in a bush or tree.
**Eggs:** 3–5, greenish-blue with reddish-brown markings.

**Mistle thrush** (*Turdus viscivorus*) 29cm (11in), wingspan 36cm (14¼in). Resident throughout most of western Europe south to northern Africa. Breeds as far north as Scandinavia and also further east. Relatively large thrush. White underparts, often smudged with an area of grey on the upper breast, and displaying a variable black spotted patterning. Pale sides to the head. Back and wings are grey. Sexes are alike.

**Fieldfare** (*Turdus pilaris*) 27cm (10½in), wingspan 42cm (16½in). Occurs in central parts of Europe, and northern Mediterranean, overwintering in the UK. White eye stripe and grey on the sides of the head. Brown band joins the wings across the back. The rump is grey. Rusty-yellow band across the breast with darker markings, Underparts otherwise white. Sexes are alike.

# Nightingale

*Luscinia megarhynchos*

The arrival of the nightingale in Europe is seen as heralding the start of spring. However, these birds are often difficult to spot, since they utter their musical calls towards dusk and even after dark on moonlit nights. Their relatively large eyes indicate that these members of the thrush family are crepuscular, becoming active around dusk. Their drab, subdued coloration enables them to blend easily into the dense shrubbery or woodland vegetation that they favour. The nightingale is only present in Europe from April to September, when it breeds, before it once again heads back to Africa for winter.

**Distribution**: From southern England and mainland Europe on a similar latitude south to north-western Africa. Over-winters farther south in Africa. **Habitat**: Woodlands, gardens. **Food**: Mainly invertebrates. **Size**: 16cm (6¼in), wingspan 20–24cm (8–9½in). **Nest**: Cup-shaped. **Eggs**: 4–5, greyish-green to reddish-buff.

**Identification**: Brown plumage extends from above the bill down over the back of the head and wings, becoming reddish-brown on the rump and tail. A sandy-buff area extends across the breast, while the lower underparts are whitish. The large eyes are dark and highlighted by a light eye ring. Sexes are alike.

# Starling

European starling *Sturnus vulgaris*

These frequently sighted birds are resident in a vast range of areas. However, some populations of the common starling, especially in the more northerly part of their range, will undertake seasonal migrations. This prompts the sudden arrival of hundreds of birds in urban areas, especially where there are groups of trees suitable for roosting. They often prove noisy in these surroundings, even singing after dusk if the area is well lit.

In flight, large flocks are adept at avoiding pursuing predators, such as hawks, by weaving back and forth in a tight formation. They are equally adept at seeking food on the ground, picking up seeds and probing for invertebrates. When breeding, a pair will often adopt the nest of a woodpecker, but in areas where nesting sites are in short supply, starlings may even tunnel into a suitable bank to create a nesting cavity. The young birds subsequently leave the nest at about three weeks after hatching.

**Distribution**: Range extends throughout Europe and north Africa, with Scandinavian and eastern European populations migrating farther south for the winter. Also present farther east into Asia, and has been introduced to North America and Australia. **Habitat**: By houses and buildings. **Food**: Invertebrates, berries, birdfeeder fare. **Size**: 22cm (8½in), wingspan 37–40cm (14½–16in). **Nest**: In a tree hole or birdhouse. **Eggs**: 2–9, white to pale blue or green.

**Identification**: Glossy. Purplish-black head with a greenish hue on the body, overlaid with spots. Dark brown wings and tail. Hens are similar, but spotting is larger and base of the tail is pinkish rather than blue, as in breeding males. Young birds are duller, brownish and lack iridescence.

# UNDERSTANDING FISH

Compared with birds, mammals or other creatures that we are used to seeing around us, few people are able to observe aquatic life to quite the same extent. There is no doubt that we still have a lot to learn about the world of fish.

Although bounded by water, fish have lives that in many ways parallel those of animals that live on land. Like all creatures, they are driven by basic instincts – the need for food, to avoid predators and to reproduce. These requirements have driven the evolution of a range of body shapes and colours. They have also affected the ways in which senses and behaviour patterns have developed in fish.

Fish are the world's most numerous vertebrates, both in terms of species and living beings. To date, some 28,000 different species have been identified and named – more than all the amphibians, reptiles, birds and mammals in the world put together.

Above: Seahorses are poor swimmers, relying on their dorsal fin beating at 30–70 times a minute to propel them along.

Left: Most fish are either freshwater or marine, these Atlantic mackerel (Scomber scombrus) are marine. Atlantic mackerel are by far the most common of the species that are caught in British waters. They travel in huge shoals, migrating towards the coast to feed on small fish and prawns during the summer, and then overwintering in deeper waters.

# EVOLUTION

*Fish are the most ancient vertebrates on the planet, and their development took place far earlier than land creatures. All other vertebrates – amphibians, reptiles, birds and mammals, including our own species – can eventually trace their ancestry back to fish.*

When the first amphibians pulled themselves out of the water on to land, the world's seas and freshwater habitats were already bursting with fish. All three of the major fish groups – jawless, cartilaginous and bony fish – had evolved long before this momentous event happened.

Fish themselves had evolved from more primitive animals known as cephalochordates. These weird-looking creatures represent a link between invertebrates and vertebrates, and are given a subphylum of their own in animal classification. Before the first fish appeared, cephalochordates were the most complex creatures on the planet. They lacked the bones that would later define fish and other vertebrates, but they had many of the other characteristics that we now associate with these creatures.

*Below: The fossilized remains of*
Pterichthyodes, *an armoured placoderm fish which swam in the planet's oceans around 370 million years ago.*

*Below:* Dunkleosteus *was the largest of all the placoderms – some specimens grew as long as a bus. A fearsome predator, it included other fish in its diet.*

*Above: The whale shark (*Rhincodon typus*) is a plankton feeder and the world's largest living fish. Like all sharks it has a skeleton of cartilage rather than bone.*

Like vertebrates, the cephalochordates had a spinal cord and V-shaped bundles of muscles along their flanks – features which had never existed in any animals before them. Cephalochordates did not need to move much to find food, but when under attack they were capable of a sudden burst of speed. They used bundled muscles to sweep their flattened tails from side to side, which would drive them through the water, like fish today.

A few cephalochordates still exist today. One group, the lancelets, look very similar to the creatures that gave rise to the first ancient fish. Lancelets are filter feeders that survive by sifting plankton from the water, and it is thought that the cephalochordate ancestors of fish lived in a similar way.

## Well protected

With such a streamlined design, the next stage in fish evolution seems almost a backward step. The first true fish were covered in heavy body armour, which limited their ability to swim much at all. Rather than darting through the water, these creatures were much more plodding and deliberate in the way that they moved. Unlike most modern fish they lacked fins, but they had retained the cephalochordates' flattened, flexible tail, albeit covered with thick, protective scales. When they did lift themselves up from the bottom and swim along slowly, it was by sweeping their tails from side to side as their ancestors had done.

These early armoured fish were the first animals on Earth to have bones. While the cephalochordates had had a flexible quill-like structure to protect their spinal cord, these first fish had true vertebrae. Other bony elements in their body structure included a simple skull, which surrounded the brain. To begin with, however, there were still no jaws or teeth. The earliest armoured fish, which lived in the seas around 450 million years ago, were like underwater hoovers, feeding on detritus which they sucked up from the bottom.

Perhaps surprisingly, considering their abundance today, fish were not an instant success. For the first 40 million years after they appeared they remained relatively rare, making up only a small proportion of all the creatures that lived in the world's oceans and freshwater habitats. The restricting factor was almost certainly the fact that they still lacked jaws. This limited their options when it came to feeding – the jawless fish that survive today are all either detritus feeders, scavengers or parasites on other fish.

As the eons passed, the jawless fish did diversify a little in shape but they never grew very large. Few of them reached more than 20cm (8in) long. These fish must have been targets for the large invertebrate predators that existed at that time, as they all retained their body armour.

## The vertebrate jaw

Around 400 million years ago a new group of fish appeared, the placoderms. Outwardly they looked very similar to the armoured fish that had gone before them but they differed in one important respect – they had jaws. The evolution of jaws gave the opportunity for these fish to expand and diversify, as now they could hunt.

Although the placoderms only existed for around 40 million years, in that time they came to dominate all of the world's aquatic habitats. A few of them grew into absolute monsters, unlike anything that had been seen on the planet before. Among the last of the placoderms was a particularly famous giant: Dunkleosteus, a huge predator that grew up to 10m (33ft) long. Although its jaws lacked teeth the Dunkleosteus had fearsome shearing edges, which could slice through the body of almost any prey with ease. Living in the waters

---

### A tale with no end

Evolution is a process that continues today. In the future the world will see new species of fish appear and then become extinct, just as they have in the past.

Many of the fish that are living on Earth today evolved fairly recently – often in response to geographical changes. The cichlids of Africa's Rift Valley lakes, for example, sprang up in the past 12 million years, after the lakes themselves had become cut off from the sea. A few ancestral species, which made their way up the rivers that flowed from the lakes, found them largely uninhabited. These pioneering fish then quickly evolved into new species to fill the many vacant niches, resulting in the great variety of cichlids that lives in the lakes today.

Above: All of the cichlids pictured here are from Lake Tanganyika. This is a young humphead (Cyphotilapia frontosa).

Below: A male black calvus (Altolamprologus calvus), another cichlid that lays its eggs in empty shells.

Above: The pearly shell dweller (Lamprologus meleagris) lays its eggs in empty snail shells.

Below: A fork-tailed checkerboard cichlid, top, (Dicrossus filamentosus) and below, a checkerboard cichlid (Crenicara filamentosa).

---

alongside the placoderms were shoals of smaller fish from another group, known as the acanthodians.

These creatures looked much more like most of the fish we know today. They had scaly bodies and they also had proper fins. These were supported by long spines and could be raised or lowered at will. More importantly, the acanthodians had teeth. Unlike the majority of fish that had gone before them, they swam in open water, rather than spending most of their lives on the bottom. They are the earliest known fish to have possessed the lateral line sensory organ which is able to detect slight disturbances in the surrounding water.

Scientists are divided over the exact position of the acanthodians in the evolutionary scheme of things. Some believe that they were the direct ancestors of the bony fish, which today make up the vast majority of fish species. Others place them in the evolutionary line leading to the cartilaginous fish, which include modern sharks and rays.

Certainly, both bony fish and cartilaginous fish appeared soon after the first acanthodians. While the acanthodians had all died out by the end of the Permian period, 245 million years ago, these other fish lived on. Bony fish were the more successful in terms of numbers, but it was the cartilaginous fish which would become the dominant predators, evolving species that would become the largest fish on Earth, no doubt a factor in their success. Today, of course, they include the sharks and rays – groups that are widespread in the oceans but less common in fresh water.

# CLASSIFICATION

*We tend to think of fish as a homogeneous mass, a huge group of animals that share characteristics which separate them from other vertebrates. However, when scientists look at fish, they see them in terms of four very different groups.*

Fish comprise four vertebrate classes: Actinopterygii (ray-finned fish), Chondrichthyes (cartilaginous fish, such as sharks), Cephalaspidomorphi (lampreys and lamperns), and Pteraspidomorphi (hagfish). Each of the other four main vertebrate groups – amphibians, reptiles, birds and mammals – has a class of its own. In other words, scientists consider ray-finned fish and cartilaginous fish to be as different from one another as reptiles are from birds.

## Ray-finned fish

The vast majority of freshwater fish belong to the class Actinopterygii, as, indeed, do most marine fish species. These fish are defined by the characteristic in their common name – all of their fins are supported by rays, which are not unlike fingers. These enable them to be opened or folded at will. In addition, the fins of most ray-finned fish have a joint where they meet the body, allowing them to be spread outward or held tight against

*Below: The roach (*Rutilus rutilus*) is a ray-finned bony fish, and belongs to the superorder Ostariophysi.*

the sides. Having such flexible fins is a great advantage and has served these fish well. As well as improving manoeuvrability in the water it allows them to turn their fins to different functions. Some ray-finned fish, for example, use their fins for display.

Most of the world's ray-finned fish, and indeed most British fish, belong to the infraclass Teleostei (an infraclass is subordinate to a subclass but superior to an order or a superorder). Better known as the bony fish, this group contains the bulk of the fish species most of us will encounter in our lives. They are not only the most common fish but also the ones most likely to end up on our dinner plates. Cod, haddock, tuna, salmon and trout are all teleosts.

The infraclass Teleostei is split into 13 superorders, 8 of which contain freshwater species. The largest of the superorders is Acanthopterygii, which includes all of the perchlike fish. Many members of this superorder are marine, such as the mackerel, mullet and seahorse. But there is also a huge number of freshwater families. Those with British members include the sticklebacks and the true perches.

*Above: Common names can be confusing. The pike topminnow (*Belonesox belizanus*) is a member of the superorder Atherinomorpha. True pike are grouped with other Protacanthopterygii.*

Another large superorder of teleosts is Clupeomorpha. Most of the families in this group are marine: those with British members include Clupeidae, which includes the herring, pilchard and shad. As these examples might suggest, clupeomorph fish are important food sources for humans. Many people in Britain make their livelihoods by catching or selling species from this group.

Freshwater clupeomorph fish are much less numerous, and most of those species that do exist spend at least some of their life in the sea. This fact is also true of most eels, which make up the teleost superorder Elopomorpha. Britain has only one eel species, the common eel (*Anguilla anguilla*), but it famously migrates from our rivers right across the North Atlantic to the Sargasso Sea to spawn.

Other teleost superorders are widespread but only some of them have species that live in or around Britain. The second largest (after Acanthopterygii) and perhaps most significant to us is the superorder Ostariophysi. This contains all of the world's catfish, including the wels (*Silurus glanis*), as well as all of the so-called carp-like fish. This latter group contains many of Britain's freshwater fish species. Carp-like fish include

*Above: The common dogfish (*Scyliorhinus caniculal) *is a type of small shark. Like all sharks it has a skeleton made of cartilage and belongs to the class Chondrichthyes.*

chub, dace, roach, and minnows, as well as carp themselves. The other major freshwater superorder in Britain is Protacanthopterygii. It contains all of the world's trout and salmon, and the predatory pikes.

Of the entirely marine teleost superorders with British representatives, perhaps the most familiar is Paracanthopterygii. This superorder contains the family Gadidae, which includes cod, haddock, and plaice. It also contains the anglerfish, deep sea hunters that lure their prey towards them, and are themselves caught by humans for sale in restaurants as monkfish.

## Cartilaginous fish

While bony fish make up the vast majority of British species, our largest fish come from another group, Chondrichthyes. Members of this class of animals are more commonly known as cartilaginous fish. This name refers to the fact that their skeletons are made of cartilage rather than bone. Cartilaginous fish include all of the world's sharks and rays. The vast majority of its members are marine

and every one of the British species is found in sea water. Britain's cartilaginous fish range from rays such as the common skate (*Raja batis*) and small sharks like the common dogfish (*Scyliorhinus canicula*, sold in British fish and chip shops as rock salmon) to

true giants like the basking shark (*Cetorhinus maximus*), the second biggest fish in the entire world.

## Jawless fish

The other two classes of fish are the most primitive and ancient, in evolutionary terms. Although they have been on Earth longer than either bony or cartilaginous fish they have far fewer living members. The two classes are often lumped together under the umbrella of the common name, jawless fish. This name refers to the fact that they lack true jaws. Instead they have a circular, almost sucker-like mouth, often surrounded by numerous small, sharp teeth. Britain's jawless fishes include the river lamprey (*Lampetra fluviatilis*) and brook lamprey (*Lampetra planeri*), and the hagfish, which are marine.

*Below: Lampreys belong to the class Cephalaspidomorphi, one of two classes of jawless fish. As this picture shows, while they might lack jaws they often have formidable teeth.*

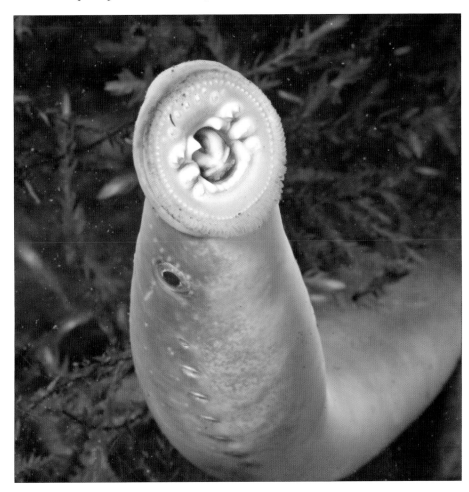

# ANATOMY

*Many people are still unsure exactly how fish are defined. Confusingly, some animals are called fish but are not fish at all – starfish and cuttlefish are just two examples of this – so it is useful to know exactly what physical features set fish apart from other animals.*

Fish are defined by certain physical characteristics. First and foremost, they are vertebrates – animals with backbones. Other vertebrates include mammals, reptiles, amphibians and birds. Fish differ from these animals in having fins rather than legs, and gills which they use to extract oxygen from the water. Unlike dolphins and whales, which are mammals, fish can breathe underwater and are not forced to return to the surface every so often to fill their lungs with air. (Some fish gulp air to supplement the oxygen obtained from the water through their gills, but none have true lungs.)

## Fins

One external feature all fish have in common is fins. These originally evolved for locomotion, to drive fish along and help them control their position in the water. In some species, however, they have since taken on additional roles. Some fish use the supporting spines of their fins for defence, for example. Many more use their fins much like flags for display.

Most fish have seven fins: two sets of paired and three single fins. The paired fins are the pectoral fins, which emerge on either side of the body just behind the head, and the pelvic fins, which emerge from the underside a little farther back. Directly behind the pelvic fins is the single anal fin. Made famous by the film *Jaws*, the dorsal fin is probably the best known fin on a fish. As its name suggests, it emerges from the back. The seventh fin is the caudal fin, sometimes known as the tail fin. It is usually split into two lobes, although it may have a rounded or straight rear edge. Generally, fish with crescent-shaped or strongly forked caudal fins tend to be fast swimmers. Those fish with rounded or straight rear fins are slower and normally live in still or very slow-moving waters.

While seven fins is the norm, some fish have a small eighth fin – called the adipose – between their dorsal fin and caudal fin. Others lack some of the fins or have evolved in such a way that their fins have merged. Eels are a good

### Gills

All fish have gills, which they use to remove oxygen from water. Gills are rather like lungs in that they have a very large surface area and many tiny capillaries for absorbing oxygen into the blood.

*Below: In fish such as pike (*Esox lucius*), the gill slits, through which oxygen-rich water passes can be clearly seen.*

example. While they have paired pectoral fins, they lack pelvic fins, and their dorsal, anal and caudal fins have grown together into a single long strip.

The vast majority of fish swim by using their caudal fin. This is swept from side to side. A few fish, such as rays, move by means of their pelvic fins, but in most fish these are used to

*Left: This a generalized anatomy of a bony fish. A vast range of body shapes and fin arrangements exist.*

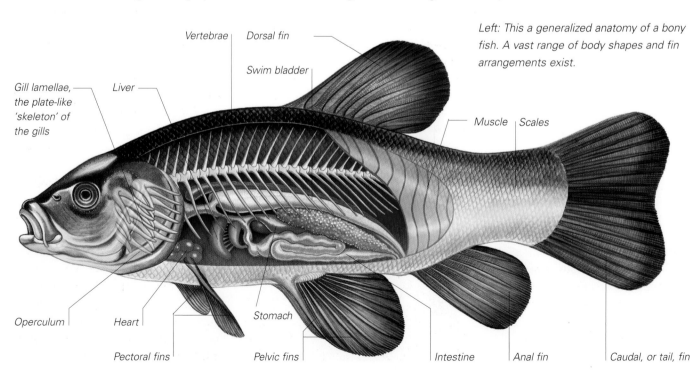

Vertebrae | Dorsal fin

Swim bladder

Gill lamellae, the plate-like 'skeleton' of the gills | Liver

Muscle | Scales

Operculum | Heart

Stomach

Pectoral fins | Pelvic fins | Intestine | Anal fin | Caudal, or tail, fin

**Fin shapes**

Above: The basking shark's (Cetorhinus maximus) triangular dorsal fin.

Above: The long, showy fins of the John Dory (Zeus faber).

Above: The Common Chub (Leuciscus cephalus) has a small dorsal fin.

Above: The beautiful fins of a blue discus (Symphysodon aequifasciata haraldi)

Above: The large, sail-like, dorsal fin of the grayling (Thymallus thymallus).

Above: The anal fin of the common eel (Anguilla anguilla) extends to the tail.

help change direction or are sculled to maintain the fish's position in the water. The dorsal fin and anal fin help to keep fish stable and upright as they swim along. These are the fins most often elaborated for display.

## Scales

All fish have fins and the majority have scales. The scales of sharks and rays (cartilaginous fish) are hard and tooth-like. They jut from the skin giving it a rough texture. Most bony fish have smoother scales, which grow from the outer layer of the skin. These scales have either rounded or comb-shaped rear edges and are only loosely attached. A few fish, such as the armoured catfish, have bony plates (scutes) in place of scales. These offer extra protection from predators.

## Internal organs

The bulk of a fish's body is made up of muscle. These slabs of flesh are the fillets we cook and eat. Beneath the muscle the internal organs are not dissimilar from our own. The main difference is the lack of lungs and the

presence of a swim bladder. This is an impermeable sac filled with gas, used by fish to control their buoyancy. The amount of gas it holds is increased or reduced, by introducing oxygen from the blood vessels surrounding it, or by absorbing oxygen back into the blood. This feature is unique to bony fish and has been lost by a few bottom-dwelling groups, such as the gobies. Sharks, rays and the jawless lampreys lack this organ completely and sink to the bottom as soon as they stop swimming.

Anatomically speaking, freshwater fish do not differ all that much from

Below: The smooth scales of bony fish overlap in a head-to-tail direction, allowing a smoother flow of water over the body.

their cousins in the sea. Many families have both marine and freshwater representatives. There are even some species that travel between the sea and fresh water, although this is rare. Fish have skin which is slightly permeable and in fresh water their bodies are constantly soaking up water, due to the level of dissolved salts in their blood being higher than in their surroundings. To avoid expanding and bursting, freshwater fish have to continually excrete water through their urine and gills – up to ten times their body weight in a single day. Marine fish have the opposite problem. In the sea they lose water from their bodies through their skins to the surroundings, as dissolved salt levels here are higher than in their blood. To survive, marine fish have to continually drink and excrete excess salt.

One anatomical difference in some freshwater fish is the presence of the labyrinth organ, which is absent from all marine fish. It is located near the gills and is made up of rosette-shaped plates full of blood vessels. The vessels let fish absorb oxygen from gulped air.

# MOVEMENT

*When it comes to moving about, the physical properties of water can be a mixed blessing. The density of water is about 800 times that of air, meaning that it offers plenty of support. However, pushing through it requires a lot of energy – swimming is hard work!*

Fish swim using symmetrical blocks of muscles arranged in a repeating pattern along either side of the body. This pattern of repetition, known as metamerism, was inherited from the common ancestor of all bony, cartilaginous and jawless fish, and is more obvious in some species than in others. Because a fish's body is supported by the non-compressible backbone, contraction of the muscles on either side causes it to flex. If the muscles on opposite sides of the trunk contract alternately, the body performs a side-to-side wiggle, pushing against the surrounding water and, thus, propelling the fish forward. The addition of median fins (the dorsal, caudal and anal fins) increases thrust to the animal's movement and also adds stability.

## Types of swimming

In long-bodied fish, such as eels, swimming involves the side-to-side undulations of the whole body, a form of swimming known as anguillaform. The undulations are greatest towards the tail end, which generates considerable turbulence, making this an very energetically expensive means of moving from place to place. Turbulence is reduced by a tapering body shape and the addition of a tail fin. The fin also increases the surface area available to generate propulsion.

*Below: Conger eels (*Conger conger*), like other eels and sea snakes, rely on snakelike movement of the body to propel themselves along.*

### Modes of swimming

The carangiform mode (shown right) is a powerful method of swimming adopted by many fish, including jacks, salmon and snappers. These fish swim using their trunk muscles, but most of the movement is in the rear half of the body while the head remains steady (1). The tail undulates in one direction, then snaps back (2), propelling the fish forward. The tail then undulates towards the opposite side, to repeat the process.

A modified and less powerful version of carangiform swimming is often described as 'oscillatory'. This is where contractions of the trunk muscle cause the body to flick from side to side (3), passing through an S-shaped wave (4).

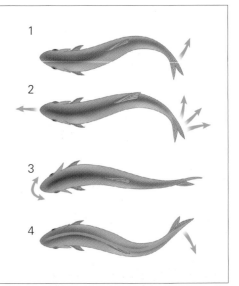

The most energy-efficient mode of swimming is that adopted by members of the family Carangidae, a group that includes fish such as the Atlantic horse mackerel. With these marine and brackish-water fish, side-to-side movements are restricted to the rear end of the fish only, and a large tail fin helps reduce turbulence and increase efficiency. When this type of swimming technique is adopted, the head remains still, helping to stabilize the fish's vision and maintain a steady direction.

A few fish use just their fins for propulsion. Examples of fish that use this swimming technique include the opah, or moonfish (*Lampris regius*), which sculls with its pectoral fins, or the batfish, which uses its pectoral and pelvic fins to pull itself along the sea floor. Seahorses and oarfish swim with the body held vertically in the water, so

*Above: The rainbow runner (*Elagatis bipinnulata*) swims in the carangiform style.*

that the dorsal fin is at the back – wave-like ripples running along the dorsal fringe and fanning movements of the pectoral fins are enough to propel the fish very slowly forward.

## Buoyancy

The lifting force exerted by water on an object less dense than itself is known as buoyancy. Objects that are less dense than water are positively buoyant and they float or rise towards the surface. Objects that weigh more than their equivalent volume of water are negatively buoyant. They will sink. The body of a fish contains several types of dense tissue, such as muscle and bone, that are negatively buoyant. For species that make a living close to the sea floor, this is an advantage – they are able to save energy simply by letting gravity take effect, and many will spend long periods resting on the bottom. They are able to raise themselves up into the water when necessary by expending energy and swimming. For fish that live in very deep water, where food is scarce, the ability to save energy is a crucial survival adaptation.

## The swim bladder

However, space is limited on the ocean floor, especially compared with the vastness of the open ocean, and so there can be advantages to life in mid water. Most pelagic bony fish have a specialized buoyancy organ, the swim bladder, that helps reduce the energy required to maintain a constant depth.

The swim bladder is a large, gas-filled chamber whose volume can be adjusted so that the fish achieves neutral buoyancy and so can 'hang' stationary in mid water. Gas can pass in and out of the bladder via a direct connection with the outside (by the oesophagus), or it can be removed by absorption into the bloodstream through a permeable area of the wall lining. Alternatively the bladder can be inflated by secretion of gas from a gland, known as the *rete mirabilis*, associated with a specialized network

Above: A plaice (Pleuronectes platessa) rests on coral. This flounder favours reefs as a habitat, although it is often difficult to see it, as it may be partially buried in sand.

Below: The red lipped batfish (Ogcocephalus darwini) moves from place to place using its pelvic and pectoral fins to effectively 'crawl' along the ocean floor.

of capillaries in animals. One of the chief limitations of the system is that the volume of the bladder cannot be adjusted instantaneously. Thus, if the fish is brought suddenly to the surface – for example on the end of a line – the abrupt decrease in pressure causes

Above: Fast-swimming schools such as these mackerel (Scomber scombrus) may swim in a diamond formation, taking advantage of the slipstream created by other individuals.

Below: Seahorses, such as this long-snouted species (Hippocampus reidi), use their dorsal fins to propel their body forward through the water. The tail is used to 'moor' when at rest.

the gas in the bladder to expand very rapidly, crushing other organs and sometimes rupturing the bladder itself. Once a swim bladder has over-expanded, the fish is so buoyant it becomes unable to return to its preferred depth.

A few types of bony fish have given up on the swim bladder. For example, mackerel rely on speed and agility to hunt as well as to evade predators, and this means that sudden changes in pressure are part of their daily lives. Their oily muscles are positively buoyant, and this goes some way to compensating for the lack of a swim bladder, but even so they must swim continuously in order to hold their position. They rely solely on the flow of water generated by swimming to deliver water to the gills.

Left: The bulge of the swim bladder can be seen in this rudd. This helps it to float in the water as it keeps the fish bouyant.

# SENSES

*Fish, like all other creatures, rely completely on their senses to survive. Without them they would be unable to detect danger or find food. Certain senses are more important to some fish than others. It all depends on where they live, what they eat and when they are most active.*

The senses that fish rely on are touch, smell and hearing. A fish's ability to sense what is around them includes an electrical sense – for a few species – or a line of receptors on a lateral line that are designed to pick up tiny movements in the water.

## Touch

One sense that all fish possess is the sense of touch. Among freshwater fish, this sense is most developed in species that are nocturnal or live in murky water. It is also important for many species that live on the seabed. The sense of touch is often enhanced by fleshy, whisker-like projections known as barbels. These invariably grow from the head and are usually concentrated around the mouth.

Several types of fish bear barbels but they are most common and exaggerated among the catfish. Most of the members of this group are bottom feeders and many are nocturnal, so they use their barbels to locate prey. Catfish have become so successful at this mode of existence that they now dominate the murky bottoms of ponds, lakes and rivers in many parts of the world – having quickly established themselves in most of the places where they have been introduced outside their native range.

*Below: As its name suggests, the electric eel (*Electrophorus electricus*) uses electricity both to sense prey and to stun it.*

## How the lateral line works

*The lateral line is used to detect pressure changes in the water. Fish use it to detect the movement of others and to orientate themselves in currents.*

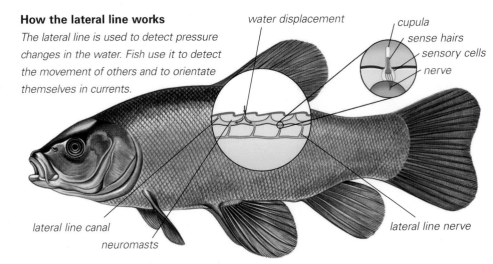

water displacement

cupula
sense hairs
sensory cells
nerve

lateral line canal

neuromasts

lateral line nerve

## The electrical sense

Touch is the sense that we would naturally associate with navigation and locating objects in the dark. Some fish, however, have extra senses that work in tandem with touch, or even replace it. One such sense is the electrical sense found in sharks, rays and in some bony fish. This can be used to detect the muscular activity of other animals, even when they are buried beneath mud. Rays use it to find prey hidden in the sediment on the bottom. Other fish with this sense find it just as useful for detecting and avoiding predators. A few species are able to use the electrical sense to navigate and detect inanimate, as well as living objects.

*Below: The nocturnal redtailed catfish (*Phractocephalus hemioliopterus*) uses its chin barbels to navigate the bottom.*

## The lateral line

Other fish have a more basic system for detecting things around them, based on the lateral line. This line is a series of tiny receptors, which usually run from the rear edge of the gill covers to the base of the tail. Each of these receptors contains microscopic hair-like projections, much like those in the human inner ear. These are surrounded by a jelly-like substance and are usually set at the bottom of a short canal or pit in the fish's skin. The lateral line picks up small movements in the water, so it can detect the presence of living things that might be out of view. It cannot detect inert objects, however, nor gauge the distance of moving objects from a fish.

The lateral line plays an important role in helping fish to sense the world around them. It is particularly useful for schooling fish, allowing individual fish to immediately judge and react to the movements of fish adjacent to them. This both helps avoid collisions and enables the synchronized movement displayed by fish shoals. All fish use the lateral line to detect movements in the water around them. Freshwater fish living in streams, rivers and other areas of flowing water also use it to orientate themselves so that they normally face into the current. This allows them to hold their position in the water and prevents them from being washed downstream. A few species use the lateral line to detect prey. Outside Britain, killifish, which feed on insects and other invertebrates that fall into the water, use it to sense the ripples made by prey struggling on the surface. Blind cavefish have large concentrations of the receptors normally found in the lateral line located on their heads. These fish, living in absolute darkness, rely entirely on these mechanical receptors to detect and home in on prey.

## Smell and hearing

Being land-living creatures, we tend think of smell as a sense that only works in air. However, fish can smell just as we can – the only difference is that they smell by detecting organic matter and other particles in water. Some species use smell to help them find food. Sharks, for example, are famous for their ability to detect minute quantities of blood in the water. It is also possible that many

---

**Compensating for blindness**

Eyes are useless in the pitch black of caves and most cavefish have lost them completely. In their place these fish have evolved an extreme sensitivity to movements in the water. The fronts of their heads are covered with the sensors normally confined to the lateral lines of fish. Cavefish use these sensors to find prey but cannot use them to navigate. Inanimate objects in their surroundings are sensed by touch.

*Below: Like most cavefish, this species from Mexico (*Anoptichthys jordani*) is blind and has little skin pigmentation.*

---

*Above: Rays have eyes like turrets on the tops of their heads. They use their eyes mainly to alert them to danger, as they find prey by touch and their electrical sense.*

*Below: The stone loach (*Barbatula barbatula*) has barbels but combines its sense of touch with vision to find food.*

freshwater fish use smell to help them find their way around. It is known that salmon use it to help them locate their home rivers when returning from the sea to breed. Every river has a unique signature odour that builds up as the water passes over rocks, sand or mud on the bottom. This odour is imprinted in the brains of young salmon and, when they near the coast as an adult, are able to follow it to the mouth of the river in which they hatched.

Hearing in fish is poorly understood but this sense is not well developed in most fish. A few species, however, can hear quite well – for example, the goldfish, which probably uses hearing to help it find prey.

## Vision

The highly developed mechanical receptor system in blind cavefish is an evolutionary response to their inability to see. The ancestors of most cavefish had perfectly good vision and some species that have only evolved fairly recently still show the remnants of

*Above: Salmon like this Atlantic salmon (*Salmo salar*) use their sense of smell to help them find their way back to their home rivers from the sea.*

*Below: Goldfish (*Carassius auratus*) are among the few fish known to use hearing to find food.*

eyes. Vision is an important sense for most fish, even those that are nocturnal or live in deep or murky waters. In subterranean caves darkness is complete but in freshwater habitats elsewhere there is always some light, even at night. Light also penetrates a long way down in the sea. While bottom-living fish may rely on touch to find food, vision can warn them of danger. The darkness caused by a predator's shadow passing overhead is enough to alert most fish.

Vision is most vital for fish that live near the surface or in shallow waters. These species tend to rely on sight more than any other sense. For active predators in particular, the ability to see is indispensable. It is hard to imagine fish such as pike living long without eyes: for these precision hunters, accurate visual targeting and the ability to quickly follow the movements of prey are vital. Plant-eating fish also rely on vision to locate food, as do most freshwater species that feed on invertebrates.

# BEHAVIOUR

*Compared with some creatures, such as mammals, the behaviour of individual fish can appear quite simple. Certainly the imperatives that drive fish are few, and boil down to the need to eat, the need to avoid being eaten and the need to reproduce. Of all these, finding food is the most pressing.*

Fish, like all animals, must eat to live. For most, however, surviving is also a constant battle to avoid becoming meals themselves. It is these two imperatives that basically govern the behaviour of all marine and freshwater fish.

## Staying alive

One of the most common behavioural responses to the threat of predation is shoaling. By gathering in groups, fish make it harder for predators to pick them off. The majority of shoaling fish belong to species that live in open water, a place where it is virtually impossible to hide. These fish use the bodies of others for cover. A predator following one individual will often see it disappear into the mass and become distracted by the sudden appearance

of others. Additionally, many shoaling fish are coloured so that their outlines seem to merge together. This makes it much harder for predators to target individuals. The other advantage of living in shoals is that they act as early warning systems. With so many pairs of eyes gathered together, predators are much more likely to be spotted before they are close enough to attack. For fish, there really is safety in numbers.

Not all fish try to avoid being eaten by shoaling. Many bottom-living fish rely on camouflage to avoid being seen in the first place. This tactic generally works as long as the fish in question keep still. Another common way of staying out of sight is to become nocturnal. Many freshwater fish hide beneath rocks or in underwater crevices by day and only emerge at

### Fish that breathe air

A few types of freshwater fish gulp air to supplement their oxygen intake. Most of these species inhabit stagnant pools, swamps or other habitats where the levels of dissolved oxygen are low. Gulping air also has another advantage – it allows some fish to cross land and find new homes. This ability is particularly useful in areas that are subject to drought, where pools often dry up or become overcrowded as they shrink under the heat of the sun.

*Below: Carp may be seen gulping air at the surface of lakes and ponds, especially when these are very oxygen-starved.*

*Above: Like other schooling clupeids, Pilchards (*Sardina pilchardus*) move in schools of similarly sized and aged fish.*

*Below: A plaice (*Pleuronectes platessa*) relies on its incredible camouflage and ability to lie perfectly still on the sea bed for defence against predators.*

*Above: Pike (*Esox lucius*) stalk their prey from behind reeds. They stay incredibly still, then launch their ambush at speed.*

*Below: Here a parasitic sea lamprey (*Petromyzon marinus*) can be seen sucking the blood from a salmon as the host fish leaps upstream to spawn.*

night to feed. This tactic is particularly effective as a defence against visual predators such as birds. Of course, this makes these fish much harder for humans to spot too. As a result, most people are unaware of the wide variety of fish living in their local rivers and streams.

## Finding food

Fish have evolved to feed on a wide range of organic matter, from detritus and plankton to other fish. Most fish spend a large part of their lives gathering food. Detritus feeders have to rummage through a lot of mud to find enough edible matter to live on. For fish that eat invertebrates, the most time-consuming part of feeding is finding their small prey. Plankton feeders are surrounded by their food – the tiny animals and algae that live in the water – but gathering and filtering out enough of these to make a meal takes time. Plant-eating fish, like plankton eaters, have little trouble finding food but need to eat a lot of it, as plants and algae are relatively low in nutrients. The only fish that spend relatively short periods feeding or finding food are the larger predators. That said, many of these spend long periods lying in wait for prey.

## Breeding behaviour

The behaviour of fish within species is fairly uncomplicated and predictable but across the group as a whole it is surprisingly varied. Nowhere is this more true than in the breeding behaviour of freshwater fish.

The vast majority of ocean fish scatter their eggs and sperm together in open water and then leave the fertilized eggs to develop and hatch on their own. This type of breeding behaviour is also seen in some freshwater fish, particularly shoaling species that live in lakes and other large areas of open water, but many others put a great deal more effort into the process of reproduction.

Many freshwater fish build nests. These vary from simple scrapes in the sand or gravel, such as the redds made by salmon and trout, to far more complex constructions. Three-spined sticklebacks, for instance (*Gasterosteus aculeatus*) form tube-shaped nests from algae. These are built by the males, which entice females in to lay. Once the eggs have been laid and fertilized, the males guard them until they hatch. They also fan the eggs to keep them well-supplied with oxygen.

*Below: An eel feeds on a worm in a river. Young eels swim upstream until they eventually reach the sea, where they spawn.*

*Above: Sockeye salmon, in mating colours of red and green, breed in fresh water.*

*Below: A male three-spined stickleback (*Gasterosteus aculeatus*) in nuptial coloration. He will later build a nest.*

Other freshwater fish use natural crevices or gaps beneath rocks as nests in which to lay their eggs. Again, the eggs are often guarded and fanned until hatching. Nest-building fish that do not guard their eggs tend to hide them by covering them with sediment.

Perhaps the most unusual of all nests are the bubble nests built by some species of freshwater fish. These are formed from bubbles of oral mucus, which float at the surface like rafts. Females lay their eggs, which are buoyant, on the undersides of these rafts; they are then guarded by the male (or occasionally by both parents).

A few freshwater fish have dispensed with nests altogether and instead brood their eggs and their young in their mouths. This behaviour is most common among cichlids, which are not found in Britain. The disadvantage is that, while brooding, these fish are unable to eat.

In the ocean, sea horses and pipefish take care of their eggs. Once the eggs have been laid they are attached to a brood pad on the male's body. He then carries them around until they hatch.

Not all fish lay eggs – a few species give birth to live young. Like mouth brooding, this strategy improves the chances of the young surviving to adulthood. Live young are much larger than eggs, however, so fewer can be produced in a season.

Many fish migrate in order to breed. This is particularly true of species that live in rivers. Breeding migrations tend to be upstream, with eggs being laid nearer the headwaters. As the eggs hatch and the young grow they gradually move down-river, until they are themselves big enough to breed. This separation between young and mature fish ensures that there is little competition between adults and fry for food, and also avoids cannibalization.

Some fish spend part of their lives in fresh water and other periods in the sea. Salmon, for instance, migrate between salt and fresh water, swimming up rivers to lay their eggs.

# FEEDING

*Feeding is an essential part of day-to-day life for most fish species. Marine food webs can be enormously complex and feeding strategies vary greatly, with one thing assured – no species is exempt from the possibility of one day becoming food for other predatory or scavenging animals.*

For fish, the endless search for food is pursued in a variety of ways; some are predators, others are prey, and some are herbivores or filter feeders.

The digestive process in fish begins in the mouth, the size and positioning of which is variable between species. Fish that engulf large prey or are active hunters usually have a mouth that opens at the front, bottom feeders have an underslung mouth, and those that pluck small prey from the surface or lie on the bottom to attack prey passing above have a mouth directed upwards.

The mouth and jaws of some species are highly modified. The tiny tubular mouth of the pipefish family (Syngnathidae) opens at the tip of a narrow snout, working like a pipette to suck up small items of food from

### Cleaning stations

Several groups of bony fish have become specialized 'cleaners'. They are adapted to feed only on the small external parasites that attach themselves to the bodies of other fish. A heavy load of parasites can place a severe strain on the body of a host, so the ministrations of cleaner fish can be highly beneficial. In fact, many large fish, even voracious predators, will wait in line for this marine valet service. Cleaners and their 'clients' develop an extraordinary level of mutual trust – the cleaners venturing close to jaws that could snap them up in an instant and the client waiting patiently while the cleaner nibbles away at gills and other vulnerable body parts.

*Below: A damselfish being cleaned by a much smaller cleaner wrasse (*Labroides *species).*

small crevices. At the other end of the spectrum, the gulper eel (*Eurypharynx pelecanoides*) engulfs small prey along with large volumes of water. Most fish that hunt larger prey have smaller but more powerful jaws, typically lined with sharp teeth.

These teeth might be excellent for snagging prey and preventing its escape, but they are not much use for cutting it up – thus the scariest-looking fish often swallow their prey whole. Often teeth of this sort flex towards the back of the throat to ease the inward passage of prey and prevent it from escaping. Teeth used for slicing and dicing, like those of sharks, which bite large prey into chunks, need to be more rigid and robust.

## Herbivores

Vegetarianism is rare among fish. Virtually all species eat other animals, especially during the early stages of life when a large intake of protein is required. However, some species do become essentially herbivorous later in life. Where insects or other

*Above: The basking shark (*Cetorhinus maximus*) is Britain's largest fish and the second-largest fish in the world after the whale shark. It feeds by swimming through clouds of plankton and sifting them out of the water with its sieve-like gill rakers.*

invertebrates are scarce, adult carp (*Cyprinus carpio*) can survive entirely on a diet of plant matter, for instance. Among sea fish, vegetarianism is more common in the tropics, where warm water and long hours of bright sunlight permit plentiful growth of marine plant material.

## Filter feeding

Bony fish have four pairs of gills located within the pharynx, or 'throat'. In filter feeding species, the bony arches that support the gills also bear long, slender rakers – rigid structures that project inwards, forming a sort of sieve through which water passing in via the mouth and out through the gill slits is strained. The size of food taken varies with the species, from algae to baby fish, squid and shrimps.

**The digestive system of a bony fish**

*The length of the intestine varies among species, but is usually shorter in carnivores. The fingerlike pyloric caecae, attached to the gut, may aid the absorption of food.*

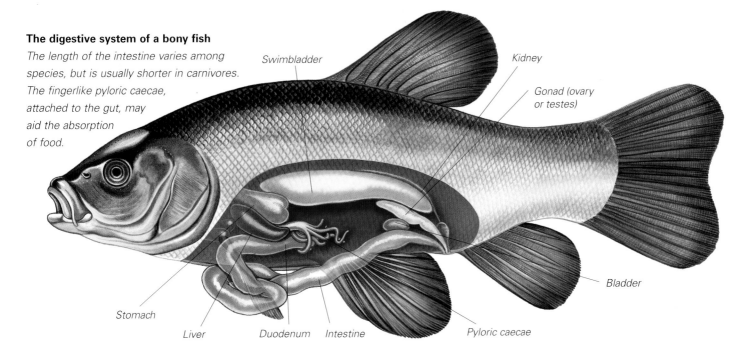

Swimbladder

Kidney

Gonad (ovary or testes)

Bladder

Stomach

Liver

Duodenum

Intestine

Pyloric caecae

## Predators

Most fish are hunters. Zooplankton and communities of small, bottom-dwelling invertebrates, including worms, molluscs and crustaceans, are an important source of food, as are fish fry. Hunting techniques among predatory fish vary from opportunistic snapping at any small passing animals to lie-in-wait ambush techniques.

Many ambush predators are very well camouflaged – the disguises of stonefish (order Scorpaeniformes) can fool the sharpest eyes. The ambush is taken a step further by some species of anglerfish (order Lophiiformes), which not only exhibit perfect camouflage, but also draw prey near with a food-like lure dangling from their head as if from a fishing line.

Ambush predators often have a relatively large mouth – when this is suddenly opened the prey is carried in with the inrushing water. Other forms of weaponry, such as stings or electric shocks, may also be used by fish for defence against predators larger than themselves.

## Parasites

There are numerous interesting twists on the predatory theme in the fish world. A number of fish are themselves parasitic – they live in close association with their prey, feeding off the host without injuring it. The key to being a

successful parasite is to avoid killing the host – once dead, it is of limited use, but kept alive it may provide a source of sustenance for life.

Some parasites are better adapted to this than others. For example, the carapid cucumberfish lives within the body of a sea cucumber, feeding off the tissues of the respiratory and reproductive systems, which

*Above: The dogfish can use its dorsal spines to pierce and poison a predator.*

*Below: Carp are onmivorous, and scour the bed for fungi, plants, crustaceans and worms.*

continually regenerate, providing an endless source of food. Not all parasites commit to physically living on a single host – many simply swim to their victim, take a single bite and swim away. Often they improve their chances of getting close enough by impersonating harmless or benign species, especially cleaners (*see* box on the opposite page).

*Above: The pipefish can probe into crevices and suck up food with its tubular mouth.*

*Below: This preserved fangtooth clearly shows the deep-sea fish's huge, sharp teeth.*

# REPRODUCTION

*Individual fish share their habitats with many others, and all must find a way to maximize their own success among the competitors, predators and potential mates. For this reason, the success of fish reproduction is often dependent on, or at least affected by, the environment in which they breed.*

Reproductive methods in fish are diverse. Gender differences are often less defined than in mammals, and unique strategies such as semelparity also affect the way they live.

Bony fish employ a large variety of breeding strategies. Often zoologists talk of oviparity (egg laying) versus viviparity (live bearing). Female oviparous fish produce eggs, which they release into the water where they are fertilized by sperm from the male. In most cases, the numbers of eggs involved are extremely large. Viviparity is far less common, and only about one in every 30 families of fish have true live-bearing species in which mating occurs and embryos develop inside the female, nourished by way of a connection to the mother.

Between these two apparently distinct strategies there is a large grey area, known as ovoviviparity, that leads to some degree of confusion. Ovoviviparity is where a female fish produces eggs that are fertilized and hatch internally so that the mother gives birth to live young at any stage from early larvae to fully formed, sexually mature offspring.

## Parental types
As well as physiological differences in reproductive biology, fish also exhibit a striking variety of behaviours and strategies, designed to maximize their chances of successful breeding. These can be grouped into three main types, or guilds, based on how the parent fish treat their offspring. These types are non-guarders, guarders and bearers.

Non-guarders are oviparous. They produce eggs and sperm, either in a single large spawning or several smaller sessions, and leave nature to take its course. In some cases, the eggs are released in open water as part of a mass spawning, while in others they are shed above a specially selected substratum – for example, gravel or weed. In both cases, the chances of any single fertilized egg developing to adulthood is tiny, so non-guarders tend to produce eggs in vast numbers.

The eggs of species that show some substratum selectivity may have a slightly improved chance of survival, and may thus be produced in slightly smaller numbers than those that are simply released to the mercy of the prevailing current.

Guarders are also oviparous, but they tend to produce fewer eggs and therefore take rather more care of them, sticking around and defending the eggs, which are typically laid in a nest or adhesive mass, to be guarded externally. Sticklebacks are one group of freshwater species that exhibit this breeding strategy.

*Above: Bullheads (*Cotis gobis*) guard their eggs, which are anchored to a nest.*

Bearers may be oviparous, viviparous or ovoviviparous, but in all examples the offspring are carried with one of the parents as they develop – either as eggs or as larvae. In oviparous bearers, the female lays eggs, but they are then gathered up into the mouth of one of the parents, who holds them there until they hatch.

## Males and females
Among mammals, the differences between sexes usually seem clear cut. The distinction is often less definitive in fish, and hermaphroditism – where both male and female sex organs develop within the same individual – is common.

In most of these instances, fish are sequential hermaphrodites – meaning they start life as one gender and then at a later stage switch to the other. For example, some gobies start out as males and become females. This makes

*Below: 'Mermaid's purses', seen here, are the egg cases of a lesser spotted dogfish (*Scyliorhinus canicula*).*

*Below: Free-swimming larvae mingle with eggs that have not yet hatched in this school of planktonic life.*

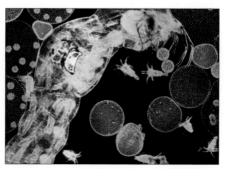

## Schooling

A 'school' is the term used for a group of similar-sized fish that move in a coordinated manner, always swimming in the same direction and reacting almost as one. There is no leader. Members of a school use sight and the lateral line sense to stay together.

There are several benefits to be gained from schooling behaviour. First, there is never any difficulty finding a mate. Second, the members of a school may help each other to find food. Finally, and perhaps most important of all is the principle of 'safety in numbers' – the greater the numbers, the better the chance of members surviving an attack from predators, who may find it difficult to target and pick off individuals.

Of course the system is not perfect – larger schools are conspicuous and some hunters specialize in herding fish together into a dense bait ball that can be taken whole. But in general, as long as the school remains larger than the average predator's appetite, the benefits outweigh the risks.

*Below: Very large schools may present predators with a formidable moving 'wall'.*

physiological sense because sperm are relatively cheap and easy to produce, even for small fish, whereas eggs require much more investment, something that is more readily afforded by large individuals.

But there can also be a sound ecological advantage to working the other way around – many wrasse and sea bass (families Labridae and Serranidae) begin life as females and become males only when they have grown sufficiently large to maintain control of a territory or a harem. Synchronous hermaphrodism, where a fish produces both female and male gametes that can function at the same time, is less common, but in species such as tripodfish this may allow individuals to self-fertilize. Hermaphroditism as a strategy is rare among freshwater fish and unknown in British species.

## Semelparity

For some fish, breeding is a once-in-a-lifetime event. These species are called semelparous, and they include eels, roughies and some salmonids, adults of which invest all their available body resources in producing large numbers of high-quality eggs to ensure a good chance of survival for their young. Spawning leaves the adults drastically weakened and with quite literally nothing else to live for.

## Seasonality

Most fish species of temperate seas and freshwater habitats are seasonal breeders – in other words, they come into breeding condition at much the same time each year. Seasonality is regulated by hormones – chemicals released into the blood by glands, such as the hypothalamus and pituitary. This allows the fish to respond physiologically to environmental conditions – the temperature, day length and lunar cycles, for example.

Some fish breed at any time of year. These tend to be species of the warm tropics, where conditions remain relatively constant all year round and so no season is particularly favourable. The same is true of deep-sea habitats, which are beyond the influence of surface temperatures and day length. It is thought that many deep-sea species off the coast of Britain are year-round breeders, though details of this are rarely understood in full.

## Larvae protection strategies

Fish larvae are highly vulnerable to predation, but most have developed at least some adaptations that help reduce the risk of being eaten.

Some larvae, for example, are almost transparent, making them hard to see. Many have large spines or filaments that make them difficult for other small animals to swallow, while others grow exceptionally fast in order to minimize the time they spend at risk from predators of a certain size. Very often, schools of larvae live in different locations or at different depths to adults of their own species, thus reducing the risk of cannibalism when the latter feeds on small organisms.

*Below: The characteristic shape of perch can already be seen in its larva (top), swimming alongside an ostracod (bottom).*

# ENVIRONMENTS

*Fish are the most widespread and numerous vertebrates on Earth. Their watery realm covers around two-thirds of our planet. The vast majority of the world's fish live in the sea, the biggest of all natural habitats, but the freshwater world is also home to a specialized group of creatures.*

New species of fish are being discovered and described all the time, both from marine and freshwater habitats. While the majority of fish live in the oceans, species diversity is greater among freshwater fish. Of the 28,000 known species of fish in the world today, 11,950 are confined to fresh water. Many of these species are unique to the rivers or lakes in which they live.

Each body of fresh water is effectively an island, surrounded by land and cut off from other lakes and rivers. Just like on islands, many of the creatures they are home to live in that area and nowhere else.

Ocean fish, by contrast, have fewer boundaries. With an average depth of just over 3 kilometres (2 miles), the sea is a habitat in three dimensions. Whereas most land-dwelling animals can only move over the surface in two directions, fish move in three directions, and exist throughout the water column. Unlike freshwater species, marine fish are not physically separated from one

*Below: The creatures who inhabit shallow waters of the world's oceans are very different from those who live in the depths.*

another; a species that occupies a particular niche on one side of an ocean is very likely to be found in a similar niche on the other side of the ocean. This means that there are very few truly rare fish found in the oceans. Many freshwater fish on the other hand are much more vulnerable, simply because the ranges they inhabit are so comparatively small.

Although there are two main environments for fish – marine and fresh water – within these there are several different variations of watery habitats, which fish have adapted to benefit from and survive within.

## Marine habitats

By their very nature, marine habitats tend not to exist in isolation as they are largely continuous. Seas and oceans often blend with each other in such a way that it can be difficult to say where one ends and the next begins. That said, many marine fish are only found in particular parts of the ocean. Some species live in the well-lit upper layers of the open ocean, for example, while others are found only in the deeper, darker waters.

*Above: While some sea creatures spend their lives swimming in the sea, others, like this hermit crab, are found on the seabed.*

Just as fish may be adapted for life in open water, so they may also be specialized for life on the bottom. In shallow waters the nature of the seabed may dictate their appearance. Rays and flatfish that live on sandy areas of the sea floor are often coloured and patterned to match that sand. Similarly, fish that live over mud or shingle may be coloured and patterned accordingly.

Marine habitats tend to be most varied near the coast. Here the seabed rises up towards the surface and may even break through it at low tide. The combination of abundant sunlight and a solid substrate allows seaweeds and other marine algae to grow. These, in turn, provide food and hiding places for invertebrates and fish. In tropical seas corals often take the place of algae. Britain has corals of its own, although these are much smaller and fewer in number than those of warmer waters.

## Freshwater habitats

Although all fish have certain features in common, as a group they are incredibly varied. This great diversity reflects their many different lifestyles. Some are bottom feeders, others find

*Above: Slow-moving rivers support a wide variety of aquatic life.*

*Above: A fast-moving hillside stream will be full of oxygen, but may lack food.*

their food in the water column, while others hunt and forage at the surface.

Sea water is fairly homogeneous wherever it is found on the planet. The main variables in marine habitats are water temperature and light. In freshwater habitats there is also a great amount of variation in water quality and flow. For instance, mountain streams run quickly, and are clear and full of oxygen. On the other hand, they are often relatively sparse in terms of food. Swamps, by contrast, are full of organic matter, meaning that food is rarely hard to find. However, the water is stagnant, and dissolved oxygen levels are low.

Freshwater fish vary immensely in colour and shape. Even within species individuals may look quite different, depending on their age, sex, and habitat. Colour may be used to attract a mate but it can also help fish to hide. Like their marine cousins, many freshwater species are camouflaged to blend in with their surroundings. Bottom feeders often perfectly match the substrates (or bottom level) where they feed – for example, those living in rocky streams tend to be cryptically patterned in various shades of brown, making them very hard to spot when they are not moving. Fish that feed in clear, open water, such as those found in lakes, are more often silvery to reflect any light that falls on them. This has the effect of helping them to disappear in the blue.

Shape as well as colour, may be used to help camouflage fish. However, shape is more often a reflection of the type of life a fish leads: for example, how it is equipped to feed. Bottom feeders tend to have rather flat, wide bodies, with mouths which are positioned quite low down on the head. Open water feeders, on the other hand have their mouths positioned at the front of the head.

Of course, the freshwater world is not inhabited by fish alone. Fish share their environment with amphibians such as frogs, toads and newts, and mammals such as otters – not to mention insects, plants and birds. The co-existence of these different types of creatures has, naturally, influenced the evolutionary process: many creatures have developed specific habits and physical characteristics that reflect their place in the food chain.

## A hidden wealth of wildlife

Britain has a great variety of aquatic creatures, just below the surface of the rockpools, rivers and lakes of Britain there exists an astonishing array of life, and below this there is even more.

*Below: Freshwater fish share their habitats with mammals such as the otter.*

# FRESHWATER CONSERVATION

*Britain's freshwater habitats are in a much better condition now than they were just a few decades ago.
Nevertheless, they remain vulnerable, particularly to the threat of pollution. Protecting them is an
ongoing effort, involving everybody from water companies to independent conservation organizations.*

Britain's freshwater habitats are home to a great range of wildlife, from fish and amphibians to mammals and birds. They are also very important to our own species, for a variety of reasons. First and foremost, they are the source of the water that flows from the taps in our homes. Although this water is treated before it reaches us, most of it ultimately comes from rivers, either directly or indirectly, via the reservoirs they feed. They are also places of recreation. We visit them for everything from swimming and angling to birdwatching and boating, and many of our larger lakes are tourist attractions in their own right.

This great interaction we have with our freshwater habitats inevitably puts pressure on them. Some people, unfortunately, are prone to leave litter,

*Below: Volunteers clear reeds from a marshland pond in Colchester to promote a healthy wildlife habitat.*

while boats can disturb wildlife, particularly boats with motors. That said, our rivers and other freshwater habitats are much healthier than they once were. Not so long ago many were contaminated with vast quantities of untreated industrial and other waste, which poured straight into them.

The change in our attitude to rivers is perhaps best illustrated by the story of the Thames. In the 1950s, the River Thames in London was virtually lifeless, polluted by raw sewage and industrial effluent, as well as hot water, which poured from the gas works and power stations along its banks. During the summer, large stretches of the river were virtually devoid of oxygen and completely absent of fish. In the 1960s, efforts began to reverse the decline in water quality and today the Thames in London is home to a huge range of fish, including species highly sensitive to pollution, such as lampreys and salmon. With the fish, birds such as

*Above: A grey heron (Ardea cinerea) waits beside an English canal for a fish to swim by. Inland waterways need protection in order to sustain important food chains.*

cormorants and herons have returned. There are even otters moving back in. So far they have yet to reach the city centre, but they have been seen around Redbridge and Richmond.

As we have cleaned up our rivers, so we have also made efforts to protect and even extend some of our rarer freshwater habitats, such as reed beds. On the Somerset Levels, for example, an entirely new area of reed bed habitat has recently been created from old peat diggings. Known as the Ham Wall Reserve, it is owned and managed by the Royal Society for the Protection of Birds (RSPB), and has already attracted such rarities as bearded tits and bitterns, both of which now breed on the site.

Other wetland habitats have been created from scratch. Towards the end of the 1990s, work began to transform an area of several small reservoirs into a new wetland habitat in London. Managed by the Wildfowl and Wetlands Trust (WWT), the project was completed and opened to the public in the year 2000. Like Ham Wall, it has attracted bitterns, along with many other species previously rare or unknown in the capital.

*Above: The River Thames has been successfully cleaned and now supports a diverse population of fish, after being seriously polluted for many years.*

*Above: One of the many stretches of British rivers that is looked after and well maintained to the benefit of both anglers and the local wildlife.*

Creating new freshwater habitats is great for wildlife, but protecting and managing existing ones is even more important. Large conservation organizations like the Wildfowl & Wetlands Trust (WWT) and the RSPB play a very important role in wetland conservation, buying up areas to maintain them for wildlife. Smaller, local groups also play their part, with volunteers clearing litter and other debris from clogged waterways.

One of the most important groups of people for freshwater habitat conservation in Britain is the nation's anglers, as the lakes and areas of rivers they use are often well looked after.

## Endangered species

Although the state of Britain's freshwater habitats has improved in recent decades, some of their inhabitants remain very rare, although in many cases these creatures have always been uncommon, due to their restricted ranges.

The powan (*Coregonus clupeoides clupeoides*), for instance, is known only from a few Scottish lochs, while the pollan (*Coregonus autumnalis pollan*) is equally isolated, occurring in just three loughs (lakes) in Ireland. Other fish are now much rarer than they once were due to fishing. Salmon, for instance, now spawn in far lower numbers than before, mainly because so many of them are caught offshore before reaching their home rivers. Other freshwater creatures in decline include the water vole (*Arvicola terrestris*). Its population has been decimated by American mink (*Mustela vison*), which became established in Britain after being released and escaping from fur farms.

*Right: The British Trust for Conservation Volunteers runs 'holidays' for volunteers working on conservation projects.*

# MARINE CONSERVATION

*Britain has a healthy enthusiasm for conservation – the Royal Society for the Protection of Birds (RSPB) alone has more than a million members. Yet despite this fact its marine habitats have long been neglected. Just why have the world's seas and their inhabitants been taken for granted for so long?*

Britain is a nation surrounded by water. Many of our most spectacular creatures live in the seas that lap our shores, yet few of us ever see them. It is said that out of sight is out of mind, and in the case of our marine wildlife that is certainly true. While many of our land animals and land habitats are protected by law, our seas are almost completely unprotected, and as such they have suffered. They are seen as something to be exploited, harvested for fish and other edible life forms, and used as dumping grounds for our sewage and other waste.

## Fishing stocks

For a long time, the importance of our seas to wildlife has been ignored and the health of our underwater marine habitats has deteriorated, often without us even realizing it. Part of the problem, of course, has been their relative inaccessibility. Although in many cases they are just a short distance from our coastal towns, they might as well be on the other side of the world in terms of how often they are visited and monitored. Perhaps surprisingly, although it has been

*Above: The busy harbour of Polperro, one of Cornwall's numerous coastal villages where fishing is still a way of life.*

*Below: A basking shark and swimmers off the coast of Cornwall. The basking shark is the largest fish found in British waters.*

mapped using sonar and other techniques, much of our seabed has never actually been visited at all by submersibles or divers.

That said, we do have other ways of telling of the changes in our seas. Perhaps the clearest indicator is the content of the nets of the many trawlers and other vessels that fish off our shores. For many decades now, the annual catch of certain species of fish, such as cod, has been dropping and so has the average size of the individual fish caught. Put simply, these species are being fished out. The largest adults

have disappeared and many of the fish caught now are too young and too small to actually breed. This is not just a concern for wildlife lovers and conservationists but also for the fishermen themselves. If fish are caught before they can breed, then their stocks

*Below: The long-snouted seahorse, (Hippocampus hippocampus) is a rarely seen British native.*

*Above: The shore of Lundy Island, where the British government imposed a no-take zone on the fishing industry in 2003. Since then the marine life in the area has consequently recovered.*

will not be replenished. Before long the fishermen's livelihood will have gone, and with it the income on which their families and communities depend.

## Quotas and no-take zones

In an effort to manage fish stocks, quotas have been set on how many fish of certain species trawlermen are allowed to catch. These quotas have been controversial, not least because they often mean that fishermen are forced to throw some of their catch (which is already dead) overboard. If they were to bring it to shore they could be prosecuted for landing too

many fish. Naturally, this is viewed as an appalling waste of fish by the trawlermen, who when they set their nets have no idea exactly how many fish of a particular kind they are going to pull up from the deep. Quotas are perhaps not the best way to manage fish stocks and protect marine habitats.

Another idea that has been tried and tested, and found to be successful, is the no-take zone. As the name suggests, a no-take zone is an area of ocean in which fishing is prohibited. This allows the marine habitat there to recover and gives fish a safe area in which to live and breed. No-take zones are considered a sensible way to manage fish stocks, because once they

*Below: The emissions from power stations and heavy industry continue to cause global warming and pollute land and water.*

have recovered completely many of the fish which hatch or grow up in them then leave and go on to repopulate the surrounding area. Britain has just one no-take zone – a small area of the Bristol Channel off the eastern shore of Lundy Island. Established in 2003, the marine habitat it encompasses has begun to recover, and other areas are being considered.

In September 2008 one of those, Lamlash Bay off the Isle of Arran, was given the go-ahead by the British government. Conservationists hope that Lundy and Lamlash Bay will be the first of many, enabling Britain's sea life to recover, just as many of our wild species on land lately have.

## Creatures in decline

No-take zones will certainly protect some species but they cannot protect all of them. Indeed, some fish are in decline not because of overfishing but because of changes in the sea itself. Perhaps the most documented of these is the lesser sand eel (*Ammodytes marinus*). This little fish used to occur in vast numbers until relatively recently and provided food for countless sea birds. In the past decade lesser sand eel numbers around Britain have plummeted. This is thought likely to be due to a slight rise in sea temperature, possibly caused by global warming. As the sand eels have gone, so Britain's sea bird populations have suffered.

*Below: A cleaner coastline, like Ainsdale Beach, shown here, is the first step to improving marine conservation.*

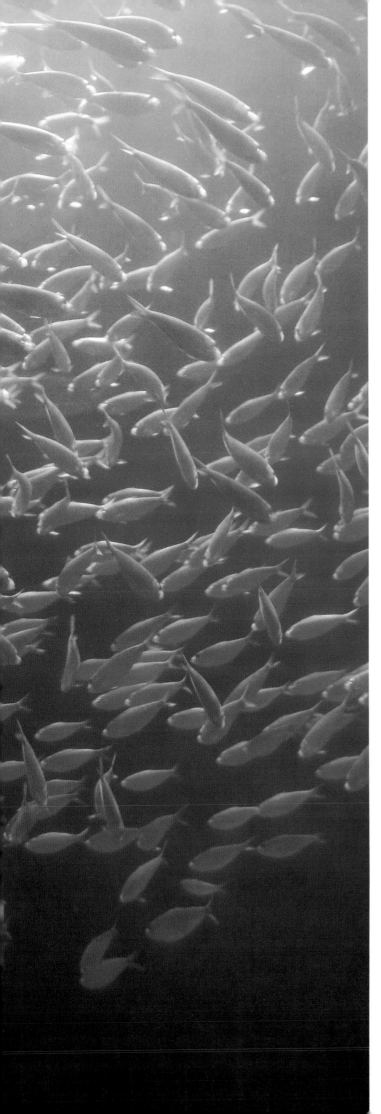

# DIRECTORY
# OF OCEANIC FISH

Wherever you are in the United Kingdom you are never more than 116km (72 miles) from the sea. Despite this, its marine waters remain largely a mystery to the majority of the British. Many may have ventured out on to them in a boat or a cross-channel ferry but very few have ever gone beneath the surface to explore beneath the waves.

As wild places go, Britain's coastal and offshore waters are wilder than anywhere on land. Here animals live in habitats that have remained virtually unchanged for tens of thousands of years. The fish that are caught to eat include some of the most common species in the sea. Herring and mackerel, for instance, are shoaling species that swim through the open ocean in huge numbers. Less common are some true giants of the waters, such as the oarfish and the basking shark.

The fish in the following pages are grouped by their habitats; first we cover the shores, coasts and estuaries of Britian, then shallow seas, followed by creatures from the open ocean and deep water.

Above: A conger eel (foreground) shares an underwater crevice with a moray eel in British waters.

Left: A small school of silver herring swim in unison, avoiding the many larger fish that prey on them.

# ESTUARIES AND COASTAL WATERS

*The world beneath the sea's surface is unfamiliar to most of us – especially if it is not represented in the daily catch that reaches the fishmonger. That said, the fish that live in Britain's estuaries and coastal waters include some that are familiar looking because they can be seen in most seaside aquaria, and a few of the smaller species can even be spotted in rock pools.*

## Tope

*Galeorhinus galeus*

**Distribution**: Temperate and subtropical oceans between latitudes 68°N and 55°S.
**Habitat**: Shallow bays and offshore waters.
**Food**: Mainly fish, such as herring, smelt, barracuda and hake; also squid, crabs, snails and sea urchins.
**Size**: 1.8m (6ft).
**Breeding**: Ovoviviparous; between 6 and 50 young born after year-long gestation.

The tope is known by many common names, including soupfin shark – a sadly appropriate name for a shark whose fins are highly prized for making shark fin soup. It is caught throughout its range, both commercially and as a sport fish. The tope adapts well to life in large aquariums. A wide-ranging and abundant species, often occurring in small schools, the tope inhabits the surf zone and deep water, and is found both on the bottom and swimming in open water. In the higher latitudes of its range, it is highly migratory, occurring near the poles in summer and moving near the equator in winter. Tope can cover 50km (30 miles) or more in a day. They have a lifespan of about 55 years, but like many sharks they mature slowly and have low breeding productivity; this, coupled with pressures of fishing, have caused numbers to decline.

**Identification**: Body slender. Head with long snout and large, almond-shaped eyes. Mouth with blade-like teeth bearing cusps. First dorsal fin much bigger than second dorsal fin. Second dorsal fin more or less aligned with anal fin and approximately same size. Terminal caudal lobe as long as rest of fin. Body colour grey to bluish above, becoming white on underside. Juveniles have black-tipped dorsal and caudal fins and white trailing edges on pectoral fins.

## Common angel shark

*Squatina squatina*

**Distribution**: Eastern North Atlantic coast (Norway to Spain); also Morocco, Mauretania and Senegal.
**Habitat**: Sandy and muddy seabeds.
**Food**: Other bottom-dwelling fish, crabs, molluscs.
**Size**: 2.4m (8ft).
**Breeding**: Ovoviviparous; bears 7–25 pups.

Lying motionless on the sandy bottom using its coloration and flattened shape to help it remain concealed from any potential prey, the common angel shark appears a placid creature. If prey comes within range, however, this ambush predator can strike with lightning speed to snatch the unsuspecting victim. It can also be highly aggressive if disturbed by divers, and when caught and landed in a boat it will snap dangerously at anything coming within range. Mostly active at night, the common angel shark frequents shallow water from about 2m (6.5ft) down to 100m (330ft) in summer, but it descends down to about 150m (500ft) or so in the winter. Also known as 'monkfish' (although not to be confused with *Lophius*), the common angel shark is popular for commercial fishing in many parts of the world.

**Identification**: Flat body with large, wing-like pectoral and pelvic fins. Mouth bearing pointed teeth located near tip of snout. Eyes on top of head. Prominent spiracles behind eyes. Small spines on snout and above eyes. Body colour mottled greyish-brown to green above, underside lighter.

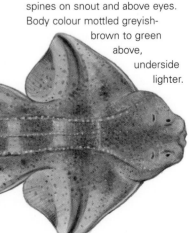

# European conger eel

*Conger conger*

Lurking in caves and crevices, the powerful European conger eel is one of several species found worldwide. This species is usually a nocturnal predator, lying out of sight until likely prey comes near, at which time it launches itself from its hiding place to snatch its meal with large teeth. Congers, landed in boats and lashing about and snapping viciously, have been known to overturn small craft as well as biting their occupants. Once sexually mature, the conger migrates from its North Atlantic coastal waters to spawn in deep ocean of the continental slope. The young eels hatch into a stage known as leptocephali and are carried back across the Atlantic on ocean currents.

**Identification**: Muscular, snake-like body lacking scales. Head with large eyes and protruding upper jaw. Both jaws have powerful teeth. Prominent, pointed pectoral fins. Long dorsal fin originates well forward, near pectoral fins. Elongated anal fin. Colour black, grey or dull brown above, often depending on habitat; creamy below.

**Distribution**: Atlantic Ocean from Iceland and Scandinavia to Mediterranean and Senegal.
**Habitat**: Among shipwrecks and rocks in both shallow and deep water.
**Food**: Octopuses, crabs, fish.
**Size**: 3m (10ft).
**Breeding**: Oviparous; spawns in deep, subtropical Atlantic Ocean; eggs hatch into planktonic leptocephali.

# Pearlfish

*Echiodon drummondii*

**Distribution**: North Sea and British Isles.
**Habitat**: Waters from about 50–400m (164–1,312ft).
**Food**: Probably small marine creatures.
**Size**: 30cm (12in).
**Breeding**: Oviparous; eggs hatch at surface and larvae are carried and distributed by ocean currents.

The 30 or so species of pearlfish, which are also known as cucumber fish, are inhabitants of tropical, subtropical and temperate seas. Many of them spend much of their lives inside other marine creatures, such as bivalve molluscs or sea cucumbers. Some species do this for protection only, while others also feed on the organs of the host. The pearlfish *Echiodon drummondii* has the typical thin, elongated shape of many pearlfish. This knife-like shape makes it easy to squeeze into the host's body through its anus. Most pearlfish have a fairly sedentary lifestyle, but their eggs hatch at the surface into glassy larvae that are dispersed widely on the ocean currents to exploit new habitats.

**Dogfish** (*Scyliorhinus canicula*) 1m (3¼ft). Atlantic and Mediterranean shark with slender body, long tail, flattened head and rounded snout. Sandy-brown above with brown spots, creamy-white below. Rests among rocks by day, and at night hunts crabs, molluscs and small fish. Reproduction involves males entwining their bodies around females.

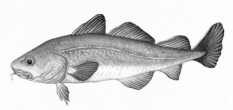

**Atlantic cod** (*Gadus morhua*) 1.2m (4ft). This is one of the world's most important food fish for humans, but it is now classed as Vulnerable due to long periods of overfishing. The omnivorous cod is found in North Atlantic coastal waters, usually in schools. The fish has a stout body with three dorsal fins, two anal fins and a large, triangular tail. The head bears a single chin barbel.

**Whiting** (*Merlangius merlangus*) 35cm (14in) Like many other species in the family Gadidae, the slender whiting has three dorsal fins and two anal fins; the first anal fin is much longer than the second. The whiting is an important commercial food fish and it is found in shallow Atlantic waters from Iceland to Spain, including the Mediterranean and Black Seas.

**Identification**: Thin, flattish, shallow, eel-like body – almost knife-like in shape; dorsal and ventral surfaces are fringed with a continuous fin. Its body is translucent, with silvery bands and patches of pale reddish pigment on the flanks, iris and operculum (gill cover). It has a silvery abdomen. Dark markings on head.

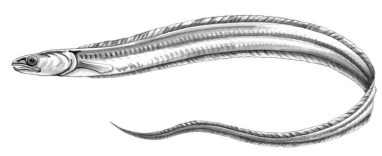

# Shore rockling

*Gaidropsarus mediterraneus*

The shore rockling is one of several species of rockling that inhabit shallow Atlantic waters. The shore rockling has a preference for algae or sea grasses in which it can hide. Like the other rocklings, the shore rockling has a long, slender body with two dorsal fins. Rocklings have sensory barbels on the snout and chin; in the case of the shore rockling, there are two on the snout and one on the chin. The similar-looking five-bearded rockling (*Ciliata mustela*), with which it can be confused, has five barbels, however. The three-bearded rockling (*Gaidropsarus vulgaris*) also has three barbels around the mouth, but it is distinguished from the shore rockling by its colour, which is reddish brown with well-marked blotches.

**Identification**: Body is long and slender with smooth, scaleless skin. First dorsal fin is short, with a prominent first ray; second dorsal fin is long. Long anal fin. Caudal fin is rounded. Head bears two sensory barbels on the snout and one barbel on the chin. Colour is dark brown; the pigment on the dorsal area may be slightly mottled in appearance.

**Distribution**: North-eastern Atlantic, including North Sea, from British Isles to southern Morocco; also Mediterranean.
**Habitat**: Among rocks and in shallow water down to about 30m (98ft).
**Food**: Crustaceans, worms and fish.
**Size**: 50cm (19½in).
**Breeding**: Oviparous; eggs hatch at the surface.

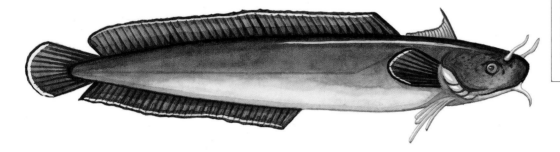

# Angler

*Lophius piscatorius*

**Distribution**: North-eastern Atlantic from Scandinavia to Morocco; also North, Baltic and Mediterranean Seas.
**Habitat**: Among rocks and sand in shallow, inshore waters.
**Food**: Crustaceans and other invertebrates, fish.
**Size**: 2m (6½ft).
**Breeding**: Oviparous; eggs float at the surface in gelatinous masses.

Sold for food as 'monkfish', the angler is a huge-headed creature with a range of unusual adaptations for capturing prey. It lurks on the bottom of the sea, its ragged-edged, flattened and mottled body helping it to blend with its surroundings. It then waves and twitches an enticing lure, which is formed from its first dorsal fin spine, to attract victims. If a fish or crab comes close to the lure (presumably believing it to be a small item of food), it is engulfed by the angler's mouth. Amazingly, even diving seabirds have fallen for this trick and have been found in the stomachs of landed anglers.

Spawning takes place in deep water and the eggs float at the surface. Once hatched, the young spend their early lives feeding on plankton.

**Identification**: Head is massive and flattened, with large, upward-facing, gaping mouth and sharp, incurved teeth. Body flattened and tapering towards tail; body much narrower than head. Head and body bordered by a fringe of lobes. Dorsal surface has several elongated rays; first bears a fleshy lobe (the 'lure'). Pectoral fins broad and large. Pelvic fins small. Colour is variable.

# Three-spined stickleback

*Gasterosteus aculeatus*

**Identification**: Pointed head with small mouth and large eyes. Body slender and flattish, tapering to narrow caudal peduncle. Three dorsal spines in front of dorsal fin. Anal fin shorter than dorsal fin. Pectoral fins with rounded edges. Pelvic fins reduced to a single spine and ray. Colour outside breeding season: silvery on flanks and white below; male in breeding colours described on the right.

Found in many parts of the Northern Hemisphere from ponds and rivers to shallow seas, the three-spined stickleback is a lively little fish immediately recognizable by the three characteristic spines on its back. The body lacks scales, but is protected by bony plates, and carries pelvic as well as dorsal spines. During breeding, the underside of the male becomes an intense red or orange colour, his back and sides turn blue-green, and his eyes become blue. When breeding, the male builds a nest and is highly territorial. The tunnel-shaped nest rests on the bottom and is made from plant material glued together with mucous secretions. Several females will lay their eggs in the nest. Once the eggs are laid, he immediately fertilizes them. The male then fans and guards them until they hatch, and protects the hatchlings for several days, until they disperse.

**Distribution**: Northern Pacific and Atlantic coasts; also Mediterranean and Black Seas; also inland in North American and European rivers.
**Habitat**: Shallow freshwater and marine habitats; preferably with gentle or no currents.
**Food**: Mainly invertebrates, fish eggs and larvae, small fish.
**Size**: Up to 10cm (4in).
**Breeding**: Oviparous; external fertilization.

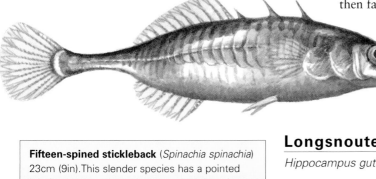

**Fifteen-spined stickleback** (*Spinachia spinachia*) 23cm (9in). This slender species has a pointed head, a long caudal peduncle and 14–17 spines on its back. It is the largest member of the stickleback family. It is usually found among seaweed in coastal areas near the shore in the eastern Atlantic.

**Shortsnouted seahorse**
(*Hippocampus ramulosus*) 15cm (6in) Like other seahorses, this species has a horse-like head and swims with its body held vertical or nearly so. The pectoral fins are situated just behind the eyes. The body is covered with bony plates. Favours habitats among the seaweeds and grasses in Atlantic and Mediterranean waters.

**Identification**: Long snout; fleshy appendages on back of neck resemble a 'mane'. Head and body bony, angular and ridged. Body elongated, especially from region of dorsal fin to end of tail. Pectoral fins and anal fin small. Pelvic fins and caudal fin lacking. Colour yellowish-green to reddish-brown, marked with blue patches and spots.

# Longsnouted seahorse

*Hippocampus guttulatus*

Among the most instantly recognizable of all marine creatures, seahorses get their common name from the shape of the head. With their strange appearance, unusual fins and habit of floating upright in the water or resting with their tails entwined around vegetation, it is not surprising that many people do not realize that seahorses are, in fact, fish. However, the mating behaviour of seahorses is even more atypical of fish. During mating, as with other seahorse species, male and female longsnouted seahorses perform an elaborate display by linking their tails and undertaking a courtship 'dance'. Then they bring their bellies together and the female transfers some of her eggs into the male's abdominal pouch. He then fertilizes the eggs. The young develop in the male's pouch for several weeks before he 'gives birth' to live young that resemble miniature versions of their parents.

**Distribution**: Eastern Atlantic from Great Britain to Morocco; also Mediterranean.
**Habitat**: Shallow waters, especially among algae and sea grasses, down to 20m (66ft); in water down to about 80m (262ft) during winter.
**Food**: Mainly invertebrates.
**Size**: Up to 15cm (6in).
**Breeding**: Male broods fertilized eggs in abdominal pouch until they hatch.

# Pogge

*Agonus cataphractus*

With its large, heavily armoured head and upturned snout, barbel-fringed mouth and narrow, tapering body, the pogge is a highly distinctive fish. It usually lives on the bottom, preferring sandy or muddy seabeds, although it is also encountered in estuaries. An underslung mouth restricts its food to bottom-living animals, and it uses the sensory barbels around its mouth to probe the substrate for small hidden crustaceans, worms, brittlestars and molluscs on which to feed. The pogge often burrows in the mud or sand, where its body coloration makes it difficult to see. From February to May the pogge lays eggs which are held fast in seaweed.

**Identification**: Head and body covered in hard, bony plates. Head large and longish, with eyes set on top of head; snout upturned and bearing a pair of hooked spines; mouth fringed with numerous barbels. Spine on each gill cover. Two dorsal fins. Body colour mottled grey-brown with four or five dark saddles across back; underside whitish.

**Distribution**: North-eastern Atlantic, including Shetland and Faroe Islands, south-western Iceland and the southern Baltic.
**Habitat**: On sandy and muddy bottoms from 5–500m (16–1,640ft).
**Food**: Echinoderms, crustaceans, molluscs, worms.
**Size**: 15cm (6in).
**Breeding**: Oviparous; external fertilization.

# Greater weever

*Trachinus draco*

The weevers have venom glands associated with grooved spines on their gill covers and in the first dorsal fin. The venom provides defence against bottom-feeding rays and large flatfish, since during the day the fish typically lie buried in the sand with just their eyes and the tip of the first dorsal fin exposed. If not disturbed, the fish stay buried all day, emerging at night to swim about in search of prey. The greater weever favours deeper water than the very similar lesser weever, which frequently occurs in the shallows off sandy beaches and is regularly trodden on by bathers. The resulting wounds are extremely painful, often causing swelling and bruising.

The greater weever is found all around the coasts of the British Isles, from the shallows to about 150m (490ft) deep. It breeds and spawns from June to August.

**Identification**: An elongated fish with a small, compressed head, an upward-slanting mouth and large eyes. The first dorsal fin is short, black, spiny and fan-like, while the second dorsal fin and anal fin are long and low, extending to the tail. It has a small tail fin, but large pectorals. There are two or three small spines above each eye, and a large spine on each gill cover. Greenish above with yellowish-white oblique stripes; paler shades below.

**Distribution**: Eastern Atlantic from southern Norway to Morocco, Madeira and Canaries; also Mediterranean and Black Seas.
**Habitat**: On sandy, muddy or gravelly seabeds, at depths of 1–150m (3¼–490ft).
**Food**: Small invertebrates and fish.
**Size**: 40cm (16in).
**Breeding**: Oviparous; eggs fertilized externally.

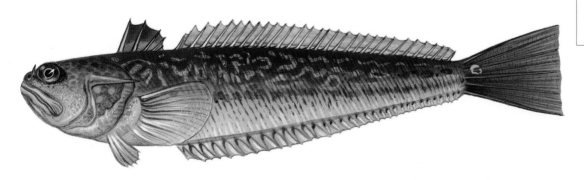

# Tompot blenny

*Blennius gattorugine*

A common fish of rocky shores, the tompot blenny is usually found from just below the low-tide mark to depths down to about 12m (40ft), where it conceals itself in crevices or under rocky ledges. It is most active at dusk and dawn, but its cryptic coloration and pattern make it hard to be seen by the small crustaceans that largely make up its diet. Young fish sometimes occur in large tidal pools on the lower shore among thick seaweed. The blennies use the same areas for spawning, with each male selecting a suitable crevice and encouraging one or more females to attach their adhesive eggs to the rock. The male then fertilizes the eggs and guards them until they hatch. The presence of tentacles above each eye makes identification of this species definitive.

**Identification**: Stoutly built with a long, high dorsal fin that is stiff and spiny at the front. It has a long anal fin and large pectoral fins, and a flattened, branched tentacle above each eye. Yellowish brown with seven or more dark brown bars on each flank; spawning males are chocolate-brown.

**Distribution**: North-eastern Atlantic from Ireland to Morocco; also Mediterranean Sea. Found inland throughout mainland Portugal.
**Habitat**: Shallow coastal waters off rocky shores, from 3–30m (10–100ft).
**Food**: Mainly small crustaceans.
**Size**: 20cm (8in).
**Breeding**: Oviparous; sticky eggs are laid in a submerged rock crevice.

# Sand goby

*Pomatoschistus minutus*

**Distribution**: Eastern North Atlantic from Norway to Spain; parts of Mediterranean and Black Seas.
**Habitat**: Sandy and muddy shallows close to shore, and estuaries, mainly from mid-tide level to about 20m (66ft).
**Food**: Small crustaceans and marine worms.
**Size**: 6cm (2¼in).
**Breeding**: Oviparous; female attaches eggs to the inside of an empty clam shell where they are fertilized by the male, who guards the eggs.

A very common fish of inshore sandy and muddy areas, the sand goby has a sleeker profile than most of its relatives and sometimes swims in small schools. Active by day, it feeds mainly on tiny crustaceans, such as copepods, amphipods and young shrimps, as well as marine worms. In turn, it is eaten by a wide variety of marine predators, including various species of cod and bass, as well as seabirds such as terns. It spawns in shallow waters in summer, the male luring the female into the empty shell of a bivalve mollusc to lay her eggs, but retreats to deeper waters in winter. Juvenile fish may enter the lower reaches of estuaries, but adults avoid brackish water.

**Identification**: A slender goby with high-set, prominent eyes. The two dorsal fins are well separated, the first with six rays. Rounded pectoral fins. Pelvic fins are fused into an oval sucker. Colour generally light sandy brown with dark dots and faint bars on the back. The male has a white-rimmed dark-blue or black spot on the first dorsal fin.

**Lumpsucker** (*Cyclopterus lumpus*) 55cm (21½in). The lumpsucker has a deep, rounded, scaleless body with four rows of bony plates embedded in it. Although the fish has two dorsal fins, in older specimens the first dorsal fin becomes incorporated into the body. The pelvic fins are modified into a ventral sucker, with which the fish attaches itself to rocks. Males in breeding condition develop a reddish belly.

**Ballan wrasse** (*Labrus bergylta*) 60cm (23in). This fish has large conical teeth for crushing the shells of molluscs and crabs. It usually forages among rocks about 20m (66ft) down, although the young often occur in large intertidal rockpools. Young fish are often emerald green. Adults are mottled greenish-brown females, but change sex to become red males.

**Stargazer** (*Uranoscopus scaber*) 30cm (12in). The stargazer has a robust, flattened head with eyes set on top, pointing upwards. Usually dark brown or blackish with grey-brown flanks, it is well camouflaged and attracts prey with a mobile lure on its lower lip. It has a venomous spine behind each gill cover, and an electric organ behind each eye. Occurs in Mediterranean and eastern Atlantic.

**Northern (shore) clingfish** (*Lepadogaster lepadogaster*) 6cm (2¼in). The powerful sucker beneath its body enables it to attach itself to rocks to resist the waves and tidal streams of rocky shores. Rather flattened, tapered, scaleless body. Head long and triangular with a 'duck-billed' snout.

# SHALLOW SEAS

*The areas of sea that surround Earth's land masses constitute only 8 per cent of the globe's ocean area. Despite this, they are home to most marine life and often include particularly species-rich reefs. In the following pages we are only looking at fish, but mammals and crustaceans are abundant in shallow seas, and perhaps here more than in any other habitat the food chain is in constant evidence.*

## Atlantic hagfish

*Myxine glutinosa*

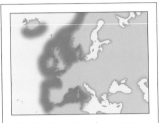

**Distribution**: North-eastern Atlantic Ocean and western Mediterranean Sea.
**Habitat**: Soft seabeds at depths of 20–1,000m (66–3,280ft).
**Food**: Marine worms and dead and dying fish.
**Size**: Up to 80cm (31½in).
**Breeding**: Separate sexes release eggs and sperm into water. Large eggs have hook-tipped filaments at each end that anchor them to each other, and to the seabed. No larval stage is known.

This is one of about 30 species of hagfish that all have the same basic body form and habits. Although blind, it is an active predator, particularly of worms. This bottom-living animal is also a scavenger. It finds carcasses or moribund fish by scent, drills into them with its jaw-like toothed plates, and then forces itself inside to eat the flesh. Its body is extremely slimy for lubrication and to protect itself from predators, and it is able to form part of it into a knot to gain extra purchase as it forces its way in for its meal. A hagfish has no stomach, and its skeleton consists of a pliable reinforcing rod, or notochord, running the length of the body. A dorsal nerve cord lies above this, terminating in a simple brain at the head end.

**Identification**: Eel-like animal with a glutinous, scaleless body and a fin-like fold of skin extending along the body and around the tail. The head end has a single nostril and mouth surrounded by short barbels, but no eyes. Greyish or reddish brown in colour, but variable depending on colour of seabed.

## Sea lamprey

*Petromyzon marinus*

Although it has no jaws, the sea lamprey is much closer to a true fish than the similar-looking hagfish. Its gills are supported by a cage of cartilage, and as an adult it has functioning eyes. Its dorsal and tail fins have fin rays, and it has a complex spawning behaviour resembling that of salmon. Yet it has a pliable notochord rather than a series of vertebrae, and instead of jaws it has a rasping tongue. It uses this to bore into the flanks of living fish such as cod and sharks, and feed on their blood and flesh. An anticoagulant in its saliva keeps the blood flowing. In total contrast, larval sea lampreys are filter feeders that live in rivers partly buried in the river bed.

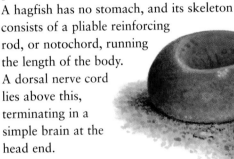

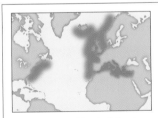

**Distribution**: North Atlantic from Norway to North Africa, and from Labrador to Florida.
**Habitat**: Shallow seas from below tide level to 650m (2,130ft), but enters rivers to spawn; larvae live in rivers.
**Food**: Adults prey on other fish. Larvae filter particles from surface of the mud.
**Size**: Up to 1.2m (4ft).
**Breeding**: Eggs released by females fertilized by males in nests in gravelly shallows. Each female produces up to 200,000 eggs. Adults then die, but larvae live in fresh water for up to seven years before migrating out to sea.

**Identification**: Eel-like fish with a rasping tongue instead of jaws, prominent eyes and seven circular gill apertures on each side behind the head. Two shallow dorsal fins, and small tail fin. Brownish yellow with black marbling on the back, pale below.

# Hammerhead sharks

*Sphyrna lewini/Sphyrna zygaena*

Britain is not known for its dangerous sharks. Every so often, however, large and potentially deadly sharks do enter our waters. Hammerhead sharks are among these species, normally found in warmer seas but occasionally drawn far enough north to swim off British shores. The scalloped hammerhead (*Sphyrna lewini*) is thought to be the most common of the several different species; it is certainly the most frequently encountered in coastal waters around the world. Often this species is found swimming alone, but occasionally it forms much larger groups. At certain times of the year schools of several hundred are known to gather. The reason for these aggregations is not understood but they may be linked to breeding. In some parts of the world the scalloped hammerhead is a largely stationary species of shark, with individuals rarely travelling far. Elsewhere, however, it is migratory, with schools swimming towards the poles in summer.

Smooth hammerhead sharks (*Sphyrna zygaena*), pictured here, are also found in British waters, and share similar characteristics with the scalloped hammerhead.

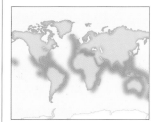

**Distribution:** Hammerhead sharks are most common in tropical, subtropical and warm temperate coastal waters and are only rarely found off British shores.
**Habitat:** Coastal waters, occasionally entering estuaries.
**Food:** Fish and squid
**Size:** 4.3m (14ft)
**Breeding:** Like many sharks, this species gives birth to live young. Each litter contains 15–31 offspring, each measuring 43–55cm (17–21½in) long

**Identification**: The head of the hammerhead shark is its most obvious feature, is very wide and flattened and from above or below does look like the head of a hammer. The eyes are positioned at either end and the mouth underneath. The front edge of the head of the scalloped hammerhead has an indentation at the centre, which distinguishes it from other hammerhead sharks.

# Tiger shark

*Galeocerdo cuvier*

This species gets its common name from the tiger-like body markings. One of the largest and most aggressive of all sharks, the tiger shark is renowned for its varied tastes in food. A powerful and fast swimmer when attacking its prey, it will swallow almost anything that will fit into its mouth, including sea lions, sea snakes, turtles, other sharks and seabirds. It has also been known to swallow items of more dubious nutritional value, such as car licence plates and tyres. It has also been implicated in attacks on human bathers. Tolerant of both marine and brackish conditions, the tiger shark sometimes enters river estuaries and is known to attack land mammals that come to the water to drink.

**Distribution**: Circumglobal in temperate and tropical oceans and seas. Common around Australian coasts.
**Habitat**: Coastal waters, including estuaries, and over continental shelf down to about 140m (460ft), but sometimes deeper.
**Food**: Very varied: scavenger as well as predator of a range of creatures including fish, marine reptiles, seabirds, mammals (such as dolphins and sea lions), crustaceans and molluscs.
**Size**: Up to 6m (20ft).
**Breeding**: 11–82 young; livebearer.

**Identification**: Fast-swimming aggressive shark. Body tapers towards tail. First dorsal fin much longer than second dorsal fin. Upper lobe of caudal fin long with subterminal notch. Head with large eyes and a broad, blunt snout. Wide mouth bears rows of large, serrated teeth. Body colour greyish with black spots and vertical bars (reminiscent of a tiger), more prominent in young individuals, pale below.

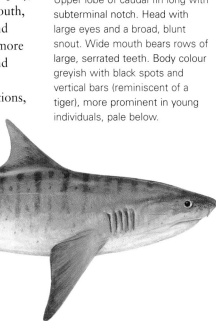

# Great white shark

*Carcharodon carcharias*

The great white, the largest predatory shark, has a reputation as a ruthless killer. Attacks on humans may occur because the shark mistakes swimmers for its natural food of seals or turtles. When a great white attacks, it usually lunges up from below, delivering a lightning-fast bite before pulling back. Once the prey has been rendered helpless, it returns to shear off chunks with its triangular, serrated teeth. Smaller prey may be taken whole. After a large meal, the shark may not feed again for several weeks. Wide-ranging and usually solitary, the great white shark breeds at about 10 to 12 years, producing live young after a gestation of about 12 months.

**Identification**: Torpedo-like body with pointed, conical snout. Mouth bears large, 7.5cm (3in), serrated teeth in both jaws. Well-developed lateral keels on caudal peduncle. Upper part of body blue-grey or brownish, lower part white. Large caudal (tail), dorsal and pectoral fins; pectoral fins with blackish tips on underside.

**Distribution**: Temperate and tropical oceans worldwide.
**Habitat**: One of the more coastal mackerel sharks, but also found in open water to depths of 1,300m (4,250ft).
**Food**: Fish, turtles, seabirds, seals, sealions, dolphins.
**Size**: Up to 6m (20ft), but occasionally larger.
**Breeding**: 2–10 young; livebearer.

# Basking shark

*Cetorhinus maximus*

This giant, the second-largest species of shark, gets its common name from its habit of cruising leisurely at the surface of the water in summer as if sunbathing, although it may also swim at depths of about 200m (650ft). Basking sharks may be found alone, in pairs or in groups. Despite its size, the basking shark feeds solely on tiny plankton, which it filters from the water using comb-like structures on its gill arches. To help it obtain sufficient food, the basking shark swims along at about 5kmh (3mph) with its huge mouth wide open, taking in thousands of litres of water per hour.

**Identification**: Huge, with pointed snout and cavernous mouth. Gill slits very large and prominent. Large caudal fin with longer upper lobe. Has small teeth, but these used for mating, not feeding. Body variably coloured blackish, brown or blue on back, becoming pale towards belly. Fins prized for making shark-fin soup.

**Distribution**: Temperate oceans worldwide. Common along Pacific coasts of US during winter months.
**Habitat**: Highly migratory species. Found inshore in surface waters, but possibly also deeper water.
**Food**: Plankton.
**Size**: 10m (33ft), but occasionally up to 15m (50ft).
**Breeding**: Little known about breeding behaviour; it may produce up to 6 young in a litter; livebearer.

# Common thresher shark

*Alopias vulpinus*

**Distribution**: Widely distributed continental shelf species. Especially prominent along eastern and south-western coasts of Australia.
**Habitat**: Deep coastal waters to open surface waters.
**Food**: Fish, squid, crustaceans.
**Size**: 6m (20ft).
**Breeding**: 2–7 young; livebearer.

The common thresher is the largest of the three species of thresher sharks. All three are recognizable by the upper lobe of the tail fin, which is almost as long as the body itself. It is thought that the shark may use its tail to lash out and stun prey before devouring it. Threshers may even join together to herd prey together with their tails before feeding on them. The common thresher is wide-ranging, swimming in deep water close to the shore as well as in open water near the surface. The thresher's breeding habits are only partly known, but like other mackerel sharks the young feed on the yolk of unfertilized eggs as they develop, which helps ensure they are well formed at birth. Threshers are hunted for their meat and fins, and their numbers have dropped as a result.

**Identification**: Muscular body. First dorsal fin much bigger than second dorsal fin. Upper lobe of tail fin almost as long as rest of body. Large, scythe-shaped caudal and pectoral fins. Body variably purple-grey to black on top, creamy white below.

# Shortfin mako shark

*Isurus oxyrinchus*

A sleek, spindle-shaped, metallic blue shark, the mako bears a resemblance to the porbeagle, but is distinguished from it by its longer body and lack of a secondary keel on the caudal fin. The mako also lacks lateral cusps on its dagger-like teeth. One of the fastest of all the sharks, the highly predatory mako can accelerate to speeds of up to 35kmh (22mph) – sometimes even faster – for short distances, and it can also maintain a higher body temperature than that of the surrounding water. An opportunist hunter, its food includes schooling fish, such as tuna and herring, but it is also known to take porpoises. The mako is a popular sport fish and is often caught on rod and line from boats; at such times, it often leaps spectacularly from the water, and jumps up to a height of 6m (20ft) are sometimes recorded. The mako may even try to attack the boat. These sharks may live up to 20 years or more.

**Identification**: Streamlined body. Head has long, conical snout. Curved teeth lack lateral cusps. First dorsal fin much bigger than second dorsal fin. Crescent-shaped caudal fin with no secondary keel. Body colour metallic blue above, white below.

**Distribution**: Worldwide distribution in temperate waters; also found in tropical oceans.
**Habitat**: From surface waters down to 150m (490ft) or more.
**Food**: Fish such as mackerel and tuna; also porpoises and turtles.
**Size**: 4m (13ft), perhaps exceptionally to 6m (20ft)
**Breeding**: Usually about 10–12 young; livebearer.

# Common skate

*Dipturus (Raja) batis*

A sought-after and now heavily overfished commercial species, the common or blue skate can grow to 2.9m (9.5ft) or more. The snout is elongated and the pectoral fins form broad 'wings', giving the flattened body a more or less diamond shape when viewed from above. Swimming with a typical undulating action of its pectoral fins, the impression of having wings is further enhanced, since the fish seems to be flying through the water. Along the dorsal surface is a series of spiny thorns that may help give some protection from predators.

The common skate can emit a small electric discharge, like the electric rays, but this is insufficient to deter predators and is probably used in courtship. Fertilization is internal, and the leathery eggs are laid in summer. The cases have tendrils to help them attach to weeds and other objects.

**Distribution**: Eastern Atlantic Ocean, from Iceland to Senegal, and western Mediterranean.
**Habitat**: Near seabed, usually down to 100–1,000m (330–3,280ft).
**Food**: Fish, crabs, lobsters.
**Size**: 2.9m (9½ ft).
**Breeding**: 1–2 eggs.

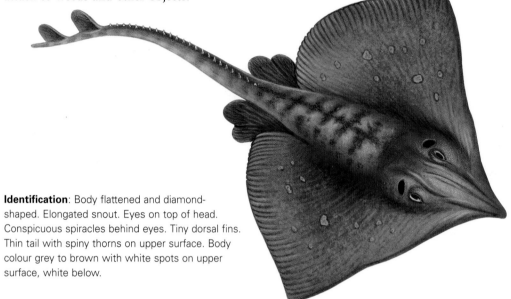

**Identification**: Body flattened and diamond-shaped. Elongated snout. Eyes on top of head. Conspicuous spiracles behind eyes. Tiny dorsal fins. Thin tail with spiny thorns on upper surface. Body colour grey to brown with white spots on upper surface, white below.

# Atlantic torpedo ray

*Torpedo nobiliana*

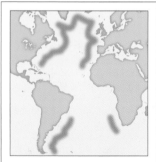

**Distribution**: Subtropical and temperate waters of the Atlantic Ocean.
**Habitat**: Pelagic but also on sandy seabeds and reefs from 2–800m (6½–2,625ft).
**Food**: Mainly small fish.
**Size**: 1.8m (6ft).
**Breeding**: About 60 young; livebearer.

One of the largest members of the family Torpedinidae, the Atlantic torpedo ray is one of 50 or more species of rays that can produce an electric current using specially modified muscle cells. In some species, including the Atlantic torpedo, the strength of the shock delivered can be up to 220 volts. Electric rays use the electricity both as a form of defence and to capture prey. Fish are the main food of Atlantic torpedos, and prey is usually caught as the ray delivers a stunning shock while wrapping its pectoral fins around it. The ray then manoeuvres the victim into the mouth. Using this method, the ray can catch even fast-moving fish. Juveniles are usually found on the bottom, but adults often swim in open water.

**Identification**: Most of body flattened and disc-like. Two dorsal fins. Paddle-shaped caudal fin. Snout short. Large spiracle behind each eye. Body colour blackish to chocolate-brown above, white below.

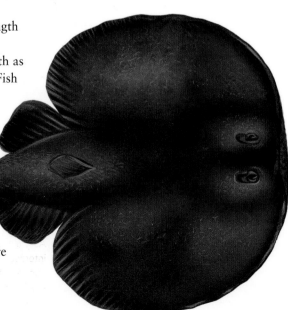

# Spotted torpedo ray

*Torpedo marmorata*

This ray's common name comes from the mottled appearance of its dorsal surface. Like other members of its family, it has the ability to emit an electric shock that will deter most predators (although large sharks are often not put off) or stun prey, rendering it helpless before being eaten. By day, the spotted torpedo usually lies buried on the seabed with just its eyes visible, but at night it hunts for crustaceans and small fish, which it first overpowers with an electric discharge. The electricity produced by these rays was used from ancient times up until around the 1600s as a form of therapy intended to cure many diseases from gout to headaches.

**Identification**: Most of body flattened and disc-like. Two dorsal fins. Paddle-shaped caudal fin. Snout short. Slightly stalked eyes on top of head. Large spiracle behind each eye. Body colour mottled brown above, underside creamy white.

**Distribution**: Eastern Atlantic Ocean from Britain to southern Africa. Also the Mediterranean Sea.
**Habitat**: Soft sea bottom around reefs and seagrass meadows.
**Food**: Small fish and crustaceans.
**Size**: 1m (3¼ft).
**Breeding**: About 5–30 young; livebearer.

# Thornback ray

*Raja clavata*

This is the commonest ray to be found in British waters. Sometimes known as the thornback skate, it makes up the bulk of all the skate sold in fish and chip shops around the country.

Like most of the world's rays, the thornback ray is a bottom-dwelling fish that finds its food with tiny sensors in the skin that detect the electrical impulses given off by the muscles of its prey. Using this information the thornback ray can locate flatfish that are buried beneath sand. Other prey, such as crabs, are also found in this way. With its eyes positioned turret-like on the top half of its body, vision plays virtually no part at all in hunting, instead its main purpose is to warn the ray of predators.

The thornback ray is a nocturnal hunter and spends its days lying still on the bottom, often largely covered with a layer of sand. It lives in relatively shallow waters around much of the British coast, and is usually found living over sand or gravel at depths of 10–60m (33–200ft). When the time comes to spawn it moves into shallower waters still. Females produce around 150 egg cases every year.

**Distribution**: Most common around Wales and southern England. Absent from north and north-east Scotland and the east coast of England. Also found in the eastern Atlantic from Iceland, and the western Baltic south to Morocco, Namibia, the Mediterranean and the Black Sea. Also reported from eastern South Africa.
**Habitat**: Coastal waters.
**Food**: Crustaceans and small fish.
**Size**: 120cm (47in) (including tail).
**Breeding**: The egg cases are laid between March and August. The young take about 5 months to develop and hatch. Empty egg cases are often washed up on the shore, and are known as 'mermaid's purses'.

**Identification**: The thornback ray is covered on its upper surface with prickles, which are present from hatching. As if these were not protection enough the prickles are interspersed with larger, backward-pointing thorns, or bucklers. Each of these has a thick, button-like base. On the females, they form a line along the back and in both sexes they extend along the tail.

# Spotted eagle ray

*Aetobatus narinari*

**Distribution**: Wide-ranging in tropical and temperate Atlantic, Pacific, Indian oceans and Red Sea.
**Habitat**: Sandy coastal regions and reefs but also found in estuaries and open water.
**Food**: Clams, oysters, shrimps, octopus, squid, sea urchins, fish.
**Size**: 2.5m (8¼ft) excluding tail; may reach 5m (16½ft) in total with tail.
**Breeding**: Up to 4 pups; livebearer.

The eagle ray's common name is due to its large size and its swimming movements, which resemble those of a flying eagle. Beautifully marked, the diamond-shaped spotted eagle ray is an active swimmer, often forming large schools as it migrates across the oceans. This large ray is also found close to the bottom in shallow water, where it digs into the substrate for food such as clams and other molluscs using its curious flat, duck-billed snout.

At the base of the long, whip-like tail the eagle ray has a battery of highly potent stinging spines. These are used in defence to deter or injure would-be predators. The spotted eagle ray can also leap out of the water when pursued. This species is no less dangerous to humans if caught and hauled aboard a boat; the lashing tail can deliver painful, occasionally fatal, stings to humans.

**Identification**: Body disc flattened and diamond-shaped. White spots on a black, grey or brown background, contrasting white below. Eyes on side of head. Large spiracles. Broad, bill-shaped snout.

# Manta ray

*Manta birostris*

This impressive fish is the largest of all rays. The largest recorded was 6.7m (22ft) across. They probably developed as bottom feeders, then became filter feeders in the open sea.

Despite its size, the manta ray eats mainly plankton. The horn-like cephalic fins in front of the head can be rolled up to form a funnel that helps channel water and food into the mouth when feeding. The word 'manta' originates from the resemblance of this ray's wide, flapping fins to a cloak or mantle. This ray is a solitary species, but individuals are often accompanied by other fish species, such as cleaner fish, remoras and pilot fish. The lifespan of the manta ray is approximately 20 years.

**Distribution**: Found throughout the world's oceans, mainly seen in tropical coastal regions of Atlantic, Pacific and Indian oceans. Also sometimes in temperate regions.
**Habitat**: Usually inshore surface waters down to 120m (390ft); occasionally farther from shore.
**Food**: Planktonic crustaceans and small schooling fish.
**Size**: 5.2m (17ft) long; width is approximately 2.2 times greater than length.
**Breeding**: 1 young; livebearer.

**Identification**: Body flattened. Large, wing-like pectoral fins. Front lobes (cephalic fins) extend on both sides of rectangular mouth. No dorsal or caudal fins. Small teeth, in lower jaw only. Gills on underside of body. Whip-like tail. Body colour variable, but usually brown, grey-blue or black above, white below.

# Arctic charr

*Salvelinus alpinus*

**Identification**: Form typically trout-like, with rounded, streamlined body. Slightly pointed snout and large mouth with teeth in both jaws. Adipose fin present. Caudal fin slightly forked. Colour highly variable according to habitat, size and time of year: often brown or greenish on back, flanks silvery with pinkish or red spots; underside paler. Spawning adults usually have bright orange-red ventral surface and pelvic, pectoral and anal fins.

The Arctic charr is found mainly in cold, northern waters. There are both landlocked, freshwater varieties and others that migrate between freshwater habitats – where they spawn – and the sea. The species is an opportunist feeder, taking food from small crustaceans to members of its own species. Spawning takes place between September and October, with the preferred site being shallow, gravelly bottoms. The female builds a nest by turning on her side and using her caudal fin to clear away an area, known as a redd, in which to lay her eggs. After a period of courtship, eggs are laid in the redd and fertilized by the male. Where charr are migratory, the young first venture to the sea after a period of between two and six years.

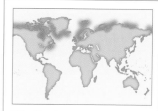

**Distribution**: North Atlantic including northern Norway, southern Greenland and Iceland. Also north-western Canada and USA; Beaufort Sea.
**Habitat**: Deep runs of rivers and lakes, and – in migratory individuals – brackish waters and shallow seas.
**Food**: Small crustaceans and fish, including other charr.
**Size**: Usually about 45cm (18in), but may be bigger.
**Breeding**: Nest builder; eggs shed in gravel beds of rivers, and fertilized externally.

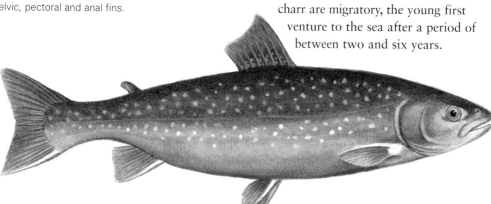

# Trout

*Salmo trutta*

Few fish are more variable than the trout. This is partly because many populations are resident in different types of waters, and isolated from each other, but also because some populations migrate downstream to the sea when adult, where they live on a diet of marine fish and invertebrates. The two types are usually known as brown trout (resident form) and sea trout (migratory form). Both are found only in well-oxygenated, clean water. They spawn in winter in gravelly shallows, the sea trout migrating back from the ocean to reach favoured sites. When mature, sea trout then migrate to the ocean, where they feed for one to five years before returning to breed. Brown trout, however, remain in fresh water. Both are prized food and sports fish.

**Identification**: Streamlined fish with small scales, an adipose fin and a square-cut tail fin. The area of the body in front of the tail fin is relatively deep and flattened. Colour very variable, ranging from brownish with black spots on the back, plus red spots on the sides, often with pale rings, to silvery with fewer spots (especially in migratory fish returning from the sea). The belly is pale coloured, and the fins are dark and only sparsely spotted.

**Distribution**: Native range mainly Atlantic: Europe and Scandinavia, and east to the Urals. Migratory group introduced to other regions.
**Habitat**: Cool, clear rivers and lakes, and – in migratory sea trout – mainly shallow seas.
**Food**: Small crustaceans and insect larvae in fresh water, plus fish; fish and larger crustaceans in the sea.
**Size**: River trout 40cm (16in); sea trout 1m (3¼ ft).
**Breeding**: Nest builder; eggs shed in gravel beds of rivers, and fertilized externally.

# Atlantic salmon

*Salmo salar*

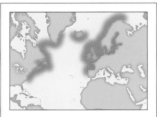

**Distribution**: North Atlantic from Canada and Greenland to Iceland, northern Europe and Scandinavia, and Barents Sea. Also adjoining rivers.
**Habitat**: Rivers when young and when spawning; mainly coastal waters at sea.
**Food**: Crustaceans, insect larvae when young in fresh water; small fish and shrimps when at sea. Spawning salmon do not feed.
**Size**: 1.2m (4ft).
**Breeding**: Nest builder; eggs shed in gravel beds of rivers, and fertilized externally.

This is one of the most famous of all fish, partly because it is a valuable food species – so much so that it is now raised in fish farms – but also because of its spectacular spawning migrations. After some years feeding in rich North Atlantic Ocean waters, adult salmon navigate their way back to the rivers where they spent their early lives, and swim upstream to reach spawning sites in shallow, gravelly streams. Here the eggs will hatch and juveniles grow through several distinct stages. Salmon do not require salt water, however, and numerous examples of fully freshwater populations of the species exist through the Northern Hemisphere.

The anadromous fish migration pattern not only involves adapting from salt to fresh water, but also navigating long distances, and travelling up rapids and waterfalls against the current. They use so much energy in the process that many die after spawning.

**Identification**: Large, streamlined fish with a relatively small head, an adipose fin and a shallowly forked tail. Breeding males develop a hooked lower jaw (kype). Adults fresh from the sea are silver-sided with greenish-blue backs, heads and fins; white below. They become darker and browner as spawning nears, with black and red spots. Young salmon in fresh water are dark, with a line of dark blotches and red spots on flanks.

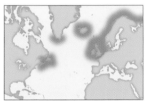

# Haddock

*Melanogrammus aeglefinus*

**Identification**: A large-eyed fish with three dorsal fins – the first triangular with long anterior rays – and two anal fins. It has a very short barbel beneath its short lower jaw. Dark greenish brown on the back, greyish silver on the sides and white below, it has a conspicuous, thumb-print-like black blotch between the pectoral fin and the arched lateral line.

One of the most heavily exploited of food fish, and now becoming scarce as a result, the haddock is a close relative of the cod (*Gadus morhua*), which feeds on the bottom in the relatively shallow waters of the continental shelves. In the north of its range the haddock feeds inshore in summer, migrating to deeper water in winter, but farther south it does the opposite.

Although adult fish feed on the bottom, their eggs are buoyant, floating near the surface. The young then feed in the plankton, often swimming with large, drifting jellyfish whose trailing tentacles provide some protection from predators. When they reach about 5cm (2in) in length, the young haddock move down to the sea bed in order to feed on worms, crabs, molluscs, brittlestars and small fish.

**Distribution**: North Atlantic from eastern Canada and New England to southern Greenland, Iceland, northern Europe, Scandinavia and the Barents Sea.
**Habitat**: Close to the seabed on continental shelf, mainly at depths of 40–300m (130–980ft).
**Food**: Bottom-dwelling invertebrates and small fish such as sandeels.
**Size**: 75cm (29½in).
**Breeding**: Eggs shed are fertilized externally and hatch into planktonic larvae.

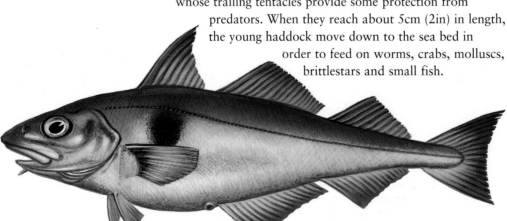

# Coalfish

*Pollachius virens*

**Identification**: A typical cod, deep in the belly but tapering towards the tail, with large eyes, a small chin barbel when young that disappears with age, three dorsal fins and two anal fins. Brownish-green back, with silvery sides and belly and a cream-coloured or lighter grey lateral line.

---

**Atlantic rainbow smelt** (*Osmerus mordax*) 30cm (12in). This small-sized relation of the salmon has a pale green back and silvery flanks with a purple, blue and pink iridescent sheen. It feeds in North Atlantic coastal waters or in large lakes when it is adult, consuming small planktonic crustaceans and insect larvae, but in spring it migrates up to about 1,000km (620 miles) against the current to spawn in rivers draining into the Arctic Ocean.

**Rainbow trout** (*Oncorhynchus mykiss*) 50cm (19½in). Familiar as a farmed food fish, the rainbow trout has been introduced to many freshwater environments worldwide, where it is also valued as a game fish. It can now be found in 45 countries on all continents, apart from Antarctica. The rainbow trout is a native of the eastern Pacific Ocean and rivers from Alaska to north-west Mexico. It resembles a European trout with an iridescent rainbow stripe along each flank, but a large, silvery migratory form, called the steelhead, lacks this characteristic stripe.

**Pouting** (*Trisopterus luscus*) 45cm (18in). This member of the cod family is a rich copper-brown above, and has yellowish-grey flanks with four or five dark bars. It has a single chin barbel and a black spot at the base of each pectoral fin. It occurs in the eastern Atlantic Ocean and the western Mediterranean Sea, and is a common sight on rocky reefs and wrecks. Young pouting often occur in large schools swimming close to the shore.

**Poor cod** (*Trisopterus minutus*) 40cm (16in). Resembling its close relative the pouting (*Trisopterus luscus*) described above, but smaller, the poor cod is a common species in the coastal waters of the eastern Atlantic Ocean and the western Mediterranean Sea. It lives in schools close to sandy or muddy sea beds, and in mid-water, and feeds on crustaceans, marine worms and small fish. In turn, it is preyed on by larger fish and dolphins.

---

Also known as the saithe or pollock, and not to be confused with the similar pollack (*Pollachius pollachius*), the coalfish lives in large schools in continental shelf seas. These waters are richer in food resources than the deep oceans, owing to the nutrients scoured up from the relatively shallow sea bed, so even surface-dwelling fish favour them. Mature coalfish feed mainly on smaller schooling fish, frequenting coastal waters in spring and summer, and returning to deeper waters in winter. They spawn from January to April, and their eggs and larvae drift into the coastal shallows where the young fish feed on planktonic crustaceans and small fish for two years before moving into deeper water.

# Atlantic hake

*Merluccius merluccius*

This moderately deep-water species, also called the European hake, lives near the bottom by day, but makes feeding forays into mid-water at night to find its prey. It feeds mainly on squid and fish, such as anchovies, sardines, herrings and small hake. After spawning in spring and summer, the buoyant eggs and larvae drift into shallower inshore waters where the young hake are less vulnerable to cannibalistic predation, and there they feed mainly on planktonic crustaceans. It is an important food species, especially in southern Europe, but has suffered from over-exploitation and is now scarce in many sea areas.

**Identification**: A slender, large-headed fish with a protruding lower jaw and large, curved teeth, a triangular first dorsal fin and second dorsal and anal fins with elongated bases. Blue-green back, silvery sides and belly, with a straight, dark lateral line.

**Distribution**: North Atlantic from eastern Canada and New England to southern Greenland, Iceland, northern Europe, Scandinavia and the Barents Sea.
**Habitat**: Schools near the surface and in mid-water to depths of 200m (650ft).
**Food**: Marine crustaceans and fish.
**Size**: 1.3m (4¼ft).
**Breeding**: Eggs shed are fertilized externally; the larvae drift in plankton.

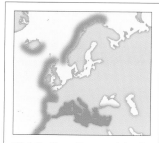

**Distribution**: Eastern Atlantic Ocean from Norway and Iceland to Mauritania; also Mediterranean Sea and southern Black Sea.
**Habitat**: Near the bottom on the middle and lower continental shelf, usually at depths of 70–370m (230–1,215ft) but occasionally as deep as 1,000m (3,280ft).
**Food**: Fish and squid, or crustaceans when young.
**Size**: 1.4m (4½ ft).
**Breeding**: Buoyant eggs shed into the water are fertilized externally; the larvae are planktonic.

## John Dory

*Zeus faber*

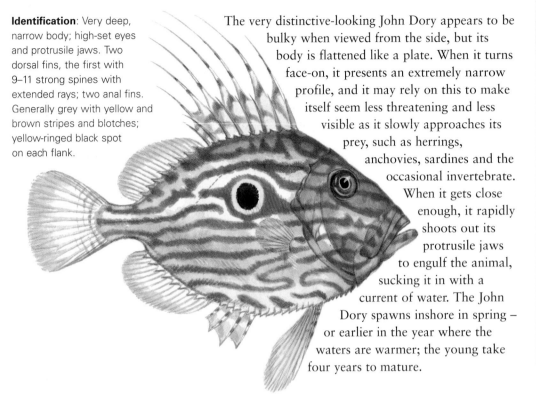

**Identification**: Very deep, narrow body; high-set eyes and protrusile jaws. Two dorsal fins, the first with 9–11 strong spines with extended rays; two anal fins. Generally grey with yellow and brown stripes and blotches; yellow-ringed black spot on each flank.

The very distinctive-looking John Dory appears to be bulky when viewed from the side, but its body is flattened like a plate. When it turns face-on, it presents an extremely narrow profile, and it may rely on this to make itself seem less threatening and less visible as it slowly approaches its prey, such as herrings, anchovies, sardines and the occasional invertebrate. When it gets close enough, it rapidly shoots out its protrusile jaws to engulf the animal, sucking it in with a current of water. The John Dory spawns inshore in spring – or earlier in the year where the waters are warmer; the young take four years to mature.

**Distribution**: Widespread in shallow temperate seas, including the eastern North Atlantic Ocean, the Mediterranean and Black seas, western North Pacific Ocean around Japan and Korea, and the western South Pacific Ocean around Australia and New Zealand.
**Habitat**: Inshore waters close to the seabed, at depths of 5–400m (16½–1,310ft).
**Food**: Schooling fish, plus occasional crustaceans, octopus and cuttlefish.
**Size**: 65cm (25½in).
**Breeding**: Eggs are shed into the water where they are fertilized externally.

## Common sea bream

*Pagrus pagrus*

Usually found on or near rocky reefs and wrecks, the common sea bream is a bottom-feeding fish that preys mainly on crabs, brittlestars, molluscs and small fish. Despite its name, it is now far less common than it once was, having been overexploited by commercial fisheries. Larger, older fish are now rare, and since this is a species that changes sex with age – from female to male – the selective removal of larger fish seriously unbalances the sex ratio. However, like many warm-water fish, the common sea bream tends to accumulate toxins in its body, through eating filter-feeding animals that have themselves ingested mildly toxic micro-organisms. The risk of becoming a victim of such poisoning, known as 'ciguatera poisoning', may make humans regard the species less favourably as a food source, and improve its chances of survival.

**Identification**: A deep-bodied, laterally compressed fish with a large, blunt head, big eyes, a spiny dorsal fin and a forked tail. Silvery red with reddish dorsal, pectoral and tail fins, and faint yellow spots on each scale giving a yellow-striped effect.

**Distribution**: Eastern Atlantic: Strait of Gibraltar to Madeira and the Canary Is; also Mediterranean and northward to the British Isles. Western Atlantic: New York, USA and northern Gulf of Mexico to Argentina.
**Habitat**: Rocky or sandy sea beds to a depth of about 250m (820ft).
**Food**: Crustaceans, echinoderms, molluscs and fish.
**Size**: 90cm (35½in).
**Breeding**: Eggs are fertilized in the water.

# Turbot

*Psetta maxima*

**Identification**: An almost circular flatfish, with a large head and both eyes on the left side. The dorsal and anal fins form a fringe around the scaleless body. Usually dull sandy brown.

The thickset, powerful turbot is an active hunter that preys mainly on other fish – particularly bottom-dwelling species such as sand eels and small members of the cod family – although it also takes a few invertebrates. It is also a prime target for commercial fisheries. Like most other flatfish, it lives mainly on the bottom, but its young swim in midwater with the aid of a buoyant swimbladder that they lose as they mature. This feature helps the young fish disperse from the spawning grounds. When they settle on the bottom they live in shallower water than the breeding adults – a fact that helps prevent them being eaten by their own species.

**Distribution**: North-east Atlantic Ocean from Arctic Circle to North Africa, plus Mediterranean and Black seas, and most of Baltic Sea.
**Habitat**: Sandy or rocky seabeds, including brackish waters, in depths from 20–70m (66–230ft).
**Food**: Smaller fish, such as sand eels, herring, whiting and gobies, plus large crustaceans and bivalve molluscs.
**Size**: 1m (3¼ft).
**Breeding**: Eggs are shed in the water and are fertilized externally.

**Plaice** (*Pleuronectes platessa*) 50–60cm (19½–23in). The plaice is one of the most familiar of the flatfish, because it is widely caught and sold whole for food. It is also one of the commonest species to be seen alive by recreational divers in northern Europe, and young plaice may even be disturbed by people paddling on holiday beaches. This is because it favours sandy shores, where it swims in with the rising tide to prey on buried molluscs and worms as they emerge to feed. It often nips off the siphon tubes of burrowing clams and other bivalves, and grazes the tentacles of fanworms, using the well-developed teeth on the left-hand, lower, side of its mouth. It is most active at night, typically spending the day lying on the sea bed partially buried by sediment.

**Atlantic halibut** (*Hippoglossus hippoglossus*) 2m (6½ft). This big, elongated, dull green-brown flatfish lives in North Atlantic and Arctic waters, where it preys on other fish such as cod, haddock and skate. There are records of it reaching 4m (13ft). This large fish is now rare due to overfishing, and the species has been classified as Endangered.

# Dover sole

*Solea solea*

The Dover sole is distinguished by the way its small, curved mouth is set to one side of its extremely rounded snout. It is largely nocturnal, but may be active on dark days or in cloudy water. It usually spends the day partly buried in the sediment, emerging at night to feed largely on small bottom-dwelling invertebrates. It sometimes swims clear of the bottom to take small fish. As with all flatfish it begins life looking like a normal fish, and lives near the surface, but its eyes move to one side as it metamorphoses into a small flatfish. It is an important food-fish.

**Identification**: An elongated flatfish with both eyes on the right-hand (upper) side of its head, a very blunt snout, a small mouth and a small pectoral fin. Medium to dark brown with irregular, indistinct dark patches on its upper side, and a dark spot on the upper pectoral fin; white below.

**Distribution**: Coastal north-eastern Atlantic Ocean from Norway to Senegal and Cape Verde Islands, western Baltic, Mediterranean and south-western Black seas.
**Habitat**: Sandy and muddy seabeds at depths of 10–100m (33–330ft), moving to deeper waters in winter.
**Food**: Mainly bottom-dwelling worms, molluscs and crustaceans, plus small fish.
**Size**: 70cm (27½in).
**Breeding**: Eggs are released into the water and fertilized externally.

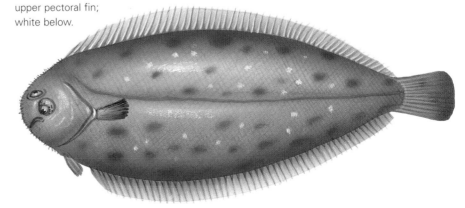

# OPEN OCEAN AND DEEP WATER

*These are the most mysterious and unexplored regions of the sea. Even in the waters just off the British coast there are parts of the seabed that have never been visited by humans. The creatures that live in these habitats are often bizarre. Deep sea fish in particular can look almost alien, but are perfectly adapted to their environment.*

## Chimera/Rabbit fish

*Chimaera monstrosa*

The common chimera is one of about 40 species belonging to the subclass Holocephali. Of these, many are deep-water specialists about which little is known. The common Atlantic species, however, is familiar to the local fishing industry. It is most active at night, when it migrates to shallower waters to feed. Chimeras, like the agnathans, have a persistent notochord – a flexible supporting rod running the length of the body. Males have a clasping structure on the forehead which may help to hold the female while mating.

**Identification**: Elongate, ventrally flattened body tapering to a very fine tail, with large pectoral fins held at right angles to the sides of the body. Dorsal fin has prominent spine; eyes large; body patterned with irregular longitudinal brown and white stripes and spots.

**Distribution**: Eastern Atlantic range, from tropical waters to northern temperate zone; also Mediterranean Sea; may be present in western Pacific, but not widely confirmed.
**Habitat**: Deep water of the continental slope descending to sea floor, at depths of 1,000m (3,280ft).
**Food**: Benthic invertebrates.
**Size**: Up to 1.5m (5ft).
**Breeding**: Oviparous, with internal fertilization; young hatch fully formed; no parental care.

## Six-gilled shark

*Hexanchus griseus*

This large shark is usually found swimming in water as deep as 1,800m (5,900ft) and is therefore rarely seen. However, between July and November the blunt-nosed six-gilled shark migrates into some shallow water locations, allowing divers a rare glimpse of it. A robust, elongate shark with a long caudal fin and a single dorsal fin, it gets its common name because it has six gill openings on each side of the head; most sharks have five pairs of gill openings. This species is a member of the order Hexanchiformes, known as the frilled sharks and cow sharks – all of the sharks in this order have six or even seven pairs of gill openings. Although a predator of small sea creatures, it will also scavenge on the carcasses of larger marine animals.

**Identification**: Body robust with a single dorsal fin set well back, close to the caudal fin. Caudal fin has a long upper lobe and a short lower lobe. Pectoral fins broadly triangular in shape. Head with blunt snout and large eyes set far forward on the head. Has six gill slits. Teeth in upper jaw are saw-like, those in the lower jaw are more pointed in shape.

**Distribution**: Widespread in tropical and temperate seas.
**Habitat**: From the intertidal zone (occasionally) down to 1,875m (6,150ft) but usually about 90m (300ft).
**Food**: Varied diet includes crustaceans, other fish, whale carcasses and seals.
**Size**: Up to 4.8m (15¾ft).
**Breeding**: Ovoviviparous, with litters of over 100 pups; gestation may take up to 2 years or more.

# Sleeper shark (Greenland shark)

*Somniosus microcephalus*

These huge members of the dogfish order are so named because of their somewhat sluggish movement, despite which they are effective predators and scavengers, occupying the top of the deep-sea food chain. Recent research suggests that sleeper sharks are one of very few predators capable of tackling giant squid. Sleeper sharks are not usually fished commercially but they turn up regularly as bycatch and are targeted by Inuit subsistence fisheries. The flesh contains high levels of urea and trimethylamine oxide. If eaten fresh it is toxic, inducing a condition similar to drunkenness, but it can be dried or carefully cooked to make it fit for human consumption. Sleeper sharks develop and grow slowly and females give birth to live young that hatch from eggs inside the uterus.

**Distribution**: Northern Atlantic and Arctic Ocean, occasional records from the Southern Hemisphere.
**Habitat**: Cold, deep water of the continental shelf down to 1,200m (3,940ft).
**Food**: Varied diet includes other fish, smaller marine mammals, squid, octopus and carrion.
**Size**: Up to 7.3m (24ft).
**Breeding**: Ovoviviparous, with litters of a dozen or more pups.

**Identification**: A very large, heavy-set shark with five pairs of gill slits that are small in relation to the animal's size. The dorsal and pectoral fins are also small, and the tail fin is asymmetrical with a notch in the upper lobe. They are generally brown, black or grey in colour, with some having dark lines or white spots along the flanks.

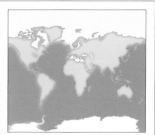

**Bramble shark** (*Echinorhinus brucus*) 2.75m (9ft). A large, deep-water shark with dark grey-brown metallic-looking skin and a scattering of spiky scales. The tail fin is highly asymmetrical. The species is best known from the Mediterranean region and the continental shelves of the north-eastern Atlantic, but has been recorded in all oceans, with the possible exception of the Indian Ocean.

**Spined pygmy shark** (*Squaliolus laticaudus*) 21cm (8¼in) This is a miniature deep-water shark that migrates to shallower depths at night to prey on small fish, squid and crustaceans. There is a characteristic spine – common to most of the 130 or so species of squaliform shark – in front of the first dorsal fin, and it has a bioluminescent patch on the belly.

**Goblin shark** (*Mitsukurina owtsoni*) 5m (16½ft). This is a bottom-dwelling species found in tropical oceans. Its exaggerated facial features account for the shark's common name, and it is characterized by having a particularly long, pointed snout that overhangs the mouth, looking like a huge nose. It is able to project its jaws rapidly forward in order to snap up prey, such as cephalopods and crabs.

# Cookiecutter shark

*Isistius brasiliensis*

This is a small shark, with a long, narrow, cylindrical body and a short, blunt snout. The lips can be formed into a sucker with which the shark attaches itself to much larger prey. The shark then bites into the flesh with saw-like rows of lower teeth and rotates its entire body to remove a neat circular chunk of meat. Cookiecutter scars are commonly seen on a variety of species of larger fish and marine mammals. The scientific name *Isistius* refers to Isis, the ancient Egyptian goddess of light. This is appropriate, as cookiecutters are bioluminescent, and the skin of the belly contains a great many photophores. These are cells containing chemicals that react with enzymes to produce an eerie, green glow. The arrangement of photophores enhances the counter-shading effect, making the fish extremely difficult to see from below. Cookiecutters lurk in deep water during the day, and migrate to shallower depths to feed at night.

**Distribution**: Tropical and temperate Atlantic, Indian and Pacific oceans.
**Habitat**: Open ocean and deep water down to 3,500m (11,500ft).
**Food**: Eats small fish and crustaceans whole; parasitic on larger fish and marine mammals.
**Size**: Up to 56cm (22in).
**Breeding**: Ovoviviparous with litters of up to 12 young.

**Identification**: Long, narrow body with an even brown colouring, except for dark collar. Dorsal and anal fins are small. Snout is short and conical; mouth has flexible, muscular lips for creating suction.

# Whale shark

*Rhincodon typus*

This, the world's largest living fish, is only just beginning to be understood. Until recently it was known mainly from shallow seas, as a seasonal visitor to reefs and coasts. But for several months a year it disappeared. Studies have revealed it to be migratory and able to descend to great depths in search of food. Like other large marine organisms, it is a filter feeder, specializing in plankton and small fish. Where food is plentiful, whale sharks may temporarily gather in groups of up to 100 or more. They are hunted mainly for their fins. Left undisturbed, they can live for more than 100 years.

**Identification**: Vast, bulbous-bodied shark with square snout and large mouth. The body has several longitudinal ridges, is dark grey to brown above, white below, marked with a pattern of white spots and horizontal stripes on back and flanks. Of its two dorsal fins, the second is very small; the pectoral fins are triangular, the pelvic and anal fins small. Its tail is large with a longer upper lobe.

**Distribution**: Tropical and warm temperate oceans worldwide.
**Habitat**: From coastal reefs to deep open ocean, down to 1,000m (3,280ft) or more.
**Food**: Plankton and small fish.
**Size**: Up to 20m (66ft).
**Breeding**: Ovoviviparous, with large litters of up to 300 pups.

# Blue shark

*Prionace glauca*

**Identification**: Long, narrow body with asymmetrical caudal fin. Dorsal fin is not particularly large, but pectoral fins are very long. Eyes appear large on conical, flattened head. Body is strikingly counter-shaded – dark blue on the back, bright blue on the flanks and paler in colour underneath.

Also known as the blue whaler because of its frequent association with dead whales, the blue shark is a species whose future may be under threat due to increased commercial exploitation – more than 10 million are killed annually for food. Blue sharks are curious and opportunistic and readily investigate any possible source of food, including divers and shipwreck victims, thus earning a reputation as one of the more dangerous shark species. However, more usual food sources include squids and small fish, such as herrings – schooling species are especially favoured in the open ocean, where feeding opportunities can be few and far between. Female blue sharks can produce a great many young. One female was recorded carrying 134 embryos, though it is unlikely all would have survived to birth.

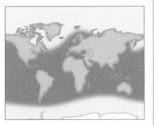

**Distribution**: Tropical and temperate oceans and seas worldwide.
**Habitat**: Open water to 350m (1,150ft) deep.
**Food**: Smaller fish and invertebrates, including octopus and squid; may also scavenge carcasses of larger animals.
**Size**: Up to 4m (13ft). There have been unconfirmed reports of larger individuals being sighted.
**Breeding**: Ovoviviparous, 4–80 pups born per litter; there is no parental care.

# Slender snipe eel

*Nemichthys scolopaceus*

The snipe eel's elongated, outwardly curving jaws are lined with tiny backward-pointing teeth. The fish cannot really bite, or even properly close its mouth. It hunts by swimming with its mouth open, sweeping the water. Once snagged by the teeth, small prey finds itself in a position it can only move in one direction – down the eel's throat. The eel is particularly efficient at catching shrimp, whose long antennae are easily snagged. The tactic can backfire and snipe eels have been found clinging to the tails of fish far too large to swallow from which they are unable to disengage. The body tapers to a thread-like tail. A dorsal fin runs halfway along the body, and is replaced by a row of short spines running to the tail. The anal fin is soft rayed all the way to the tail.

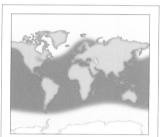

**Identification**: The strange, almost bird-like head is by far the thickest part of the body, with large eyes and long, slender outwardly curving jaws. The skin is dark brown above, almost black on the belly.

**Distribution**: Tropical and temperate seas and oceans worldwide.
**Habitat**: Deep mid-water down to 2,000m (6,560ft).
**Food**: Pelagic crustaceans and small fish.
**Size**: Up to 1.3m (4¼ft).
**Breeding**: Oviparous, with planktonic leptocephali larvae typical of eels; no parental care; spawns only once in its lifetime.

# Gulper eel (pelican eel)

*Eurypharynx pelicanoides*

It is not difficult to see why the gulper eel is so named – this fish has a huge, gulping mouth. The jaws are greatly extended and the soft tissues of the mouth are highly elastic, giving the fish a truly gargantuan gape and allowing it to take in enormous quantities of water from which prey is filtered out and then swallowed whole. Not surprisingly, the gulper is not a particularly fussy eater and will take anything unlucky enough, and small enough, to come within range – in practice this means mostly deep-water shrimps and other crustaceans, small fish and squid. There is no tail fin as such – the body tapers into a long whip-like tail with a swollen tip containing light-producing cells. Adult gulper eels appear to enter a rapid decline and die shortly after spawning. Fertilized eggs develop into planktonic larvae, like those of other eels, known as leptocephali.

**Distribution**: Temperate and tropical oceans and seas worldwide.
**Habitat**: Very deep water down to 7,500m (24,600ft).
**Food**: Small fish and invertebrates.
**Size**: Up to 1m (3¼ft).
**Breeding**: Oviparous; no parental care; spawns only once in lifetime.

**Spiny eel** (*Notacanthus chemnitzii*) Up to 1.2m (4ft). Spiny eels are large, elongate fish distinguished by a row of spines along the back and another row on the belly in front of the anal fin. They live in deep, temperate waters of all oceans and feed mainly on bottom-dwelling invertebrates, especially sea anemones.

**Bobtail eel** (*Cyema atrum*) Up to 15cm (6in). A rather obscure relative of the snipe eel, found in very deep mid-water of all oceans. The bobtail has a moderately elongated body and long, narrow, curving jaws.

**Longneck eek** (*Derichthys serpentinus*) Up to 40cm (16in). A cosmopolitan, deep-dwelling eel with a long, snake-like black body. The head is separated from the body by a narrow neck, behind which the dorsal and anal fins form a continuous fringe running the entire length of the body and around the tail. Longneck eels eat small fish and planktonic crustaceans.

**Identification**: Gulper eels lack scales. The skin is smooth and slippery and that of the huge mouth is very stretchy. There is a single long dorsal fin running the length of the body and tail and a long anal fin. The long, narrow tail has terminal light organ.

# Atlantic herring

*Clupea harengus*

Herrings are adapted for long periods of rapid swimming and have a body plan that has not changed for million of years. Atlantic herrings live in large schools, mainly feeding by night either on individual items or on planktonic copepods strained from the water with specialized gill rakers. They retreat to deeper water by day. Vast schools of herring attract the attentions of predators, whose approach triggers a behaviour known as 'bait balling', in which every fish tries to hide in the middle of the crowd, creating a dense, swirling mass. This schooling behaviour is also exploited by trawlers, with almost certainly unsustainable numbers taken each year.

**Distribution**: Temperate waters of North Atlantic Ocean.
**Habitat**: Mainly coastal waters, down to about 200m (650ft).
**Food**: Plankton.
**Size**: Up to 45cm (18in).
**Breeding**: Oviparous; spawns annually (timing varies), eggs sink and adhere to weed or the substratum.

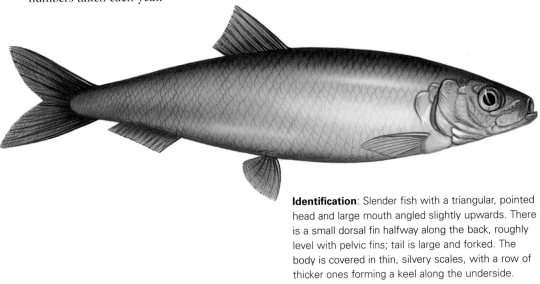

**Identification**: Slender fish with a triangular, pointed head and large mouth angled slightly upwards. There is a small dorsal fin halfway along the back, roughly level with pelvic fins; tail is large and forked. The body is covered in thin, silvery scales, with a row of thicker ones forming a keel along the underside.

# European pilchard

*Sardina pilchardus*

**Identification**: A small, spindle-shaped fish with a single, small, delicate dorsal fin and inconspicuous pectoral, pelvic and anal fins. The tail is deeply forked. The body is counter-shaded – steely grey above and bright silver below. Some fish display a series of dark spots on the flanks. Has typically oily skin which can give off a beautiful shimmer of colour when seen underwater.

A small cousin of the herring, the pilchard is intensively exploited by commercial fishing interests, and is eaten either fresh or canned as 'sardine'. Strictly speaking, a sardine is a young pilchard. As well as by humans, the species is also exploited by a large number of marine predators, including dolphins, sharks and larger bony fish such as tuna and mackerel. Pilchards feed close to the surface at night and retreat to deeper water by day. Different populations spawn at different times of year, with the main peaks in spring and summer. Females produce tens of thousands of small, floating eggs at a time, which hatch into larvae within 2 to 4 days. Like other schooling clupeids, pilchards spend their entire life in a school of similar aged and sized fish.

**Distribution**: Temperate waters of north-eastern Atlantic Ocean.
**Habitat**: Pelagic; in open oceans as well as close to shore, occasionally entering estuaries, from 10–100m (33–330ft).
**Food**: Plankton.
**Size**: Up to 25cm (10in).
**Breeding**: Oviparous; no parental care.

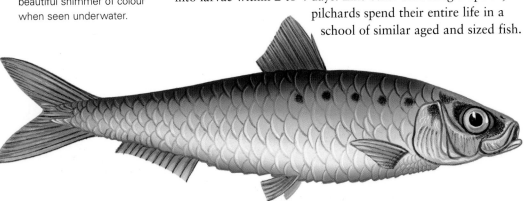

# Viperfish

*Chauliodus sloani*

**Identification**: Body long and gently tapering, covered with thin, iridescent scales that allow dark brownish-blue coloration to show through. First dorsal fin is soft but tall with a very long first ray. Paired pectoral and anal fins are long and narrow. Head relatively large, with large eye and mouth full of long, pointed teeth.

The viperfish has teeth so large that it cannot fully close its mouth. The teeth are adapted for impaling prey rather than for cutting or tearing flesh. Once the prey is caught, the teeth tilt inwards on slightly flexible roots to aid the swallowing process. The jaws can be dislocated and the stomach expanded in order to accommodate prey that is very nearly as large as the viperfish itself. A circular, light-emitting photophore situated under the eye serves to lure potential prey close to the animal's deadly fangs. Smaller light-emitting cells are arranged in rows along the belly and scattered over the body. The viperfish migrates from the depths to shallower water on a regular basis, rising at dusk from a daytime depth of about 2,000m (6,560ft) or more to night-time hunting grounds at about 600m (1,970ft).

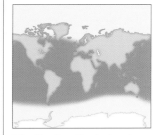

**Distribution**: Tropical and temperate waters of all oceans, and some adjoining seas.
**Habitat**: Deep water down to 2,500m (8,200ft).
**Food**: Smaller fish and pelagic crustaceans.
**Size**: Up to 35cm (14in).
**Breeding**: Oviparous, with external fertilization and no parental care.

# Stoplight loosejaw

*Malacosteus niger*

**Distribution**: Tropical and temperate zones of the Atlantic, Indian and Pacific oceans.
**Habitat**: Deep water down to 2,500m (8,200ft).
**Food**: Bony fish and crustaceans, including deep-water shrimps and copepods.
**Size**: Up to 24cm (9½ in).
**Breeding**: Presumed to be oviparous, but details of its breeding are unknown.

Another deep-sea oddity, the stoplight loosejaw is named for the photophores under and behind the eyes, which glow red and green respectively. The lights probably serve to attract prey and to illuminate it so it can aim its attack.

Like other members of its family, the species has enormous jaws – far longer than the skull. When the fish opens its mouth, the lower jaw dislocates and extends forward – a row of sharp, backward-pointing teeth hook into prey, which is then dragged back into the mouth. Rather than being enclosed within a sheath of flesh and skin, the skeleton of the lower law is exposed. This reduces drag and allows the lower jaw to shoot quickly forward without creating a pressure wave that might alert the prey.

**Atlantic menhaden** (*Brevoortia tyrannus*) Up to 50cm (19½in). A schooling, pelagic fish, deeper-bodied than other herrings but ecologically similar. Schools are generally restricted to warm surface waters where they provide an important food resource for larger fish and cetaceans.

**White barracudina** (*Arctozenus risso*) Up to 30cm (12in). Also known as the ribbon barracudina, this fast-swimming, silvery grinner favours the cold waters of the North Atlantic. It hunts alone or in large schools, using speed to ambush pelagic shrimps and smaller fish.

**Grideye fish** (*Ipnops agassizii*) Up to 15cm (6in). This long, narrow-bodied relative of the tripod fish has large, short-based fins with soft rays. It, too, lives close to the sea floor at abyssal depths of 1,500–4,000m (4,920–13,120ft) down.

Upper jaw

Lower jaw

**Identification**: The elongated body tapers to a tiny, laterally flattened tail fin. The paired fins are very narrow, the median fins are larger but very delicate. The jaws are longer than the skull. It has a red comma-like photophore under the eye and a green circular one below it. The head and body are black. The fish is shown here with mouth open, the lower jaw swinging down to reveal the gape between the jaws.

## Silver hatchetfish

*Argyropelecus aculeatus*

Hatchetfish are named for their body shape – they are flattened laterally, with a narrow tail and very deep front end, resembling the handle and blade of a hatchet. The species is able to hide even in open water thanks to a combination of shape, reflective scales and blue-emitting photophores that make its silhouette disappear when viewed from below. Hatchetfish lurk in the deeper part of their range during the day, rising at dusk to 100–300m (330–1,000ft) to feed on a variety of small planktonic animals – copepods and the larvae of other crustaceans and fish are all taken, but best of all are ostracods.

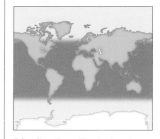

**Distribution**: Tropical, sub-tropical and warm-temperate areas of the Atlantic, Indian and Pacific Oceans.
**Habitat**: Pelagic in open ocean at depths 100–600m (330–1,970ft).
**Food**: Zooplankton.
**Size**: Up to 8cm (3in).
**Breeding**: Fertilization is external; there is no parental care.

**Identification**: The body is flattened laterally and is deeper in the front half. Its fins vary greatly in size and shape. The eye is very large and the mouth so steeply oblique as to be almost vertical.

## Tripodfish

*Bathypterois grallator*

Among the deepest dwelling of all fishes, the tripodfish spends most of its time 'standing' on the sea floor, propped up on three elongated stiffened rays from the pelvic and caudal fins. Food is scarce at such great depths, and this characteristic posture, facing into the current, offers a low-energy alternative to swimming. The tripodfish can swim, and when it does so, the fin rays trail behind. The eyes are greatly reduced in size. Adult tripodfish live solitary lives in a habitat where it can be difficult to find a mate. As a result, they have evolved to be simultaneous hermaphrodites – both male and female reproductive organs mature in the same body at the same time, making it possible, if necessary, for a single individual to fertilize its own eggs.

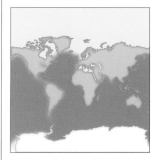

**Distribution**: Tropical and temperate Atlantic, Indian and Pacific oceans and deep adjoining seas.
**Habitat**: Deep-ocean floor to 3,500m (11,500ft).
**Food**: Nekton (deep-water plankton), mostly copepods.
**Size**: 40cm (16in).
**Breeding**: Simultaneous hermaphrodism.

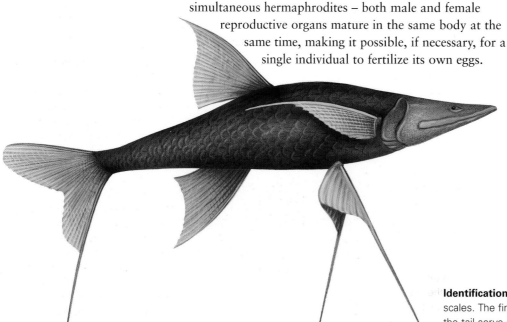

**Identification**: Body has a diamond pattern of dark scales. The first ray of each pelvic fin and the last ray of the tail serve as tripod supports. The pectoral fins form streamers while the dorsal fin stabilizes the body.

# Longnose lancetfish

*Alepisaurus ferox*

With its super-streamlined body and tall dorsal fin, the lancetfish is built for acceleration. Two or three fin rays in from the front, there are several over-long rays that form streamers. The mouth is armed with sharp teeth and two prominent fangs used for snatching prey – mostly smaller fish, but also invertebrates. Feeding adults may venture into sub-arctic waters, where prey can be abundant during the short summer, but they return to the tropics and sub-tropics to breed. Juveniles have undifferentiated gonads that may have the potential to develop into functional male or female sex organs, or perhaps both, although not at the same time.

**Distribution**: Atlantic and Pacific oceans and the adjoining seas.
**Habitat**: Deep mid-water down to 2,000m (6,560ft) or more.
**Food**: Fish and invertebrates.
**Size**: Up to 2.15m (7ft).
**Breeding**: Oviparous; possibly asynchronous hermaphrodism; external fertilization; no parental care.

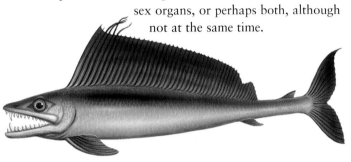

**Identification**: The body appears silvery, but all the fins are either black or dark brown. The first dorsal fin is very large, and the third, fourth and fifth dorsal fin rays may extend to form long, distinctive streamers. Second dorsal fin is very small. The tail fin is deeply forked, with an elongated first ray.

# Opah

*Lampris guttatus*

Also known as the spotted moonfish, the opah is a resident of open water with a laterally flattened body that appears almost round when seen in profile. Opahs grow very large – the heaviest individual on record weighed in at 270kg (595lb). Opahs are generally solitary but are often seen in the company of fast-swimming mackerel or tuna.

Despite their ungainly proportions, opahs can produce a good turn of speed using a rigid flapping of their sharply tapering pectoral fins. They eat mainly small fish, crustaceans and small squid. The mouth is small and lacks teeth.

**Distribution**: Tropical and temperate Atlantic, Pacific and Indian Oceans, and some adjoining seas.
**Habitat**: Mid-water at 50–500m (150–1,600ft).
**Food**: Smaller fish, crustaceans and squid.
**Size**: Up to 2m (6.6ft).
**Breeding**: Oviparous; spawning occurs in spring.

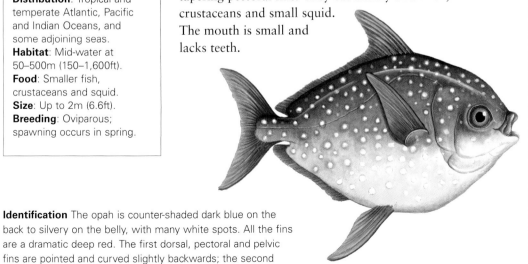

**Identification** The opah is counter-shaded dark blue on the back to silvery on the belly, with many white spots. All the fins are a dramatic deep red. The first dorsal, pectoral and pelvic fins are pointed and curved slightly backwards; the second dorsal and anal fins form a fringe above and below the tail.

**Greeneye** (*Chlorophthalmus acutifrons*) 30cm (12in).
Greeneyes live near the sea floor, where they hunt small fish and invertebrates. Their eyes are large and iridescent. There are iridescent patches on the head. Greeneyes appear to be hermaphrodites. They are thought to form schools for spawning. Greeneye larvae live in mid-water, sinking deeper and adopting a bottom-dwelling lifestyle as they reach adulthood.

**Jellynose** (*Guentherus altivela*) 2m (6½ft).
The jellynose lives close to the sea floor of the continental slopes of the eastern Atlantic and eastern Pacific oceans. It has a plump body that tapers to a pointed tail and feeds on other smaller fish. The second dorsal and anal fins form an almost continuous fringe around the tail.

**Snaggletooth** (*Astronesthes gemmifer*) 20cm (8in).
A long, black, scaleless fish found in all the world's oceans. It produces violet light from rows of light-producing organs on its flanks and two more close to each eye. It has long, sharp teeth.

**Pearlsides** (*Maurolicus muelleri*) Up to 8cm (3in).
This small but striking fish lives in the Atlantic and Pacific at intermediate oceanic depths of about 1,500m/4,920ft, migrating vertically to shallower waters at night to feed on plankton-dwelling invertebrates, such as copepods. Its flanks are covered with silvery scales.

**Lightfish** (*Icthyococcus ovatus*) Up to 5cm (2in).
A deep-bodied fish, generally brownish-yellow with silvery flanks. The body tapers sharply to the tail and the caudal fin is small. Dorsal and anal fins are small, soft rayed and delicate. Photophores in two rows along underside.

# Oarfish

*Regalecus glesne*

The oarfish may well be the longest species of fish –
specimens up to 17m (56ft) long have been reported,
though the largest reliable record is of a specimen 11m
(36ft) long. This extraordinary creature is thought to be the
inspiration for many myths of sea monsters – including the
Loch Ness monster. Oarfish are most often encountered
washed up on land – sightings of live individuals are rare.
Two recent accounts suggest that the fish maintains a
vertical position in the water, propelling itself slowly
with rippling movements of the
dorsal fin, which runs the
entire length of the body. The
long, ribbon-like pelvic fins,
meanwhile, are held out to the
sides as stabilizers. Oarfish have
no teeth and instead of scales
their skin is covered with a
fine coating of guanine, the
material that gives all fish
their silvery colour.

**Identification**: The long body is
laterally flattened, silvery in colour
with dark bluish-grey markings.
The fins are crimson. The first
dozen or so rays of the long
fringing dorsal fin form a
spectacular crest. Each fin is a
single soft ray.

**Distribution**: Recorded in
Atlantic Ocean and
Mediterranean Sea, also in
Indo-Pacific waters and
eastern Pacific Ocean.
**Habitat**: Mid-water of open
oceans from 20–1,000m
(66–3,280ft).
**Food**: Pelagic crustaceans,
small fish and squid.
**Size**: May exceed 11m (36ft)
in length.
**Breeding**: Oviparous; larvae
known from surface waters.

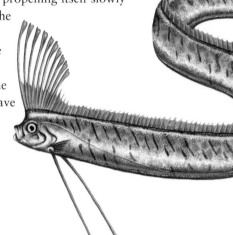

# Abyssal grenadier

*Coryphaenoides armatus*

Also known as rattails because of the way the body tapers to a long, narrow, pointed tail,
grenadiers are among the most abundant fish of the deep oceans, with a collective biomass
estimated at several million tonnes. Their abundance is a consequence of being very long-
lived (60 years), as the rate of reproduction is actually very low. Grenadiers grow slowly –
the rate of maturation depends on the availability of food. If necessary, a grenadier can go
several months without feeding, but this inhibits development. It seems likely that the species
is semelparous, meaning individuals have only one chance at reproduction – adults die soon
after spawning for the first and only time. The sex ratio in some populations weighs heavily
in favour of males. There is a small light-emitting organ on the animal's belly.

**Distribution**: Deep areas
of all tropical and temperate
oceans worldwide.
**Habitat**: Deep mid-water to
4,700m (15,400ft).
**Food**: Deep-sea crustaceans,
sea cucumbers, squids and
other fish.
**Size**: 1m (3¼ft).
**Breeding**: Oviparous;
probably breeds only once in
its lifetime.

**Identification**: Large conical head
with small chin barbel. Body tapers
from pectoral region to very narrow
tail. Dorsal fin has two long spines,
followed by a short fringe of soft rays
running the length of the body. Most
of body is silvery brown or pink,
becoming bluish on the belly.

# Giant sea devil

*Ceratias holboelli*

This is the original sea devil – the first and largest deep-sea angler to be so described. Prey, in the form of smaller fish, is attracted by the sea devil twitching a fishing lure (the esca), formed from the modified first spine of the dorsal fin (the ilicium), and is then engulfed by the angler's huge mouth. Needle-like teeth ensure there is no escape. The other dorsal fin rays form distinctive knobbly protuberances, called 'caruncles', along the back. Females produce eggs that float in rafts of jelly and hatch into tiny larvae that live as plankton. Males remain very small, and when mature seek out the much larger mature females, which release chemical signals to guide suitors in the dark water. The male latches on to her with sharp teeth and over time becomes permanently fused. He extracts nourishment directly from her blood supply, through an intermeshing of blood vessels, and produces sperm to fertilize her eggs as needed.

**Distribution**: Tropical, sub-tropical and temperate oceans worldwide.
**Habitat**: Mostly deep water to 2,000m/6,560ft.
**Food**: Smaller fish.
**Size**: Females 1.2m (4ft), males 16cm (6¼in).
**Breeding**: Males form parasitic attachments to females. Eggs fertilized externally, no parental care.

**Identification**: Female has a bulbous body. Mouth is huge and opens upwards. Dorsal fin is modified into a fishing lure.

# Giant oceanic sunfish

*Mola mola*

**Distribution**: Tropical to temperate waters of Pacific, Atlantic and Indian oceans.
**Habitat**: Open ocean, close to surface, but may dive to 500m (1,640ft) or more.
**Food**: Jellyfish, fish, molluscs, crustaceans and echinoderms.
**Size**: 3.3m (11ft).
**Breeding**: Produces hundreds of millions of tiny eggs which are fertilized externally; these drift in the oceans with no parental care.

This is the world's largest bony fish, weighing in at anything up to 2,300kg (5,070lb). The vast, disc-shaped body is laterally compressed and stabilized by tall dorsal and anal fins. The name refers not to the fish's shape, but to its habit of 'sunbathing' while floating on its side near the surface. There is no tail; instead the body ends with a rounded rudder (the clavus) formed from the last few rays of the dorsal and anal fins. The skin is scaleless and tough. The sunfish has well-developed teeth, which are fused to form a sort of beak. The jaws are powerful enough to bite through shell and bone, but the mouth is small and the sunfish is not a fast swimmer, so it preys mostly on slow-moving or drifting animals. Mature females produce an astonishing number of tiny eggs, which drift the oceans – the chances of any one being fertilized and surviving infancy are small.

**Identification**: Very large truncated body, lacks tail. Caudal and pelvic fins are absent, dorsal and anal fins are tall, providing some stability and steering when swimming.

**Dealfish** (*Trachipterus arctica*) 3m (10ft). One of several deep-sea ribbonfish species, the dealfish has a long, laterally flattened body that tapers steadily from head to tail. Confined to Arctic and north Atlantic waters, it eats smaller fish and squid and has a very slow reproductive cycle – taking 14 years to reach sexual maturity.

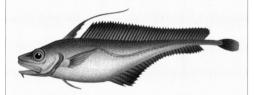

**North Atlantic codling** (*Lepidion eques*) 45cm (18in). A medium-sized cod relative of temperate waters, with a large head and large, bulging eyes. The body tapers to a narrow tail with a small caudal fin. Codlings are predatory, feeding mainly on crustaceans and polychaete worms.

**Bullseye grenadier** (*Bathygadus macrops*) 50cm (19½in) A moderately deep-dwelling fish of the tropical and subtropical north Atlantic. Occasionally caught and eaten, but not in large numbers.

**Deep sea cusk eel** (*Barathrites iris*) 65cm (25½in). A deep-sea 5,300m (17,390ft) relative of the commercially important cusk eels, *Barathrites* has much the same shape – a small head and long, tapering body with a continuous dorsal-caudal-anal fin fringing the tail. Atlantic distribution; also present in Indian and Pacific.

## Needlefish

*Belone belone*

This is a fish of many common names – it is informally known as the garpike, sea pike, sea needle, greenbone and mackerel guide. This highly distinctive species is fished commercially as well as for sport – when hooked it fights hard, leaping clear of the water. It feeds mainly on schooling pelagic fish, such as smaller herrings and mackerel, and migrates along with these species – summering in the northern Atlantic and Baltic and retreating to warmer waters during the winter months. Female needlefish produce eggs that float at the water's surface, often becoming attached to floating weed or other debris by long tendrils. Needlefish of all sizes are eaten by a variety of fast-moving predators, including tuna, swordfish and seals.

**Identification**: Athletic fish with a greatly elongated, cylindrical body shaped by well-developed swimming muscles. Long, narrow snout and large eyes. Lower jaw is longer than upper jaw. Dorsal and anal fins set well back on body, close to the tail with a forked caudal fin. Silvery body. Sometimes confused with similiar species *Belone svetovidovi*.

**Distribution**: North-eastern Atlantic Ocean, also Mediterranean and Black seas.
**Habitat**: Open water close to surface; may occasionally enter estuaries.
**Food**: Smaller fish, especially sardines and anchovies.
**Size**: 95cm (38in).
**Breeding**: Oviparous; no parental care.

**Tapetail** (*Eutaeniophorus festivus*) 5cm (2in). A bizarre little fish belonging to the small order Cetomimiformes. Occurs in all tropical and temperate oceans but is not common in any of them. Body is elongate, with large fins. The pelvic fins are situated forward of the pectorals, at the throat. The tail ends in a long streamer.

**Pilotfish** (*Naucrates ductor*) 70cm (28in). The pilotfish is a boldly patterned relative of the jacks. Its body is a dark-blue colour or black with seven or eight broad, evenly spaces white vertical bands. It lives in the surface waters of tropical and subtropical seas worldwide, and it is associated with floating objects, such as seaweed and jellyfish.

**Identification**: Head and mouth large, body short and deep with lateral line lying within a groove along the flank from eye level to the midline of the tail. Colour uniform dark brown to black.

## Fangtooth

*Anoplogaster cornuta*

The common fangtooth, also know as the ogrefish, is named for its unpleasant gape full of needle-like teeth. It is a prickly customer in other ways, too – the body is covered in scales bearing short spines, giving it the feel of coarse sandpaper. The dorsal, anal, pectoral, pelvic and caudal fins all have conspicuously unwebbed fin rays. The lower fangs fit neatly into cavities in the palate when the mouth is closed. These cavities extend up inside the head, either side of the brain. The teeth are used for snagging smaller fish and invertebrates, but despite its fearsome appearance, it frequently falls victim to larger predators, especially tuna and albacore.

**Distribution**: Tropical and temperate oceans worldwide.
**Habitat**: Close to sea floor in deep areas, from 500–5,000m (1,640–16,400ft).
**Food**: Smaller fish and invertebrates.
**Size**: 15cm (6in).
**Breeding**: Oviparous; larvae develop in surface waters; no parental care.

## Yellowtail amberjack

*Seriola lalandi*

Yellowtail amberjacks are a familiar sight on reefs and in coastal waters, but they also live in open ocean – juveniles, in particular, often live in schools far out to sea, having been carried with ocean currents as larvae. Large adults are more often solitary. All jacks are efficient swimmers – the carangiform mode of swimming, where the head stays still and the tail sweeps from side to side, is named after this family. The tall, forked tail fin offers powerful thrust without excessive turbulence. Amberjacks are predators of smaller fish species and invertebrates, which are ambushed and caught with a burst of speed.

**Identification**: Long, torpedo-shaped body with large, forked tail. Body is dark blue above and white below; tail fin is yellow or dark with yellow trailing edge. Single dorsal and anal fins are small with a triangular leading portion and an elongate fin base reaching nearly to the tail.

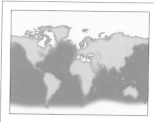

**Distribution**: Tropical and warm-temperate waters worldwide.
**Habitat**: Coasts, reefs and open ocean, usually close to sea floor, from shallows to 825m (2,700ft).
**Food**: Small fish, cephalopods and crustaceans.
**Size**: 2.5m (8¼ft).
**Breeding**: Oviparous; no parental care.

## Northern bluefin tuna

*Thunnus thynnus*

This is probably the largest of all the tuna species. The largest known individual was 4.58m/15ft in length and weighed 684kg/1,508lb. This enormous size is achieved through an insatiable appetite for smaller fish and invertebrates, which the bluefin hunts day and night outside the breeding season. Bluefin tuna live in schools often containing a mix of species, but all members of the school will be of similar size to avoid accidental cannibalism. These 'warm-blooded' fish migrate north in summer and spend winter in the tropics, where they breed. Their huge swimming muscles make them exceptionally meaty, and as a fish that tastes very good they have been hugely over-fished to supply the demand for their flesh, particularly for sushi. The species is now being commercially cultivated off the Japanese coast. Although it is not listed as endangered, as the southern bluefin tuna is, it is thought to be seriously threatened as it is caught indiscriminately at all stages of maturity, thus preventing the establishment of wild communities.

**Distribution**: Northern Atlantic, Mediterranean and Black Sea. Sub-population off coast of South Africa. American range extends from Canada to Brazil.
**Habitat**: Oceanic, usually in surface waters, occasionally down to 3,000m (9,840ft); visits coastal waters.
**Food**: Smaller fish and pelagic invertebrates; will also take benthic animals and kelp close to shore.
**Size**: 4.5m (15ft).
**Breeding**: Oviparous, spawning up to 10 million floating eggs a year.

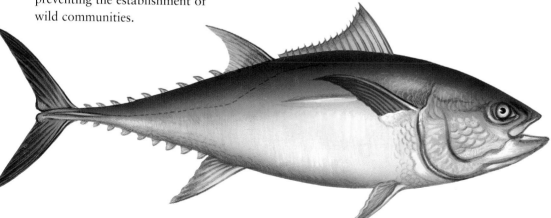

**Identification**: Large, torpedo-shaped fish, two dorsal fins followed by series of finlets on tailstock. Pectoral and pelvic fins short, anal and second dorsal fin highly falcate (sickle-like), caudal fin a stiff, symmetrical crescent with darkly pigmented lobes. Body counter-shaded – bluish-grey above, silvery below.

# Albacore

*Thunnus alalunga*

These fish move around their distributional range in schools, performing extensive migrations in search of food or to spawn in tropical waters in summer. They often congregate at thermoclines – depths where the water changes temperature, where upwelling currents bring nutrients up from below and prey is more abundant. Large albacore tend to live deeper down than small ones.

Albacore have a strong schooling instinct and often form mixed schools with other types of tuna. As with other tunas, over-fishing is a concern. The flesh is considered to be excellent and is sold as high-quality canned tuna. Also worrying from a consumer's perspective is the tendency of the species to accumulate high levels of mercury in the flesh.

**Distribution**: All tropical and temperate oceans and seas including Mediterranean. Very common off Australian coast.
**Habitat**: Pelagic in open ocean, mainly in surface waters to 600m (1,970ft).
**Food**: Smaller fish.
**Size**: 1.4m (4½ft).
**Breeding**: Oviparous; spawn in tropical waters during the summer.

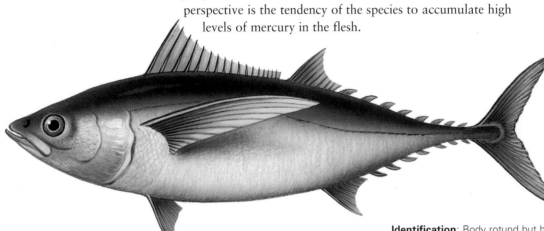

**Identification**: Body rotund but highly streamlined with pointed snout and tapering tailstock. Eye is large. Two dorsal fins and dorsal and ventral rows of finlets. Pectoral and anal fins are small; dark-blue caudal fins form a shallow crescent-shaped tail with pointed tips. Pectoral fins are very long. Body steely blue above, silvery white below.

# Atlantic mackerel

*Scomber scombrus*

Schools of this species tend to remain in deep water in winter, but in summer feed close to the surface, travelling in search of suitable prey. Plankton, crustaceans and fish larvae make up the bulk of the diet, but the mackerel is also well adapted for pursuing small fish such as sand eels. Mackerel lack a swimbladder, and rely on lightweight oily musculature as well as continual, fast swimming to stop them from sinking. Their gills are ventilated by the force of water passing into the open mouth rather than by any kind of pump, so if they stop swimming they die. The species is highly commercial and supports large fishing industries.

**Identification**: Slender, near cylindrical body with pointed snout and tapering tailstock. Tiny scales; body is silvery green to white on belly, marked with vertical or slightly oblique black bands on back and flanks. All fins are small, tailstock bears tiny finlets, caudal fin forms a pointed crescent.

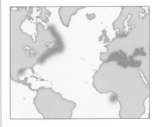

**Distribution**: Parts of northern Atlantic, also Mediterranean and Black Sea. Western Atlantic range is from Labrador to Cape Lookout, Oregon.
**Habitat**: Oceanic, in surface waters to 200m (650ft).
**Food**: Zooplankton and small fish.
**Size**: 60cm (23in).
**Breeding**: Oviparous; larvae feed actively and attain lengths of 25cm (10in) in first year.

# Frigate mackerel

*Auxis rochei*

The frigate mackerel is a shoaling fish of open water. It is most common in seas over the continental shelf, which stretches out for up to 500km (310 miles) from the coast. It is a fish of warm waters, but occasionally it occurs off British shores.

The frigate mackerel is sometimes referred to by its alternative common name of bullet tuna, it actually belongs to the same family as both and has characteristics of each. Like the common mackerel (*Scomber scombrus*) it is relatively small and has dark, wavy bars on its back. Like a tuna, it is quite deep-bodied and has a very shallowly sickle-shaped tail.

The frigate mackerel is both a predator and prey in the ocean. It forms schools for protection from larger fish and dolphins, both of which count it as food. Smaller fish on the other hand, such as anchovies, are eaten by it. Other prey include swimming crustaceans, crab larvae for example, and small cephalopods, like juvenile squid.

**Distribution**: Normally found in warmer seas worldwide, this fish is a rare visitor to British shores.
**Habitat**: The open ocean.
**Food**: Small schooling fish, squid and crustaceans.
**Size**: 60cm (23in).
**Breeding**: Spawning occurs at different parts of the year in different regions. The eggs are scattered into open water and develop unguarded.

**Identification**: The body is bullet-shaped and round in cross section. There are two well separated dorsal fins, the second followed by eight small finlets. The anal fin is small and also has finlets behind it. The caudal fin is narrow, with the two lobes forming a shallow sickle shape. The scales on the rear half of the body are larger than those at the front. There is a series of about 15 dark wavy bars on the back.

**Horse mackerel** (*Trachurus trachurus*) 70cm (27in). A widespread schooling fish of the Atlantic and western Pacific Oceans. The body is a greenish-grey colour above and silvery below, and it has large keeled (ridged) scales on the flanks. The horse mackerel gets its common name from the legend that other smaller species of fish could ride on the back of it over great distances. It feeds on crustaceans, squid, and other fishes. There are two main populations: the west stock which spawn in the eastern Atlantic off the coasts of western Europe, and the north stock which spawn in the North Sea, where it is fished commerically.

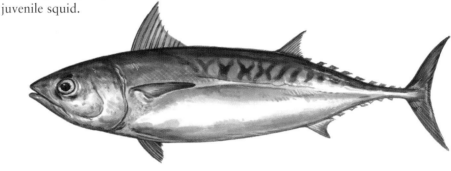

# Swordfish

*Xiphias gladius*

The scientific names *gladias* means 'sword', as in gladiator. The bill of the swordfish is flat with sharp edges, and is used as a deadly weapon, to kill and slice prey into pieces small enough to swallow. Swordfish tackle a wide variety of prey, mostly other fish, but also pelagic invertebrates. They travel long distances, overwintering and spawning in warm waters in spring, then heading for cooler waters to take advantage of seasonally abundant prey over the summer. Juveniles have a fully developed sword by the time that are 1cm (½in) long, and begin hunting immediately. Females grow slightly faster than males and reach a larger size. Swordfish is a tasty food fish; however, it has a tendency to accumulate dangerously high levels of certain marine pollutants, especially mercury, so frequent consumption is not recommended.

**Distribution**: Tropical and temperate oceans and seas worldwide.
**Habitat**: Pelagic in mid-water from 200–800m (650–2,620ft).
**Food**: Fish, cephalopods, crustaceans.
**Size**: 4.5m (15ft).
**Breeding**: Oviparous; spawns in spring; larvae grow rapidly.

**Identification**: Body tapers from head to tail, which bears long caudal fins forming a crescent. Pelvic fins are absent, pectorals are long and low slung. Single dorsal fin is tall and single anal fin is small – both are falcate. Head is large with large eyes and the upper jaw is modified into a long, blade-like bill.

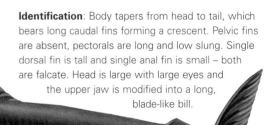

# DIRECTORY
# OF FRESHWATER
# FISH

In Britain fresh water is never far away. Every valley has its river and every hillside its streams. There are lakes too, some of them quite significant in their size. These habitats are home to a wide range of wildlife. Foremost among the vertebrates are fish.

Britain's freshwater fish are far more diverse than one might imagine. They vary in size from the tiny minnow to the wels – one of the largest freshwater fish on Earth. Like oceanic fish, Britain's freshwater fish also vary in their behaviour. Some are solitary while others shoal. Some are predators while others feed largely on plants.

Because they live underwater, freshwater fish can be hard to observe in the wild. The most commonly seen are those that live in shallow water – such as the brown trout; many others are so well camouflaged that they are hard to see at all. A few, such as the pike, combine camouflage with an ability to be almost motionless, rendering them all but invisible.

*Above: Telford Bridge in Invermoriston, Scotland. The cool inland waterways of the British Isles are teeming with life, although much of it is unseen by the human eye. Conservation projects and awareness of pollution are important to protect the wildlife.*

*Left: A pike swims in the waters of a lake. The northern pike is the archetypal freshwater predator of British waterways.*

# PRIMITIVE FISH

*Lampreys and lamperns are the most primitive living vertebrates. Like sharks and rays, they have skeletons made of cartilage rather than bone, but unlike them they lack jaws and true teeth. Sturgeons, an ancient group of fish that has barely changed since the time of the dinosaurs, were once present in British waters, but are now rarely, if ever, seen.*

## Lamprey

*Petromyzon marinus*

This fish spends part of its life in fresh water and part in the sea. In many ways its life cycle is a mirror image of that of the eel (*see* page 249), which it resembles. Adult lampreys enter fresh water to breed, swimming up rivers to spawn over gravel shallows before returning to the sea. The young fish, known as prides, are filter feeders, sifting algae and tiny invertebrate animals from the silt on the river bottom. They remain prides for six to eight years, before developing into sub-adults and heading downstream to the sea. Adult lampreys are parasitic, attaching themselves by means of their sucker-shaped mouths to the bodies of other fish and feeding on their blood. In Europe, this species has become uncommon, due to pollution in the rivers where it breeds.

**Identification:** The body is long and eel-like but the mouth is a sucker-shaped disc. The tooth plate of the adult, at the front of the disc, has between seven and nine large, sharp cusps. There are seven separate gill openings, which run in a horizontal line on the side of the head. There are no paired fins. The upper side is olive to yellow-brown and heavily blotched with darker brown. The underside is much lighter.

**Distribution:** Most of coastal Europe; many of the Atlantic-draining rivers of North America's east coast.
**Habitat:** Large rivers and coastal waters.
**Food:** Young: filter feeders; adults: blood of other fish.
**Size:** Up to 1.2m (4ft).
**Breeding:** Spawning occurs in the middle of summer. Each pair makes a pit in the riverbed, where the eggs are laid. They are then left to develop unguarded.

## Brook lamprey

*Lampetra planeri*

This fish closely resembles the larger lamprey, but spends its entire life in fresh water. As its name suggests, the brook lamprey is an inhabitant of small streams and is usually found in the upper reaches of rivers. The young are filter feeders, eating tiny organisms sifted from the mud. Adults live just long enough to breed and then die, their rotting bodies returning nutrients to the streams in which their young will grow. The brook lamprey spawns in nests dug on the bottom in shallow water. Wherever possible, these tend to be positioned in shade and sites under bridges are often used. Sometimes several pairs will spawn in the same nest.

**Identification:** Closely resembles the lamprey but has a smaller sucker disc containing small, blunt teeth. The colour ranges from dark brown to dark grey above and lighter below, usually yellowish, sometimes white. There are seven gill openings and no paired fins. During spawning, the areas around the mouth and anus turn rusty red.

**Distribution:** Throughout northern Europe as far south as central France.
**Habitat:** Streams and, rarely, lakes.
**Food:** Algae and small invertebrates.
**Size:** Up to 25cm (10in).
**Breeding:** Larvae become adults at 6 or 7 years old. Spawning usually occurs in sandy or gravelly areas.

**Lampern** (*Lampetra fluviatilis*) Up to 50cm/19½in. Halfway between the lamprey and the brook lamprey in size, the lampern has a similar life cycle to the former, spending its adult life at sea and entering fresh water to breed although it is sometimes called the river lamprey. It inhabits coastal waters and rivers of north-western Europe, but is now rare.

**Sturgeon** (*Acipenser sturio*) Up to 3.5m (11½ft). This fish has been hunted to near extinction for its highly prized caviar. The River Severn was once Britain's main sturgeon river but the Common Sturgeon is rarely found in any UK waters now. It has also disappeared from many European rivers and is extremely rare in those where it remains.

# SALMON, TROUT AND RELATIVES

*Salmon and trout are shoaling fish and, in the main, migratory breeders. Some of them spend part of their lives in the sea, and therefore appear in both this and the marine sections of this book. The salmon and brown trout in particular are prized by both anglers and gourmets. In western Europe, these two species are more common on restaurant menus than any other freshwater fish.*

## Salmon

*Salmo salar*

The salmon, or Atlantic salmon, as it is known in North America, is one of the world's most familiar fish. It is caught wild and also widely farmed. It is an important sports fish too, particularly in Scotland. The salmon also has its own place in mythology. In Ireland's ancient Celtic myths, for example, Bradán Feasa (the Salmon of Knowledge) was caught by the poet Finn Eces and prepared by the hero Fionn mac Cumhaill (Finn McCool). When hot fat from the fish was sucked off his thumb, the knowledge Finn gained thereby enabled him to become leader of the fabled Fianna tribe.

**Identification**: The tail fin is slightly forked and has clear, well defined rays. There is a small adipose fin. The corner of the mouth extends to directly below the rear edge of the eye. Adults and large juveniles (smolts) are silvery with small x-shaped marks on the flanks. The underside is white. Young fish (parr) have between eight and eleven dark rounded marks on each flank, with orange spots between these marks.

**Distribution**: Northern Europe, Iceland, southern Greenland and the east coast of North America.
**Habitat**: Rivers and the sea.
**Food**: Invertebrates and small fish.
**Size**: Up to 1.5m (5ft).
**Breeding**: Adults enter rivers from the sea. Spawning occurs in November or December in shallow riffles.

## Brown trout

*Salmo trutta*

**Identification**: The base of the tail is thick compared with that of other trout and the caudal fin has a relatively square rear edge. There is a small adipose fin. The corner of the mouth extends behind the rear edge of the eye. Although called the brown trout, the colour of this species varies. Freshwater individuals tend to be brownish with numerous black and rusty red spots. Sea trout are silvery with an orange-edged adipose fin.

The brown trout is another very familiar fish. Although native to Europe it has been widely introduced to other parts of the world as far distant as North America, Australia and the Falkland Islands. In Europe, this is the species most often caught by fly fishermen. They use lures made to look like mayflies, which they dance over the surface of the water. This fact betrays the brown trout's predilection for flying insects. It can often be seen jumping or breaking the surface of lakes and slow-flowing rivers, particularly at dawn and dusk when these insects are most abundant. The brown trout is considered good eating and in some places is farmed as a food fish.

**Distribution**: Native to Iceland, the British Isles, mainland Europe and parts of Russia. Widely introduced elsewhere.
**Habitat**: Rivers, streams, lakes and the sea.
**Food**: Invertebrates and small fish.
**Size**: Varies: in fresh water around 30cm (12in); in the sea up to 1.4m (4½ft).
**Breeding**: Females dig shallow depressions in which they spawn. Marine individuals (sea trout) enter fresh water to spawn.

# Arctic charr

*Salvelinus alpinus*

Two forms of this fish exist in the wild. One inhabits deep mountain and highland lakes in central and northern Europe (including Britain and Ireland). It shoals in open waters not far above the bottom. The other form, found in the northernmost reaches of Europe, is migratory, breeding in rivers but spending its winters at sea. The two forms look quite different. Landlocked Arctic charr are darker and smaller, and rarely exceed 30cm (12in) long. The Arctic charr is one of Britain's rarest freshwater fish but it is quite common in the rest of its range. In Siberia it is known as golets.

**Distribution**: Lakes in Europe and rivers and the sea around the Arctic, from Scandinavia and Russia to Alaska and Canada.
**Habitat**: Lakes, rivers, sea.
**Food**: Aquatic invertebrates and small fish.
**Size**: Up to 1m (3¼ft).
**Breeding**: Mostly in tributary streams of their river homes; winter or early spring. Eggs are laid in gravel redds and develop unguarded.

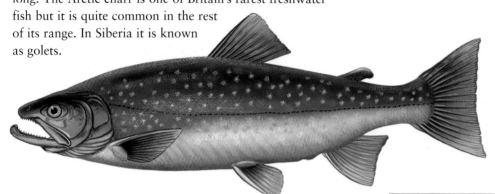

**Identification**: The base of the tail is relatively narrow. The caudal fin is large and quite deeply forked. There is a small adipose fin. The scales are very small. Fish that spend the winter at sea are silvery, with bellies of orange or red. Lake fish are greeny-brown, with red and white spots on their sides. Both forms have white edges to their pectoral, pelvic and anal fins.

**Schelly** (*Coregonus laveretus*) 30cm/12in. The schelly inhabits a few isolated highland lakes in England, Scotland and Wales, as well as lakes in the Alps and rivers flowing into the Baltic Sea. It feeds mainly on planktonic invertebrates, filtering them from the water using its gill rakers. It was formerly found in the eastern North Sea but is now thought to be extinct there, due to pollution and over-fishing.

# Huchen

*Hucho hucho*

**Identification**: Similar in appearance to the salmon, but with a thicker tail base. The huchen has very small scales and a slightly pointed head. The corner of the mouth extends beyond the rear edge of the eye. There is an adipose fin and the caudal fin is shallowly forked. During the breeding season both sexes turn coppery red.

This large fish is native to the Danube River and is sometimes known as the Danube salmon. It is a protected species and fry raised in captivity are frequently released to boost the wild stock. It has been introduced to several other European rivers including some in Britain, although less successfully than hoped. The huchen occasionally reaches lengths of around 1.5m (5ft) and weights of 18kg (40lb), but historically it grew much larger.

The huchen is a territorial species, but not solitary, with large individuals occupying and defending territories such as a large pool, which may be inhabited by several other individuals. These fish undertake short migrations upstream for spawning between April and May. Juveniles feed on invertebrates such as insect larvae, while adults prey mostly on fish, but also on amphibians, reptiles, small mammals and waterfowl. The huchen is listed as Endangered by the IUCN.

**Distribution**: Danube River and its tributaries, introduced to some British and other Northern European rivers.
**Habitat**: Rivers.
**Food**: Freshwater invertebrates, fish and amphibians.
**Size**: 1m (5ft).
**Breeding**: Spawning occurs in early spring over gravel. As with the brown trout and salmon, the female digs a shallow nest (redd). The eggs are left to develop unguarded and hatch after 5 weeks.

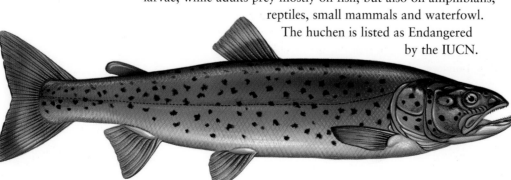

## Vendace

*Coregonus albula*

The vendace is one of the UK's rarest freshwater fish, and also one of the oldest – dating back to the Ice Age. Other common names for this species include 'whitefish' and 'European cisco', and 'fendas' in Welsh. Until recently the only surviving vendace in the UK were found in the Lake District, but in the 1990s they were successfully transferred to Loch Skeen, a remote loch near Moffat in south-west Scotland, where stocks have increased. It is also found in lakes in northern Europe, especially Finland, Sweden, Russia and Estonia, and in some lakes of northern Germany and Poland. It is found also in diluted brackish water in the Gulf of Finland and the Gulf of Bothnia of the Baltic Sea.

Vendace mainly feeds on zooplankton, such as small crustaceans and their larvae. The fish live in schools made up of large groups of individuals. They generally breed in the autumn, laying their eggs on pebbly or sandy ground, but in several North European lakes distinct spring-spawning populations of vendace exist, some of which have been described as separate species.

**Distribution**: Northern Europe including Finland, Sweden, Germany and Poland. In UK only in Lake District and southwest Scotland.
**Habitat**: Lakes.
**Food**: Small crustaceans and larvae.
**Size**: 35cm (14in).
**Breeding**: Autumn spawning, laying eggs on sandy ground.

**Identification**: A small, streamlined and slim fish with a bluish green back, a white belly and silvery flanks. The fins are grey in colour becoming darker towards the margins. It has large eyes, a relatively small mouth and an adipose fin

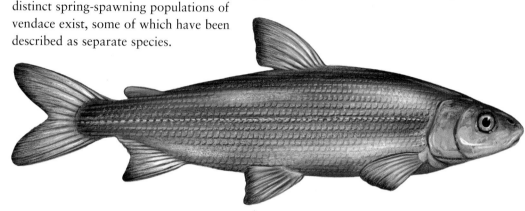

## Pollan

*Coregonus autumnalis*

**Distribution**: This fish is found only in four lakes in Ireland: Lough Ree, Lough Derg, Lough Erne and Lough Neagh.
**Habitat**: Lakes.
**Food**: Freshwater invertebrates.
**Size**: 63cm (25in).
**Breeding**: Spawning occurs in November or December. The eggs are scattered into open water and settle on the bottom, where they eventually develop unguarded.

The pollan is one of the few freshwater fish native to Ireland. It is absent from the rest of the British Isles and the rest of Europe. The pollan occurs in Ireland's four largest lakes, including Lough Neagh, the largest lake in Britain. Its limited distribution and the fact that it occurs elsewhere in the world as a saltwater fish (when it is known as the Arctic cisco) suggests that it was one of the first, if not the first fish to colonize Ireland's lakes at the end of the last Ice Age, around 10,000 years ago. As the global temperature increased, Ireland's ice sheets melted and their weight was lifted off the land beneath. With the ice disappearing this land slowly rose and the lakes, which had previously been linked to the sea, were isolated, along with their fish.

Today, pollan numbers have declined, particularly in Lough Erne, Lough Derg and Lough Ree, as they compete with other fish, notably the roach, for food. The healthiest population by far now exists in Lough Neagh. Here there was once a thriving pollan fishery and although this has now long since gone, pollan remain numerous enough for their young to be the principal bait of Northern Ireland's eel fishermen.

**Identification**: The pollan ranges in colour from blue to dark green, occasionally brown, above. The rest of the body is silvery. The dorsal and caudal fins are dusky, while the fins lower on the body are lighter in colour.
The body is robust, but at the same time highly streamlined. The head is small, making the eyes appear larger than they actually are. The mouth is relatively small and opens right at the tip of the snout.

# LOACHES, CATFISH AND BURBOT

*All of the fish on these pages are bottom-dwellers and as a consequence are rarely seen in the wild, even where they are common. Although they vary greatly in size and diet, they have similar patterns of behaviour, hiding out by day and becoming active at night. This helps them to avoid herons, otters and other predators who do their hunting by day.*

## Spined loach

*Cobitis taenia*

**Identification**: The body is long, slender and slightly compressed in the vertical plane. The head is small with the eyes placed high on the sides. The mouth is small and surrounded by six fleshy barbels. There is a short but sturdy backward-pointing spine beneath each eye (hence the name). This has two pointed tips and is usually retracted into the skin. The sides are marked with conspicuous rows of dark, oblong blotches.

This little fish is widespread throughout Europe but rare in most of the places where it is found. It also occurs in Asia, where it is thought to be more common. The spined loach is an inhabitant of still and slow-moving waters. It lives on the bottom, where it feeds on tiny invertebrates and other particles of organic matter. These are removed with the help of mucus as it filters water, laden with sediment, through its mouth. This fish tends to be most active at dawn and dusk. It spends the daylight hours hidden beneath mats of algae on the bottom or buried in the mud. It has large gills, an adaptation which helps it survive in waters with low oxygen levels. It is also able to absorb oxygen through its gut wall and occasionally gulps air.

**Distribution**: Most of Europe, apart from northern Scandinavia. It is absent from Ireland and in Britain is restricted to a few eastward-flowing English rivers.
**Habitat**: Swamps, ponds, lakes, rivers and streams.
**Food**: Detritus and tiny invertebrates.
**Size**: Up to 13.5cm (5¼in).
**Breeding**: Spawning occurs during May and June. Eggs are usually laid on mats of algae or around the bases of aquatic plants.

## Stone loach

*Nemacheilus barbatulus*

**Distribution**: A huge range, being found throughout most of Europe and as far east as China. Introduced into Ireland.
**Habitat**: Streams and rivers.
**Food**: Small aquatic invertebrates.
**Size**: Up to 15cm (6in).
**Breeding**: Spawning occurs from April until June. The eggs are laid in two or three batches over the same spot, often among vegetation or gravel. They are guarded by the male until they hatch.

**Identification**: The body is relatively long and slender, but the front is more rounded than the rear half, which is vertically flattened. The head is quite large compared with most other loaches but the eyes are quite small. There are six barbels around the mouth but no spines beneath the eyes. In colour it is olive-brown above, with darker blotches, and yellow below.

The stone loach is a fish of streams and small, fast-flowing rivers. It is often found in the same stretches of water as bullheads (*see* p.240). It spends the day hidden among the stones and other rubble on the bottom, hence its common name. Like the spined loach, it becomes active as the sun goes down. It hunts throughout the night, seeking out mayfly larvae, stonefly larvae and other invertebrate prey while most of its own predators are inactive. Although a common fish, it is rarely seen, being beautifully camouflaged even when it is out in the open. Although several individuals may be found within the same area of river, this fish tends to be solitary, only gathering with others to breed.

LOACHES, CATFISH AND BURBOT **239**

# Wels

*Silurus glanis*

This gigantic creature holds the title of world's largest freshwater fish. One individual, caught in Russia's Dnieper River in the 19th century, measured 4.6m (15ft) long and weighed an incredible 336kg (740lb). No fish caught anywhere in fresh water since has come close to beating this record. The wels is a type of catfish that lives in large, slow-flowing rivers and areas of still water, such as oxbow lakes. It is mainly nocturnal, spending the day lying still amongst tree roots or beneath overhanging river banks. Not all wels are giants but most older individuals are very large fish. It is a carnivore. The bulk of its diet is made up of other fish but it also eats amphibians, waterfowl and small mammals.

**Distribution**: Native to larger rivers of northern Europe and Russia. Introduced into England, France Spain and northern Italy.
**Habitat**: Large rivers, lakes and marshes.
**Food**: Fish and other aquatic vertebrates.
**Size**: Up to 4.6m (15ft).
**Breeding**: Spawning occurs from May until July. The female lays her eggs in a shallow depression made by the male, who then guards the eggs.

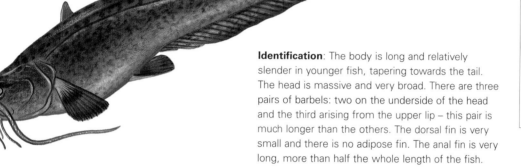

**Identification**: The body is long and relatively slender in younger fish, tapering towards the tail. The head is massive and very broad. There are three pairs of barbels: two on the underside of the head and the third arising from the upper lip – this pair is much longer than the others. The dorsal fin is very small and there is no adipose fin. The anal fin is very long, more than half the whole length of the fish.

# Burbot

*Lota lota*

**Distribution**: Found across most of the temperate and sub-polar regions of the northern hemisphere.
**Habitat**: Slow-flowing rivers and lakes.
**Food**: Aquatic invertebrates and fish.
**Size**: Up to 1m (3¼ft).
**Breeding**: Spawning occurs in mid-winter, often under ice. The eggs are scattered over gravel and left to develop unguarded.

This fish is the only member of the cod family to live in fresh water. It has an enormous range, occurring right across the northern parts of Europe, Asia and North America. There are plans to re-introduce this freshwater member of the cod family back into British waters, where it is thought to be extinct. If it does still survive, the counties of Cambridgeshire and Yorkshire (particularly the River Derwent or River Ouse) seem to be the strongest candidates. It is mainly nocturnal and spends the day lying still in a sheltered nook on the bottom. By night it scours the beds of rivers and lakes for invertebrates and small fish. In North America it is also known as the eelpout and the lawyer, although the origins of these curious names are sadly lost in history.

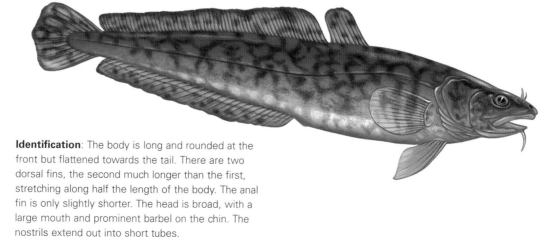

**Identification**: The body is long and rounded at the front but flattened towards the tail. There are two dorsal fins, the second much longer than the first, stretching along half the length of the body. The anal fin is only slightly shorter. The head is broad, with a large mouth and prominent barbel on the chin. The nostrils extend out into short tubes.

# STICKLEBACKS, BULLHEADS AND MINNOWS

*Sticklebacks, minnows and bullheads are named for their physical characteristics. Sticklebacks are named for their spines, Bullheads are so called because their prominent eyes and flattened heads give them a slightly bovine appearance, and minnows are named for their size.*

## Three-spined stickleback

*Gasterosteus aculeatus*

**Identification**: The three spines that give this fish its name are its most obvious distinguishing feature, running along the back in front of the second, more complete, dorsal fin. The body is torpedo shaped and quite streamlined, and the eyes are large. The pelvic fins, like the first dorsal fin, are reduced to spines. The general colour of freshwater individuals is greenish brown. The male's belly turns red during the breeding season.

The three-spined stickleback is a great fish to watch in the wild. Its preference for still shallow water and its fearless nature make it easy to observe, and its breeding behaviour is quite absorbing. In spring and early summer, males build nests from algae and plant fibres on the bottom. These nests are shaped like little tunnels and the males entice the females into them to lay their eggs. The males then guard the eggs and keep them well-oxygenated until they hatch by fanning them with their fins. During the breeding season males become quite territorial but at other times of the year these fish can often be found in small shoals. Interestingly, the three-spined stickleback is also found in coastal marine waters. There the males make their nests from seaweed.

**Distribution**: Throughout Europe, from Iceland to the Iberian Peninsula, southern Italy and the Black Sea. Also found in North Africa; widely introduced throughout the world.
**Habitat**: Rivers, lakes, ponds, ditches and coastal waters.
**Food**: Aquatic invertebrates and fish fry.
**Size**: Up to 10cm (4in).
**Breeding**: The male builds a nest into which he entices the female. He then guards the eggs until they hatch.

## Bullhead

Miller's thumb *Cottus gobio*

**Distribution**: Ranges from southern Scotland to the Black Sea. More common in Britain than on the continent; absent from Spain and Portugal.
**Habitat**: Streams and small rivers with rocky bottoms.
**Food**: Aquatic invertebrates and fish eggs.
**Size**: Up to 17cm (6½in).
**Breeding**: Spawning occurs March to May. The female attaches her eggs to the underside of a rock. The male guards them until they hatch.

This fish lives in rocky streams and small rivers. By day it usually hides beneath large stones or in the gaps between pebbles, its dappled colours making it virtually invisible unless it moves. As the sun starts to set it emerges to find insect larvae and the eggs of other fish, holding itself steady in the rushing current with its large pectoral fins. The bullhead is rarely active throughout the night, usually settling after an hour or two of feeding, and then foraging for another hour or two around dawn. This crepuscular behaviour is driven by the fact that it is a visual predator that is itself quite vulnerable to predation. Although it can grow larger the bullhead rarely exceeds 10cm (4in) long. In parts of England it is called 'miller's thumb'.

**Identification**: The body is slightly flattened, a typical adaptation of bottom-dwelling fish in swift water. The head is quite broad and the body, seen from above, tapers from the temples to the tail. There are two relatively long dorsal fins. The anal fin is positioned directly below the second dorsal fin and is slightly shorter. The pectoral fins appear unusually large.

# Minnow

*Phoxinus phoxinus*

**Identification**: The head and the body are both rounded and the snout is blunt. The body is covered with small scales and there is an obvious lateral line, curving down towards the belly. A line of dusky blotches runs along the side – these become darker towards the tail. During the breeding season the male's belly reddens and his throat turns black.

The minnow is famous for being small. It is not the smallest freshwater fish but it is the smallest native fish in Britain to spend its whole life in fresh water. A shoaling fish of streams and small rivers, it is most common in waters where the temperature is quite low and the oxygen levels are high, although it is sometimes found in the shallows of slower-flowing, warmer waters. It is an omnivore, feeding on everything from algae and water plants to insect larvae. It is itself prey for a wide range of larger fish and an important food source for the brown trout (*see* page 236) and the kingfisher (*Alcedo atthis*). This fish is considered a good indicator of water quality in rivers and streams, being absent where pollution levels are high.

**Distribution**: Widespread throughout Europe, including Ireland, where it has been introduced. Also found in Russia, where its eastern range extends to Siberia.
**Habitat**: Streams and rivers.
**Food**: Algae, plant matter, aquatic invertebrates.
**Size**: Up to 12cm (4½in).
**Breeding**: Spawning occurs from April to June. The eggs are shed into open water over gravel and left to develop unguarded.

# Bitterling

*Rhodeus sericeus*

**Distribution**: Native to the Danube basin and central Europe but has been widely introduced into western Europe, including England.
**Habitat**: Lakes, ponds and overgrown, slow-flowing rivers.
**Food**: Planktonic crustaceans and insect larvae.
**Size**: Up to 9cm (3½in).
**Breeding**: April to August. The female lays 30–100 eggs inside a mussel. The fertilized eggs remain here until they hatch 3–4 weeks later.

This fish has a very unusual but successful method for protecting its eggs – it lays them inside a living freshwater mussel. As the breeding season begins, the male sets up a territory around a mussel, which he defends from other males. He attracts a female who then lays her eggs in the mussel's inhalant siphon, which leads into its gills. (She does this using an ovipositor, a delicate tube which she develops during the spawning season.) The male then sheds his sperm over the inhalant siphon, which sucks it in.

**Identification**: The body is deep, with large scales. The mouth is small. The dorsal, caudal and anal fins are significantly larger than the others. The lateral line is visible only in the first five or six scales behind the gill cover. The body is greyish-green on the back and silver on the sides and belly. Breeding males turn purple and develop small turbercles on the forehead and snout.

**Ten-spined stickleback** (*Pungitius pungitius*) 7cm (3in). Slightly smaller and less cosmopolitan in its distribution than the three-spined stickleback, the ten-spined stickleback is less well-known to most Europeans. Nevertheless, it is a relatively common fish with similarly fascinating breeding habits. This stickleback tends to be found in areas more choked with the stems of water plants than its three-spined relative, and it can survive in waters with much lower oxygen levels. It ranges through the coastal regions of most of the temperate and sub-polar northern hemisphere, including North America. There it is known as the Newfoundland stickleback or nine-spined stickleback. The latter name is telling. This species can have as few as eight spines along its back and does not always have ten, as might be expected.

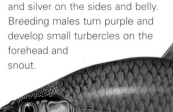

# ROACH, GUDGEON, RUDD AND BARBEL

*Roaches and rudds are commonly found in weedy lakes and rivers, where they live in shoals. Medium-sized members of the carp family, they are most often seen on the end of a hook. A few populations are fished commercially for food but generally speaking they are considered sport fish and of more interest to anglers than gourmets.*

## Roach

*Rutilus rutilus*

**Identification**: This fish is moderately deep bodied with a relatively small head. The body has fairly large, almost diamond-shaped, scales but the head is scaleless. The flanks and belly are intensely silver and the back blue-green to brown. The pelvic and anal fins range from orange to bright red. The iris of the eye is also red.

This common and easy-to-catch fish is very familiar to European anglers. It has been introduced to many parts of the continent where it is not native, including Ireland, Scotland and Wales. It is a schooling fish, most common in still or very slow-flowing waters. An omnivore, it eats large amounts of plant matter and tends to be particularly abundant in areas of thick weed growth. It is no giant but it can grow to quite a respectable size – as much as 1.8kg/4lb. It is rarely eaten, however. Angling for roach is mostly a sporting pastime and fish tend to be put back in the water after they have been unhooked and, possibly, weighed.

**Distribution**: Native to eastern England and most of Europe, including Russia as far east as the Ural Mountains.
**Habitat**: Ponds, lakes and slow-flowing rivers.
**Food**: Plant matter and aquatic invertebrates.
**Size**: Up to 53cm (21in).
**Breeding**: Spawning occurs from April until June. Eggs are shed over vegetation, which they stick to, and are left to develop unguarded.

## Gudgeon

*Gobio gobio*

Although unfamiliar to most people, the gudgeon is a relatively common little fish. It lives in a wide range of habitats, including canals, and is much more tolerant than most fish of disturbances, such as regular boat traffic. As a result, it is often the first type of fish caught by budding anglers. It prefers still or slow-moving waters but may be found in areas with moderate or even relatively rapid currents. As its body form suggests, it is a bottom-dwelling species, locating small invertebrate prey partly by touch as it grubs around in the silt. (In still waters young gudgeon feed on planktonic organisms in open water). Gudgeon tend to form small shoals. Unusually for fish, they are capable of producing squeaking sounds, which they appear to use to maintain contact within the shoal.

**Identification**: The body is long and slender and the back slightly curved. In cross section it is almost circular, but compressed somewhat towards the tail. There is a single barbel at each corner of the mouth. The head is scaleless but the body is covered with rather large scales, with between 38 and 44 in the lateral line. The dorsal, anal and caudal fins are covered with small, dark spots.

**Distribution**: Native to the whole of Europe apart from Ireland and the Iberian Peninsula. It has been introduced into both of these places.
**Habitat**: Lakes, rivers and canals.
**Food**: Aquatic invertebrates.
**Size**: Up to 20cm (8in).
**Breeding**: Spawning occurs in shallow water at night in early summer. The eggs are scattered, usually over gravel, and are then left to develop unguarded.

# Rudd

*Scardinus erythrophthalmus*

**Distribution**: Occurs throughout Europe, ranging from England to the Ural Mountains. Introduced to Ireland and Wales.
**Habitat**: Sluggish rivers, ponds, lakes and other areas of still water.
**Food**: Invertebrates and plant matter.
**Size**: Up to 45cm (18in).
**Breeding**: Spawning occurs from April to June. Eggs are shed over vegetation, which they stick to, and are left to develop unguarded.

The rudd was named, in the 17th century, for the colour of its fins. The word for red has obviously changed a little in England since then (although the word ruddy, meaning reddish, is still in use.) The fins are brighter in colour in clearer water. The scales are a reflective silver to gold colour. This is a schooling fish, found in oxbow lakes and large, slow-flowing rivers. Its popularity with anglers has seen it introduced to a wide range of freshwater habitats, including ponds, lakes, reservoirs and canals. It survives in waters with fairly low oxygen levels so tends to thrive wherever it is introduced but it requires abundant vegetation and a gentle flow of water.

**Identification**: Resembles the roach in many respects and is often confused with it. The rudd, however, has its dorsal fin set farther back and has a keel on its belly (the belly of the roach is rounded). The dorsal and pectoral fins are grey with a reddish tint. All of the other fins are bright red or orange. The back may be bluish green; the sides are pale gold and the underbelly is a paler, silvery colour.

# Barbel

*Barbus barbus*

**Identification**: The body is long and almost circular in cross section, although the belly is flattened. The snout is pointed and the eyes rather small. The lips are thick and have two pairs of barbels. The body is a soft greenish brown on the back, golden yellow on the flanks and lighter on the underside. The scales are fairly small and well embedded in the skin.

The barbel was known in medieval times as the pigfish, for its habit of rooting around for food. The word barbel is commonly used to describe the whisker-like organ at the mouth that enables this and other types of fish to forage by touch. It hunts for invertebrate prey at night and is relatively inactive by day, although it will happily take bait during daylight if offered it. It is a great favourite of anglers, being renowned for its fighting spirit once hooked. This popularity has led to it being introduced into many rivers. Once caught, it is usually weighed and then put back in the water, as it is not generally considered good to eat. Despite its size and the fact that it often schools, the barbel can be difficult to spot as its coloration camouflages it against the bottom.

**Distribution**: Native to eastern England and most of continental Europe. Introduced to other parts of England and Wales.
**Habitat**: Clean rivers with good stretches of gravel.
**Food**: Aquatic invertebrates.
**Size**: Up to 91cm (36in).
**Breeding**: Males and females congregate in shallow water and spawn as a group. The eggs are scattered over clean gravel and are left to develop unguarded.

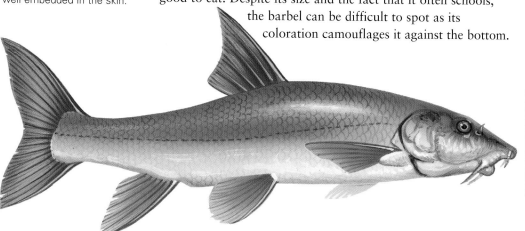

# CARP, CHUB, DACE AND TENCH

*These fish include some of the larger members of the carp family found in Europe. Some are regularly stocked in lakes, reservoirs and flooded gravel pits, and are familiar to anglers. Others are less commonly seen. Considering their size, all of these fish eat relatively small creatures. With the exceptions of the chub and dace, they also feed on plant matter.*

## Carp

*Cyprinus carpio*

**Identification**: The mouth is toothless, with two pairs of barbels emerging from the upper lip – those nearer the corner of the mouth are longer. In most wild fish the body is fully scaled but there are varieties such as the leather carp and mirror carp in which most of the scales are absent. The head is always scaleless. The dorsal fin is long, stretching along more than half the length of the back.

The carp is a potentially large and long-lived fish that thrives in still and slow-flowing waters around the world. It is a sport fish for anglers as well as a source of food. Its preference for plant matter and invertebrates means that it poses no threat to other fish, which has made it a popular choice for stocking new ponds and lakes. In some areas where it has become established, however, it is considered a nuisance. In captivity it has been known to reach 47 years old and a weight of 36kg (80lb).

**Distribution**: Native to the Danube basin and much of Asia as far east as China. Widely introduced in western Europe (including Britain) and elsewhere around the world.
**Habitat**: Lakes, large ponds and slow-flowing rivers.
**Food**: Aquatic invertebrates and plant matter.
**Size**: Up to 1.5m (5ft).
**Breeding**: Spawns spring and summer in shallow water. Scattered eggs are left to develop unguarded.

## Chub

*Leuciscus cephalus*

**Identification**: The body is thickset and rounded with the head and 'shoulders' unusually broad. The mouth is wide and the snout quite blunt. The dorsal and anal fins have relatively short bases and are similar in shape and size, although the outer edge of the anal fin is more rounded. The scales on the back and sides are green to greyish-brown and are clearly outlined.

The chub is a truly European fish, being found throughout the continent apart from the very far north, from Wales to the Ural Mountains. It is sometimes found living alongside the carp in still or slow-flowing waters but is more common in large rivers with moderate flow. Young chub form schools for protection, but the adult fish are usually solitary. The chub is a carnivorous fish and extremely adaptable, feeding on a wide range of small creatures. Prey items vary from insect larvae and crustaceans such as crayfish to frogs, small fish and even young water voles. Although not as large as the carp, the chub can reach a respectable size and is often caught by anglers. The largest specimens landed have weighed around 7.25kg (16lb).

**Distribution**: Absent from Ireland but otherwise found throughout Europe, apart from the very far north.
**Habitat**: Rivers and, less commonly, lakes.
**Food**: Aquatic invertebrates and small vertebrates.
**Size**: Up to 61cm (24in).
**Breeding**: Spawning occurs in May and June in shallow water. The eggs are scattered over water plants, which they stick to, and left to develop unguarded. The hatch after around 8–10 days.

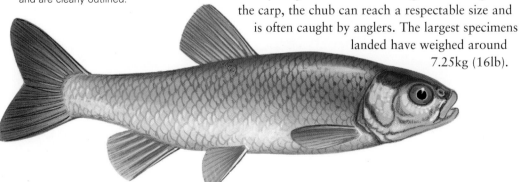

## Dace

*Leuciscus leuciscus*

**Distribution**: From Britain through northern Europe and Russia, as far east as Siberia; no farther south than the Alps. Introduced to Ireland.
**Habitat**: Rivers and large streams.
**Food**: Invertebrates, particularly insects.
**Size**: Up to 30cm (12in).
**Breeding**: Spawning occurs in shallow waters early in spring. Eggs are deposited over gravel and left to develop unguarded.

This northern Eurasian fish is found in rivers, most commonly in the relatively clean water of their middle and upper reaches. That said, it may also be found in slower-flowing stretches downstream and has even been known to enter brackish water at the edge of the Baltic Sea. It is a shoaling fish and feeds on invertebrates, particularly insects, eating both the aquatic larval forms and adults as they lay their eggs at the surface. It also eats other invertebrates that fall into the water. The dace is a very active and relatively fast-moving fish. In some places it is known by the alternative common names of dart or dare.

**Identification**: The body is slim and the head and mouth are relatively small. The lateral line is clearly visible, beginning at the back of the gill cover, level with the centre of the eye, and curving downward then back up again, mirroring the curve of the belly. The iris of the eye is yellowish and the pectoral, pelvic and anal fins pale orange or yellow. The other fins are grey.

**Crucian carp** (*Carassius carassius*) 51cm (20in). This widespread fish ranges from east England to central Russia. It is smaller and more deep-bodied than the carp and lacks barbels. Purebred fish are rare as this species interbreeds with the carp and also with the goldfish (*Carassius auratus*). It is a fish of still or slow-flowing water. It can tolerate low oxygen levels and is often found in waters with heavy plant growth.

**Ide** (*Leuciscus idus*) 1m (3¼ft). The ide (*above*) is similar in appearance to the dace but grows much larger. It lives in schools in the lower reaches of the rivers of northern Europe, including their estuaries, and is also common in flood plain lakes. Young ide are plankton feeders. Adults feed on invertebrates and occasionally small fish.

## Tench

*Tinca tinca*

This fish is able to tolerate much higher temperatures and lower oxygen levels than most of its relatives. It is found mainly in still water, although it also inhabits very slow-flowing backwaters of rivers. It can also be found in brackish water. The tench is usually the most common large fish in very silty or overgrown bodies of fresh water in its range, and will rarely venture into clear waters. It is a favourite of anglers, with record fish measuring 70cm (27½in) and weighing around 6.4kg (14lb). Fishing for tench is a summer pursuit; the species tends to lie inactive near the bottom during the winter.

**Distribution**: Native to most of Europe, including England and the western part of Russia. Introduced into Ireland, Wales, parts of the USA and Australia.
**Habitat**: Lakes, marshes and the backwaters of rivers.
**Food**: Invertebrates and plant matter.
**Size**: Up to 70cm (27in).
**Breeding**: Spawns late spring and early summer. Eggs are shed over vegetation and develop unguarded.

**Identification**: Most easily told apart from its relatives by its very small scales. These are deeply embedded in very thick skin, the surface of which is often slippery, like that of an eel. The eyes are small and have reddish irises and there is a single pair of barbels, one at each corner of the mouth. The body is rounded and the base of the tail rather deep.

# BREAMS, BLEAK AND PERCH

*These members of the carp and perch families tend to be found in running water, particularly the lower reaches of rivers. They all feed on small prey and some are an important food source for larger fish. Although most of these species feed in relatively deep open water they tend to spawn in the shallows, usually where the bottom is covered with weeds.*

## Bream

*Abramis brama*

**Identification**: This fish has flat sides and a high, arched back. The head is small with a mouth that can extend to become tubular. The head is scaleless but the body is covered with many small scales. The back is grey or dark brown and the flanks more golden brown. The fins are greyish-brown: those on the underside are tinted with red.

The bream is a schooling fish that spends the day in deep water. At night it moves into the shallows to feed. Like many members of the carp family this fish is a bottom feeder, eating insect larvae, crustaceans, worms and other small invertebrates. It catches its food by sucking it up from the bottom, using its down-turned, tubular mouth.

Despite the size of its prey it can grow into quite a large fish; the biggest may weigh as much as 9kg (20lb). It is found throughout much of Europe and is popular with anglers. Bream spawn in shallow water among dense vegetation, mostly at night. Young bream are a silvery colour, which makes it difficult to differentiate them from silver bream.

**Distribution**: Native range extends from Wales eastwards to the Ural Mountains and from the northern Baltic to the Alps. Widely introduced elsewhere, including Scotland, Ireland.
**Habitat**: Lakes and deep, slow-flowing rivers.
**Food**: Aquatic invertebrates.
**Size**: Up to 80cm (31½in).
**Breeding**: Spawns late spring and early summer. Yellowish sticky eggs adhere to stems and leaves and are left to develop unguarded.

## Silver bream

*Blicca bjoerkna*

**Distribution**: Widely distributed throughout Europe from eastern England to the Caspian Sea, between the Baltic states and the Alps.
**Habitat**: Large rivers.
**Food**: Aquatic invertebrates.
**Size**: Up to 36cm (14¼in).
**Breeding**: Spawning occurs in small schools in summer. The eggs are shed among water plants, and will stick to their leaves. They are left to develop unguarded.

Although it belongs to a different genus and is smaller, this fish closely resembles the bream in shape, hence its common name. It eats planktonic creatures in open water but also searches for larger invertebrates on the bottom. The silver bream is a schooling fish like its namesake. It may reach weights of up to 1kg (2¼lb) but is usually smaller. Its size has made it unpopular with commercial fishermen, who complain that it competes for food with larger, more profitable freshwater fish. This fish is also known as the white bream or flat bream. In the Danube the silver bream has been known to hybridize, but this has never been recorded in British waters. It is found all over Britain except Scotland and Ireland.

**Identification**: The body is predominantly brilliant silver in colour, although the top of the back is usually light olive-brown. The pectoral and pelvic fins are orange with grey tips; all of the other fins are dusky. The body shape is similar to that of the bream but the scales are larger and the mouth is not tubular. The head is small and, as with other cyprinids, scaleless.

# Bleak

*Alburnus alburnus*

The bleak is a relatively small shoaling fish, and a member of the carp family. It is often found in turbid waters and slow-moving reaches of rivers where there is little oxygen. It is also found in clear waters in some lakes and streams. It feeds on planktonic animals in the water column. It also takes advantage of its upward-pointing mouth to take flying insects that land on the surface. Shoals often spend much of their time near the surface during the day and head down into deeper waters at night. Because of its size, the bleak is not really sought after by anglers. Nevertheless, it is frequently caught, being quicker than many other fish to take bait in open water. Despite its ability to tolerate low oxygen levels, it is very sensitive to pollution and has declined in many European rivers as a result.

In Eastern Europe, the bleak's scales are used to make artificial pearls.

**Identification**: A relatively shallow, slender body. The head is slightly pointed with the opening of the mouth on its upper side. The eyes are large and the lateral line clearly visible. The scales are quite big, but are thin and fragile, and are easily dislodged. The back and upper flanks are turquoise in colour and the underside is white.

**Distribution**: Found throughout most of Europe apart from the Iberian Peninsula. It is native to eastern England and has been introduced into some rivers in the west.
**Habitat**: Lakes, rivers and, occasionally, streams.
**Food**: Aquatic invertebrates.
**Size**: Up to 20cm (8in).
**Breeding**: Spawning occurs in shallow water during May and June. The eggs are scattered, often over weeds, and are left to develop unguarded.

# Perch

*Perca fluviatilis*

**Identification**: The body is usually slender and the head quite short (making up about a quarter of the total length). There are two dorsal fins; the first has spines protruding from its upper edge. The pelvic fins are set close together and each has a spine on its leading edge. The back is greenish-brown and there are dark vertical bars on the sides. The underside fins are deep orange.

The perch is widespread within northern Eurasia, with a range extending from Ireland as far eastward as Siberia. It is naturally a fish of lowland lakes and slow-flowing rivers but has been widely introduced into other areas of still fresh water. Young perch feed on planktonic creatures and form shoals for protection from predators, but as they grow older they become more solitary. Adult perch hunt small fish, including other members of their own kind. They also eat insect larvae and other invertebrates. The perch is a popular fish with anglers. It rarely exceeds 2kg (4½lb) in weight but occasionally may reach up to 4.75kg (10½lb). It is relatively long-lived, sometimes reaching 22 years of age.

**Distribution**: Most of Europe north of the Alps and Pyrenees. Also occurs throughout much of Russia.
**Habitat**: Lakes and rivers.
**Food**: Young: plankton; adults: aquatic invertebrates and small fish.
**Size**: Up to 51cm (20in).
**Breeding**: Spawning occurs in April and May in shallow water. Strings of eggs are laid and woven around aquatic plants. They are left to develop unguarded.

# ZANDER, RUFFE, PIKE AND GRAYLING

*Pike and Zander are both predatory fish of some notoriety. Pike will lie in wait behind reeds for unsuspecting prey to past before lunging at them, whereas young zander will hunt in packs, surrounding their prey. The ruffe and grayling are two more species of freshwater fish that are much sought after by anglers. All these fish are carnivorous.*

## Zander

*Stizostedion lucioperca*

**Identification**: The body is long and slender and the head rather pointed. The mouth is large and filled with many small, sharp teeth. There are several longer fangs at the front. The two dorsal fins are clearly separated. The front fin, like that of the perch, has spines emerging from its top edge. The anal fin is about half as long at the base as the second dorsal fin.

This large, streamlined fish is a solitary predator, hunting other fish in large rivers and lakes. It tends to be more common in cloudy waters than clear ones and is most active around dawn and dusk. It lives and hunts in open water and tends to avoid the weed beds favoured by other predators, such as the pike (*see* opposite). Larvae feed on tiny planktonic invertebrates but move on to larger invertebrates and small fish as they grow older. This fish was introduced into England in the 1960s and has since spread, possibly to the detriment of native fish. Like the pike it is a favourite target of experienced anglers. Large zander can weigh as much as 19kg (42lb).

**Distribution**: Native to parts of Sweden and Finland, eastern Europe and western Asia. Introduced into English rivers, lakes and canals.
**Habitat**: Lakes, rivers and canals.
**Food**: Aquatic invertebrates and fish.
**Size**: Up to 1.3m (4¼ft).
**Breeding**: Spawning occurs from April until June. The eggs are scattered over stones or vegetation and left to develop unguarded.

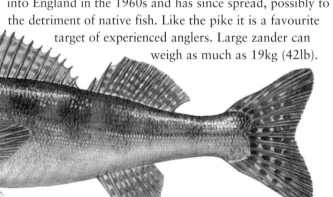

## Ruffe

*Gymnocephalus cernuus*

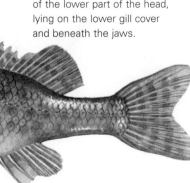

**Distribution**: Native to most of Europe north of the Alps. Occurs through Russia and central Asia as far as China. Introduced Scotland and North America.
**Habitat**: Lakes and slow rivers.
**Food**: Aquatic invertebrates and fish eggs.
**Size**: Up to 30cm (12in).
**Breeding**: Spawning occurs from March until May. The sticky eggs are scattered over plants or stones and left to develop unguarded.

This is a schooling fish of slow and still waters, usually over soft mud. It only occurs naturally where the flow is very gentle. It feeds mainly on aquatic invertebrates, which it snaps up from the bottom, both during the day and at night. Bloodworms (midge larvae) make up the bulk of its diet but it also eats other insect larvae and, sometimes, fish eggs. It is widespread in continental Europe and western Asia, but in Britain it is native only to eastern England. It has been introduced to Scotland and parts of North America. In the Great Lakes of the latter it has become a pest, out-competing local fish for food. It is a prolific breeder, which has made it impossible to eradicate where it has been introduced, accidentally or otherwise.

**Identification**: The body form is not a great deal different from that of the perch and is similarly slender. The first and second dorsal fins, however, are united to form one, long, continuous fin. Another distinguishing feature of this fish are the several large cavities visible beneath the skin of the lower part of the head, lying on the lower gill cover and beneath the jaws.

# Pike

*Esox lucius*

The pike is the archetypal freshwater predator. Its huge mouth and long, streamlined, yet powerful body mark it out as a hunter, and it is very good at what it does. It catches other fish unawares, holding its position in the water column among weeds so that it blends in with the background. As soon as its prey swims into range it strikes, darting out from cover to snap it up. The pike can reach quite an impressive size. Females may grow to as much as 1.3m (4¼ft) long and weigh up to 24kg (53lb). The males are significantly smaller, rarely exceeding 69cm (27in) long. The pike is one of the most widespread fish in the Northern Hemisphere and also occurs in North America, where it is known as the northern pike.

**Identification**: The body is long and muscular and the mouth very large. The lower jaws contain several massive fangs while the palate has hundreds of much smaller sharp teeth. Seen from the side, the head is pointed. From above, the snout appears flat. The dorsal and anal fins lie very far back on the body. The body is greenish-brown on the back and green on the flanks. Patterning varies between individuals.

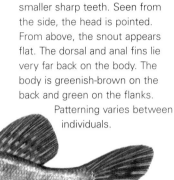

**Distribution**: Throughout Europe (north of the Alps and Pyrenees) and northern Asia, from Ireland to eastern Siberia. Also found Canada, northern states of the USA.
**Habitat**: Lakes, canals and slow-flowing rivers.
**Food**: Fish, amphibians, small mammals and water birds.
**Size**: Up to 1.3m (4¼ft).
**Breeding**: Spawns early spring. Females may be joined by more than 1 male. Eggs are shed over water plants, develop unguarded.

# Grayling

*Thymallus thymallus*

This is a shoaling fish of cool, clean, well-oxygenated rivers and lakes. It feeds on invertebrates that live on the bottom as well as insects that fall into the water. Classified by some authorities as a salmonid, the grayling is a member of the same family as salmon and trout. Most, however, give it and its close relatives a family of their own, Thymallidae. Indeed, its appearance more closely resembles some cyprinid fish rather than trout or salmon. The grayling has quite a wide natural distribution but its range has been extended by anglers. Unlike many fish caught by anglers, the grayling is often eaten and its flesh is said to have an excellent flavour.

**Distribution**: Found naturally from Wales as far east as the Ural Mountains and from southern Sweden south to France. Introduced elsewhere.
**Habitat**: Lakes and rivers.
**Food**: Invertebrates.
**Size**: Up to 50cm (19½in).
**Breeding**: Spawning occurs in pairs from March until May. The eggs are shed into a shallow depression dug by the female in sand or gravel and are left to develop unguarded.

**Eel** (*Anguilla anguilla*) 1m (3¼ft). With its long, sinuous body, the eel looks more like a snake than a fish. Since it sometimes comes out of the water in wet weather to travel short distances over land, it might even occasionally be confused for one. The eel is remarkable for its behaviour as well as its appearance. Although it spends most of its life in fresh water, it spawns in the Sargasso Sea, on the far side of the Atlantic Ocean. The young then make their way back to Europe's fresh waters, entering rivers as young, transparent 'glass eels' and migrating upstream. As they travel they grow darker (then called 'elvers'). They then spend anything from 6 to 20 years growing to sexual maturity before heading downstream and into the ocean to begin the cycle again.

**Common goby** (*Pomatoschistus microps*) 6.5cm (2½in). The common goby is a marine fish that enters estuaries and the lower reaches of rivers. It is also found in brackish coastal marshes but tends to spend the winter in deeper waters a little way out to sea. Like most other gobies it is a mainly solitary creature that feeds on aquatic invertebrates, seeking them out between rocks or snapping them up from the muddy bottom. Most people who have seen this fish in the wild have seen it in rock pools, where it is often trapped by the retreating tide. The common goby breeds throughout spring and summer, with females laying their eggs beneath the shells of bivalve molluscs, such as mussels.

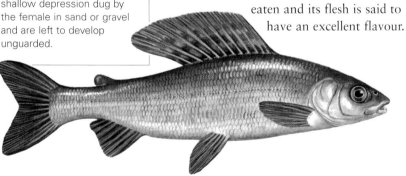

**Identification**: The most striking feature of this fish is its flag-like dorsal fin, which is particularly large in the males. The other fins are relatively small and unspectacular. There is an adipose fin present. The head is quite small and the snout rather pointed, with the mouth on its underside. The greenish-brown to steel blue body is covered with moderately large scales.

# SHAD, SMELT, MULLET AND SEA BASS

*All of the species here are principally marine fish that enter fresh water. The flounder is a bottom-dwelling fish, but all of the others tend to be found swimming in open water. Some have populations that are entirely land-locked. Some, such as the sea bass, are sought-after game fish or are hunted commercially for food.*

## Allis shad

*Alosa alosa*

**Identification:** The body is flattened and the underside has a greater curve than the back. The belly has a keel made up of sharp, backward-pointing teeth. The head is relatively large and all of the fins, apart from the caudal fin, are small. The back is metallic blue in colour, and the flanks golden, shading into silver. There is usually a dark blotch just behind the gill covers at the same level as the eye.

This fish spends most of its adult life in the sea, only entering large rivers to breed. In spring it gathers at river mouths in shoals which then journey upstream, usually travelling some distance upriver, before spawning at night. They never leave the main channel. Once hatched, the young fish remain in fresh water, moving down to the brackish water of estuaries during autumn. They feed on planktonic crustaceans and other tiny invertebrates living in the water column. Adults eat larger invertebrates and small fish. The Allis shad can grow to a significant size; weights of 2.7kg (6lb) are not uncommon. Its size and the fact that it shoals have made it a target for commercial fishermen.

**Distribution:** Coastal waters from Norway to Morocco, as well as the western Mediterranean. It spawns in the rivers that flow into these areas.
**Habitat:** Rivers and the sea.
**Food:** Aquatic invertebrates and small fish.
**Size:** Up to 60cm (23in).
**Breeding:** Spawning occurs in May in swift water over gravel. The eggs are shed in open water and left to develop unguarded.

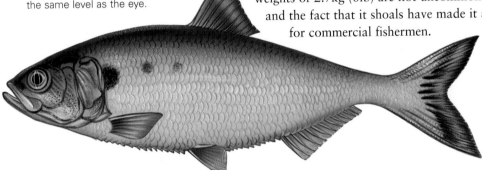

## Smelt

*Osmerus eperlanus*

**Identification:** The smelt looks not unlike a trout or salmon in its general form but is much smaller. The mouth is relatively large, with the lower jaw longer than the upper. Both jaws contain sharp, backward-pointing teeth: these are larger in the lower jaw. There is an adipose fin. The back is light olive brown and the flanks metallic purple to silver. The underside is white.

In terms of habitat, the smelt is an unusual fish. Some populations are confined to freshwater lakes, which they never leave. Others are marine and only enter fresh water to breed. Like the Allis shad, the smelt is a shoaling fish and one that is caught commercially. Smelt is often smoked before being sold for consumption. It is also used to make fish oil. All smelt tend to spawn over sand banks or gravel. Occasionally they shed their eggs over plants. Once the eggs have hatched (after three to five weeks) the larvae make their way downstream. Rather than entering the sea straight away they spend some time in the brackish waters of estuaries, feeding on planktonic invertebrates, then moving on to shrimps and other larger crustaceans as they grow.

**Distribution:** Occurs from the west coast of Ireland to the Baltic states. Abundant in parts of the North and Baltic seas.
**Habitat:** Lakes, rivers and coastal marine waters.
**Food:** Aquatic invertebrates and small fish.
**Size:** Up to 30cm (12in).
**Breeding:** Spawning occurs late winter and early spring over sand or gravel, and occasionally vegetation. Eggs are shed in open water and left to develop unguarded.

# Thin-lipped grey mullet

*Liza ramada*

The thin-lipped grey mullet is essentially an ocean fish but adults often enter estuaries and the lower reaches of rivers to feed. This species eats a variety of small invertebrates as well as algae, often grazed from pilings sunk into the bottom, such as those used to support jetties. Invertebrates are usually sifted from mud, although they may occasionally be snapped up in open water. Despite the diminutiveness of its prey, this can be quite a sizable fish, weighing up to 2.9kg (6½lb). It is a popular game fish among sea anglers. It is also caught commercially and, in some places, farmed as a food fish. In the wild, the thin-lipped grey mullet tends to form small schools, which move slowly as they search for food.

**Identification**: The body is torpedo shaped, the head pointed and the caudal fin large. There are two small, well separated dorsal fins: the first is shaped rather like the sail of a Chinese junk; the second is more triangular. The pectoral fins are quite high on the body, almost level with the eye. There is often a dark spot at the upper part of the base of the pectoral fin.

**Distribution**: Throughout the Black Sea, Mediterranean and western Atlantic as far north as Scotland and southern Sweden.
**Habitat**: Coastal marine waters, estuaries and rivers.
**Food**: Algae and aquatic invertebrates.
**Size**: Up to 60cm (23in).
**Breeding**: Spawning occurs at sea in coastal waters from September until February. The young then colonize shoreline habitats and estuaries.

---

**Twaite shad** (*Alosa fallax*) 56cm (22in). This fish looks similar to the Allis shad but is less deep-bodied and has a distinct notch in its upper jaw. It is a predominantly marine species that enters rivers to breed. There are also land-locked freshwater populations in some Irish and Italian lakes. It feeds on planktonic crustaceans and small fish. It occurs from Iceland and southern Norway to Morocco as well as throughout the Black and Mediterranean Seas.

**Flounder** (*Pleuronectes flesus*) 51cm (20in). The flounder (*right*) is the only flatfish found in fresh water in Europe. Large adults live on the bottom of the sea at depths of 25–40m (82–131ft), but young fish enter rivers and migrate upstream, beyond the reach of tidal waters. Flounders found in rivers are rarely more than 20cm (8in) long. Over this size, they move downstream and re-enter the sea.

**Big-eyed sandsmelt** (*Atherina boyeri*) 9cm (3½in). This little fish is best known from populations in brackish lakes and lagoons along the coast of the Mediterranean, but it also occurs in the sea. As well as the Mediterranean it is found near the shore in Atlantic waters, ranging north to the Netherlands and the southern coast of Wales. It forms large, tightly packed shoals for protection.

# Sea bass

*Dicentrarchus labrax*

This large species is probably known to most people in Europe as a food fish. A predominantly marine species, it is fished commercially off the south coast of England and also, in larger numbers, off France, Spain and Italy. It often enters estuaries and is occasionally found quite far up tidal rivers. The young in particular may be found schooling in estuaries, hiding from predators in the murky water and feeding on the shrimps and other crustaceans that are often abundant here. Adults are less gregarious than the young and often search alone for larger invertebrates and fish.

**Identification**: The body is torpedo-shaped and the head rather large. There are two well separated dorsal fins: the first has eight or nine strong, slender spines and is longer at the base than the second. The anal fin lies almost directly beneath the second dorsal fin and is similar in both shape and size. The mouth is large and the rear edge of the gill cover has two flattened spines.

**Distribution**: Throughout the Black and Mediterranean seas and in Atlantic coastal waters from Denmark to north Africa.
**Habitat**: Coastal marine waters and estuaries.
**Food**: Aquatic invertebrates and small fish.
**Size**: Up to 1m (3¼ft).
**Breeding**: Spawning occurs from March to May in coastal waters. The eggs are buoyant and the larvae tend to head for estuaries soon after hatching.

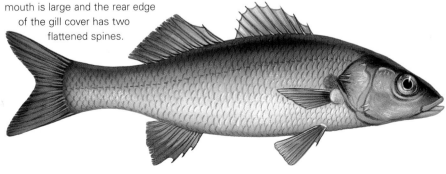

# INDEX

PICTURE ACKNOWLEDGEMENTS

Images in the book belong to Anness Publishing, with the exception of the following, which are reproduced with permission of Alamy: pp2, 96t&b, 99, 16t, 177tl, tr, bl & br, 178t & b, 179t & b, 180t, 181all, 182m, 183tl, tr, ml, mr & b, 184, 185tl, tr, ml, mr & b, 186ml, mr, & bl, 187b, & m, 188t & b, 189 ml, mr, bl & br, 190bl, br & t, 191b, 192t, 198, 199, 232.